D1506944

Rocking the Boat

Paul Wilson

SRL Publishing Ltd

SRL Publishing Ltd
Office 47396, PO Box 6945
London
W1A 6US

First published worldwide by SRL Publishing in 2021

ISBN: 978-183827983-7

1 3 5 7 9 10 8 6 4 2

This book is affectionately dedicated to the memory of my mother, Patricia Wilson.

19 September 1937 - 28 April 1996

Men are afraid to rock the boat in which they hope to drift safely through life's current, when, actually, the boat is stuck on a sandbar. They would be better off to rock the boat and try to shake it loose - Thomas Szasz

Table of contents

Chapter 1

Lincolnshire life

I felt like I was at the mercy of a giant as my tiny hands clutched the coarse mane of my horse, Maisie. My chubby legs splayed out horizontally in my childish attempt to keep from sliding off her back.

I was never in any danger, something my Grandad made sure of as he slowly led the gentle black and white cart horse to the stables for a well-earned nosebag after the day's chores were finished.

We could often see Grandad at the reins of the blue "float", which was a large two wheeled wooden box cart hitched to Maisie. Sometimes he would let me ride in the float. If I were lucky, I would even get to clutch the reins.

At the end of the day, Grandad would hoist me onto her back for the long trot back to the stables. After she was secure, we would walk back to the house together, where the warm and comforting smell of my mother's cooking would be waiting to greet us as we walked in the door.

My mother Pat, younger brother, Steven and I lived with Grandad, who was known in our village as Bert. My mother worked tirelessly to make sure we always had everything we needed. Besides the typical household tasks of cooking, cleaning, shopping, sewing, and washing, she also worked long, arduous hours in the fields and factories to make ends meet.

Many in our village were farm labourers, but Grandad was a shepherd who looked after the many sheep and cows on the farm. Our home was a "tied cottage" because it was tied to Grandad's job, for which he had dedicated thirty-five years of service.

That was the nature of life in not only our village, but in many of the villages surrounding the market town of Boston, Lincolnshire, located seven miles to the north. Many farm workers were tied to their homes because their employers supplied it with the job. Unfortunately, this system, which had developed in the 1800s, placed many farm workers in a precarious situation. They were beholden to their employer, because if they lost their job eviction would soon follow.

Joseph Ward was Grandad's employer and landlord. Mr. Ward was a rather impatient man, but because our entire livelihood depended on him, Grandad worked hard to make sure he stayed happy, even at the risk of his own health.

Our home was set back from the road, behind a farmyard and seated amid green paddocks frequented by a stable of fine Arabian horses owned by Mrs. Ward. Our home was one of the many quaint, comfortable little houses scattered along a road colloquially known as the 'seven-mile straight' in the sparsely populated, leafy, rural village of Carrington.

Those were happy times, but they would be short-lived. Eventually, Grandad's health became so bad it forced him to retire. Mr. Ward would not be moved. If Grandad could not work, we could not stay in our home, and that was a matter in which he would not budge.

I sat in a chair next to Grandad's bed, watching as he slept. I had never seen him look so weak. A sudden loud knock on the front door made me jump. Grandad let out a moan, but his eyes stayed closed. The front door opened, and I heard my mother's soft voice respond to a much deeper, stronger, voice. It was a voice I had become familiar with. It was the farm manager, stopping by once more to discuss when we were likely to move out. As the days went on the threats continued, until they started compounding Grandad's health issues and our family doctor felt forced to intervene, following which the threats deceased and Grandad could remain in his home.

~~~~~

My parents were barely out of their teens when they fell for each other. My father, Jimmy, was one of the many African Americans stationed with the US Air Force at nearby RAF East Kirkby. He had grown up in the public housing projects of Stamford, Connecticut. My mother was a white English woman working as domestic help for a wealthy Jewish family in Boston, Lincolnshire.

With society the way it was in 1958, their short-lived romance stood little chance. Miscegenation was frowned upon in polite English society, and racial segregation and lack of opportunities were an intrinsic reality for the African American in the States.

At the behest of his Station Commander, with no thought given to his new English family, they dispatched Jimmy back to the United States. My mother was left to raise me in difficult circumstances but aided by her supportive family.

Mother had always tried her best to prepare me for what would inevitably come my way. Her understanding of the 'colour' issue was not surprising. She had pushed back the boundary of acceptability by walking the streets of Boston on the arm of a jazz-loving black man in the 1950s.

At seven years old I would often spend Saturday mornings seated on the scullery floor, peering up at my mother as she stood in front of a large, white sink washing clothes by hand. It was during these times that she would tell me stories about my Dad. Her stories sometimes touched upon the difficulties that some white people had with 'coloureds'.

She would often conclude these tales with, "You are coloured, Paul. Your Dad is coloured. There are some people who will try to hold you back because of your colour."
In those early years, I did not grasp the meaning of what she was saying. But as I grew older, I appreciated her wise counsel and factored 'colour' into my everyday experiences.

Growing up, I regularly hung out with friends from surrounding villages and colour never seemed to be an issue. We would start a game of football wherever we found a patch of green grass, using our jackets and jumpers as goal posts.

By the age of ten I was already 5'9 and 12 stone, so I always passed for being much older than I was. This, I am sure, endeared me to some of my older friends and I was a popular figure in our group.

My size did not just give me the advantage of being popular with my friends. Starting around the age of nine, it also helped supplement our family income. During my summer holidays, I accompanied Mother to her job in the fields where she picked potatoes on the local farms.

Lincolnshire was well known for its potatoes, but few appreciated the hard work involved in getting the spuds to the retail outlets at home and abroad. Long rows of potatoes were spun out from the earth by a special rotating appliance attached to the front of a tractor. Once the potatoes had been exposed, groups of all-female potato pickers would be allocated a stretch of the potato row, about twenty-five yards that was marked by two wooden pegs in the ground. Mother was one of those women.

With back bent and legs straddled across a small wicker basket, she would reach down with both hands to scoop up and propel the exposed potatoes into the basket. When the basket was full, she would grab an empty basket that had been strategically placed nearby and continue the process until she completed her stretch of the row.

The problem was, by the time she finished her allocated stretch, the tractor and spinner were already finished with the next row. This meant she had little or no time to rest before repeating the picking process. This went on from 8:30am to 3:30pm, with a thirty-minute lunch, in large open fields that offered no respite from the harsh summer sun.

Since I was on summer holiday, I would often accompany mother to pick her allocated stretch of potatoes. I soon became very adept, which did not sit well with the other women, who resented Mother for having it easier than them, because of her unofficial helper.

The farmer, Mr. Epton, came up with a solution. He began giving me my own small stretch of potatoes to pick, for which he paid me a few pounds per week. From that point on, I could always obtain employment in various jobs on surrounding farms during my school summer holidays.

~~~~~

The nearby town of Boston was a familiar destination for me when I was growing up. Every Saturday, Mother would take me with her on 1.20pm bus to do the weekly shopping. Her stiletto shoes would rapidly click across the pavement as I ran behind her, my small legs barely able to keep up with her quick pace.

As I grew older, Mother began allowing me stay at the local recreation park by myself while she did her shopping. But by the time I was ten, the swings and slides were not enough for me anymore. I started venturing out to explore the local sights and sounds of the busy shipping port.

During these little jaunts of freedom, small groups of black men would sometimes approach and surround me. They were African seamen whose ships were visiting Boston's docks. It was such a rarity to meet anyone of colour in Boston that they always took a great interest in me, shaking my hand, asking me questions about where I was from and who my parents were, and handing me pocket money before they left.

My long-held assumption that I was the only 'coloured boy' in Boston was dispelled one Saturday afternoon as I walked along the high street. A young Michael Jackson look-alike began approaching from the other side and I was so taken aback I did not know what to do, so I did nothing. I averted my eyes until I had passed him, then quickly turned my head to look back at him. He did the very same thing and we both started laughing. We stopped and shook hands and chatted. His name was Trevor, and he ended up becoming a friend with whom I would sometimes discuss issues of colour.

When I was young, I honestly believed that being a 'coloured boy' in the town was a positive thing. That was my experience. Everyone seemed to know who I was, and I attracted the attention of those who did not. That all changed when I started secondary school at eleven years old.

~~~~~

The end of the summer holiday meant a new beginning for me at William Lovell School in the neighbouring village of Stickney. It was a big occasion. For the first time in my life, I had to wear a school uniform. I despised the green jacket and found the tie almost unbearable, but I wore them for the sake of my mother.

I looked the part that first morning as I cycled with friends to the crossroads in the village. I leaned my bike against a large tree in someone's front garden and waited for the school bus to pick us up for the two-and-a-half-mile journey. I was excited both at the prospect of making new friends and, as my older friends had reassured me, being chosen to play for the school football team.

Our bus entered the school gates and stopped inside the grounds. As the doors opened, twenty excited children jumped off the top step and sprinted to the playground area.

I asked my village friends if there were any black kids at the school and they assured me there were none. As I ambled through the playground looking for my friends, I realised they were right. I did not see anyone that looked like me, but that was not an issue. Or so I thought.

"Hey, Cuba, Cuba."

I turned around. A dumpy, fair-haired boy was staring intently at me. He was chewing on a piece of gum like a cow chewing its cud. His uniform tie was pulled down and hanging loosely around his neck.

He looked around to ensure other boys were within range to hear his next turn of phrase.

"You know you look like a big Cuban cigar?" he shouted.

The boys surrounding him laughed as if he were some playground comedy legend instead of a smirking, pudgy faced little twerp.

A rush of thoughts clouded my mind as I moved towards him.

Who the fuck do you think you are talking to, you fat bastard?

I watched for any sign that he might punch or kick me, but he did neither. I grabbed him by the throat with my left hand and pushed his head against the rusty wire mesh fence that surrounded the tennis court. His eyes sank into their sockets as his fat cheeks reddened and bottom lip quivered.

I raised my right fist in the air. "Don't you ever speak to me again, because if you do, I'm going to smack you in the teeth, understand?" I yelled in his face.

"Yeah, bloody hell, okay!" he gurgled as my grip tightened.

I released my grip, turned around and walked away like nothing had happened.

The news circulated throughout the four hundred pupil school like wildfire.

"That coloured first year boy threatened to beat up Peter Johnson from third year!" they whispered amongst themselves. First-year pupils were supposed to be meek and mild, especially on their first day at school.

Despite getting off to a rough start on the first day, things soon settled into a state of normalcy. I attended my first German language class. My friends had warned me it was a tough class with an unforgiving teacher, so I was already nervous as I walked into the small classroom on the first day. The hair on the back of my neck stood up as I looked at the unrecognisable words chalked on the blackboard.

I pulled out a chair and slid my chunky thighs under the small desk. As I tried to decipher the German words on the board, a long-haired boy scraped the floor with his chair as he sat down next to me.

I glanced over at him and the dark stubble that peppered his chin. I stroked my small, wispy moustache that I trimmed with an old razor once a month.

He's already shaving at age eleven, I thought to myself.

Our teacher, Frau Langstaff, shouted out names while looking at her attendance sheet.

"Alan Coote," she said in her light Dutch accent.

"Yes, Miss," responded my bearded neighbour. I leaned over to him.

"Alright, Alan?" I asked.

"Yeah," he calmly responded as he peered over at my textbook.

"What's that you've got written on your book?" he asked.

"Slade," I replied. "I like them."

I also liked Symarip, Dave and Ansil Collins and Max Romeo. My favourite tune, *Liquidator* by Harry J and the All Stars, always played at the end of a Boston Utd home game.

Alan pushed his textbook under my nose.

"Nah, you need to listen to these!" he said.

I read the list of new, captivating names on the cover of his notebook, 'Junior Walker and The All Stars', 'The Temptations', 'The Four Tops', among others.

Later in the week, I borrowed my Uncle Stan's new transistor radio, determined to listen to the artists Alan had told me about.

Late at night I would hide under the bedcovers and twiddle with the dial until I found Radio Luxembourg. The first tune I enjoyed was the belting sound of Bill Cosby's 'Little Ol' Man', a rendition of Stevie Wonder's

'Uptight'.

I quickly forgot Slade. I was a soul music convert.

Aged fourteen I learned to dance to soul music by watching the older boys on Saturday nights at Boston's Assembly Room, a large popular music venue on the banks of the river in the marketplace.

My first visit to the Assembly Room was a meticulously planned adventure on my part. I had saved up money from my Saturday morning job as a stable boy and used it to buy a new outfit from Insiders, a small fashion boutique in Boston.

Since none of my friends were allowed out late on a Saturday evening, I walked through the huge double entrance doors of the Assembly Room alone, paid my entrance fee and walked up the ornate staircase (since everyone knew all the action took place on the upper floor).

I reached the top of the stairs and an intimidating, brightly lit bar, populated by older boys and girls, came into view.

Straight ahead was the main dance hall, and I instantly recognised the sound of MFSB's 'The Sound of Philadelphia'. The spacious dance floor was packed with boys and girls just a little older than me, and it stayed that way for the rest of the evening.

I lacked the confidence to get out there myself, but I spent much of the evening watching the different dancing styles in wonderment. I went over to the bar and ordered a Coke several times, but then always quickly retreated to the safety of the darkened main hall.

It was getting late, the lights suddenly dimmed, which I knew meant the DJ was about to spin another romantic 'slowie'. Earlier in the evening, this had prompted a mass exodus from the dance floor.

A young girl brushed past me, then stopped and turned to me.

"Are you going to ask me for a dance?" she asked.

In the dim light of the dance hall, I struggled to see her, but I could make out that she was tall, had a pleasant smile and short dark hair.

"Yeah, okay," I replied.

I put my arms around her small waist, and we swayed awkwardly to the music.

"What is your name?" I asked.

"Shirelle. What is yours?"

"Paul."

As our bodies moved in sync to the melodic strains of Bloodstone's 'Natural High', I was certain she could hear my pounding heart above the strains of the record. As the song ended, Shirelle leaned forward and kissed me passionately on the lips for what seemed like an eternity. My head started spinning. When did stars fall out of the sky and lodge behind my eyes? If someone had asked me my name right then, I probably would have drawn a blank.

The glaring lights came back on and shook me back into reality. Under the harsh ballroom lights, I realised a generous amount of face powder disguised Shirelle's brown skin, but her full lips and short afro hair were in full view.

"Excuse me, but I'm going to go over there and see my friends," Shirelle said, pointing to a small group of girls on the other side of the dance floor who were staring at us.

"Okay. I'll see you. What do you say, same time and same place next week?" I asked.

"Yeah, okay," she said.

Despite our agreement to see each other the following week, Shirelle and I never met or spoke again during my time in Boston.

~~~~~

A few months later, now full of confidence, I was walking through the bar area of the Assembly Rooms when a young girl with dark curly hair approached me.

"Hello, my name is Rosemary and my friend over there likes you. Do you want to meet her?"

I looked over to where she was pointing. A tall, slim girl with long, fair hair smiled at me and discreetly waved. She was wearing a pencil skirt and white blouse, and I found her attractive.

"Sure," I said. I guess I could do this favour for Rosemary.

I walked over, introduced myself and struck up a conversation with the beautiful girl. Her name was Gillian, she was my age, and she went to Boston High School. Even though she didn't share my passion for soul music, and seemed awfully mature for her age, we soon started dating.

Every weekend we would meet up at a favourite pub on West Street or watch a film in the back row at one of the town's two cinemas. We arranged times to talk on the phone during the week, and I always looked forward to these conversations, even when I would have to spend over an hour in the village phone box on a chilly night.

My mother was very happy about my relationship and would ask me questions about her family. Had I met them yet? What were they like? The truth was I hadn't met them, and I always made excuses about why. My mother would just look at me like she didn't believe my story. But personally, I refused to believe that the reason I hadn't met Gillian's parents was anything other than innocent.

Gillian lived on the outskirts of town, so after our evening out together I always walked her home. Well, not exactly home. We never actually reached her house. We would stop at a bus shelter just around the corner from where she lived, say goodbye, and she would continue the rest of the way alone.

This went on for a few months until one day Gillian suggested I visit her house the following Sunday afternoon. I was surprised but also thrilled and excited to see where she lived and meet her parents for the first time.

On Sunday afternoon I took a bus into Boston and met Gillian in the town centre. It was a sunny day, so we walked. After about fifteen minutes we reached the Wyberton West Road, close to Gillian's home.

Gillian suddenly froze in her tracks and stared intently at a slowing oncoming car. I did not know what she was doing.

"Oh my God!" she shouted, doubling over, and placing her head in both her hands.

The car screeched to a halt a few yards from where we were.

Gillian was sobbing hysterically.

I gently placed my hands around her waist. "What's the problem?"

She looked up at me in horror. "It's my Dad," she cried.

A middle-aged man in a suit got out of the car and ran towards us. His face was bright red, veins protruded from his temple, and he was huffing. He got in my face.

"YOU! You leave my daughter alone. If you carry on seeing her, I will put you in the hospital, I promise you!" he shouted.

He turned to Gillian and pointed his finger. "You get home. I'll talk to you later."

He turned and walked back to his car.

I was speechless and confused. I got along well with everyone. No one had ever threatened to beat me up. A numbness rose from the pit of my stomach as my entire body shivered as I fought back the tears.

I looked over at Gillian, who was still shaking and crying profusely.

"It's my colour. Your dad is colour prejudiced! Why didn't you warn me?"

Gillian nodded. "I-am-so-sorry," she said in short, rasping breaths. "I'm afraid to go home. Can we talk?"

"Yes, as long as it's anywhere but here," I replied. "I want to talk to you, too."

We turned around and walked back to the town centre, both of us still in shock. After we were finished talking, we continued walking in silence. Gillian was too physically and emotionally worn out to walk all the way back home by herself at that point, so she got on a bus to go home. I stood and watched her leave, then walked the streets by myself for an hour or so.

My hands shoved firmly in my pockets, I stared at the pavement as I wandered around aimlessly, oblivious to my surroundings. My mind replayed what had happened in a continuous loop until I got tired and headed for home.

I got to my bus stop early. My bus was already in, and the driver was sitting inside reading a newspaper. He looked up as I approached.

He laughed. "Hello Paul. You alright? Boston United lost again I see."

I nodded and climbed the steps.

All the drivers knew me, that is how it was, everyone knew me, I was popular and that made the threats so difficult for me to accept.

I walked to the back of the bus, sat in the corner, and gazed out the window as the bus engine started up. I was lost in my thoughts through the whole twenty-five-minute ride. The driver's voice momentarily shook me out of my mental fog.

"This is your stop, Paul! You asleep?" he shouted.

I stood up and walked off the bus the same way I had walked on, but now feelings of sorrow had turned to anger.

~~~~~

After the racial incident, I would become very subdued whenever my mother mentioned Gillian by name. I could sense she knew something had happened, but I never discussed it with her because I did not want to upset her. Because of her own previous experience of inter-racial dating, it was not hard for her to put two and two together.

That was not the end of my relationship with Gillian, though. We continued seeing each other for a few more months. We arranged clandestine meetings off the beaten track, down darkened side streets and away from crowds where we might be recognised. I even met Gillian's mother, a lovely lady who was embarrassed and apologetic about her husband's behaviour and threats. But in the end our courtship was just not sustainable, and we eventually went our separate ways.

I left school at age sixteen with a clutch of average qualifications and began applying for various jobs. This was during a period when jobs were plentiful, yet they turned me down for each one I applied for. Mother was convinced it was because of my colour. She certainly proved to be right on at least one occasion.

I applied for a job as a weighing scale technician. It was an extremely attractive package, offering a higher-than-average salary for that area and the opportunity to pursue college education and the promise of a vehicle. The interview had gone so well that the interviewer had even discussed with me some additional perks of the job, such as servicing the weighing machines in Skegness, a popular seaside resort, during the summer months.

It felt as though I was being given the job there and then. All they required of me was a passport-sized photograph for head office administrative purposes.

However, a few days later I received notification in the post that I had been unsuccessful in my application. Disappointed, I went to my career adviser's office within Boston's Public Library.

I entered the small office and the adviser invited me to take a seat. He leaned across his desk.

"Sorry Paul, I got some feedback from the Regional Manager who told me that his Head Office in Leeds saw your photograph and instructed him not to employ you as they do not want coloured people," he whispered.

Racism was still an alien concept for me. That was something that happened to other people, not me. I enjoyed reading and had familiarised myself with the Civil Rights movement in the United States, but while I had been on the receiving end of a few racist words, this was hugely different.

This was about my livelihood and the fact that someone who had never met me denied me the right to work because of the colour of my skin.

I walked out of the Career Adviser's office with the same nausea and numbness in the pit of my stomach I had felt when my girlfriend's father had threatened to beat me up because he did not want his daughter dating a coloured boy. My thoughts turned to those many Saturday morning conversations with my mother.

"You're coloured Paul and some people will try to hold you back."

Those words reverberated in my head as I walked down the library steps and through the doors out into the bright sunshine. I looked up at the blue sky and made myself a promise. Never again would I allow racism to depress or get the better of me.

Some of my friends attended Boston College of Further Education, but that wasn't an option for me. After I turned sixteen, my family expected me to work and assist with the bills, further education never entered my head.

I explained this to my career adviser at Boston's public library. I had to work to help my mum out with the household bills. The career adviser accepted my reasoning without batting an eye.

Soon after, I secured a position with the East Anglian Optical Company in Boston.

I worked as an optical mechanic, glazing lenses for acrylic spectacle frames of various shapes and sizes. But after a couple of years, I started feeling like I desperately wanted to expand my horizons. Numerous shopping expeditions and nightclubbing excursions to large cities across the Midlands and North of England had opened my eyes to the multicultural nature of city living, with all the attendant entertainment and socialisation on offer.

By that point I realised that a quaint, sleepy town like Boston, with a population of only 25,000, just was not going to offer me the excitement and racial diversity I so desperately longed for.

Ironically, my younger brother Steven had left home shortly before to join the Royal Air Force Regiment. I looked over recruitment material for both the armed forces and the Royal Air Force Regiment and considered joining one or the other. I changed my mind once I concluded that military life would place too many restrictions on my social life, which was an unimaginable outcome for me to consider.

The music of Black America was a hugely important factor in my decision-making process, it had become a staple in my life. It was the only conduit I had to a black culture that seemed so remote and so far beyond the reach of a young black guy from a small village in Lincolnshire.

Almost all my friends were white and many still clung to the Motown-esque soul music of the 1960s Mod era, commonly known as northern soul. But as I reached my mid-teens, I became very conscious of being a minority within a minority as my taste in music had developed, now favouring hard-edged jazz and funk-oriented rhythms. These contemporary, unapologetic, and brash sounds of Black America were at odds with Berry Gordy's 'Sound of Young America' that continued to pervade local nightspots.

In the absence of any black media representation, role models or black community in Boston, my music was like a comfort blanket. It allowed me to embrace my blackness and presented me a window into another world through which I gained and maintained a positive sense of identity. Subscriptions to music magazines such as *Blues & Soul*, *Black Music Magazine*, and *Black Echoes* were delivered to our door by the newspaperman and unwittingly funded by Grandad. I voraciously read them from cover to cover.

Radio was important too: I discovered at a young age that Radio Luxembourg would frequently play black music, and later there were programs such as Radio London's Saturday morning soul show hosted by Robbie Vincent - an absolute must.

Spurred on by a desire to move, job hunting became a nightly ritual when I turned nineteen. After arriving home from work, I avidly leafed through the Daily Express newspaper, scouring the columns listing the various job vacancies on offer. The Express was a newspaper my Grandad had delivered to our door daily – something I always thought unusual given his staunch support for the Labour Party – but I did not mind, as it carried a healthy selection of job adverts and I was in the market for a new job.

However, I did not want just any job; it had to be one that would take me far away from my native Lincolnshire. Preferably into a large city, although I had not given the destination that much thought.

Chapter 2

Leaving home

Everything changed one night in 1979. I was sitting at the kitchen table, gazing at the job adverts in the newspaper, just as I had done every night for at least five months. Suddenly, a large advert caught my attention.

'Metropolitan Police, New Scotland Yard, London, require clerical assistants to work in our many departments.'

I quickly scanned the small print and saw that I met the educational requirements. The salary, however, while more than I was making, I guessed it was not a lot to live on in London.

I set the paper aside and went about the rest of my evening. But that advert kept lingering in the back of my mind, and the more I thought about it, the more excited I became. By the time I went to bed, all I could think about was moving to London.

How would I make that work? Where would I live? I had no contacts or relatives in London, or even anywhere remotely near London. I would have to make it on my own, but how?

The next morning, my excitement was mixed with a big dose of reality. First, I would have to get the job. Then, I would have to find somewhere to live, which could be a huge hurdle, but it was worth a try. I mailed in my application and waited. I decided not to tell anyone in my family or in my workplace until I had secured the job.

If I am unsuccessful no-one will be any the wiser.

Days went by without a response. Maybe it was all just wishful thinking. If I didn't get the job, I would just pursue other avenues. I had lost nothing by simply filling out the application and mailing it in.

One evening I came home from work, Mum was standing in front of the kitchen sink washing dishes. She looked over at me and smiled.

"Welcome home. There's a letter for you, over there on the table."

"Great. Thanks Mum." I went and sat down at the table and picked up the letter. I wasn't expecting much. I received many letters, so this wasn't exactly an unusual occurrence. It was probably another one of those letters record dealers sent out, with lists of the latest vinyl imports for sale.

But when I looked at the envelope, something told me this was different. It had an air of being something official. Could it be?

I took the letter and ran upstairs to my room. I sat down on the edge of my bed. My heart was pounding, and my palms were feeling sweaty. I could hardly contain myself. I carefully yet anxiously opened the envelope and immediately saw the Metropolitan Police headed paper and crest.

'Dear Mr. Wilson...... we would like to invite you to a selection interview.'

Yes! I threw my arms into the air like some demented goal-scorer.

That evening I changed into my jogging gear and went for a long run. This was not unusual for me, but this time it was to help me clear my head and use up some pent-up nervous energy I had from my earlier excitement.

The day of my interview, I booked a day off work to take the train to London. When I left the house that morning, I told Mother that I would probably work a little late. On the train to London's Kings Cross Station, I kept consulting the little map that had been sent with my letter from the Metropolitan Police. This map detailed the various routes that might be taken to the location of the selection interview: Peel House, 105 Regency Street, Pimlico, SW1.

Peel House was a large old building at the very end of Regency Street. I arrived early and was shown into a waiting area by a young lady.

"Would you like some tea or coffee?" she asked.

"No thanks. May I just have some water, please?" I replied. It worried me that I would spill coffee on my brand-new white shirt.

A few minutes later another lady came in to get me and take me to the office where the interview was to be held.

Two smartly dressed ladies sat behind a long table in the middle of the room when I walked in.

"Hello, Paul. Did you have a pleasant journey?" one of them asked.

"Yes, thank you," I said, taking a seat at the table.

As we began talking, my nerves calmed down. I had not thought about the questions they would ask, but I didn't need to worry. The conversation was casual. I felt very much at ease, almost like I was talking to two friends and not two people who would decide whether my dream of working there would come true. Then I was hit with a lightning bolt.

"Paul, if you are successful in gaining a position with us, where would you live?" one of them asked.

There it was. The question that would be the undoing of my trip to London and my dreams.

I quickly gathered up a nervous response.

"Of course, I would need to look for accommodation, most probably a room or a bed-sit."

Even as the words came out of my mouth, I knew full well that the salary they offered would barely cover either.

The same lady that asked smiled sweetly at me added, "Well, what we do for young people is offer you a place in a Civil Service hostel. These are large buildings in central London where young people working for Government departments share accommodation. You'll be provided with two hot meals a day and the rent is very reasonable. What would you think of that?"

My heart did a triple somersault. I wanted to leap across the table, hug and smother both of them with kisses. I had never in my wildest dreams imagined this would be the outcome to my dilemma.

I took a deep breath to control my excitement. I could yell, shout, and jump around all I wanted when I got home, but here I needed to stay professional.

"That sounds great. Thank you," I said calmly.

I left Peel House feeling like things had gone well. I still had to wait to be officially offered the job, but I felt very hopeful. I went back home and waited. I thought I would hear something in a few days at the most.

Three days went by and I got concerned. Maybe it was just taking a little longer than I thought. Then three days turned into four… five… six. Then one week turned into two, and with each passing day I grew increasingly concerned at the lack of communication from the Metropolitan Police.

Finally, I received a letter that looked like the one I had received inviting me for an interview. Just like before, I ran to my bedroom to open it in private. This time my nerves were more on edge than ever before. I quickly opened it and scanned the words on the page.

'Dear Mr. Wilson,

We write regarding our letter offering you a position with the Metropolitan Police. As we have not received your response, we can only assume you are no longer interested …......'

"What letter?" I shouted, jumping to my feet.

I ran downstairs and looked through the shelf above the sideboard in the hallway where old letters were often kept.

Nothing.

I looked over at the clock. 5:00 PM. Maybe there would still be someone in the office. I ran out the front door and to the telephone box about four hundred yards away at a crossroads in the village.

"Hello, this is Paul Wilson and I've just received a letter from you, but I definitely did not receive your job offer letter," I said breathlessly.

"Well, Mr. Wilson, the position is yours. However, arrangements are in place that the position has to be filled within eight days. I'm sorry about that."

"No, problem," I interjected, "I can do that."

"Are you sure? We can always put things back until later in the year?"

"No, I'll be okay. I want to do it now," I said anxiously.

"Will you require the hostel accommodation discussed at your interview?"

"Yes, please,"

I left the telephone box and walked very slowly back to my house as I mulled over what I was going to tell my mother.

I opened the back door, stepped into the kitchen, and blurted out,

"Mum, I'm leaving home, I'm going to live in London, working for the police!"

Mother was seated in her favourite chair in the corner by the window and with arms folded she looked up at me with no trace of emotion on her face.

"What on earth are you talking about, Paul?"

"I'm leaving, Mum, next week. I have to start my new job."

"No, not you, too." she said. My brother had left home only a few months earlier, and Mother was still adjusting to that.

I sat down with my Mother and tearfully explained everything that had been going on. After things were calm, I sensed she was relieved. For several months she had watched me become increasingly reclusive. I would often lock myself away in my bedroom and play music at a high volume. Whenever I was questioned or chastised, I would complain about having nowhere to go and nothing to do. I had clearly been depressed.

A few days later I received another letter from the Metropolitan Police with information and instructions about my hostel accommodation.

I was to arrive at 44-46 Leinster Gardens, Bayswater, W1 by 1:00 PM for my booking in procedure. I could bring one large suitcase and one small piece of hand luggage. I looked at my map of London and found Bayswater. I realized I would only be a short walk from Oxford Street and Notting Hill. I had little knowledge of Central London, so these two iconic areas would serve as my point of reference.

The following weekend I said goodbye to my family and friends. Many of my friends did not understand what I was doing or why. Many of them would never move beyond the borders of Lincolnshire, and certainly not to live in London, or 'the Smoke' as they sometimes called it. But I was not like most people. I was different.

With all my worldly possessions piled snugly inside my cherished brown 1970 Triumph Herald, I lingered for a long while, giving my dear mother a long hug. I kissed her cheek and, with tears in my eyes, climbed into my car and drove away.

As I set off down the seven mile straight towards Boston, I reached over and shoved a cassette into the player. A favourite Dean Parrish soul record from my school days played. Through my tears and sobs, I sang along at the top of my voice.

"Can't take it anymore.... here I go, I'm on my way, off to the city... and now I'm gonna live, gonna find me a girl.... I'm on my way."

Blinking my tears away, I looked in my rear-view mirror at the large trees on both side of the straight road, their leafy branches touching to form a canopy, like some green guard of honour recognised this auspicious occasion in my young life.

Hours later I turned into Leinster Terrace, London, W2, and pulled my faithful Herald up outside a hugely impressive large white building that resembled a Skegness seafront hotel. I walked up what appeared to be marble steps and approached two large front doors. Driving non-stop in the hot July sun, sweat trickled down my face as I pressed the bell.

A lady who looked like British actress Peggy Ashcroft opened the door and grinned. "You must be Paul. What time do you call this?"

"Sorry, I've been driving all day. I had some problems."

"Well, never mind, park your car around the corner on a meter and bring your stuff in, your room is ready." The Peggy Ashcroft look-alike said.

A few minutes later she showed me to my room, which contained three single beds. She pointed towards one of them.

"That one is yours, and that is your wardrobe and chest of drawers over there," she pointed out.

A sash window at the end of the room provided light as well as a view of the garden to the back of the premises.

"You've got Queensway over there, a busy shopping area two-minutes' walk away," said Peggy as she pointed at the window, "but before you do anything else, go downstairs and get some food, you'll get to meet your two roommates soon enough."

In the dining room downstairs, large silver trays were lined up on tables down one side of the room. Smartly dressed staff stood on the other side, ladling food onto the plates of the young men standing in line. I got in line, was served my dinner, and went and sat down at a table by myself to eat. Afterwards, I went back to my room and tried to sort my clothes and belongings into the little space I had.

Prior to leaving home, I had done my research on my new neighbourhood and discovered from a recent copy of Blues & Soul magazine that Fangs night club was below the Great Western Hotel in Paddington. According to the advert, that night the well-known DJ Froggy would make a guest appearance. I was tired from driving all day, but such an opportunity on my doorstep was too good to miss.

A short time later, I drove through the narrow streets of Bayswater into Paddington and parked close to the Great Western Hotel. At the entrance to Fangs, I paid an entrance fee and entered a small basement area packed with punters. There was a healthy sprinkling of young black people on the crowded dancefloor, which was something I had never witnessed in all my clubbing experiences. Huge speakers adorned the area in front of the DJ console. Behind the decks, an animated Froggy chatted away on the microphone.

I picked my way through the crowded basement dance floor and over to the general area in front of the bar. Froggy busily announced forthcoming events over the PA system, but it was the opening strains of Wilbert Longmire's 'Black Is The Color', a firm favourite of mine, that stopped me in my tracks. Motionless and propped up against the bar, I felt tearful as the enormity of the day's events flooded my senses and with the realisation that this was the first tune that welcomed me to London, my new home.

I left Fangs around 2:00 AM, emotional and exhausted. I returned to the hostel and made my way upstairs to the communal bathroom down the corridor from my room. I showered and changed into pyjamas that I had carried in my car. I quietly entered my room, not switching the light on, and slid under the bedcovers.

"Hello, Paul is it?" a distinctive Welsh voice said.

I opened my eyes, blinked, and saw a young white guy standing by the bedroom door.

"Hi, I'm Glyn, just going down for breakfast,".

"Hi Glyn, nice to meet you," I said, "I'll be down soon."

Glyn worked at a bank and Andy – who travelled home at weekends – worked at the Victoria & Albert Museum. They were to be my roommates for the next six months.

Chapter 3

New Scotland Yard

The following Monday I again walked into a basement room at Peel House but this time for new staff induction.

The rows of desks that took up most of the room reminded me of my school days. I smiled at the realisation that I was here to begin my career, not learn math equations. I was a bonafide adult now.

Each desk had a folder, personalised with our name and department. Men and women of various ages began sitting down and looking at their folders. A middle-aged man with greying hair sat down next to a young woman who looked to be about my age. My desk was in the row right in front of them. I sat down and picked up my folder. Right under my name were the words "Solicitor's Department". I was not sure what that entailed. I looked around for someone to ask, but before I had a chance a lady walked up to the front of the room.

"Good morning everyone. Welcome to the Metropolitan Police. My name is Wendy. Let's get right into things this morning. First, I am going to go over our organisational structure, then we will take some questions."

Thirty minutes later, when Wendy was finished speaking and answering questions, she dismissed us for a fifteen-minute break. Everyone stood up and scattered, but I decided to use this opportunity to ask a question I had not wanted to bring up right in front of everyone. I walked up to Wendy, who was at the water cooler filling her cup.

"Hi. Can I ask you a quick question?" I asked.

"Sure," she said, taking a sip of her water.

"I noticed I'm the only one here going to work in the Solicitor's Department. What exactly do they do?"

Wendy raised her eyebrows and glanced at the folder in my hands. Was it really that surprising that I wanted to know what I was going to be doing for a living?

Finally, Wendy's face relaxed and she smiled.

"The Metropolitan Police Commissioner employs a solicitor to prosecute cases on behalf of the police. That solicitor employs several people to help carry out that function. Police staff are employed in the department to help support that work."

"Oh," I said.

"Yes," Wendy continued. "Solicitor's is seen as one of the more prestigious departments at New Scotland Yard. They even have their own particular career structure."

"That sounds great. Thank you," I said.

"You're welcome. Let me know if you have any other questions."

I got a drink of water and went back to my desk. As the day progressed, I grew more and more excited about my new job. I carefully planned out everything I would do to ensure that my first day went smoothly. At the top of my list was making sure I got there on time. I hadn't yet been in the midst of London's morning commute, but I knew that leaving early was a must.

Later that day, I did a practice run to make sure I did not get lost on my first morning. I quickly realised that I need not have bothered as St James underground station was just across the road from my new workplace.

The next morning, I sat on the crowded train marveling at the intensity of the 'rush-hour' and London's smartly dressed workforce, mostly unsmiling, not uttering a word and focusing straight ahead. Like me, their thoughts probably consisted mostly of just getting to work on time. At each stop, many of them rushed off the train only to be replaced just as quickly by more smartly dressed, unsmiling, quiet commuters.

Since it was a sunny morning and I had given myself plenty of time, I decided to get off early at Victoria station and walk the ten-minute remainder of my commute. People walked back and forth at speed, a bit drone like, as they made their way to their own destinations.

From the pavement of Victoria Street, I peered up at New Scotland Yard. The daunting skyscraper of a building was a far cry from the two-storey converted house where I had worked just a few days ago. The tinted glass structure glistened in the early morning July sunshine. For two years, I had dreamed of this day when I would begin a new job in one of the largest cities in the world.

I crossed the road and walked towards the revolving New Scotland Yard sign. I had seen it so many times on the evening news programme, 'News at Ten', but in real life it seemed much bigger and altogether more impressive. A group of Japanese tourists congregated under the sign. They too understood its iconic nature and the importance of the building behind it.

A young man from the group walked over to me. "Will you take our photograph, please?" he asked.

"Sure," I said.

The group stood close together and smiled as I took their picture. I wanted so badly to tell them that I was just starting work at 'The Yard' that morning but decided against it. I gave the camera back to the young man and made my way towards the large glass entrance doors, which had been wedged open. I guessed it was to allow ease of access to the scores of visitors filing into the building.

A line had formed in front of the reception desk, where two ladies sat processing paperwork. I got in line to await my turn, relieved that I had given myself so much extra time that morning. Around the edge of the building's entrance hall, many more people sat waiting to be called back for their appointments, interviews, or any other kind of business they had there.

When my turn came, I took a deep breath and smiled.

"Morning, my name's Paul Wilson. I've been instructed to report to the Solicitor's Department, General Office on the 11th floor," I said, handing the lady my authority, a form presented to me at my induction.

She looked at the form, smiled and pointed, "That's fine, just go through there and the lifts are on the right and left."

I shared the lift with three other young people, all of whom stayed silent during my quick journey up to the 11th floor. Like the people on the train and on the pavements, everyone was preoccupied with getting to work and there was little time for small talk.

I entered the General Office and introduced myself to the front desk receptionist. She instructed me to have a seat while she made a phone call. A few minutes later a man came out and shook my hand.

"Hello Paul, I'm John Goldsmith. I'm the office manager here," he said.

"Nice to meet you," I replied.

He motioned with his hand. "Follow me and I'll help you get settled in."

John showed me to a desk and gave me some basic clerical and filing duties to help me acclimatise to the office environment.

Later in the morning John pointed to a stack of papers over to the side.

"Don't file those yet, Mr. McCrorie has to sign them first."

"Mr. McCrorie?" I asked.

"Yes, he's the big boss. He's head of all non-professional staff in this department. You probably won't see much of him; he doesn't spend much time here. After you finish filling out those papers, just give them to me, and I will make sure they get to him so he can sign them."

A few days later, I was standing next to the office door when it suddenly opened. A thin man in his early sixties with slicked back dark hair and hawkish facial features had one foot in the door and was barking something indecipherable to John Goldsmith on the other side of the office. The man quickly retreated down the corridor without so much as a glance at the admin staff. He walked with a slight stoop which I would come to believe was probably from years of sitting behind a desk. I quickly deciphered that the man was William McCrorie, the Senior Principal Legal Executive. Just like John had predicted, I did not see very much of him for a while after that.

During my first few weeks of working in the General Office I was the dog's-body, scurrying around making sure all the prosecuting solicitors had the correct Magistrates' Court cases listed in their diary for the next day. After a short time, I was given more responsibility. Each morning I would telephone every Magistrates' Court in London and try to calculate how many prosecuting solicitors would be required to prosecute over the next few days. It was not an exact science and occasionally we had insufficient solicitors available to deal with the listed cases, and prosecution cases would be dismissed by frustrated magistrates.

My colleagues in the General Office were mostly Londoners and very friendly and welcoming for the most part. Anita shared my desk space. An 'East Ender' with the commensurate cockney accent, she was a devout West Ham football supporter who spent many Saturday afternoons down at the Boleyn Ground. When she was not drooling over Paul Brush, West Ham's wonder-boy, she would tell me what Greg Edwards was playing on his Capital Radio Soul Spectrum show. She loved Greg and was forever encouraging me to visit the Lyceum Ballroom in The Strand for the 'soul nights' which I knew were extremely popular. However, I wasn't a big fan of Greg's as I felt much of the music that he played was at the commercial 'disco' end of the soul music spectrum. This was the main reason I never did attend the Lyceum Ballroom in the Strand. I was already an elitist music snob.

"You want to go to Maccy D's at lunchtime, Paul?" Anita asked me one day.

"Where?" I asked.

She smiled, "McDonalds.".

"What's that, a wine bar?" I asked.

"No!" she shrieked. "It's a burger restaurant. Where are you from?"

~~~~~~~

From the time I first arrived in London, I frequented 'Crackers' nightclub in London's Wardour Street, Soho, somewhere I had grown familiar with prior to my arrival in London. Its position as the place to be on a Sunday evening was well documented in all the Black music periodicals. With a policy of playing the latest, best, and hardest jazz-funk tunes, DJ George Power, was worshiped by a clientele at the pinnacle of London's esoteric clubbing scene. It was one of the few clubs in London's West End that admitted black people in great numbers. In fact, the Crackers' clientele was almost exclusively black.

The dancing was frenetic, creative with certain moves bordering on the balletic. I learned that some of the better dancers attended jazz dance classes in Covent Garden to gain that important edge on the dance floor. It was a far cry from what I was used to and far from the scene I imagined at the Lyceum Ballroom in the Strand. Club life in London at that time was largely segregated along racial lines, and this was very much a fact of life or considered normal by almost everyone that I met.

In addition to the segregated nature of the night life, after living in London for a few weeks, it began to sink in that black people were not represented as commuters on the underground trains I used to get to work. I noticed the same when I was out and about during my lunch break in Victoria. It did not take long for me to realise that limited access to decent jobs had far-reaching ramifications for London's black community.

On a lighter note, maybe this explained the striking difference in fashions. Back home in Lincolnshire all my peers were aware of the fashion-conscious London youth. In the mid-seventies I had marvelled at the smart clothes worn by Arsenal's football supporters visiting Nottingham Forest's City Ground. The guys were wearing clothes that, if I could afford them, I would wear on a night out but never at a football match. It was insignificant to me at the time that all the visiting supporters were white youths. Now here I was a few years later, observing the fashion trends of black youth inside Crackers and noting the tight-fitting denims and military style shirts favoured by many of the patrons.

Hardly the trendy fashion worn by the (mainly white) 'Soul boy' tribes who frequented the fashionable underground suburban soul clubs in Essex and Kent. This inconsistency, I surmised, was probably since most black youth that I met didn't have access to the same well-paid jobs as their white working-class contemporaries and this also explained why most young black women that I met didn't own or drive a car.

For someone from outside of London, raised in a white community, coming to terms with the starkly contrasting lifestyles experienced by young black and white people was painful for me to accept as normal.

Eventually I agreed to attend a midweek West Ham match with Anita. A 2nd Division club, West Ham's East End working class support was fanatical and infamous for hooliganism.

"Let's watch the match from behind the goal," Anita said when we arrived.

Surrounded by very lively young West Ham fans, by kick-off, the terraces were filled nearly to capacity, with everyone wedged in shoulder to shoulder. I looked around and quickly noticed that I was the only black face in that section of the ground.

As the teams ran out onto the pitch, memories of my time at Boston Utd as a ten-year-old suddenly came flooding back. The opposing side has a black player. This was like showing a red flag to a bull. Each time he got the ball, the whole terrace were standing erupted in unified chants of '*nigger*'.

I turned and looked at Anita. Her face was bright red, and she looked like she wanted the earth to swallow her up. She looked like that for most of the match. She was embarrassed, but I also thought it was naïve of her to have not foreseen this outcome since she mixed with these people on a regular basis. I knew from what I had seen in my files at work that the right-wing racist group, the National Front, frequented the Boleyn football ground in large numbers.

"I'm so sorry," said Anita when we sat down in the office the next morning. She never spoke of the match again and certainly did not invite me to any more games.

A few weeks later, I noticed John Goldsmith showing a young, black female around the office. She was given the desk opposite of mine, and I learned her name was Rosemary and she was a seventeen-year-old school leaver. She wore a box pleated skirt and high collared blouse, a style favoured by young black females. She quickly settled into office life.

Rosemary was initially incredibly quiet and clearly very new to the office environment. I would later discover that she was also unused to being in the company of so many white people. As the months went by, I noticed a gradual change in her demeanour as she befriended her white colleagues who all seemed brash and that much louder. She would join the rest of the female office staff on lunch breaks at the McDonalds on Victoria Street. I watched Rose develop into a confident and assertive young lady who became a popular and reliable worker in the General Office. We became good friends.

"You're a novel one, aren't ya?" Rose said to me one day.

"What do you mean?" I asked.

Rose laughed. "You sound like you're trying to speak like the white solicitors."

It was true that I was conscious of my Lincolnshire accent and did unconsciously mimic the speech pattern of professional solicitor colleagues. Rose noticed this and enjoyed playfully teasing me about it.

Eventually, Rose invited me to her parent's home in New Cross, South East London for dinner. Rose's parents were Jamaicans, and the food reflected that. Her mum was fascinated by my heritage. It was still highly unusual in those days to meet the offspring of a black man and a white woman.

Rose became a regular girlfriend and helped introduce me to the West Indian culture of food, house parties and dancing. Dancing to reggae, particularly 'lover's rock', with a female partner was so alien to the soul music culture I'd grown up in where guys danced largely by themselves. It was a pleasant, exciting, cultural awakening.

'Lovers' was a softer style of reggae music that was very popular in the late seventies and early eighties. The lyrics often related to lost love or difficult relationships between men and women. It was a style which was particularly favoured by young black women and was often the staple at house parties where couples would dance together in a tight embrace, hips undulating to the rhythm. It was a very intimate experience and one that my hips, unused to a reggae beat, took a little time to get used to. However, with the willing instruction and help of numerous dance partners, it quickly became second nature.

The Solicitor's Department offered a career structure and assistance with further education. It was an attractive offer that I decided to take advantage of. I began attending evening classes at Brixton College, funded by the department. Within nine months I completed an 'O' level in *the General Principles of English Law*. From there I attended evening classes at South London College, where within another ten months I successfully completed my 'A' Level in *English Law*. I had a law degree course firmly in mind.

Eventually, my daily work involved visiting William McCrorie's office to provide him with information from the daily list of prosecutions around London. It was sparsely furnished, with piles of files neatly stacked in every conceivable space. He would often be sitting behind his desk, the telephone wedged between his shoulder and ear, shouting instructions to the poor soul on the other end while typing with two fingers at breath-taking speed.

When I would enter his office, he would peer at me over his horn-rimmed spectacles and nod for me to take a seat while he continued typing and shouting into the phone. After he got off the phone, he would often engage me in conversation, usually about the weekend's football. He and his close friend Robert Birch, the Metropolitan Police Solicitor, were avid season ticket holding Crystal Palace supporters.

I found our brief, three-minute chats to be highly motivational. I felt privileged to be in this genial man's company, even for such a short period. For the most part, he seemed genuinely interested in me and my welfare. He would continue to ferociously prod the typewriter keys in woodpecker fashion as he asked me questions about where I lived and how I got to work. And each time he would inevitably end up asking me, "Can you type yet?"

The penny finally dropped. I had to learn to type in order to progress to Law Clerk, the next rung on the promotion ladder.

~~~~~~~~~

After enjoying hostel life for about six months, I was persuaded to share a flat in Tooting Broadway with a few friends from the Hostel. That lasted for one month as the guys refused to take responsibility for keeping the flat tidy, so I found myself a small bed-sit on the top floor of a large Edwardian house owned by an Algerian family in Balham. I paid eighteen pounds a week for rent and had access to a small gas meter in an adjoining toilet where I would deposit twenty pence coins to run a small cooking stove in one corner of my room.

Balham was an area you had to move through carefully. I felt uncomfortable visiting the local pubs, particularly The Bedford pub in nearby Bedford Hill which was frequented by prostitutes. They would visit from far afield, walking the streets from Balham station towards Tooting Common and Streatham Hill to ply their trade. But one huge plus about Balham was Austin, who owned the local West Indian barbershop. He and his young assistant, Starsky, knew just how to cut and style my hair.

On Sunday nights I received my education in hard-core reggae from Frontline International, a sound system from nearby Brixton, at Studio 200, which was a three-minute walk from my bedsit. This was not a lightweight venue for the fainthearted and smoke averse, and I must have stuck out like a sore thumb. I did not have dreadlocks for starters, and my clothes bought from the Kings Road in Chelsea were fashionably stylish, unlike the black outfits, hoisted trousers, and heavy shoes favoured by the largely Rastafarian clientele.

"You're here every week, but you don't look like a reggae lover," a white barmaid said to me one night.

"I just live around the corner and coming here is better than the pub or watching the telly," I said.

My foray into Studio 200's heavy reggae set was to come to an end when I discovered the Wessex Suite in Clapham Junction was hosting regular funk and soul nights each Sunday. The thirty-minute walk home across Wandsworth Common into Balham at 1:00 am was a small price to pay for a great evening out.

One Saturday afternoon, my mother made the four-hour journey from

Boston on National Coach to visit me in Balham. As she climbed the stairs and entered my artfully arranged and exceptionally clean bed-sitting room, she looked around and smiled.

"We all have to start somewhere," she said sweetly. She was always one to see the positive.

One day, while walking around Balham's food market, I looked up and saw a sign that would lead me on a journey that would provide me with an invaluable skill set and change my professional life forever.

Martin Luther King School of Typing

~~~~~~~~~~

With William McCrorie's increasing interest in my ability to type swirling around in my head, I entered the grubby looking door below the sign. I walked up the stairs onto the first floor, which opened into a classroom setting with a chalkboard at one end and fifteen wooden desks and chairs neatly facing it, each with a typewriter.

I knocked on the closed door of an adjoining room. A lady opened the door.

"I want to learn to type. Or rather, I need to learn to type to do my job," I said.

She smiled. "We can certainly help you there. We run a beginners Pitman course at 10:00 am Saturday morning for people such as yourself."

The following Saturday morning I arrived promptly at 10:00 am. She had lied as there wasn't anyone like me among all the students sitting behind their typewriters. For one thing, some of them showed a frightening level of competency. For another thing, they were all females.

Despite the obvious drawbacks, I decided to stay. I was painfully slow at first, navigating the keyboard at a snail's pace. The teacher was wonderfully patient and would occasionally chastise the young ladies, who would laugh at my efforts. I suspected I was something of a novelty to them. But I persevered, attending class each Saturday morning for what seemed like an eternity.

Unfortunately, when it came to the final exam, I failed. I was unable to complete the exercises with sufficient speed in which to pass. However, I gained a competency and confidence that would help me in the forthcoming keyboard age of my chosen career.

Confident that I was ready for promotion, I applied for a position as Law Clerk and was invited for an interview. John Clark, a Principal Legal Executive at one of London's Crown Courts, chaired my promotion board.

"What do you think should happen to Ronald Biggs?" he asked right away.

I knew enough about New Scotland Yard's politics to give an answer that would have pleased all law abiding and God-fearing people. Biggs, the notorious Great Train robber who escaped from prison in 1965, was now leading an untouchable life of leisure in Brazil.

"…and it's important to bring him back to England as justice must, as always, be seen to be done," I concluded a few moments later.

I detected a half smile from John, probably relieved that he had not got one of those black militant types to deal with.

The next day I was sitting at my desk in the General Office, when William McCrorie walked in. He did not peer over his glasses to bark instructions at John Goldsmith this time. Instead, he walked towards the back, where my desk was located. The room became deadly silent as everyone looked down at their desk and pretended to work.

McCrorie walked over and slapped an envelope on my desk, his index finger momentarily pinning it down as if to stop it from blowing away. He smiled slightly, turned around and walked out of the office, avoiding eye contact with anyone.

Everyone in the office was now looking at me as I picked up the envelope with my name on it and opened it. I held my breath as I read the words:

'Result of Promotion Board: Fitted for Promotion.'

I was ecstatic and felt that all my hard work attending evening classes and typing classes on a Saturday morning had paid off.

Within a few days I was transferred to Middlesex Guildhall in Parliament Square to begin my new career as a Law Clerk at Middlesex Crown Court. My job was to prepare simple cases on behalf of the Metropolitan Police Solicitor, for Crown Court trial, where barristers instructed by the police would serve as the prosecution. This work offered me a closer insight into the world of policing, albeit from my rarefied work environment. My new colleagues helped me understand what was expected of me.

My duties at Middlesex Guildhall, an impressive Grade 2 building that had served as a Crown Court since the early 1970s, brought me into contact with many police officers, particularly Criminal Investigation Department (CID) officers, who would have to seek me out at Court and would often be reliant upon my help as the prosecuting solicitor's representative. I became friendly with a few of these officers but soon realised they wanted something from me, something that their career progression and credibility demanded; a successful conviction at Crown Court.

Chapter 4

The Law Clerk Years

In early Spring of 1981, two friends from my Bayswater hostel days, Ossie and Neil, approached me about sharing a rented flat with them. As they were keen to leave the hostel and I was ready to move on from my current arrangement, the timing was perfect. Between us we found an ideal flat on Kingswood Road, near to the top of Brixton Hill in South London. By this time, I was settled into my work at Middlesex Guildhall. Each morning I would catch a bus to Brixton underground station and take the Victoria line to Victoria, where I could walk along Victoria Street to Parliament Square in about fifteen minutes. I enjoyed both my role and the ease of travel from my new home.

My flat mates and I all got along well, both had West Indian heritage, Ossie from Montserrat, and Neil's parents were Barbadian. We would often sit around in the evenings, relaxing and talking about our lives, including our jobs. Neil worked for the Ministry of Defence at Empress State Building in Earl's Court, and Ossie worked for the Metropolitan Police's G10 Crime Statistics in Buckingham Gate. They also knew what I did for a living, which is probably why their faces registered such shock the first time I said, "I get paid to watch porn at work, what did you do today?"

This happened occasionally on cases that involved the seizure of obscene material, usually films but sometimes books, which would be committed to our Crown Court by the Clubs and Vice Unit's Obscene Publications branch. In the instances when I would be delegated to the courtroom as the prosecuting solicitor's representative, I would take a customary seat behind the bewigged prosecuting barrister.

In these porn cases, I would watch with interest as the jury was sworn in. How would these ordinary folks react once the judge told them they would have to watch hour after hour of hard pornography, via the large screen and cinematic equipment set up in the court room? You would think this would elicit reaction from at least some of them, but never once did I detect any emotion from the assembled jurors. The defence counsel's strategy was simple. They hoped that by showing the jury hours of film footage they would become either bored or desensitized. Because of this they would view the material as unlikely to deprave or corrupt and return a verdict of not guilty.

Like all Crown Courts, mine had a police room and a contingent of police officers appointed to the Court to perform security duties. In our case, that was usually from the neighbouring Cannon Row, one of London's most famous police stations. I would often get into conversations with these officers as they went about their daily business. It was during one of these chats I was told that, as a member of the Metropolitan Police civil staff, I had the privilege of using the gymnasium in the basement of the Cannon Row police station.

Since the police station was on the opposite side of Parliament Square, I ventured across during my lunch break. I approached the police constable on back gate security duty and showed him my civil staff police pass.

"Where's the gym, Officer? I'm interested in using it."

He yawned and pointed into the corner of the station yard.

"Down that stairway", he said flatly.

"Thank you," I said.

He nodded and gave me a half smile. I had a feeling that getting one visitor looking for directions was about the most exciting thing that had happened to him that day.

I entered the police station yard and walked down the steps, into a small area that housed a changing room. Just past that was a much larger room, with a boxing ring in the centre. Scattered around the boxing ring were various metal contraptions fixed to the outer wall, along with iron discs stacked on metal racks. I would later discover these were weight training machines. From that day on I would visit the gym regularly, keen to bulk up my lanky slender frame.

The gym soon became an especially important place for me, for the weight training but mostly for the social aspect. I gained the impression that for some isolated black staff scattered in so many differing New Scotland Yard branches and departments it served as a useful social hub. The weight training facilities were mostly for police civil staff members of the Comets Weight Training Club managed by Bob Viner and Keith Murray, both of whom occupied senior positions in New Scotland Yard's (C3) Fingerprints department. Very few police officers used the gym's facilities.

The gym attracted several characters who enriched my social life over the next few years. There was Detective Sergeant John Streeter, a member of the Special Branch and personal protection officer to the Attorney General. While in the changing room, he would open his briefcase and remove a handgun. The first time he did this, I stood there watching, mesmerised. I had never seen a handgun before. He would then lock it away in one of the metal lockers that seemed to be the preserve of older members.

It was in this same room that I received my first serious encouragement to join the Metropolitan Police as a uniformed officer.

~~~~~~~

One afternoon I was sitting on a bench in the changing room, pulling on my training shoes.

"God knows, things have got to change," a deep voice said.

I looked up. A tall white man stood at the other end of the room, wearing a towel around his waist, and dripping with water from the communal showers he had just come out of. There was a small group of us getting changed out of our office clothes to use the gym. Everyone stopped what they were doing and looked at the man to see who he was talking to.

"We need to get more people like yourself into the job," he continued.

He did not mention me by name, but it was apparent he was talking to me, and by people like me he was referring to black people. I gave a half nod to acknowledge I heard him, but I was not about to get into a serious conversation about what was a prickly subject for me. And I certainly was not going to discuss it in the changing room with a stranger wearing only a towel around his waist.

I went back to pulling on my shoes, wanting that to be the end of the matter. But in the corner of my eye, I could see he was still looking at me. I looked over at him again. He continued to stare at me with a look of pain etched across his face.

He's pleading with me! Well, I'm not having it, I thought.

I had my views on joining the police as a constable. They were views that were largely influenced by my work in the Solicitor's Department General Office at New Scotland Yard, where many of the files on my desk had the word 'Sus' written on them. Police officers had to apply to our office for the assistance of a prosecuting solicitor for any forthcoming Magistrate's court trial. Once the application form was received, we'd place it in a buff folder and write an abbreviation of the offence on the front of that folder. 'Sus' was a word that I and other colleagues in the General Office would regularly write. It was an abbreviation for Suspected Persons, taken from an

Act that was introduced to control returning soldiers from the Napoleonic wars that ended in 1815. Often destitute and homeless, they would wander the streets, sleeping in public spaces, and causing anxiety among the elite classes.

'Every suspected person or reputed thief, frequenting any river, canal, or navigable stream, dock, or basin, or any quay, wharf, or warehouse near or adjoining thereto, or any street, highway, or avenue leading thereto, or any place of public resort, or any avenue leading thereto, or any street, or any highway or any place adjacent to a street or highway; with intent to commit an arrestable offence - Section 4, Vagrancy Act 1824.'

Repeatedly I would read applications for legal assistance and time and time again the same well-worn template seemed to be used by the arresting officer. Hundreds of these files went across my desk in my few months at the General Office, saying things such as 'the suspect was a young black male who had been seen trying car door handles or looking into handbags at a bus stop'. Not once did I ever see any mention of witnesses or victims. No, it was sufficient for one or two officers to witness such *offences* and usually achieve a conviction.

I knew from my friends and associates that there were undoubtedly some young black guys out there on the street, robbing people. But the sheer number of these template statements suggested to me that there might have been an undercurrent of police *controlling* young black men who, in the words of some officers I would accompany and chat with at court, failed the 'attitude test'.

In addition, when our Court would get backlogged with cases, the Lord Chancellor's Department would transfer Middlesex cases to St Albans, Hertfordshire, or Watford. In these instances, I would sometimes travel back into London by train with the police officers in my case. On occasions during our long conversations on the train, they would drop their guard, forgetting my colour and position and openly discussed sorting out the 'sooties' as they referred to black males.

If I were right, then these cases and convictions would seriously limit the potential of black youth in the career market and often keep them in low standard public housing. Not to mention this would continue to stoke and inflame the historical bitterness many black people felt towards the police. It was a vicious circle and not one that I wanted to contribute to. This was especially true after the Brixton riots[1], which as far as I could see was a

---

[1] The rioting was sparked by antagonism between black youths and the police. On Friday April 10, 1981, two police officers were attempting to help an injured young black man in their car when a group, misinterpreting the officers' actions as harassment, attacked the vehicle. Two days of rioting ensued on the streets of Brixton, 299 police were injured, along with at least 65 members of the public. 61 private vehicles and 56 police vehicles were destroyed. 28 premises were burned and another 117 damaged.

backlash by black youth against a police force that was continually fabricating cases against them.

~~~~~~~~~~~

One image from the Brixton riots catapulted into the headlines. An officer stood with blood trickling down his face from a head wound under his helmet. This photo was carried in all the tabloids but was particularly

recognised for being emblazoned across the *News of the World* newspaper with the headline *The Bloodied Face of Brixton*. A few weeks after the riots I learned that the man in the picture, injured by a flying brick, was none other than Inspector Dennis 'Dinger' Bell, the man who had stood in my gym changing room with a towel around his waist and had encouraged me to join the police as a constable.

It was at the Cannon Row gymnasium that I met Cleo Sandiford, a member of the Police Forensics Department who would become a good friend of mine. He would often instruct me in the science of weight training, something he had mastered in his home country of Barbados as was evidenced by his impressive shoulders, biceps, and a chest that bore glowing testament to years of pumping iron. Having worked for the Metropolitan Police since the mid-seventies, he knew a lot of people and he introduced me to some of them.

Cleo worked alongside Marian Edwards, the sister of Capital Radio DJ Greg Edwards. Before long we were both invited to a house party at Marian's family home in Acton. Attending house parties in the black community was a regular and welcome occurrence. These parties would last all night, with food such as curried goat and rice, fried fish or jerked chicken often being served at 4:00 A.M. They provided a necessary social outlet for black people who were often discouraged or excluded from attending night clubs in London's West End. "It's a private party tonight, lads," was often a greeting that myself and others experienced at the doors of mainstream night clubs in London, as an innocuous means of preventing us from entering. Because of this, clubs that either had no such door policy or were owned or managed by black people became enormously popular.

Cleo also introduced me to his friends, Vince Daniels and Winston Baird, who were both from the Caribbean. Winston worked in Clubs & Vice, and like Cleo was a Barbadian. Vince was a former soldier and boxer who now worked in the Fingerprints Department. He was in his thirties, but still maintained a physique that even twenty-year-old's would envy. But it was Eddie who always made me smile and captivated my attention, for two reasons. First, he sported a giant wild afro at a time when it was unfashionable. Second, he was head barman at New Scotland Yard's in-house bar, suitably named 'The Tank'.

The Tank was a large, oblong shaped room on the ground floor, close to the reception hall. The furnishings and décor were bland and minimal, with a few sets of tables and chairs and a couple of portraits adorned the wall. No one cared about that because they were too distracted by the centre of attraction and the reason they were there. Down one side of the room was a generously stocked liquor bar, and behind that bar most evenings was Eddie, serving a diverse selection of New Scotland Yard detectives and assorted police staff. He was the only black person in The Tank on occasion. This and his wild, untamed afro and ability to laugh at everything and everyone made him a legendary figure.

On Friday nights The Tank would be in its full glory, with constant chatter, clinking glasses, and the smell of beer that would drift into New Scotland Yard's lobby and reception area. Against a backdrop of raucous laughter, detectives would try to impress young ladies from their typing pool as they spun colourful yarns about 'nicking armed blaggers' and other shady characters from yesteryear.

It was in The Tank that Winston and Cleo introduced me to Mount Gay rum, a favourite tipple from their island home of Barbados. A few glasses would have a transformational effect on my *Bajan* friends, and I would watch in wonderment as it occurred. Winston's volume would increase, as would his ability to tell animated, jaw-dropping stories that I so wanted to believe were true. Add to this the fact that he was also being buffeted by fellow drinkers in various states of inebriation the whole time, and it was quite the sight to behold. The later it got, the more freely the drinks would flow. Then around 10:00 PM many would make their way on unsteady legs across the road to St James Park London Underground Station.

~~~~~~~~~~

Several events preceded my decision to apply as a constable with the Metropolitan Police. Both Inspector Bell's words in the gymnasium changing room and my friend Cleo's constant encouragement were contributory factors. But I had also gained an invaluable insight into policing from my own work. Each day I would sit in the courtroom, observing and critiquing the way police officers presented their evidence, dealt with the cross examination, and acquitted themselves in a number of courtroom scenarios.

A mildly eccentric barrister named Edward Grayson was another influential figure in my life during this time. We would exchange views on policing and criminal evidence matters. Grayson often confided in me after a trial and shared his disappointment at the poor standard of evidence presented by police officers in the witness box. Grayson was always keen to discuss remedial solutions to improve rates of conviction. The worst bone of contention for him were cases thrown out by the judge due to lack of a continuity statement involving the submission of drug samples to the police forensic laboratory.

In moments of frustration after yet another loss in court, Grayson would insist that I join the police, if only to improve areas of police evidence submission. I would laugh, but the truth was the more we talked about it and the more time I spent watching various officers, the more I began taking his suggestion seriously. After all, the major impediment to my joining, the *sus* law, had since been repealed.

All these things were in the back of my mind one night when I picked my friend Cleo up and we headed out for a fun evening in London's club land. We were driving across Clapham Common, which at midnight was not particularly busy, talking about what we were going to do.

"Which club should we grace with our presence tonight?" Cleo asked.

"I don't know, but the best ones are over the river. We'll head for London Bridge and figure it out when we get there," I said.

"Sounds good," Cleo replied.

We were halfway across a junction in the middle of the Common when a speeding car came out of nowhere and ploughed into the side of my pale blue Vauxhall Viva. I never even saw it coming. The car and us spun like a dodgem car at the fairground. When it came to a stop, I got out and began walking around slowly to inspect the damage. My car was drivable but had sustained serious body damage, with the side stoved in where we had been hit. The offending vehicle suffered some front-end damage but had certainly come out the better of the two.

A young, white man walked towards me. "I just didn't see you, man," he said.

At that moment, a police van started driving towards us. I went out in the middle of the road and waved my arms. The van stopped, and six officers climbed out the rear door as I approached them. I explained to the officer driving the van what had happened. The other officers then began questioning both myself and the other driver. Finally, they instructed both of us to exchange the necessary information. All but one of them then climbed back into the police van. The one that was left stood close by without making eye contact with me.

"No one completed an accident report. To make sure one gets done, go to Clapham Police Station and report the accident," he whispered.

"Thanks," I whispered back.

The offending driver began getting back into his car.

"My insurance company will be in touch," I said.

"Sure, no problem," he said, before starting his car and speeding off across the Common.

A few minutes later I pulled my battered car into the parking lot of Clapham police station, parked, and walked into the front office.

"I've just been involved in an accident on Clapham Common. It was the other bloke's fault and now I want to report it," I said to the solitary officer on reception.

Before that officer had a chance to respond, a sergeant walked up (recognisable by the three stripes on his jacket tunic).

"Yeah, I heard that on the radio. Our van dealt with it."

I thought about what the officer had advised. "Yes, but now I want to make an accident report," I said.

"No need, the van driver will have completed one," The sergeant said with a touch of annoyance in his voice.

I left the station feeling like I had been fobbed off.

I got back in the car and told Cleo what had happened and how frustrated it made me feel.

"You should have told him you worked for the Job Solicitors," he said.

He's right, but why should I have to? I thought.

Monday morning, I went to my insurance company's office in Streatham and completed a full report of Saturday night's events. They called me back the next morning.

"I'm afraid the driver of the other vehicle reported it stolen on Sunday morning. Police have since found it burned out on Mitcham Common," the insurance clerk told me.

"The police questioned him at the accident scene. Shouldn't they have completed an accident report by now?" I asked.

"I asked them, and they said that one hadn't been completed because neither driver made any allegations," the clerk responded.

"That's absolute bollocks," I said. "Where does that leave me?"

"Well, he's not admitting any guilt regarding the accident and there were no witnesses so I'm afraid with your third-party fire and theft cover you have little chance of getting anything."

"Ok, and the other guy, theft of car, burnt out, he's going to get a full pay-out I guess?" I asked sarcastically.

"I really can't say sir, is there anything else I can help you with?"

"No, thanks," I said, crashing the phone into its cradle.

I looked through my wallet until I found the scrap of paper with the offending driver's name and address. Leafing through the telephone directory, much to my surprise, I found his name and telephone number. I dialled the number, *he's probably at home, unemployed,* I thought. The phone rang about half a dozen times until it was picked up.

"Can I speak to Mick?" I asked.

"Yeah, Mick speaking."

"I'm the guy you ploughed into on the Common on Saturday night," I said.

"Oh, yeah. You know my car was nicked early Sunday; the Old Bill found it burnt to cinders on Mitcham Common?"

I ignored his fairy-tale. "So, are you going to give me a statement for my insurance, since you admitted it was your fault?" I asked.

"Can't afford to mate," he said.

"You know this will leave me well out of pocket, don't you?" I said, raising my voice.

"Get yourself a can of petrol, mate," he said before hanging up the phone.

For a few fleeting moments I pondered over his inferred suggestion that I torch my car and claim on my insurance, but the prospect of going to prison quickly brought me to my senses.

Chapter 5

Joining the Met as a Constable

Six months after the accident, I completed an application to join the Metropolitan Police as a fully attested police constable. In my typical fashion, I decided I wouldn't tell anyone about my decision until it was approved.

~~~~~~~~~~

One evening two weeks later I was at home, relaxing with my flat mates. I was sprawled out on the sofa watching television, Ossie was sitting in an armchair and Neil was stretched out on the floor reading a newspaper.

A sudden knock on the door made me jump to my feet. No one ever knocked on our door. I walked to the door, saying a silent prayer that it wasn't the police regarding my application. Back in those days, police constable applicants would receive an unannounced home visit to determine whether they were 'fit and proper' for the job.

When I opened it, a police inspector in full uniform stood in front of me.

"Paul Wilson?" he asked.

"Yes, that's me," I said.

"I'm Inspector Hambleton from Clapham Police. I'm here regarding your recent application to join us. I just need to come in and look around. Is anyone else here with you?"

"Yes, my flat mates are here. But they have no idea I've done this," I said.

"Well, I'll need to ask them a few questions, too. That's how we do things," he said.

I turned and bounded back into the living room. Ossie and Neil looked up at me, slightly bewildered.

"What's going on, man?" Neil asked.

"Okay guys, here's the deal. I applied to join the police and they want to ask you some questions," I blurted.

I had barely got the words out of my mouth before the Inspector was by my side.

"Right, lads. I need to get your full names and date of birth," he said.

I could have sworn I heard Neil kiss his teeth as he stared at the Inspector.

"Why?" he asked.

I stood behind the Inspector, clasped my hands in a praying position and mouthed the word *please*.

Neil complied and Ossie (the quiet one) gave a half smile before he too gave the Inspector the information he asked for.

The Inspector gave a quick look around the flat, thanked us for our time and left.

"I owe you guys a drink," I said.

"You owe us a lot more than that! How could you?" Neil laughed.

Three days later I was notified to come down to Paddington Green police station to take the police recruitment test and have an interview. I arrived early and was taken into a classroom with twenty other applicants. Each table had a folder with a name on it. I found mine and took a seat.

"When the bell goes off, turn over the paper and answer all the questions on the paper," said the invigilator.

An hour later, I put my pen down and sighed. *Those questions had nothing to do with policing.*

Later on, they showed me into a large office for my interview. Seated behind a large desk were two male uniformed officers. One was a Chief Superintendent and the other was a Chief Inspector. After three and a half years of working for the police, I knew how to recognise ranks.

"Mr. Wilson is it?" asked the Chief Inspector.

"Yes, Sir," I replied.

"Tell us in your own words why you want to be a police constable," he said.

You need me more than I need you, was the first thought that came to mind, but of course I kept it to myself. Instead, I drew on my previous experience working in the Solicitor's Department and my preparing prosecution cases for the police.

"The police must reflect London if they are to gain and maintain the confidence of all London communities," I concluded.

The Chief Superintendent leaned forward. "And is you that

representation?" he asked, mimicking a poor West Indian accent much like Chalky White from comedian Jim Davidson's sketches.

"I believe I can make a difference, Sir," I said.

At the conclusion of what was a bland interview barbed with racist remarks, I got up and left the room, where a member of the police staff stood waiting.

"Wait here, please," he said, before going into the interview room and shutting the door.

A few minutes later the door opened and stepped back out, holding out his hand.

"I'm pleased to tell you that you have been successful and will receive formal notification in due course," he said, shaking my hand. "We just need to complete your pension transfer form. You have three years and a half years of police Civil Staff pension. We can either give you two-and-a-half years of police officer pension or two thousand pounds in cash."

"I'll take the pension in time, thanks," I said, although the thought of the cash to upgrade my aging Ford Capri was a fleeting temptation.

At that point I knew that I only had to endure twenty-seven and a half years before I could claim my full 'thirty-year pension'.

A week later I received a formal notification for my commencement at Police Training College in Hendon, North London, which would begin in two months.

Chapter 6

Police College, Hendon

Two months later, I climbed the steps of Colindale Underground station with a battered suitcase in one hand and a map in the other. As I stepped into the North London sunshine, I turned left toward Hendon Police Training College. They had offered me an overnight option, to assist with the 9AM start on my first day, but I turned it down. I was not concerned by a 9AM start. In fact, I was early as usual. My primary concern that morning was whether my new haircut was still within the regulation length. A few minutes later, I turned a corner and looming right in front of me was a large building. I approached the uniformed guard standing next to the gate.

"Excuse me, mate, is this the training school for new recruits?" I asked.

"No, take the next right," he replied.

I walked a few more minutes until I came upon some rather imposing concrete tower blocks surrounded by spacious grounds. I approached the security guard at the gate and showed him my introductory letter.

"All your classmates arrived last night," he said, ticking me off his list.

"Yeah, but I live in South London. I didn't see the need to spend another night here when I'll be here for long enough."

The guard laughed and pointed down the drive. "That's fine. The office is down that way. They will get you checked in."

As I walked down the drive, I approached the main buildings and came upon what looked like a huge car park. Around two hundred uniformed police officers, standing in rows stood at attention. Their helmets glistened in the early morning sun as a sergeant stood nearby barking out instructions.

"Ten shun!" he shouted. Two hundred boots slammed the ground in unison.

How did they get those razor-sharp creases? I thought as I made my way past the rows of smartly dressed constables, who were now watching me. The sergeant turned gave me a cold, disapproving glare.

Then I saw her. How did I miss her before? The one black face in a sea of 199 white faces.

We made eye contact and smiled at each other. *That is a powerful picture,* I thought.

I felt the heat rise in my face and turned my eyes away in embarrassment. I kept walking until I reached the reception area. From there I was shown to my living quarters on the 10th floor of one of the towers I had seen earlier.

"This is where you'll live for the next six months. The shower and bathroom are just down the corridor," a staff member said as we stood in the small, box-like room with a single bed, wardrobe, desk and a small sink in the corner. It was so small I was just impressed that we could stand in it at the same time.

"Thanks," I said, throwing my suitcase on the bed.

"Get settled in and then meet in the courtyard in twenty minutes. You will get further instructions from there," he said, turning to leave.

After he left, I laid down on the bed and stared at the ceiling, thinking about the one black face that I had seen on the parade.

What have I done?

Twenty minutes later I was standing in the middle of the courtyard surrounded by forty other young men milling around, talking, and laughing. As I looked around, I made a quick observation.

They are all white!

Or so it seemed, anyway. A few minutes later, two guys walked up and introduced themselves to me as Charlie and Johnny. Charlie was Anglo-Indian and had a strong South London accent. Johnny was from Iraq. We stood there talking for several minutes getting to know each other.

Charlie looked around. "Looks like we represent the ethnic minority," he said. The three of us laughed.

A few minutes later we were shown into the classroom and took our seats at the same desks we would use for the next six months. There were eighteen recruits, including two female constables.

"To start, I would like everyone to introduce themselves," the instructor said.

Everyone took turns sharing a little about themselves. I learned that Charlie had worked for the police as a motor mechanic at the Police Traffic Garage in Croydon, South London. I had only known him a few minutes, and I could already tell he had a wry sense of humour.

When Johnny announced he was from Iraq, the instructor replied, "You lot are losing". Everyone laughed, including Johnny. This was a reference to the ongoing war between Iran and Iraq.

When we weren't in the classroom receiving instruction on various elements of criminal and traffic law, we were outside doing practical exercises in various parts of the sprawling estate. They designed these sessions so we could put what we learned in the classroom into practice. Scoring well on the classroom test is one thing but dealing with a real-life crime on the streets is another matter. On paper you might have all the right answers on how to handle the unlawful possession of drugs, but how will that translate when you are in the middle of that situation?

These mock incidents would be staged on one of the estate roads, and everyone sooner or later would be called up to take charge of the "situation". The first time, I made it a point to stand behind the group and try not to catch the eye of the instructor. This only works for so long, especially when other students are trying to do the same thing.

"Wilson, out!" yelled the instructor.

I came out from the safety of my classmates and walked towards the road. I was on centre stage, an actor who was yet to come to terms with my role. My actions would be open for all to see, scrutinise and learn from. We had two instructors, a Sergeant and a Constable, the instructor would often play the "criminal" or occasionally a member of the public seeking assistance. He loved to keep us on our toes with all the different incidents he came up with. At the time it was painful, other times it was funny but considering that we would be on the streets in less than six months, in the presence of the public, these exercises were invaluable.

Twice a week we would do drill marching or drill classes. I could never get my head around why we did this. I had never seen police march anywhere! It seemed to me that it was just an excuse for semi-retired sergeants who had previously served in the army (in particular the Guards Regiments) to impart their fading memories of a military bonded by parade ground drill on unsuspecting fresh-faced police recruits.

With those drills came the need for an immaculate uniform turnout, razor-sharp creases in the trousers *and* the sleeves of the tunic jacket. This I could manage, but I struggled with the requirement for shoe toecaps to be *bulled* to a mirror-like sheen. Fortunately, each class had someone who had served in the military and was familiar with things like marching and bulling shoes. In our class that person was Tony Popham, or "Pop" as he was known, a 29-year-old former soldier who was now our class captain.

Pop was not the only ex-military man in our class. There was also Andy Verrier, who had previously served as a member of the Territorial Special Air Service (SAS) but refused to disclose any details about his experience. In his introduction on the first day, he did not hold back on explaining what his goals were.

"I didn't join the police for free McDonald's burgers. I joined to climb the ranks, as I think I can best serve the police and our communities as a senior officer."

A few weeks into training, 'Pop' gave Andy the nickname "Trapper" not because of any hunting prowess but because of his ability to secure a date and begin a relationship with Emma, one of the two female recruits in our class.

Every morning was the ritual of the parade where all classes, in full uniform, assembled in rows on the parade ground to await inspection by a senior officer, usually an Inspector. I couldn't help but think about that first day when I had walked by the parade on my way in and made eye contact with the one black face in the crowd.

During each inspection, the senior officer would walk slowly up and down each row, stopping occasionally to pick a piece of fluff off a jacket or to point out that the constable's hair was touching the collar of their shirt and must be cut before the next parade. I prayed the inspector would pass by me without comment. Each morning I would wet my hair and within minutes it would shrink tightly to my head, giving the appearance it was short as it fitted neatly under the tall helmet. Once the parade was finished and we could relax a little, I would go into the men's room and flick my hair out with a steel afro comb. It never once dawned on me to think that anyone might ask why I had all that hair in the classroom but short hair on parade.

We also had physical exercise (PE) and self-defence classes during the week where I would try to master the complex art of Jiu-Jitsu and other martial arts, which was fun but also incredibly time-consuming. There were a lot of different moves to remember, and I was always sceptical about how useful it would be in dealing with a pub fight on a Saturday night.

But what I really disliked was swimming, which usually involved having to climb and jump from the highest diving board. I did not like heights. Johnny Banham was one of the PE instructors and a former boxer who had represented England. I knew him from my days at Cannon Row gym where he would coach the Metropolitan Police boxing team. For some reason, Johnny would not acknowledge that he knew me previously and often gave me a hard time as I battled the many life-saving exercises in the pool. I felt these were particularly pointless as I had often heard that no one should voluntarily jump into London's heavily polluted Thames river as it would almost certainly be the last thing you ever did.

Banham was also responsible for arranging a milling session for new recruits, which was an exercise adapted from the military where two officers stand head-to-head in an informal boxing ring and pummel one another until told to stop. Now here is where I could shine. Fighting was in my DNA or so I imagined. My brother Steven was a highly accomplished boxer and instructor whose achievements and prowess had earned him the nickname 'boxer' in the RAF Regiment. My Uncle Tony and Uncle Robin had also been title winning boxers in the British Army. Unfortunately, Uncle Robin later gained notoriety as a street fighter. He had a particular penchant for throwing punters through pub windows, a life choice that earned him numerous spells inside various prisons.

During my time at the Cannon Row gym, I had never once set foot in the boxing ring. But I had often whiled away the time watching Banham's expert tuition. I reckoned if I could just remember a couple of the basics, I stood a good chance at quickly knocking the other guy down. When my time came, I was matched with a recruit from another class, who had previously served in the Royal Marines.

"All right," said Banham, standing between us. "When I say go, start throwing punches until I tell you to stop."

I stood with my chin tucked down between my gloved fists in an orthodox boxing stance. I felt ready to explode.

"Go!" Banham shouted, quickly stepping out of the way.

I delivered a straight right followed by a haymaker of a left, neither of which contacted my opponent's head. However, he did stumble backward with a look of surprise on his face. Brimming with confidence, I swung two more punches, but those did not make contact either.

"Ok, that's enough!" shouted Banham, stepping between us.

As usual, he avoided eye contact with me and told us both to go and get changed. He gave no explanation of why. I felt cheated. I'd watched my other classmates go toe to toe for around forty-five seconds.

One morning we had our Physical Exercise class with a female instructor I had never seen before.

"Okay, line up!" she shouted.

After we were lined up, she walked down the line tapping each of us on the head and counting loudly. I was number twelve.

"I want all the odd numbers to stand directly in front of the even numbers," she shouted.

Everyone looked at each other like she must be crazy, but we complied.

"Odd numbers, I want you to grip the waistband of your partner's shorts. On my command, pull down your partner's shorts," she said.

A ripple of laughter spread around the room.

The instructor then walked up to me.

"I've heard you people are blessed down there," she said loudly, "so I'm going to stand right here to see for myself."

Everyone laughed again. I forced a sarcastic smile.

If she wanted to have a look all she had to do was ask, I thought at first.

But no, this is about dominance and humiliation. A reminder of days on the Plantation.

"Go!" she shouted. Within a split second, I gripped my partner's wrists to prevent exposure.

Despite these occurrences, my day-to-day life at Hendon was mostly uneventful and boring. Most evenings were spent in my room, swotting up for the inevitable classroom test the following morning. But on occasion, there would be a knock on my door from someone telling me I had a phone call. Each floor had a phone fixed to the wall. Its loud ring could often be heard all over the floor. Whenever it was for me, it was usually Jennifer.

Jennifer was a nineteen-year-old of African Caribbean heritage who joined a few weeks after me. She was experiencing a multitude of issues. Often, I would answer the phone only to be met with loud sobbing. She was finding the learning particularly challenging and had failed a couple of the 'progress tests', causing her to fear she might get back classed by her uncaring and unsympathetic instructors. There were also family pressures, as her Dad was not happy with his princess being exposed to the dangerous life of a police officer. We would talk for ages and eventually, Jennifer would calm down and adopt an assertive voice, making it clear that she wasn't about to give up. We became firm friends.

I found the learning difficult, too. It was unlike anything that I had ever experienced. Huge chunks of legalistic text had to be memorised and recited like a parrot. Mnemonics were used extensively to aid our memory and application of the legislation and police practices.

"Wilson, come out and deal with this man who has been knocked down by a car," shouted the instructor. "I want you to kill the cow."

COW was a useful mnemonic to be applied at the scene of a road traffic accident. C = Casualty, O=Obstruction and W=Witnesses. There were so many, almost all extremely helpful in the practical scenarios that would come our way.

Many of my class colleagues would somehow find time to do their homework and spend time in the downstairs Peel Bar, a fully equipped bar and lounge for use by the recruits. I did not like the bar and its atmosphere, so when I had time, I would leave the estate and drive to Kilburn to experience a different environment. This was something I felt was necessary, as a form of escapism from what was for me an alien, disciplined, and sanitised environment that knew or cared little about the multicultural London I had grown to love over the previous few years.

As the six-month course progressed, I grew increasingly confident and began to enjoy the daily rituals in a way that I guessed masochists enjoy flagellation. The syllabus made unsuccessful efforts to ensure that police recruits were equipped to relate to diverse sections of the community in a way police had failed to do in years gone by. These involved classroom sessions around human awareness, colloquially known as HAT (human awareness) training. Included in this was a project whereby, in couples, we were asked to present to the class on a particular community-related subject of our choice.

My project was post-war immigration to the UK and my partner was Charlie. We spent time together in the evenings preparing, but as time went by, I noticed that I had begun to unilaterally influence the content of our project. I know Charlie tried his best to retain a sliver of what had been agreed at the outset. But in an autocratic leadership style that was to surface on more than one occasion in the future, the end project had morphed into an analysis of the *Rastafarians in Britain.*

I became familiar with Rastafarians and their culture during my lengthy induction into London's reggae music scene. From what I had seen and heard, they were often misunderstood and unfairly stereotyped and bore the brunt of both serious and low-level racism at the hands of police. I felt that the police needed to have a better understanding of them and their culture to slow down these occurrences, or better yet prevent them altogether.

One night Charlie leafed through my notes in preparation for our presentation.

"How did we get to this?" he asked.

"You know it's something you wanted to do," I said, trying to keep a straight face.

Charlie shook his head. "No, I don't think so."

The morning of the class presentations, we waited patiently while our colleagues presented their projects. I could not help but notice that they all carefully steered away from anything that might be construed as even slightly controversial.

They will certainly sit up and take notice when we do ours! I thought.

When it was our turn, I was just about to stand up when a loud explosion rattled the windows. We all looked at each other in shock. The only time I had ever heard anything that loud was in the agricultural fields of Lincolnshire when industrial-strength explosives or *crow-scarers* were used to frighten the birds away from the young crops.

"Verrier, go check and see what happened!" shouted the instructor.

Andy ran out of the room and returned two minutes later looking crestfallen. As soon as I saw his face, I knew something serious had happened.

"There's been an explosion!" he shouted. "People are hurt and bleeding."

"Alright, class. Quickly make your way down the stairs and assemble in the driveway," the instructor barked.

Everyone started running down the stairs at the same time. Someone tripped and fell headlong down six steps. We helped him to his feet, saw that he was okay and kept going. Once we reached the ground floor, I ran through one of the open fire exit doors. A female officer sat on the grass, clutching her bloodied leg. Her black tights were ripped to shreds, and she was being tended to by another officer.

As we all gathered outside, a headcount was completed. Then we found out what had happened. It was not a terrorist attack, as many of us had feared. A workman repairing the roof of a neighbouring classroom with hot asphalt had inadvertently caused his gas bottle to explode, showering people below with fragments of building debris.

As the dust literally settled, our class was dismissed for the day. Charlie and I would not have a chance to present *Rastafarian's in Britain*, a project I had laboured over for three weeks. I had a feeling Charlie was not too bothered over this loss.

The end of course final examination was hyped so much by our instructors that all of us were living on the edge. We talked of nothing else. We would create a mock test for ourselves and sit around in lounge areas relentlessly questioning each other on every aspect of our learning over the past five months.

Finally, the big day came. To everyone's relief, all recruits in both of my intake classes passed the exam. There were no casualties. We could now look forward to our graduation dance at some remote hotel in the Hertfordshire countryside. But before that, there was the matter of performing the security detail, a responsibility thrust upon those who had successfully completed the last step necessary before becoming a full-fledged police constable. This meant patrolling the perimeter of the Peel Estate every evening and throughout the weekend.

My weekends were sacrosanct, a time for socialising with non-police friends and spending time with Grace, my girlfriend, whose Barbadian parents would always cook me the best Sunday lunch imaginable. I tried to block out the thought of not being able to leave the estate for one whole week, but as the time neared, I became increasingly depressed and agitated. I tried to convince myself this was the final hurdle and an easy one at that. Soon I would be free from all this nonsense. I remained unconvinced and made arrangements to present my dilemma to senior officers.

One morning, I stood in front of the Training College Chief Inspector pleading my case.

"Sir, I've made it this far in what have been challenging circumstances for everyone. But for me, and I suspect other black officers, we experience additional and different issues and pressures because of our background, colour, family, and friends. To be honest with you, the weekends and evenings away from this place have played a key part in my being able to cope."

The inspector listened intently, made a few notes, and nodded. I was excused security detail and allowed to go home that weekend.

The following Sunday, as I enjoyed a traditional West Indian dinner of chicken, rice, and peas with my Grace and her parents, I shared with them my experiences of the past six months. And for the first time, I shed a tear. It was a combination of happiness, sadness, and most of all relief that I had survived what had seemed at the time to be a cult-like experience designed to mould us into an unquestioning homogeneous group of young people, devoid of self-expression.

The next morning, I returned to Hendon, where we would all learn what police station we were to be posted to.

"Woolwich?" I said to the instructor, upon receiving the information about my post. "Don't they know I live in Brixton?"

"It's south of the river Thames. What's the problem?" he asked.

"Not exactly an easy journey for me, is it?" I protested.

"Have a word with our Personnel office. They make the decisions," he said.

A short time later, I bumped into Johnny Banham as I was walking into the Personnel office. For the first time in six months, he looked me in the eye and held out his hand.

"Congratulations on passing the final exam," he said.

I was surprised but shook his hand. "Thanks," I replied.

"Sorry I didn't speak to you on the course. I didn't want anyone to think I was favouring you," he explained.

"I see. Well, I really must get something sorted out. Bye," I said dismissively, walking past him to enter the office.

"How can I help you?" an officer at the desk asked.

"I've been posted to Woolwich, but I live in Brixton. Can I have something closer?"

The officer tapped his pen against the desk. "Hmm. Well, it just so happens that we posted an officer to Croydon who said he would prefer to be closer to his home in Greenwich," he said.

"That's understandable since Greenwich is close to Woolwich. I'm more than happy to swap with him," I said.

And so, it came to be. I was posted to the Croydon Police Station, referred to in police circles by its designated letters of 'ZD' or more commonly, using the phonetic alphabet, Zulu Delta.

The irony that I would refer to myself as a Zulu Delta every day for the next few years made me smile. It was meant to be.

Chapter 7

Croydon Police Station

One early December morning in '83 I sat at my kitchen table eating breakfast and reading the newspaper. In only a few more days, I would begin my life as a police constable at Croydon police station. I was spending the interim getting caught up on rest and phoning friends to find out which bus I should catch from Brixton Hill to Croydon town centre. I was unfamiliar with the route having very rarely ventured south of Thornton Heath pond during my time in London. Reading anything I thought would help me in my new career, I was keen to keep abreast of current affairs and would avidly read a quality newspaper each day.

As my eyes scanned the page, the words *PSI Report* caught my attention. In the article, the writer was responding to a report published a few weeks earlier by the Policy Studies Institute (PSI).

I had previously read about the PSI report while at Hendon. Commissioned by the metropolitan police, the PSI had been conducting a large-scale study of the relationship between the metropolitan police and the community for four years. The recent findings in this report were disturbing, something to which the author of the article seemed to agree.

"The PSI found that racial prejudice was pervasive, and that the Met was preoccupied with ethnic differences".

The PSI researchers, embedded with operational police officers for two years, had found the relationship between police and ethnic minorities particularly concerning. But of particular interest to me was that PSI researchers found that terms such as 'monkeys', 'spooks,' and 'coons' were widespread in both private conversation and on police personal radio.

It was against this backdrop that my career as a uniformed police officer began.

On my first day at Croydon, in company with two colleagues, Guy and Clive, I entered the Chief Superintendent's office for the customary 'welcome to Croydon' chat.

"Glad to have you with us, lads. What has taken you so long to join, PC Wilson, I see you've been with us for a few years? Anyhow, you three probationary constables have arrived just as we have lost three officers," was his opening comment and a reference to the weekend's car bomb that exploded outside Harrods department store in central London, the blast killed three police officers and three civilians and injured 90 people.

My first few days were very much about getting familiar with the station and the management structure. Just before Christmas, it was a very relaxed time for us new probationary constables and it was explained to me and the others that we would undertake a strictly supervised 'Street Duties' programme following the Christmas period and before we were set loose on Croydon's unsuspecting public.

After a few days of familiarisation, I learned that the police canteen was a social hub for officers as well as the place they would often sit and write their arrest notes. With time on my hands, I'd sit in the canteen sipping coffee and observing the antics of officers that I'd soon be working alongside. One morning I was standing at the counter waiting for my food when a black guy in plain clothes sidled up to me.

"You here?" he asked.

"Yes," I said, with a hint of sarcasm.

"No, I mean at Croydon."

"Yep."

He raised his eyebrows and let out a small chuckle before walking off to join his colleagues. I later learned he was Detective Constable Clay Neblett.

My colleagues described him as a "good bloke", so it seemed strange to me that he appeared reluctant to engage me in conversation for more than a few seconds. I would later learn that black officers avoided socialising with other black officers at work for fear of attracting spiteful comments from white colleagues.

Such cultural nuances were unfortunately not discussed with black recruits attending Hendon Police Training College otherwise I would have been made aware of the inherent danger in inviting a black friend to a police social function. That was something I had to learn the hard way when my girlfriend, Grace, accompanied me to a Croydon police Christmas party at a local pub. By this time, I had only been at the station for a few days and had not yet been assigned to a team but nevertheless I felt being seen at a Christmas social would help me integrate into station life.

Grace worked at a high street bank, the only black employee, so I felt she wouldn't feel out of place at a police social. She was attractive and intelligent, which I believed would help endear her to my new colleagues who I was certain would refrain from using vulgar language in her presence.

As we arrived in the function room of the pub there were a few cursory nods and glances as we sat down at the long table in the centre of the room. Everything was fine at first, the drinks flowed freely as everyone waited for the food to arrive. But as more drinks were consumed the mood began to change, it began as harmless banter that went back and forth between numerous colleagues seated either side of the table. Then things gradually went downhill as stories about recent arrests and other encounters with the public were recounted in increasingly loud voices. These accounts were littered and peppered with racial slurs such as "nigger," "coons," and "spades".

I looked at Grace, she rolled her eyes.

"Are these people your friends?"

"No, colleagues, I haven't actually started working with anyone yet," I said to distance myself from what was unfolding.

I tried unsuccessfully to block out the raucous chatter by engaging Grace in conversation, but she remained silent and slowly picked at food with her fork. Her eyes were glossy and her pale brown cheeks blushed crimson. I could tell she was distressed, and it filled me with sadness, shame, and guilt. How could I have been so recklessly naïve? Why hadn't I foreseen this outcome?

Finally, she turned in her chair, placed her fork on the table and glared at me. Her expression screamed, "get me out of here."

I put down my knife and fork, wiped my mouth with a napkin and nodded towards the door. Grace got to her feet and avoiding eye contact with anyone at the table quickly walked to the exit. I slightly nodded to a couple of surprised colleagues and followed her out the door.

On the drive home, I feebly attempted to explain the rationale behind attending the Christmas party.

"I honestly believed it was better to try to fit in by attending than not," I blurted.

Grace sat with her arms folded, staring straight ahead and not responding. In fact, she didn't speak to me for several days after that.

Following my Street Duties course of close supervision, I was posted to a 'Relief' as teams are known in police circles. Inspector John Simons was my Relief Inspector. A Scot with a burly physique and fatherly demeanour who was very precise and meticulous in his dealings with people and paperwork alike. I was told he was a former Sergeant in the Traffic Unit. It was good practice for Inspectors to welcome newcomers to the team, and I did not think I was treated any differently. His welcome chat was very thorough and reassuring.

"You'll never be as rich as a police officer but do well and you'll always be well off compared to the rest. And don't forget if you have any money problems at all don't keep it to yourself. Tell me about it and we'll see what we can work out. You do not want to get behind on your rent or mortgage payments or anything else that can get you into trouble. Will you let me know?"

"Yes, Sir," I said.

A few months later I found out that there had previously been a black officer on my team who was arrested and subsequently sacked because of "money problems".

In those early years, an Inspector was a god-like figure who held your career progression in his hand to do as he (or more rarely, she) saw fit. John Simons was often brusque and a man of few words, but he had a fairness about him I grew to admire. He would walk into the parade room where we assembled to hear the latest intelligence and news, along with postings for the shift.

"You all know what you're doing?" he would always ask in his Scottish accent when we were about to file out the door and onto the streets.

The relationship between Inspectors and Constables was an aloof one in those days. The Constables did the heavy lifting and Inspectors managed, often nudging the helm when necessary.

My favourite shift was 11pm to 7am. I would get home by 7:30am, sleep for a few hours and be up and around again by 1pm. That left me all afternoon to work in the garden, go shopping, and do other things that normal nine to fivers could not do during the week. Working those quiet hours also allowed me to walk the streets by myself and have some personal reflection. I would often ask myself deep and introspective questions such as *why have I joined the police?*

Chapter 8

The Axe Man

One night I was working my beat on Lower Addiscombe road at 1:00 AM. Since policing Croydon's night clubs was a drain on manpower, especially on the weekend, doubling up on foot patrol was forbidden until clubs closed at around 2 or 3 o'clock. For this reason, and because numbers were scarce on night duty anyway, I was on foot patrol by myself.

As I slowly walked through the drizzling rain, I longed for the time when I would have enough service under my belt to drive a police car so I could stay warm and dry on nights like this.

Out of the darkness a police car slowly approached me on the opposite side of the road. I recognised it as Inspector Simon's car. He made a U-turn and pulled up alongside me with the window rolled down. As he got out of the car, I felt the warmth from his vehicle as a short-lived respite from the chilly night air.

I really need to be an Inspector, I thought.

"Everything alright, Paul?" he asked.

"Yes, Sir, all correct," I said. This was the usual police parlance when asked questions by an Inspector or above.

"Bit quiet tonight, maybe when the clubs kick out it'll liven up a bit."

"Yes, Sir, let's hope so."

As Inspector Simons returned to his car, he paused before opening the door and pointed down the street.

"I passed a tall bloke up there wearing a long coat. He's coming this way. It looks like he's carrying something under the coat. Give him a pull."

With that he got in his car and drove off into the night.

I stepped back into the shadows to await this potential suspect. A couple of minutes later a tall figure in a long coat began walking in my direction. I leaned back against a low wall and tried my best to blend into someone's garden hedge. As the man neared me, I stepped into the centre of the pavement, blocking his way. His coat was unbuttoned, and he looked like a "biker" type with long hair and heavy boots.

"Bit cold tonight," I said.

"Yeah," he responded.

With my left hand, I reached over and tugged back his coat. A long-handled axe hung from the waistband of his trousers. It was the same type of axe I had used as a boy to split wooden logs for our open fire. I grabbed the wooden shaft of the axe and pulled it away from his waistband. At that very moment, a car drove by and I could only imagine the conversation they might be having.

"What's this for, mate?" I asked, holding the axe at arm's length.

"Someone tried to rape my girlfriend earlier," he said calmly.

"Okay, but why the axe?"

"I know who it was and I'm going to sort him out."

I called for a police van and arrested the man for carrying an offensive weapon. A small gathering of officers was waiting in the station yard when we arrived, just in case axe man tried to escape. Given the nature of the offence coupled with the allegation of attempted rape, my night duty CID colleagues took over the investigation of both matters.

For reasons best known to the investigating officer and the Custody Sergeant that night, the axe man was bailed to his home address following the charge. An hour after his release, I heard a call transmitted over my personal radio.

"Officer to deal please, disturbance in progress on private premises........."

The address given by the police control room was the axe man's address.

"That is my axe man from earlier this evening, approach with caution," I shouted into my personal radio.

Within thirty minutes the axe man was back in police custody. Apparently, when he returned home, he discovered that the man who had attempted to rape his girlfriend had returned for a second attempt. The axe man beat the rapist into a bloody mess, kicking him in the head numerous times with his heavy boots. He was arrested a second time and the rapist was taken to Croydon's Mayday Hospital and admitted to intensive care. He survived.

Chapter 9

Complaint

As a young constable walking the streets of Croydon, I drew interest from the sizeable black community who, for the most part, welcomed my presence. Older men often approached me and shook my hand. However, that was not the response I received from young, mostly black, guys.

They would walk down Croydon's North End in small groups and as they passed me there would be a loud, unified "kissing of teeth". This was an audible sign of distaste in the black community. Others would shout "traitor!" from the open window of cars as they drove past me. I was mostly immune to name calling.

One Friday night with other officers from Croydon I was posted 'up town' to Trafalgar Square, outside of the South African Embassy (which had been the target of weekly 'anti-apartheid' protests) when I was approached by a young, black woman. She got within inches of my face.

"What do you think you're doing? Don't you realise this evil apartheid regime treats you like a third-class citizen? Yet here you are, protecting and sustaining it!" she shouted.

I dearly wanted to engage in a discussion with her, but I was on duty, so I trotted out a stock answer.

"I'm here to prevent disorder, protect property, and keep the peace. While I might sympathise with your cause, I have a job to do," I said.

"You're all the same! You make me sick!" she said before storming off to re-join the small group of noisy protestors congregated outside of the vacant South Africa house.

Our brief interaction stayed with me more than any of the usual name calling and I would revisit it in my mind time and time again over the coming years.

The Morrison's were a black family that lived on a council estate in West Croydon. They had three teenage sons, none of whom I believe had a job. The Morrison brothers were well known to the police for petty theft and for being found in possession of cannabis. They would hurl verbal abuse at me like it was a favourite pastime, especially during my first few months on the street and particularly when I was working alone. Their vehicle, a Rover 3.5, rarely had a valid tax disc on display, so I would sometimes stop them, which only served to further poison things between us. One day I was called into my Inspector's office.

"Paul, you got your first complaint," he said, looking down at a paper on his desk.

My mouth dropped open and I stared at him, speechless. I was horrified that someone would go to all the trouble of putting pen to paper in order to complain about me.

"In due course you'll be interviewed by someone from the complaints department," he said, handing me a Form 163.

My eyes quickly scanned the page. The complaint was from the oldest Morrison brother. I had recently been to his house to arrest him for an assault offence, as we had a statement identifying him as a suspect. After a loud exchange of words at the front door, I entered the residence to remove him physically. His complaint was that I had gone into his house without a warrant.

When it came time for my interview with the Complaints Department, I had to attend Clapham Police Station where I waited outside Chief Inspector Ron Hope's office. A Sergeant from the Complaints Unit sat down next to me.

"Just tell the Chief Inspector exactly what happened and what paperwork you completed. I think you'll find him to be a reasonable bloke. Try not to worry."

Finally, I was called into the office. Chief Inspector Hope sat behind a large desk looking up at me sternly. We had never met before, but he was well known as being the most senior black officer in the Met.

"Sit down, PC Wilson," he said.

What followed was a most uncomfortable interview. Chief Inspector Hope informed me that he had established I had failed to complete the *premises searched* form following the arrest. After he finished, he pointed at the door.

"Wait outside and we'll be with you shortly."

I left the office and waited outside while the Sergeant remained and talked to the Chief Inspector. A few minutes later the Sergeant came out and handed me a statement of what had been discussed.

"You need to sign this," he said.

After reading the paperwork I signed it and handed it back to him. He smiled. "Alright, that is all over with. Just make sure you enter a record of the search in the register when you get back to the station. The next step will be for us to meet with the complainant. Chief Inspector Hope would like another word with you before you leave."

I went back into the office and sat down. Chief Inspector Hope looked more relaxed and not stern like before. He started asking me about my career, my aspirations, and how I was finding things. We had a good conversation.

As I got up to leave, he reached out his hand. "If you need a mentor, you know where to find me," he said.

I shook his hand and left the Complaints Unit in a much better frame of mind than when I arrived.

A month later, I received an internal memo telling me to call Chief Inspector Hope. When I called, he answered right away.

"PC Wilson, I need to update you on your complaint. Unfortunately, the complainant is dead. Someone stabbed him through the heart. It might be drug related but it's too early to tell as there is still an ongoing murder inquiry. What this means for you is that the complaint made against you will be discontinued."

"Thanks for letting me know, Sir," I said.

I was stunned. We had our differences but not in a million years would I have wished for this outcome.

Chapter 10

Resentment

Sometimes white members of the public were unhappy to see a black officer. One day my personal radio crackled with a message from our control room.

"Someone to deal with a theft person, Surrey Street junction with High Street."

"Zulu Delta from 826, I'll deal Mandy, I'm quite close by," I shouted into my personal radio.

I walked towards the location given by my Control Room colleague, Amanda Cousins.

Must be that group of people straight ahead, I thought.

There were about five people standing in a tight group on the pavement. I knew that 'theft person' was likely to mean there had been a 'mugging'. As I neared the group an elderly man stepped away from the rest

"I don't know why they sent you. It was one of your lot that did it," he said.

"A police officer did it? Really? Did you get their number?" I asked sarcastically.

The man just glared at me. My attempt at humour had done little to placate him.

"You'd better get one of your mates because I'm not talking to you," he said.

"Look, sir, tell me what's happened here so I can help you," I said seriously.

He turned his back on me and carried on talking to his group. I approached another member of the group and tried to get an understanding of what had occurred.

"If there's been a mugging here then I need to get the description of the suspect circulated as quickly as possible."

"He was black so you're not going to get him, are you?" the elderly man said sarcastically.

Ignoring him, I reached for my personal radio.

"Zulu Delta, 826 here, I need the Section Sergeant to join me in the High Street as soon as possible."

A few minutes later Sergeant Ken Sheehan arrived.

"Sarge, I think this elderly chap is a victim of theft, but he won't talk to me because he has a problem with my colour."

A look of anger came over Sergeant Sheehan's face. He stepped into the middle of the group of people who were still chatting away to each other.

"Look, PC Wilson here is going to investigate your complaint," he said loudly, getting their attention as they all stopped and stared at him.

He continued. "If you don't want him to deal with it then I'll make a note and the police will consider the matter closed. We are too busy for any nonsense. Now, what will it be? Will you let him do his job or shall we call this matter closed?"

My Sergeant's intervention did the trick, and I was able to do my job.

Chapter 11

Coal Miners' Strike 1984

Prime Minister Margaret Thatcher's decision to mobilise large numbers of police officers from the Metropolitan Police and elsewhere to help manage the picket lines of the 1984 coal miner's strike was met with glee by a sizable police fraternity.

Police discussions in the canteen and elsewhere focused primarily on the huge potential for overtime. Some estimated their monthly pay would be enhanced one hundred percent. As the number of officers receiving orders to go "up north" increased, huddled discussions began taking place in Croydon police canteen about the number of rest days you could work and how much money you were likely to make.

As the strike progressed with little sign of the miners' resolve being buckled by swarms of unsympathetic police officers, a rumour percolated the station that one Croydon officer had enjoyed so many tours of duty at the mines and had earned so much money he was able to build an extension on his house which he named the "Arthur Scargill" room.

Stories of impressionable local girls from financially decimated mining communities being taken advantage of and exploited by cash rich police officers were commonplace. In fact, stories about the sexual exploits of officers were secondary only to the stories about overtime payments earned.

The most popular local story involved a young lady from Yorkshire who had recently travelled down to London and showed up at the Croydon Police Station's front counter, pregnant and asking to see a young Sergeant she claimed was the father of her child.

While many police officers emanated from a working-class background any such loyalty and empathy were, in my experience, quickly lost on joining the police and so it was with the striking miners.

In the enormously popular Duties Office, PC Jim Tyler and his Sergeant juggled available manpower to meet the increased demand for police officers to attend the Miner's dispute with local policing needs.

One day I poked my head in the office. "Any possibility I could go up to the mines, Jim?" I asked sheepishly, knowing my request might very well be rejected. Probationary constables (those with less than two years' service) were not to be deployed on such 'Aid' commitments. I also had not bothered to bring a "bottle" like some of my older colleagues had advised might help influence the outcome of my request.

Jim looked up over his black rimmed spectacles.

"How much service you got in?" he asked.

"Nearly eighteen months," I lied.

"Alright, it's such a bleeding drain on manpower, I don't see any option but to send you probationers up there. Better not mention it to the guv'nors though."

At that time, I was still trying to save money to buy my first property, while also trying to survive my probationary period, so his approval was a tremendous relief to me.

"Don't you feel any sympathy for the plight of working-class mining families?" one or two white friends asked.

Any empathy I might have had quickly dissipated when I thought about the numerous occasions when I had seen working class men from Nottinghamshire and Yorkshire at Selhurst Park Football Stadium as they regularly hurled vile racial abuse at John Fashanu and Vince Hilaire, two of Crystal Palace's black players.

Excited to get out of London and earn a decent amount of overtime pay, I packed enough clothes for seven days on a camp site just outside a remote Nottinghamshire village.

I boarded our coach, one of a number that travelled in convoy from central London to Nottinghamshire. The boredom of the long motorway journey ended when we reached our destination at dusk. We eagerly piled off the coach with suitcases under our arms and followed the local police officer guide along dimly lit paths to a group of portacabins sitting side by side.

"This is where you'll be staying all week lads, make yourself at home," shouted the guide.

The portacabin I stayed in was a bland characterless room that smelled of disinfectant. It was divided into two sections and offered a little more privacy than some of the others I'd seen. We had tables, a few chairs and a couple of desks. A large pile of mattresses sat neatly stacked in one corner of the room, underneath a pile of thick, coarse, grey folded blankets.

As the probationer in our group, I carefully watched as my colleagues, some of whom were veterans of the Miners' dispute, walked up to the mattresses, grabbed a blanket in one hand and tugged the mattress across the floor until happy with their location. I took what remained even though it meant I was sleeping in the middle of the room, in what I thought was probably the busiest and noisiest spot.

I had seen the television newsreels and listened to lurid police canteen stories about police being assaulted by picketing coal miners, so I was not sure what to expect. Other, less contentious, stories circulated involving groups of officers from provincial forces that tended to march everywhere, even to breakfast. Metropolitan police officers found this hilarious and enjoyed mocking them by marching in uncoordinated, comedic fashion around the campsite. For these reasons and more, Metropolitan police officers on duty in the mining communities were often singled out for derisory comment by both provincial officers and the local communities.

We started early the next morning. Eight of us sat on a minibus as it toured various picket lines at scheduled times of the day. Our remit ensured the pickets stayed within their legal obligations by not harassing miners who wished to continue working during the strike.

"Scab" was the term loudly echoed in unison by animated and angry pickets whenever miners risked a lifetime of derision to cross the picket line and exercise their right to work.

After three days of working double eight-hour shifts, I began having serious reservations and questioned my decision to volunteer for this duty. It was mind-numbingly boring. I missed the buzz of social life in London. Some of my colleagues found the time and energy to frequent a local pub but the prospect of getting assaulted by drunken miners did not appeal to me.

It seemed that as metropolitan police officers our reputation preceded us. The local police, intent on adding to my misery, instructed us not to leave our vehicle unless necessary.

I sat at the back of the minibus and stared blankly out the window. My only saving grace was my Sony Walkman that I wore every day. As a probationary constable I had been busy preparing for the end of probation exam. I had recorded myself reading large chunks of police policy and procedure and now I listened to the tapes. It was an invaluable tool and helped alleviate boredom.

My colleague, Stephen Poyle, seated next to me, leaned over.

"That's why your little gadget is so popular, it allows you to listen in private, without disturbing others."

I turned my head slightly and nodded.

"Very important in these type of scenarios," he whispered.

I nodded again.

"Then why the fuck is it that the whole bus can hear everything that you're listening to?" he yelled.

I snatched the headphones from my ears, sat bolt upright and looked at my fellow passengers.

"Really?" I asked, looking around anxiously.

Stephen smiled mischievously. "No, but I can."

I liked Stephen. His dry humour kept me in stitches.

Later that night, I retired to our portacabin. We were all exhausted from a boring sixteen-hour shift, but four of us decided to stay up and have some drinks together.

After a few beers, the alcohol had reduced our normal inhibitions and the conversation turned to race. Namely, mine.

"I just don't see Paul as black," said one officer.

"Well, I've never thought of him as anything other than black," said Stephen.

"Really? Well, I guess you could say he is, but he doesn't talk like your usual IC3 (police code for black person) from West Croydon," said another.

As a young constable still on probation, I had to be careful not to overstep the mark of what was deemed acceptable, regardless of the subject matter. This was frowned upon because, like small children, probationary constables were to be seen and not heard.

At the same time, I could not just sit there and listen to this exchange and say nothing. Emboldened by the drink and impassioned by the subject matter, I leaned forward on the edge of my chair.

"Well guys, I've always been black. I've never seen myself as anything else and I don't want to be anything else," I said.

"Yeah, but your skin isn't black, it's light brown," one of them said.

My adrenalin started rushing and for a moment I forgot where I was.

"Some of the most famous black people in history had light skin. Many light-skinned black people have been lynched by the Ku Klux Klan. In none of those cases did anyone ever once say "hey, let's not lynch him, he's not really black.""

The group stared at me in silence.

I continued. "No, when it suits you, we're black." I yelled to no one in particular.

The portacabin door that divided the space opened and Cyril walked in. His bleary eyes and messy hair suggested we had woken him up.

"Will you shut up?" he shouted "I'm trying to sleep and all I hear are arguments about whether he's a nigger or not. Of course, he's a nigger, now go to fucking sleep."

Without waiting for a response, Cyril walked back out and slammed the door behind him.

Stephen smiled that familiar mischievous grin of his. "I wouldn't have put it in those terms," he whispered.

A short time later as I lay on my makeshift bed trying to go to sleep, I thought about what Cyril had said. He had a habit of saying what others were thinking. I hated the 'n' word because it was introduced to dehumanise black people. That word recalled a painful three-hundred-year history of enslavement, oppression, torture, and murder when African ancestors were traded and treated as livestock. But if I were to survive my probation, I would somehow have to learn to live with that term and not respond the way I had earlier.

Chapter 12

Broadwater Farm

On the afternoon of October 5th, 1985, I opened the front door of my Streatham flat and welcomed the cool breeze that blew in to meet me as I stepped outside, locked the door behind me and climbed into my red Ford Capri. As I made the four-mile drive to work to begin the Late Turn shift I mulled over recent events that had caused me a great deal of introspection. These were unprecedented times. Brixton had just recovered from a spate of rioting following the accidental shooting of Cherry Groce by a police officer. Conversations in the canteen over the past few weeks had become more racially charged than usual. It had become commonplace to hear running commentary whenever disturbances involving predominantly black communities unfolded around the country.

"I see the spades are rioting in Toxteth. No surprise there."

"It's beyond me why the local Old Bill are trying to stop a load of coons from burning down their own neighbourhood."

"I see a guvnor accidently let one go in Brixton yesterday and shot a spade woman. Expect the natives to be up in arms, burning and looting soon."

I had successfully completed my two-year probation and was now beginning to enjoy my work and make friends, but the recent intensification of racial slurs was getting to me. I would share my dilemma with close friends who would then ask me the inevitable; why stay in such a racist institution? I constantly wrestled with this question, particularly during night duty when I would often patrol the streets on my own and reflect on the many questions and accusations from friends that I had to deal with on an increasingly regular basis of late. In the absence of any help, support, or recognition by white police managers that the police culture militated against black people, I had unconsciously adopted my own coping mechanisms.

Enjoying a black persona outside of the workplace was something that I keenly revelled in. It was a survival technique to retain my sanity and sense of equilibrium, and I used it to maximum effect. I immersed myself in London's black night life scene at clubs such as Gossips, Night Moves, La Prison, Columbo's, Kareba, Gullivers, Mingles, Dougies, and All Nations where I would enjoy reggae and soul music until the early hours. These venues offered me sanctuary and an antidote to the harsh and sometimes brutal reality of a racialised work environment.

"What did you do this weekend, Paul?" colleagues would ask me on Monday mornings.

I would usually reply "The Park in Kensington," or "Studio Valbonne in Soho," or other nightclubs in the West End that were considered *white* and therefore acceptable. Sometimes I would visit these *police friendly* venues to give authenticity to my stories.

Later that evening I was walking toward the Duties Office when two young officers walked out rubbing their hands together. One of them stared at me with a big smile on his face.

"Less than eight for me tomorrow," he said.

"Why? What's going on?" I asked. 'Less than eight' meant that his rest day had been cancelled with less than eight days' notice. This was a situation that attracted a significant enhancement in pay, plus another day off in lieu. It was a dream scenario for many police officers.

"Earlier today they were searching a house on Yankee Tango's ground when a black woman collapsed and died. We're going up there tomorrow to deal with the looters," he said, rubbing his hands together again to make a point. His colleague gave a throaty laugh as they walked off down the corridor towards the canteen.

I stuck my head into the Duties Office.

Jim, the Duties PC, looked up. "Before you ask, I'm sending the warning notice out now. You are on the Serial we're sending up to Tottenham tomorrow as we expect it to all kick off."

The following morning, I climbed aboard the police coach parked outside the back gate of Croydon police station and took a seat near the back by myself.

"It's that fucking rabble rousing scumbag Bernie Grant! Someone should top him," one of my colleagues said as he walked down the aisle of the coach. His remark was met with a loud chorus of laughter.

I gazed out the window, trying not to listen as my colleagues continued to make racist jokes about Tottenham councillor Bernie Grant. Our Sergeant, Don Haines, was seated at the front of the bus. He often liked to remind us of his unswerving Christian faith yet on this day did nothing to curtail the vile remarks.

We made our way to our destination, St Anne's school in Tottenham, North London. Our journey took us through Brixton, where black community tensions were still high following the recent Cherry Groce shooting. When we turned onto the High Street, I moved away from the window. I did not want the sight of a black police officer to spark a violent reaction from Brixton's large African Caribbean community.

When we reached St Anne's school, we disembarked and made our way into a classroom. A large assembly of officers were gathered for a briefing regarding the current situation. I had already heard that an early morning protest outside of Tottenham Police Station had raised concerns among some senior police officers that violent protests would soon ensue.

The local Chief Inspector went up to the front to speak.

"For those of you visiting from other parts of London, Broadwater Farm is a large council estate in Tottenham with 3,500 residents. Yesterday, some of our officers had cause to search a house occupied by Cynthia Jarret, a 49-year-old Afro-Caribbean woman who is also the mother of a suspect that we had arrested earlier. During the search, Cynthia Jarret collapsed and died from a heart attack. Once news of this spread last night, local police came under sporadic attack from mainly black youths on the estate who threw bottles and bricks at them."

The assembled officers listened intently, some taking notes while others silently shook their heads after learning about the escalation of violence on 'the farm' as it was known to local officers.

After the briefing we had some refreshments and waited for our assignment. We hadn't been waiting very long when an Inspector approached our table.

"Zulu Delta, you'll be on mobile patrol, looking after our petrol stations, vulnerable premises, and serving as a reserve should we need you on the hurry up."

I immediately thought back to the Miners' strike, *what is it about mobile patrol assignments?*

As our coach circled *the farm* I watched as plumes of black smoke billowed above the sprawling concrete council estate.

"That's from torched cars," Sergeant Haines shouted, bending down to peer out the window. He had previously been walking up and down the aisle of the coach having nerve soothing chats with younger officers but had avoided eye contact with me.

Our coach stopped and parked next to a petrol station. We watched and waited to be ready if youths should show up and try to purchase petrol in cans.

"There's someone at the pump putting petrol into a can, Sarge!" shouted an officer sitting next to the coach driver.

Sergeant Haines turned and looked.

"Don't worry, he's the wrong colour," he said.

Laughter from about half the coach followed our devoutly Christian sergeant's remark.

As the day progressed, the shouts from protestors and the dull thud of exploding petrol bombs could be heard with increased frequency from inside the Broadwater Farm estate.

"Fucking spades are dropping concrete blocks on PC's!" shouted a colleague who was monitoring the police radio at the front of the coach.

Later in the evening Sergeant Haines jumped up from the front of the coach and made an announcement that sent shivers down my spine.

"A police constable has been stabbed to death by rioters on the Broadwater Farm estate!" he shouted.

The raucous chatter of colleagues on the coach ceased. In its place was an eerie silence. I shrank down in my seat. On the inside I seethed with anger and fear.

The silence was broken by a loud voice from a few seats in front of me.

"Enoch was fucking right. They should've listened to him."

Under normal circumstances I would have taken the other officers to task over the tirade of vile, racist remarks that followed, but these were far from normal circumstances. I sat in silence, worried at how any intervention, even jokingly, on my part would be received. My God-fearing Sergeant was obviously of a similar opinion as he too sat in silence at the front of the coach.

Moments later our coach pulled into St Anne's school for refreshments and a toilet break. As the coach came to a halt, a colleague named Harry stood up and pointed out the window.

"I don't believe it. A wog with pips!" he shouted.
The other officers stood up and looked in the direction Harry was pointing. I looked out to see what they were looking at and saw a police inspector of Asian origin walking along the pavement below.

A few minutes later I sat by myself in the school canteen sipping hot tea and reflecting on everything that had happened. Loud conversations took place all around me and the air was thick with the tension of fear and anger. There were rumours of guns being fired at police officers, which further instilled the sense that we were in a war zone. I had never experienced anything remotely like it.

I felt very lonely as I sat there alone. I had been ignored, talked over, and made to feel that my feelings didn't matter. Even colleagues who I had considered to be friends spewed insulting comments. I thought about the young American soldiers in Vietnam who had been exposed constantly to so much of the horror and barbarism of war that they had been desensitised to any sense of compassion or humanity. I had witnessed that today.

As the news of PC Keith Blakelock's murder spread, many of the protesters and rioters began to slowly disperse. Shortly after our refreshment break our unit was ordered to stand down and we made the long journey back to the sanctuary of South London.

I arrived back home in the early hours of the next morning. I was exhausted but I couldn't sleep. I was replaying the day's events over and over and kept thinking about the murdered officer and how that could have been me if I had been the one facing that mob. I would have been singled out as a 'traitor' and attacked. As sunlight began breaking through the bedroom curtains, I finally fell asleep.

Chapter 13

A Dog's Life

In 1986 I was given the opportunity to become a qualified driver of police vehicles, after completing my two-year probation period. My team Inspector put me forward for the intense, three week driving course. I like to think he chose me because of my industrious nature and a return of work that placed me ahead of a few colleagues in the pecking order.

Our driving instructor was Geoff, who was also a keen motor racing fan. He would take us on long drives across the south of England, where he would put us through our paces. We would have to drive at high speeds along winding country lanes, where we were taught the art of roadcraft, braking, and road positioning, all while having to double clutch. It was a cumbersome, outdated, and totally unnecessary driving technique but like so much of the world of policing it seems we had to do it simply because that is what had always been done.

As a reward for successfully completing the course, I soon found myself sitting in my panda car on a cold, wet night in Croydon. My colleague, Andy, and I were on a mobile patrol to keep Croydon's streets safe, except that on this night there was absolutely no one else around.

They say be careful what you wish for, but I never once associated that with my desire to drive a police vehicle until this fateful night.

"Panda 2, can you look at a disturbance in Old Town, near the Youth Club. A man with a dog," the voice over the police radio crackled.

Andy grunted affirmatively into his radio and off we went.

Driving a police vehicle gives you access to many calls that foot patrol officers are unable to respond to because of distance. Those of us lucky enough to be driving a police car had a distinct advantage over young officers on foot patrol who were constantly frustrated by this limitation. At least that is what I thought.

As we reached the location, I slowed down. Andy pointed out the window.

"There he is!" he shouted.

In the distance a young white man stood by the side of the road with a dog at his feet. I stopped the car and opened my door. The streetlights were so dim it was hard to see what he was doing. I could tell the dog was big and black but otherwise could not make out what breed it was.

I got out and walked towards the man with the intention of talking to him and finding out the nature of the call. Andy followed close behind me. When I got around ten feet away, I stopped.

"Hi there. Can we have a word?" I asked.

Just as I finished speaking, the dog lunged towards me like guided missile. It happened so fast I had no time to process what was happening before the dog's head hit my groin. I staggered backwards, then regained my balance. I was just about to step forward when I felt a liquid trickling down my left thigh.

"Oh my God!" I shouted. I turned and ran back to the car, tears in my eyes, fearing the worst. I opened the back seat and flung myself across the double seat. I opened my car coat, unbuckled my belt, and unzipped my trousers. I looked down to see the front of my light-coloured boxer shorts covered in blood. Tears welled uncontrollably as by now I felt sure the dog had bitten into my manhood or worse. I pulled out the waistband of my shorts and peered down to assess the damage, praying it was all in one piece. The lights were so dim it was too hard to see and I was afraid to touch anything.

"Andy, get me to Mayday Hospital. Now!" I shouted.

Even though Andy was not police qualified, he jumped in behind the driver's seat, put on the blue light and got me to the A&E entrance of the hospital within minutes.

I hobbled into the reception area, ignored the booking-in formalities, and walked over to where patients were being seen in various booths. I had become familiar with this hospital during my career.

A middle-aged black nurse smiled at me. "Can I help you officer?"

"Yes, I've been bitten by a dog," I replied.

"Let me take a look," she said, walking behind me.

"No, not there. Here," I said, pointing at my groin.

"Oh. I really don't want to look at that this time of night. I'll get someone for you," she said, walking off.

A couple minutes later a man in a white coat walked out and introduced himself to me as the night duty A&E doctor. I told him what had happened.

He smiled. "Was it a male or female dog?" he asked.

I knew from experience that A&E staff shared the same dark humour that was commonplace among the police, but I was not interested or impressed on this night. I was not in the mood for stupid jokes when my love life was at stake. I ignored his question and followed him into a private room, where he instructed me to take off my trousers and underwear and sit on the bed.

"Officer, you have two small indentations on the penis shaft where the skin has been broken," he said, after examining me. "These marks are consistent with what you describe. The dog's teeth appear to have made it through your car coat and police uniform trousers. Your penis is naturally full of blood and the vice like pressure of the dog's jaws caused blood from the shaft to flow out. That is why you can see so much of it on your boxer shorts."

He then went on to casually describe what options I had in the event of a worst-case scenario. These included prosthetics, pumps and all manner of surgery that would enable me to 'live a normal life'.

"So, everything will work okay?" I asked hesitantly.

"Yes, you'll have no problems. Just wait here until we can give you a tetanus shot," he said.

While I waited, PC Dave Sutton, one of my Croydon colleagues, appeared at the door.

"Are you all right Paul? We heard you were rushed to the hospital?" he asked.

"Yeah, I'm fine."

I unbuckled my trousers and slowly lowered them to reveal the blood-stained shorts.

His mouth dropped open and he turned and left without another word.

After I returned to the station, I approached the supervisor on duty, Sergeant Stella Newton, remembering that: '*If any police officer receives any injury while on duty it must be reported to a supervising officer who must make a full entry in the injury on duty book*'.

"Sarge, I've got an injury on duty to report," I said.

"I heard about that. Wait here while I get the book," she said.

I braced myself for the barrage of jokes that were common police humour, but they never materialised. Sergeant Newton meticulously took down every single detail of the incident without so much as a smirk. That level of professionalism will long remain with me.

A week later I got to put the doctor's assurance that *everything will work just fine* to the test. I thought it best not to share my recent experience with my date when we arrived at my Streatham flat. She had no idea what trepidation and sheer terror surged through me at the thought of what may or may not happen. We later went to bed and our lovemaking progressed unhindered to a natural and satisfactory conclusion. I lay on my back, hands behind head, with a bigger than usual smile of satisfaction on my face, as a feeling of absolute relief gently washed over me.

Chapter 14

Crime Squad

I did not intend to spend my whole career as a police constable. My goal was to be a Sergeant by the age of thirty and I developed a plan to make that happen. This included registering for the promotion exam and enrolling in evening classes at nearby Sir Ranulph Bacon House in Sylvan Hill, Upper Norwood, South East London.

It was during these classes that police tutors would test our understanding of large chunks of criminal law and police procedure. The police promotion exam in the 1980's was largely unscientific. If you were able to memorise paragraphs of dry legal text pertaining to police powers and procedures and then fashion it legibly into an answer to the questions on the exam paper, you were home free.

The other deciding factor was the number of sergeant vacancies, and this was very important. Being promoted depended not only on your ability to answer the exam questions but on the number of available vacancies. The older officers would talk about the promotion exams in the 1970's when the metropolitan police required so many sergeants that just turning up and sitting for the exam assured you a promotion. Whether that is true or not has never been confirmed.

Shortly after the completion of the annual promotional exam, New Scotland Yard's Personnel Department would usually announce the number of sergeant vacancies. The lead up to the announcement, fuelled by rumours of expected vacancies, guaranteed that nerves were shredded.

Tensions were particularly high for the many perennial exam takers, including many Criminal Investigation Department (CID) colleagues. Some of them never adequately prepared for the exam because they incorrectly felt that their enhanced knowledge of criminal law would get them through.

"I tried to study for the exam, but a huge setback interrupted everything," a detective colleague told me one day.

"What happened?" I asked.

"I had to change trains at Camden Town," he said.

I somehow managed to keep a straight face as he basically told me, looking as serious as could be, that he started studying for the promotion exam on the train, *on the way to take the promotion exam* at the police college in Hendon. He might have been joking, but in my experience, this was very much the reality for some of his colleagues.

In 1988 I attempted the sergeant's promotion exam for the first time. Although I didn't achieve a sufficient enough mark to place me within the band of available vacancies, it wasn't a complete failure. My league table placement put me just outside of the required band of competitive places, which means I was deemed to have 'qualified'. A 'qualifier' was given access to a local promotion board comprised of senior officers.

The problem was I perceived this route to be a very subjective selection process where several unwritten variables came into play. These ranged from previous policing experience, golfing handicap, masonic lodge membership, and generally being a 'good 'ol boy'. Whether that was right or wrong, I chose not to subject myself to that humiliation. I felt that the chances were slim to none that a young, black officer with less than five years of service could achieve promotion this way.

The next step of my preparation for promotion strategy was to gain experience outside of the normal uniform foot patrol policing. I applied for and achieved a place on the Crime Squad, a plain clothes arm of the Criminal Investigation Department (CID) where officers could develop their skills in crime investigation before graduating to a fully-fledged CID officer. I enjoyed my time on the Squad, especially since I did not feel the same pressure to succeed and impress as some of my colleagues, whose goal was a lifetime in the CID.

Many of the tasks we undertook were not glamorous by any means. There was lots of surveillance work, night after night in cramped and sometimes, unsavoury conditions.

One week we were staking out a hair salon and the next week we were sitting in a smelly portacabin in a dark alley that was supposedly an office but rumoured to be a storage facility for carcinogenic chemicals. We sat, bored silly, waiting for a prolific burglar in Croydon's George Street to strike. These are not the kinds of things that endear you to a life in the CID.

The following week when we were assigned to sit overnight in an Estate Agent's office by Detective Sergeant Putman, there was a collective moan about how boring it would be. But I for one was more than happy at that point to be bored in a warm, clean office.

It was me and two other guys, all in our early to mid-20's. Scotty was the youngest but had served as a Crime Squad officer the longest. He was desperate to become a fully-fledged CID officer. He had what I felt was an unhealthy fixation on the recently released movie 'The Highlander' featuring Christopher Lambert and Sean Connery. He would frequently recite the movie's dialogue in his native Scottish accent or sing the musical score. That was annoying enough, but then he decided to alleviate our boredom by inventing a quiz to showcase his knowledge of the movie. I found the flickering streetlights across the road to be much more entertaining.

"What is the name of the alias Connor used when he came to New York?" Scotty asked.

Before anyone could respond, a sudden noise came from downstairs. I put my finger on my lips to signal both men to stay quiet. I walked across the dark office to look down the stairwell leading to the front door. I watched in disbelief as the front door slowly opened and the silhouette of a man appeared.

The dark figure slowly climbed the dark staircase. When he was halfway up, one of my colleagues turned on the office lights, illuminating the intruder, who froze like a rabbit caught in a car's headlamps.

Over at Croydon, news of the arrest reverberated around the management floor. We were briefly lauded by senior officers who had experienced hostility at local chamber of commerce meetings.

My time in the CID office was made more comfortable by officers such as DC Gerry Woolmoor, a seasoned and well-respected detective. Gerry had a natural ability to talk to people in a manner that I am sure endeared him to colleagues and members of the public alike. I got to know him very well when we sat next to one another at the sergeant promotion classes at Sylvan Hill. If I ever had problems putting together a case file, Gerry was the first CID office I sought out.

Not long after I became a member of the Crime Squad Gerry popped over to see how I was doing.

"Let me introduce you to a few people," he said.

I followed him around the main CID office as he introduced me to staff. As we were walking towards the Detective Inspector's office, Gerry stopped a short middle-aged CID officer who was walking in our direction.

"This is Paul. He works on the Crime Squad now, so you'll see him around," said Gerry.

The detective did not look at me or extend his hand like the other officers I had just met.

"I guess every company has its house nigger. Now we have ours," the man said before walking off.

Gerry looked at me and shrugged his shoulders. "Wanker doesn't know any better," he said.

In addition to surveillance, another fundamental investigative task that fell to the crime squad on a regular basis was the door-to-door enquiry. This was a staple of many major crime investigations and just another job tailor made for budding detectives.

Such inquiries were included in a range of tasks designed to track down the Croydon rapist, a man that would lure young women into his car just as night clubs were closing by claiming to be a mini cab for hire.

As is the case in many aspects of policing, it was invariably the mundane foot slogging and dogged enquiry that paid dividends and made it all worthwhile. So, it was with this case that our inquiries unearthed a name for our suspect and that enabled us to approach local schools to establish whether our suspect had attended one of them. During one such call we were passed to the school secretary who had worked there for years and immediately recognised the suspect's name.

Not wanting to tell her the nature of our inquiry, we asked if she remembered any friends of that individual. Indeed, she could and before long we were paying a visit to an associate of our suspect. The crimes had been prominently featured in the local news media, so when the associate learned of the urgent and serious nature of our visit, they gave us a phone number. Phone numbers leave audit trails so within a few hours a team of Croydon CID and West Midland's officers crashed through a small bed-sit door in Birmingham, and arrested an unsuspecting and surprised rapist.

Chapter 15

A Black Social Club

One afternoon while sitting at my desk on the first floor of the CID office, an innocuous event occurred that had an important and profound effect on my thinking.

I looked up to see a young black guy walking towards me, carrying a notepad. I recognised him as a Sergeant from a neighbouring station.

"Hi, my name is Paul Ramsay," he said, extending his hand.

"Paul Wilson," I replied, shaking his hand.

"It's nice to meet you," he said. Then looking back and forth he lowered his voice almost to a whisper. "I have a question for you. Would you be interested in joining a social club for black officers?"

Without really thinking about why he was asking such a question and suspecting that surrounding CID colleagues might be in earshot, I whispered back.

"No, we get far too much attention as it is."

"Okay," he said stoically. He scribbled something in his notebook and promptly left the office.

My terse response to Paul Ramsay's question troubled me for some time afterward. Why didn't I engage him in conversation to find out why he was asking me that question? Was I so consumed by my increasing involvement in the CID that I was failing to see the bigger picture?

Several years later I talked to Paul Ramsay about this incident. He told me he had been asked by a senior officer to conduct a survey to establish whether a 'social club' might be of benefit to black officers. Maybe, those at the top of the police hierarchy suspected that being a black police officer at that time could be an isolating experience. Regardless of the good intention, it suggested to me that white officers at that time had no clue what black officers had to do to fit into a police culture condoned and perpetuated by the vast majority.

After nearly four years working as a constable in a culture that brazenly spewed forth racial slurs on a regular basis, I had seen no improvement. I attempted to rationalise the behaviour of colleagues and recognised that after being on the street day in and day out, you would inevitably become exposed to an 'underclass' of people whose way of life was vastly different from most of the British population. Constant contact with a small swathe of the socially excluded encouraged stereotypes and a cynical attitude when dealing with what were commonly referred to as 'slag', 'scrotes', 'scum' and 'lowlife'. *It's the constant and often confrontational exposure to black youth on the streets that's led to the racialised behaviour I witnessed on a daily basis,* I thought to myself.

This behaviour was not confined to a particular class or section of poorly educated officers, either. This was confirmed to me when a middle-class, grammar school educated Sergeant sitting opposite me in the police canteen said of Croydon's Chief Superintendent; "He's off to another community meeting this afternoon. Got to keep the niggers happy."

Charlie, one of my team Sergeants, grimaced and stared at him while trying to subtly nod his head in my direction, to remind him of my presence at the table. But it didn't matter because I was considered inconsequential. Such was the nature of a culture that normalised these exchanges. A social club for black officers was not going to help. In fact, it would have aggravated matters and fuelled conspiracy theories that black officers were somehow plotting to cause trouble, or even worse change the way things were, and *the way things had always been.*

That is how it was in the 1980's. This was confirmed when I innocently invited my good friend Cleo Sandiford to an after-work soiree organised by my Relief. Cleo, a black guy of Barbadian heritage, had been a member of the Metropolitan Police civil staff since 1972. He had also been one of the earliest Special Constables from a West Indian background. Yet as he arrived to join me at the bar of the restaurant where the team had arranged to gather, Harry, a team member and colleague nonchalantly walked over with a look of incredulity on his face.

"Fuck me, what's going on here, a riot?" he yelled.

I was one of three black officers at Croydon in the 1980's. Fitting into the culture and not 'rocking the boat' was vital to survive and attain any form of standing within the local team of officers you came to rely upon daily.

While you certainly did not want to ingratiate yourself by joining in with the racist banter, challenging such behaviour would surely lead to ostracization or worse. Nevertheless, there were occasions when it was so blatant that a challenge was necessary. When I would point out racism in their speech, it always inevitably was followed by the usual responses.

"We don't mean *you*."

"You're on *our* side."

"He didn't mean it."

Sometimes the responses were tinged with anger and a general attitude of 'how dare you challenge the way we behave'. But for the most part their responses were presented with humour, probably to calm me down so my temper would not escalate. I always felt that I wasn't exposed to more serious episodes of overtly racist behaviour because I was 6'2 and looked like I could take care of myself in any physical altercation. Sometimes that proved true on the weekends at closing time outside of Croydon's nightclubs, too.

Chapter 16

The Den

Millwall Football Club was a southeast London club that Croydon officers would often assist in policing, in addition to our local team, Crystal Palace.

It was at 'The Den', Millwall's stadium, that one Saturday matchday me and a small number of Croydon officers were posted to the rear of a seated area of Millwall supporters. As we were making our way to take up our positions, one of my colleagues pointed up in the stands towards a seated Danny Baker, TV and radio personality and ardent Millwall fan. As the game progressed, with no real crowd problems, a colleague came up to me. He nodded towards a plume of smoke rising from the midst of several seated fans. He leaned over and whispered in my ear.

"Can you smell the whacky baccy? I think it's coming from over there," he said.

I moved slightly closer to the smoke and instantly recognised the smell; it was undoubtedly cannabis. At that time, many black youths on the streets were being arrested and charged with possession of cannabis. This crowd was all white, but if they had been black, I am most certain the reaction by colleagues would have been significantly different. But in all fairness, this was Millwall football club and their fans' notorious reputation preceded them. This may have had a numbing effect on my young police officer colleagues as we were greatly outnumbered, without any protective equipment or personal radio.

Why I had no such qualms or concerns as I began to make my way towards the offending pale of smoke by myself would probably have been revealed after several psychiatric therapy sessions.

"Excuse me mate, can I get through?" I said, edging between the seats.

"Mind your back I need to get through."

I took off my helmet and carried it under my arm, so it would not be knocked off my head. A cop's helmet was a prized possession and most likely would have been passed overhead throughout the stadium for the rest of the game.

I eventually reached the seats from where the offending smoke rose towards the roof. The offenders were a group of white men in their 30's and 40's who were now looking at me. I was not going to arrest anyone; I was not that foolhardy. Discretion was a powerful tool in my armoury and I fully intended to use it on this occasion, but they didn't know that.

"Okay lads, put it out or you won't see the rest of the game, understand?" I bluffed.

Four or five men stared at me in silence as they stubbed out their cigarettes on the back of the seats or on the soles of their shoes.

My job was done, so I turned and walked back to the aisle where my colleagues were standing. Just as I reached them the entire seated section, comprised of around one hundred supporters, erupted into *monkey chants*. No spoken words, just loud *monkey chants*.

None of my colleagues reacted to the chants but they probably wondered why I had caused trouble and put their safety in jeopardy. However, I did glean sneaking looks of admiration from some for going in among these fans on my own to deal with what was clearly an offence that might have even been instigated to 'take the piss out of the Old Bill'. Reckless and foolish? Maybe. Who is to say? But it certainly did not do any harm to my reputation.

Football matches in the 1980's were hot beds of violence coupled with a general hostility towards anyone that looked differently than the overwhelmingly white working-class supporter.

During this period, black football players often bore the brunt of sickening racist behaviour. As a result, black football supporters were effectively frightened away and relegated to watching matches on television.

Chapter 17

Charlton Athletic V Newcastle Utd

On April 7th, 1984, an incident occurred that demonstrated for me the sometimes-confused nature of racism in society and my chosen profession, with key actors behaving in a most unexpected manner and not according to stereotype.

Charlton Athletic was playing at home to Newcastle Utd, a second division match. It wouldn't normally attract too much police attention, but Newcastle was known to have a huge and passionate following. Assistance from neighbouring police was commonplace for such events.

It was full-time and Charlton's hooligan element of fans were loud, boisterous, and angry at having been beaten three goals to one. A few had invaded the pitch, vastly outnumbered by Newcastle fans, some of whom were intent on attacking the Charlton fans. Skirmishes involving young men lashing out with fists and boots, seemed to be happening all around.

My colleague that day was Bill Parker, a twelve-year policing veteran and former Merchant Navy seaman. He loved to tell the tale of his central disciplinary board where it was alleged that while he was a driver for S08 (or Flying Squad as they were colloquially known) he had taken home the Squad's vehicle.

An unproven element of that central disciplinary board was that Bill parked the police vehicle, including the radio and other contents, unsecured outside a non-police premises while he was drunk.

Bill found himself confined to uniformed duties for a long period following that hearing, but they could never take away his ability and love of driving powerful police cars on a regular basis.

I once found myself as Bill's 'operator' on a six-week posting to 'Zulu Two', Croydon's high-performance response vehicle. An operator sat in the front passenger seat and managed calls on the police radio, keeping a detailed log of all activities and taking notes when arrests were made. I always associated Sade's hit single 'Smooth Operator' with my numerous stints in that posting.

I got to know Bill quite well during this time and I found him to be quick witted and roguishly entertaining. We would often go out for drinks after our eight-hour tour of duty together. His elderly mum lived in flats overlooking Crystal Palace football ground and we would sometimes drop by to check on her. Bill was no angel and he had undoubtedly sailed close to the wind in his career, but he had a heart of gold. On his days off he would volunteer to drive a minibus for elderly and infirm members of a local community centre.

One night he confided in me after a few glasses of whiskey at his home.

"Black officers were hated in the seventies. No one wanted anything to do with them," he said.

This was not a provocative statement designed to anger me. It was a fact that he felt compelled and comfortable enough to share with me. Perhaps it was also his way of saying, "look how times have changed. You're in my house."

The afternoon that Bill and I walked onto the turf at Charlton's Valley ground there were fights going on all around us. We quickly established that a Charlton supporter was causing the biggest threat, as he lashed out with his boots at anyone wearing a black and white scarf.

"Let's get him, Paul!" Bill shouted.

The combination of excessive tours of duty behind the wheel plus his passion for drinking had taken a toll on Bill physically, so it was up to me to make the arrest. I jumped on the Charlton supporter and tried to grab his arms and wrestle him to the floor.

"Leave off you fucking black bastard!" he screamed in his South East London accent.

After a brief effort in which he continued to lash out and struggle, he was restrained and taken before the charging sergeant. He listened intently and looked the offender up and down while I explained the situation that led to the man's arrest.

"It was racially motivated as well. He called Paul here a black bastard," Bill said to my surprise.

While that was true, I had unconsciously omitted that from my report to the sergeant. That language was so commonplace when making arrests at football matches that it almost went unnoticed and did not seem worthy of bringing to the attention of the charging sergeant.

"Is that right officer?" the sergeant asked me.

"Yes, Sarge," I muttered. I looked over at Bill, who flashed me a grin from the other side of the charge room.

The offender was duly charged with football disorder offences.

A few days later, I received notification that the case was scheduled for trial at a Magistrates' Court. This was surprising to me because most football related arrests ended with a guilty plea and no reason for the arresting officer to attend court.

I immediately called Bill and told him that we had a day out at the Magistrates Court.

"If it's a night duty we might get some overtime out of it," he said.

It turned out the court case was not listed to coincide with our night duty shift. As usual we both signed on duty for a nine to five shift. This was a policy that had been put in place to reduce the potential for officers to make overtime for attending Court.

Bill and I arrived at the Magistrates Court on the morning of the court case, which was to start at 10:00 AM. We were both called upon to give evidence, and this time I included everything.

As usual, the accused person was almost unrecognisable. As he sat there in a fashionable suit and tie, he cut a quite different figure from the football hooligan I had arrested that Saturday afternoon.

After I finished presenting my evidence, I was subjected to a lengthy cross examination by the defence solicitor. He did not dwell much on the public order charge but seemed intent on undermining my recollection of the evidence that portrayed his client as a racist. I stuck to my account of what had happened and refused to accept any other explanation.

"Thank you, PC Wilson. That is all."

When it came time for Bill to appear in the witness box, his version of what took place matched my own. Once again, the defence tried to undermine Bill's account of the racial element of the evidence. Like me, Bill was having none of it and solidly stuck to the facts.

Finally, the defence called the accused to the witness box.

The defendant appeared nervous and unsure of himself as he tried to explain that his actions that day had been in self-defence. He claimed that he had been attacked by opposing fans and was only violent because he was trying to defend himself. He denied the racial element, stating that he would never use that kind of language and I must have been mistaken. He said there were a lot of violent skirmishes going on that day and that I must have heard someone else say it. He held to this defence throughout cross examination by our solicitor.

After the cross examination, I expected the three Magistrates to retire to consider their verdict, but no. Surprisingly, the defence still had another witness. I looked over at Bill who just smiled and shrugged his shoulders. He knew as much as I did about this surprise witness. Who could it be? Was it one of his friends? Was it someone who had evaded arrest that day and was now helping a mate out?

As the witness walked towards the box, I took a deep breath and shook my head while looking at the floor. A young black guy raised the Bible with his right hand and read from a card held in front of him by the Court's usher.

"I swear to tell the truth, the whole truth, so help me, God."

The witness introduced himself to the Court and explained that he was the accused's brother-in-law and had been at the match that day. Not only that, but he claimed that he ran onto the pitch to help the accused who was being attacked by several Newcastle supporters.

"Did you hear your brother-in-law shout a racist comment at PC Wilson?" the defence solicitor asked.

The man looked him straight in the eyes and said "No, definitely not."

It didn't escape my attention that the man had avoided making eye contact with me the entire time. But in the end, it didn't matter because this clever but perjurious intervention by the defence planted enough doubt in the minds of the Magistrates that they saw fit to acquit the accused on all charges.

I walked out of court that day feeling confused and frustrated about what had just taken place in the court room. Not only in terms of the black witness who lied to the Court to protect his racist brother-in-law, but also regarding my colleague Bill who had felt it necessary to highlight the racist element of the offence during the initial charge. In doing so, he stepped outside of a police culture that viewed racism in football grounds as an inevitable consequence of life and certainly not something police should be bothered with.

Chapter 18

Off Duty

There is sometimes confusion among the public over a police officer's power to make an arrest while 'off duty'. The truth is a police officer is 'on duty' twenty-four hours a day, every day of the year. They will not look the other way and ignore a crime in progress any more than an off duty doctor would ignore someone having a heart attack or stroke. In much the same way, the bulk of an officer's responsibilities are not diminished by being off duty. However, seasoned police officers have learned to develop a sixth sense to avoid trouble on their days off. When I was a young and eager officer, I had yet to develop those same sensibilities.

In 1984, The Kings Arms pub in Sloane Square was not only a formidable structure and a decent pub, but was a popular place to meet up with friends since it was located just across the Square from the Underground Station. One evening I arranged to meet my old friend, Ossie, to catch up over a couple drinks. We thought afterwards we might move on to other entertainment in the fashionable Kings Road, Chelsea.

I arrived first so I ordered a drink and sat down on one of the luxurious seats in the main bar area to wait. I looked at my watch. Was he late or had I become so disciplined at time-keeping that it was making me overly sensitive?

A couple minutes later Ossie walked in looking slightly dishevelled, like he had rushed all the way.

"I can't believe I'm late," he muttered, walking towards me.

"Yeah, we did say 8 o'clock, not ten minutes past," I said, pointing to my watch.

I went back up to the bar to order Ossie a drink. By this point the pub had filled up nicely, probably because it had been raining the last couple hours. Ossie's wet clothes confirmed it had not stopped.

I brought Ossie his drink and had just sat back down to enjoy my own, when shouting began just outside the pub.

"You better go sort that out," Ossie said, laughing slightly.

"Not a chance mate. I've just got the round in," I said, sipping on my almost full glass of beer.

Whatever notion I had of being off duty and oblivious to whatever altercation was happening outside ended abruptly when a young, white man's head and shoulders crashed through the plate glass window facing the pavement.

People began screaming and moving away from the shattered window. Slivers of glass lay sprinkled over empty seats.

"Well, here goes. Wait here," I said.

I ran outside and saw a small group of young men huddled together by the large, gaping hole in the window. One of the men had a bloodied face. I reached into my back pocket and pulled out my police warrant card.

"Police! Everyone stay right where you are!" I shouted, walking towards them.

One of the men turned and ran.

"Stop!" I shouted.

As I gave chase it briefly crossed my mind that the time and effort spent ironing my shirt, shaving, showering, putting on nice clothes, and the journey here to spend a relaxing evening with my friend was now being sacrificed to chase a suspect, in the rain, who was weaving back and forth into the darkness along the puddled pavement.

My adrenalin kicked in and I narrowed the distance between us. Stretching out my foot I clipped his heels and he stumbled forward, striking his head against a parking meter. Thinking he must have the wind knocked out of him, I offered him my outstretched hand.

"Okay, mate. You've had enough. Let's go back to the pub, shall we?"

He grabbed my hand and pulled himself back to his feet. Then he turned and sprinted into the darkness.

I followed him as he turned and ran into an alleyway that ended up being a dead end. With nowhere to go he stopped running. His hair and face were covered in a mixture of sweat and rain. He put his hands on his hips and tried to catch his breath as I walked towards him. His bleary, red eyes seemed to stare right through me.

"What are you going to do now?" I asked, reaching out my hands to grab hold of him.

He took an unsteady step forward. It was clear that he had been drinking. He lifted up his right fist and aimed it towards my head. I instinctively leaned backwards, avoiding his fist. My reflex response of

91

straight right hander connected with his cheek and he collapsed onto the ground.

Using a hammer lock, I held his arm firmly up his back and lifted him to his feet. My self-defence instructors at Hendon College would have been proud of me. I was surprised by how effective it was, to be honest.

I marched him back to the pub where a police van was waiting. After placing him into the van, I poked my head into the main bar of the pub. Ossie was still sitting there, oblivious to everything that had just transpired.

"I hope you're okay, Ossie. Not too bored, are we?" I shouted sarcastically across the nearly empty bar. "I have to go to Chelsea Police Station and complete a statement and I'll be back. Hopefully, it won't take too long."

At the police station I explained to the Custody Sergeant what had happened.
Later, in the writing room, I had just finished my statement when an Inspector walked in.

I stood up. "All correct, Sir."

"PC Wilson is it?" he asked.

"Yes, Sir."

He looked at me sternly. "I have just finished speaking with your suspect. He doesn't know whether to make a complaint against you or congratulate you on your right hook."

Before I could respond, he continued. "Fortunately for you he decided not to make a complaint." he said, before turning and leaving the room.

Since I was finished, I went to the front office of the police station to talk to the Station Officer.

"Will you arrange to send a message to Croydon please, booking me on duty?" I asked.

On a rest day too, I thought, thinking of the nice monetary reward that would come to me as a result. This helped make up for the lack of acknowledgment or even a simple thank you from the Inspector for having my evening ruined, my clothing splattered with blood, and for putting myself at risk.

~~~~~

There were advantages to living at the top of Brixton Hill in 1985. Supermarkets, pubs, a Chinese restaurant, a launderette, and a bus stop were practically at my doorstep. The Brixton Underground station which was only a nice little stroll away probably topped the list. As nice as all of that was, it was still not a place I wanted to leave my old (but precious to me) Ford Capri

XL with vinyl roof while I went on my much anticipated and long-awaited three-week holiday to the United States.

I arranged to park my car on a quiet tree lined street next to my friend Cleo's flat in Drewstead Road, Streatham Hill. I felt it was less likely to attract attention there. I went on my holiday and did not give it another thought.

Three weeks later I stepped off the plane at Heathrow airport, the memories of my adventures in the United States still buzzing in my head. I had a great time, but it was good to be home.

I cleared immigration, collected my suitcase, and went to a public phone to call my friend Cleo.

"Hello mate, welcome back. Did you have a good time?" Cleo asked.

"Yeah, definitely. I can't wait to tell you all about it," I replied.

"Okay, but I'm afraid I have some bad news. Some bastard's put your Capri on bricks and nicked the wheels, two nights after you left."

I was speechless for a moment as I processed the shock of what Cleo just told me.

"Okay, mate. I'll take a look when I get home," I finally said.

I went home to my flat to drop my suitcase off and get cleaned up, then I took a 109 bus to Streatham Hill rail station. I got off the bus and ran over to where my car was parked.

My heart sank. The Capri's chassis rested on piles of bricks. The nice expensive alloy wheels were gone. My head throbbed with pain as I walked around the car, taking in what I was seeing. The black, vinyl roof was splattered with bird droppings, which was something I hadn't considered when I parked it under a tree. To make matters worse, the local council had placed a notice on the windscreen threatening to remove it under the abandoned vehicles legislation.

"Hello mate. You interested in that?" a voice behind me asked.

I turned around. A white man in his early thirties stood on the pavement smiling from ear to ear.

"Why? What is it to you?" I asked.

"It belongs to a mate of mine. He's willing to sell any parts you want for a couple hundred quid."

"Is that right?" I said.

"Yeah, just let me know what you want, and we can work something out, know what I mean?"

I reached into my back pocket, took out my warrant card and held it up.

"All I know is that you are nicked for attempted deception," I said.

"You've got to be fucking joking," he replied.

I grabbed his arm and tried to push him toward the main road, where I would get assistance. He struggled violently, causing both of us to fall onto the pavement.

"Help me! Help me!" he shouted. He knew people would draw one conclusion when they saw a black man wrestling with a white man.

"Get off him!" shouted a motorist who had slowed down next to us.

"Call the police!" I shouted.

Onlookers slowly gathered around, making comments like 'black cunt, leave him alone.'

Wrestling in the gym at Hendon Police Training College had been a favourite pastime for me. That certainly came in handy now as I wrestled with the suspect on the pavement. My very skilful opponent and tutor, Bob, had brought out the best in me and taught me how to quickly shift my weight to my advantage. This guy was no Bob, and it was not long before I had him pinned down in what I knew to be an uncomfortable position.

The sound of police sirens came from down the street. It was like music to my ears. Someone had made the call. The cavalry was coming at last. The police vehicle parked across the road and two officers got out and started walking towards us.

"Here's the Old Bill. They'll sort him. Probably give him a good kicking," an onlooker shouted.

I sprang to my feet as the officers ran towards me, still holding onto the man with my right hand. I reached into my pockets with my left hand and fumbled around for my warrant card, but it wasn't there. It must have fallen out during our roll-around. I was concerned that I might not be recognised as a police officer since I was unshaven, my hair was untidy, and I had thrown on some comfortable old scruffy clothes before leaving my flat.

"PC 826 from Zulu Delta!" I shouted. I knew the use of police jargon would immediately identify me as a cop, which it did. It also helped that one of the officers recognised me.

A short time later the station van arrived, and my prisoner was taken before the Custody Sergeant at Streatham police station. He was interviewed by CID officers and his home address was searched. Much to my relief, he was charged with attempted deception.

A few weeks later someone placed a newspaper clipping from 'The Argus News' in my correspondence tray at Croydon. The headline read '*Man convicted for trying to sell Police Constable his own car.*'

Chapter 19

Racist CID officer

"826, can you deal with a damage-only on Lombard roundabout?" asked the voice crackling over my personal radio. It was not so much a question as it was a directive from an officer in the control room. A damage-only meant there had been a collision between two vehicles but there were no injuries. Lombard roundabout too far away for foot patrol officers to reach so it was usually panda drivers who took calls for that area.

"Received," I replied. This meant not only that I had received the message but that I would act on it.

When I arrived at the scene both drivers were standing next to their vehicles calmly exchanging information. One was a white woman and the other was a black man.

The black man's car had taken a serious knock and the radiator had leaked fluid onto the road. I asked them both questions to find out what happened and report it in my yellow Accident Report Book if necessary. After talking with them I established that no offence had been committed by either party, no injuries had been sustained and they had exchanged names and addresses for insurance claim purposes. Their legal obligations had been discharged.

I moved to the other side of the roundabout to conduct some Police National Computer enquiries on my personal radio. While I was busy on my radio another vehicle pulled up, and a black guy got out. He walked over and began talking to the black motorist who had been involved in the collision. Two minutes later another vehicle stopped close by. I recognised it as a police general purpose vehicle belonging to our CID. Two CID officers got out and walked towards me. I did not recognise either of them but the taller one was red in the face. A fleeting thought crossed my mind - *I had seen similar ruddy complexions among my white colleagues after a bout of heavy drinking.*

"Why the fuck have you left a bunch of spades with that white woman?" he shouted, pointing across the roundabout at the two black men, the white woman and two young black schoolboys who had been taken an interest in the aftermath of the collision.

In my experience it was not unusual for passers-by to take an interest in a road traffic accident. It was a harmless enough occurrence, but the inflammatory remarks made by this CID officer were made to imply that it was not safe for the white woman to be in such close vicinity to four black males, even with a police officer a few yards away.

This was one of those rare moments in my career that the proverbial red mist descended and clouded any rational behaviour. With no thought to the consequences, my career, my livelihood, or even the risk of incarceration, I lunged at the officer. I so wanted to grab him by the throat and punch him in the nose with my right fist.

But before I could execute my plan, the second CID officer, a much shorter man, jumped between us and shouted something unintelligible. I snapped back to reality. He turned and grabbed his red-faced colleague by the lapels and ushered him back to their vehicle. They left the scene and never reported the incident to my Duty Inspector, nor to my knowledge did they ever mention it to their CID colleagues.

What would have happened if the second officer hadn't stepped in? It's hard to say. I might have been disciplined but I am not convinced it necessarily would have meant the end of my police career. There was a code of honour in the CID. To 'grass-up' a police officer colleague, even a black one, regardless of the severity of the offence would not be well received in the CID, where they enjoyed a tight 'culture within a culture.'

For the CID officer, a formal report to a senior officer would have meant ostracization at best and almost certainly an end to his CID career with the prospect of 'going back to uniform.' The associated stigma that carried, coupled with the inability to earn copious hours of overtime (a particular skill honed by many CID officers) were huge deterrents and ensured that CID officers remained wedded to the norms of their culture, occasionally disregarding the legality of the issue at stake.

For these reasons, it is really no mystery as to why the two CID officers never breathed a word to anyone about what happened that day.

Chapter 20

Public Order Training

With my holdall flung over my shoulder, I climbed the steps of the coach sitting outside of Croydon police station's back gate. It was my turn to attend a two-day public order refresher training at the Police Public Order training facility in Hounslow Heath, West London. All public order trained officers were required to attend these on a regular basis.

The training was realistically played out in a purpose built complex comprised of authentic streets and buildings, much like a film set, along with street furniture, traffic junctions and purpose-built rooms where some of the indoor exercises took place. The physical nature of the training exercises appealed to me. Running around the streets in fire retardant overalls, NATO helmet and a long, Perspex shield wrapped around my arm was a welcome break from walking the streets of Croydon. In my experience, the training was useful in preparing us for the extreme violence we occasionally encountered in public disorder situations.

A favourite training scenario that I had frequently practiced over the years, colloquially referred to as 'the nutter', involved a small team securing entry to a room in a house in order to subdue and arrest an individual with a disposition to commit violent acts against police.

The role of the 'nutter' was played by a heavily padded police instructor, who clearly enjoyed the power it gave him. He would taunt and pull at our shields and use a heavy wooden baton to strike our helmets, all at a pace that rendered us exhausted within a few minutes.

Out on the realistic streets of the training centre, we were put through punishing routines.

"Get into formation, shields up, heads tucked behind the shield and stick together," shouted our instructor.

Our group of five consisted of three who manned the shields and two that huddled behind, their arms forcing the shield men together liked some rugby scrum formation.

An instructor would then, with great enthusiasm, launch a petrol bomb in our direction. Fire from the bottle neck flickered in the wind as it fell about six feet in front of us.

"Petrol bomb!" we shouted, slowly edging forward in our formation.

From behind my NATO helmet visor, I watched the arc of another Molotov cocktail that had been lobbed from behind a wall that hid instructors playing the part of violent protestors.

This one was a direct hit, I thought.

We bowed our heads and tucked our chins down towards our chests as flames engulfed our shields. The exploded bottle seeped enflamed petrol through the gap underneath the shields and caught my right boot on fire. A colleague with a fire extinguisher quickly doused the flames. With no harm done, our unit kept in formation and shuffled forward in readiness for the next missile.

"Well done lads. Nice work," shouted our instructor.

Later we were taken to an underground bunker where we were each issued a military style gas mask and lined up in readiness to take our turn in the bunker.

The instructor smiled wryly. "Put on the mask and on my signal climb down the steps into the bunker. When I release the tear-gas, I want you to remove your gasmask and shout your name and warrant number. Then you'll be allowed to leave the bunker."

Time and time again, I watched red-faced and tear stained officers choke and gag as they stumbled out of the bunker. When it was my turn, I slowly walked down the steps into the dimmed light of the bunker, determined not to appear nervous in front of the instructor.

The dull thud of something hit the floor of the bunker and a mist quickly enveloped me. I could not see a thing through the gas mask goggles. As instructed, I tugged at the bottom of the mask, ripped it off and shouted my name and warrant number. This allowed the gas to enter my mouth, throat, and lungs. It felt like super strength West Indian hot pepper sauce had been injected into my eyeballs and poured into my windpipe. The pain was worse than I ever imagined. Every pore of my body felt like it had been infiltrated with gas. I cried uncontrollably as I stepped out of the bunker. I no longer cared about maintaining a sense of decorum in front of my colleagues. A mixture of tears and snot ran down my face.

"Quickly, get that overall off!" barked the instructor.

He splashed some liquid into my eyes and instructed me to head to the changing room. The exercises were concluded for the day.

I was still suffering the effects of the gas a little while later as I stuffed my overalls into my canvas holdall. I was later advised not to do this. There had been complaints of wives receiving secondary gassing from taking their husband's overalls out of their holdall to wash.

After that day I swore to myself that I would never subject anyone, not even my worst enemy, to the horrendous pain of tear-gas.

Chapter 21

'No-one likes a chocolate Smartie'

As a probationer, I was often expected to walk the streets by myself until at least 3:00 AM. It was a rare treat to be officially posted on the station van as a probationary constable, a posting described by team colleagues as 'riding shotgun'. When it was offered to me, I was thrilled however, I knew from the duties roster posted on the station notice board that Cyril was posted as the station van driver.

Night duty was usually a busy time for the station van. It was a mobile resource that was used to handle a variety of jobs. Most notably, it was used to ferry prisoners from the arrest site to the police station.

At the beginning of every shift, officers were assembled into a parade where they were to be inspected and given their duties for the next shift. During these times, the Section Sergeant would provide nuggets of useful information concerning persons of interest and local crime patterns. This information would be eagerly recorded in notebooks for preparation in the event it was needed.

Following the parade, I signed out a personal radio and walked across the station yard to the parked van to wait for Cyril. A few minutes later he walked across the station yard in a manner that befitted John Wayne, except instead of a holstered pistol, a personal radio was slung around his waistband, its long-flexed mouthpiece dangling by his ankles.

Cyril was a scruffy looking, twelve-year veteran. He was tall, stocky, with dark, thinning, unkempt greasy hair and a beard. He had the slightest of a west country accent and was immensely proud of his posting to the Special Patrol Group (SPG) in the seventies. As a nonconformist, Cyril regularly pushed back the boundaries of acceptability and got away with it. I had once witnessed him saunter into the parade room, five minutes late, with ruffled hair, no tie, and heavily creased uniform trousers. The Sergeant stared at the ceiling, sighed heavily, and nodded for him to take a seat.

He was a caricature of the loud, bad mouthed police officer (the type that did not exist according to New Scotland Yard's media machine). I'd heard about the notorious SPG bully tactics and always associated them with sparking the '81 disorders in Brixton. Cyril had often joked in my presence about how his SPG Unit was 'nowhere near Blair Peach', the demonstrator who subsequently died from a suspected blow to the head from a police truncheon in the Southall anti-racism demonstrations of '79. It was well known that numerous SPG Units were on duty at that demonstration.

He reached the driver's side and slid his bulky frame into the seat. I climbed into the passenger side and closed the door. He ignored me while he conducted a cursory cockpit check. When he was finished, he turned to me.

"Look, no-one likes a chocolate Smartie, so just keep quiet and do as you're told," he said.

That's an improvement on 'nigger', maybe things are looking up, I thought.

As the van pulled out of the station yard, I stared straight ahead. I had been conditioned not to respond. Racial epithets had been indelibly etched into my psyche and served to strengthen my resolve to be a better police officer. I would work harder, be smarter, get promoted and hoist myself above the daily diatribe of racially charged rhetoric, I would constantly tell myself.

Thankfully, we were so busy on this night that our conversations were of the normal, work-related, variety.

"Zulu Delta 2, (the van's call-sign) can you make your way to West Croydon rail station? A member of the public has seen a bearded IC1 (police code for white) male with what appears to be a handgun," crackled a voice over my personal radio.

Cyril flicked on the blue light and headed towards West Croydon at an accelerated speed. I grabbed my seat belt and made sure I was strapped in firmly as we hurtled along the High Street, running through red lights along the way. The van finally skidded to a stop across from the Fox & Hounds public house.

Cyril leaned forward and peered through the windscreen.

"There he is."

I watched in disbelief as Cyril hopped out of the van and ran across the road towards the West Croydon Station entrance where a bearded, tall white man stood talking to two women.

Just as I feared, Cyril jumped the man and brought him to the ground with his arms pinned behind his back and his cheek pressed against the asphalt.

The voice of Amanda in the Croydon control room came over the radio. "Zulu Delta 2 you can stand down - Zulu 2 has made a positive stop in London Road."

Cyril's radio had reverted to its customary position around his ankle and he had not heard the message from the control room.

From the middle of the busy road, I shouted, "Cyril."

He looked up, as he levered the man's arm up his back and pressed his face further into the gritty asphalt surface.

I shook my head, "It's not him."

At once, Cyril released his grip on the man, pulled him to his feet and walked back to the van as if nothing had happened.

I watched as the tall man brushed himself down and spoke with a large crowd of interested onlookers. *A complaint is coming Cyril's way,* I thought to myself as I turned and climbed back into my seat.

We continued our patrol and at the conclusion of our shift, the West Croydon incident had not been mentioned nor had it been reported to the Duty Inspector as a complaint against police. Maybe a testament to a type of behaviour the public had grown to expect from its police service.

A few weeks later my team was on night duty, but since I had probation classes that week, I had been taken off night duty and posted to the early shift which started at 7:00 AM.

It was wintertime and still dark when I left my Streatham flat at 6:15 AM. I parked in a side road next to the police station and entered through the back door. I walked into the still empty locker room and began changing out of my clothes. That is when I noticed my shoes and gasped in horror. In my half-asleep state, I had put on one black shoe and one brown one.

For some people this might just be another funny story to share around the office after running home to get the right shoes. That was not the case with me. In my profession, this was serious. I was still on probation and the Sergeant on the early shift did not know me. The most likely scenario was that he would send me home and tell me to return for the 3:00PM shift.

Feeling like I had no other option, I changed into my full uniform knowing full well I would be laughed out of the parade room with dire consequences once they saw my shoes.

That is when Cyril walked up. He had just finished his night duty and was getting into his locker, which was close to mine.

"Guess what I've done, Cyril?" I said, pointing at my shoes.

His reaction was just as I expected. He looked down at my feet and guffawed, bending over and slapping his knee,

"Can you help me out," I said, expecting a derisory comment in response.

He reached into his locker, pulled out a pair of black Chelsea boots and tossed them to me.

"Try these," he said.

I pulled them on, and they fitted perfectly. Cyril had saved me from what was sure to be a humiliating experience. And to my further amazement he never once brought it up in my presence in canteen discussions.

Chapter 22

District Support Unit

In 1987, I decided to apply for a six-month posting on the District Support Unit (DSU). This was an opportunity to put my public order training into practice. I told one of my team colleagues, Glen, about my plans.

"You must be mad. They're going to love you," he said, laughing.

I could only imagine what his response meant but I felt sure he was referring to my colour and the fact that the DSU had a reputation for giving black people a hard time, even if they were officers. Nevertheless, I was keen to acquire a broad range of policing experience that prepared me for promotion.

The DSU's vehicle was a specially equipped minibus staffed by about ten police constables and supervised by a sergeant. It had a roaming remit to respond to any incident where many police officers might quickly be required. The DSU for 'Z' District offered support to police stations serving Epsom, Sutton, Wallington, Kenley, Croydon, Norbury, South Norwood, Shirley, and Addington. It was supervised by Sergeant Gerald Steele who had a reputation for being unconventional while delivering on difficult tasks. Grammar school educated, with a rugby prop forward build, Sergeant Steele's disdain for the public and police colleagues alike was well known. He sometimes used methods that occupied that grey area between right and wrong.

"Don't get on his bad side," colleagues warned.

It quickly became apparent that work on the DSU offered a totally different perspective to policing the streets of Croydon.

Our Unit was often called upon to deal with large fights at nightclubs and public houses. We would also be sent to help our colleagues at Selhurst Park Stadium. Ejecting football fans for rowdy and disorderly behaviour was a popular task with DSU officers as it required little paperwork.

Sergeant Steele was a colourful character, but I found his bark to be worse than his bite. He was an intelligent man, but for some reason he would find it necessary to purposely dumb down and act oafish in front of both police colleagues and the public.

A few days into my posting, it became apparent to the crew that Sergeant Steele had taken a liking to me, for reasons best known to him.

One evening we were cruising the streets of New Addington, a large, sprawling public housing estate near Croydon, when a call came into the police radio situated at the front of our bus.

"Sarge, we've got a call in Epsom. A man is waving a sword from a bedroom window, shouting abusive language and threatening passers-by," shouted the officer with responsibility for managing the radio.

"Alright you lot. Get kitted up," Sergeant Steele commanded.

What he meant by this is that we were to put on our flame-retardant overalls (colloquially known as 'baby grow'), NATO helmets and protective gloves.

Our adrenaline rushing, we struggled into our protective clothing while being thrown around the cramped bus as it swerved and rocked through the Addington suburbs at high speed with the siren blaring.

The bus finally screeched to a halt outside of the address where the disturbance had been reported. A local police panda car and the police Duty Inspector for Epsom were on site.

"Stay on the bus," Steele shouted as he slid back the passenger door and stepped out of the bus.

Steele approached the Inspector who was looking up at the first-floor window at a man energetically waving a large sword from side to side. I opened the window to hear their conversation.

"Alright guv, we'll take it from here," Sergeant Steele shouted at the Inspector.

The Duty Inspector looked bemused. He had probably expected a conversation or at the very least a couple of questions to determine who this person was and what awaited us inside that house.

Sergeant Steele walked past the Inspector and stood under the first-floor window where the man waved the sword.

"Hey you! If you do not come down, we're coming to get you," he shouted.

This was not exactly the textbook approach advocated by the training staff at the Hounslow Public Order Training Centre.

As if incensed by his demand, the sword arm waved energetically.

"Alright, you've had your chance," Steele barked.

He walked back to the bus, stuck his head inside the open door and pointed at me.

"Paul get a round shield. You and I are going in first," he said.

I immediately clipped the NATO helmet strap under my chin. Then I grabbed one of the small round Perspex shields from its storage space, jumped out of the bus, and followed the sergeant, who had already put his own gear on.

We walked past onlooking local officers and into the neat rear garden of the semi-detached, three-bedroom house, where four colleagues carrying long shields joined us.

"Me and Paul will go up first and take down the bedroom door and you lot jump on him," he said to the officers behind us, who had probably been expecting a more comprehensive briefing. They nodded and we headed towards the door. At this point it occurred to me that small round shields were not best suited to the tactic described by our sergeant as they offered little protection from a proficient swordsman. I kept my mouth shut and followed orders.

I pushed the handle on the back door, it opened, and we entered the quiet, darkened house single file.

I found the staircase and Sergeant Steele and I quietly and slowly climbed up the carpeted steps side by side, keeping our eyes on the bedroom doors off the landing the entire time.

When we reached the top, Sergeant Steele pointed a gloved finger in the direction of the bedroom door farthest from the stairs.

"It's got to be that one," he whispered.

I turned to the colleagues behind us and raised the palm of my hand to signal them to stop.

"At three, me and Paul will rush that door, hit it with our shoulders and take it down. Did you lot get that?"

The sullen faced colleagues behind us nodded.

"1-2-3," whispered Steele.

We rushed forward, the momentum of our combined weight striking the door and taking it clean off its hinges.

We both fell forward, lying across the unhinged door. Our swordsman lay trapped underneath the door, pinned down by the weight of two large metropolitan police officers, his sword quickly wrenched from his grasp by colleagues.

The six months I spent on the Z District DSU with Sergeant Steele and crew was both educational and developmental, the absence of a racially charged work environment undoubtedly added to my enjoyment.

Chapter 23

Promotion

I carefully watched the books balanced precariously on my knees as I sat in the London Underground train carriage bound for Colindale station. From there I would walk the short distance to Hendon Police College, where I was due to take the annual Sergeant's promotion exam.

My anxious mind raced with questions. Had I studied enough? Had I done enough revision? Across the crowded carriage, another police officer sat reading a study book. Like me, he was doing some last-minute cramming in the hopes that it would stick.

As nervous as I was about taking the exam, I was also looking forward to getting it over with and out of the way. I had put my social life on hold for nine months and I was ready to get back out there again.

After the exam, I went back home to my flat in Streatham and sat at my kitchen table jotting down as many exam questions as I could remember. After researching the answers to those questions, I felt confident that I had probably done well enough to achieve a competitive pass. This went a long way in calming my nerves, since it would be several days before the results came back.

A few days later I was sitting at a desk in the CID office when one of my colleagues approached.

"The results are out. I think you might have passed," he said.

"What do you mean, might have?" I asked, feeling slightly annoyed. I needed a clear answer, not a guess.

I stood up and looked around for a supervising officer, but none were available. I walked downstairs to the office of the Chief Inspector in charge of personnel and stuck my head in his door. He looked up from his desk and smiled.

"Congratulations, you got it!" he said.

"The Sergeant's exam?" I asked.

"Yes," he replied.

I should have been elated, but instead I felt flat. It felt very anti-climactic, like it had not quite sunk in yet that I had achieved a competitive pass in the sergeant's exam.

A few days later I was made temporary Sergeant at Kenley police station, located in a leafy suburb of Croydon. Most of the excitement that went on around there was generated at the pool table during refreshment breaks. After that it was back to Hendon Police College for my Sergeant's induction course. It was during that course that I was notified of my first official posting in the rank of Sergeant. I was going to Catford, in the South London Borough of Lewisham. From a policing and social perspective, Catford was much quitter than Croydon. After working in Croydon for six years, the absence of a large shopping centre struck me as unusual, but the quaint, if not rather antiquated, Catford Centre overlooked by the giant black and white fibreglass feline that sits atop the Catford Shopping Centre sign, seemed a popular shopping destination for locals of all backgrounds.

On my first day at my new station, I walked into Catford's rather small (compared to Croydon's large well-appointed 24-hour cafeteria) and shabby canteen. Before I had a chance to order any refreshments, I was approached by a black female police officer. I was immediately struck by her beaming smile; unknowing to her it served to warmly welcome me into this very different environment.

"Hello Sarge, I hear you are joining us at Catford," she enquired, hardly able to stifle the obvious pleasure written across her face.

"Yes, I am, this is my first day, really pleased to be here."

"Oh, that's really great to hear, I'm WPC Gray, or Denise out of uniform," she said, her face radiating genuine warmth and as I was later to learn - relief.

In my new rank of Sergeant, I quickly fitted into my role as team supervisor of about 12 constables. In addition, I enjoyed spells of duty as Custody Sergeant where I would make decisions regarding the reception, charge, and detention of persons arrested. After a few weeks and still learning the ropes, I was invited for a drive around my new ground by a fellow sergeant who usefully used our time together to give me a quick synopsis of each of my new team members, including skills, strengths, work ethic, and perceived weaknesses.

"You'll have noticed that Denise is our only black WPC?"

"Yes, it hadn't escaped my attention," I replied with a hint of sarcasm.

He glanced at me as he changed gears and pulled up our vehicle at the traffic lights outside Lewisham Town Hall.

"Yeah, well she seems to be settling in OK now, but there was a time during her probation when the blokes would interrupt her personal radio transmissions with monkey chants - you know how the blokes are?" said my sergeant colleague in a matter-of-fact manner while not commenting on the inappropriateness of such behaviour and, why would he, it was part and parcel of the 'no harm meant, just a bit of banter' culture.

During the remainder of my time at Catford, I did not hear any monkey noises over the personal radio as described by my sergeant colleague. Maybe my arrival and presence had helped curb a behaviour commented upon by Policy Studies Institute (PSI) researchers, embedded within the metropolitan police over a period of two years. Their final report, published in 1983, disclosed that the transmission of monkey noises over the personal radio was a not uncommon form of behaviour for many officers.

One day while working in the Custody suite, my Inspector, Mick Botting, approached me.

"Superintendent Crosbie would like to see you, Paul. I think he has some news for you."

Brian Crosbie had been my Chief Inspector at Croydon. We had a bit of a history due to the bollocking I had received from him on two different occasions. The first time was for going on one of my frequent visits to the United States without notifying Croydon Magistrates that I had a case listed during that period. The second time was after he introduced rules for staff parking in the upstairs car park. I had received a couple of warnings for leaving my red Toyota MR2 on the access ramp to the car park. One evening after a hard day's work I went to my car and found a big, yellow clamp on the back wheel, courtesy of Chief Inspector Crosbie.

After he was promoted to Superintendent and posted to Catford, we met and had a friendly chat. We agreed to put aside our previous history. So, I did not understand why he now suddenly wanted to see me.

Crosbie was sitting at his desk when Inspector Botting and I walked into his office a few minutes later.

"Paul, you're going to Bristol for a couple of days. The job has organised a seminar for all our black and Asian officers to attend. I'm afraid it's compulsory," he said. He handed me a notice with further instructions and leaned back in his chair.

Mick Botting stared at me with a totally gob-smacked expression on his face. He must have wondered why I was suddenly smiling from ear to ear. This news was like manna from heaven for me. After all, it was only a few months ago that I had visited Washington DC and attended the Congressional Black Caucus[2] where I was introduced to Presidential candidate and civil rights icon, Jesse Jackson. In order to publicly express my solidarity with the work of the Congressional Black Caucus, I ensured that my visit and photograph with Jackson was reported in 'The Job', the Met's fortnightly internal newspaper. Therefore, my immediate reaction to the Bristol Seminar should have come as no surprise to my management colleagues at Catford. And while I had no idea what the seminar was about, I knew that somehow it signalled a watershed moment. This would hopefully be the beginning of a new, enlightened era for the Metropolitan Police. Why else would they summon all black and Asian officers, if not to try to address the rampant racism we all endured?

As we left Crosbie's office, Inspector Botting mumbled something about black officers needing to be careful and *not cause trouble*. I went into the Sergeant's locker room, made sure no one was watching, and had a little dance.

---

[2] The Congressional Black Caucus was established in 1971 to put forth policy and legislation that ensured equal rights, opportunity, and access for Black Americans and other marginalised communities. It is a non-partisan body made up of African American members of Congress.

Chapter 24

Bristol Seminars

Over the next few weeks, I learned that several senior police officers shared the same misgivings as Mick Botting. Day after day, I heard stories where these senior officers expressed grave concerns about *their* ethnic officers going away for a couple days. *What are they going to talk about?* They would ask.

This reaction from my white colleagues was hardly surprising in an environment where it was generally frowned upon for two black officers to sit next to one another in the station canteen. I was more surprised and disappointed to hear that some black police officers were doing everything in their limited power to *get out* of being sent to Bristol. *Such is the pervasiveness of the internal police culture*, I thought.

However, the memorandum issued by Assistant Commissioner Wyn Jones had not been an invitation but a direct order to all black and Asian officers to attend the seminar. Perhaps it was a draconian measure, but I also saw it as a necessary one. Given the overt, subtle, and subliminal pressures black and Asian officers faced to not involve themselves in anything that might open up to scrutiny the hitherto hidden and racist nature of the police culture, I felt something like this was long overdue.

Several conspiracy theories began making the rounds, along with suggestions that the seminars were to be postponed or even outright cancelled. But this was all put to rest upon the announcement of a Bristol Seminars briefing to be held at New Scotland Yard. I took a deep breath as I read the note advising me to attend. It lifted my spirits and made me hopeful that the briefing would calm nerves and convince the doubters that this exercise was in the best interest of all black and Asian officers.

The day of the briefing, I arrived at New Scotland Yard, nervous yet excited. I walked into the entrance hall, showed my warrant card, and was ushered through. Several smartly suited, black and Asian, male and female officers milled around the foyer. I joined them and exchanged handshakes, smiles and quick introductions. I sensed that many of them were also nervous, as no one knew exactly what to expect.

When it was time to take the lift to the upstairs briefing hall, I got in with about four others. Just as the doors began closing, a white guy rushed in. He set his briefcase down and looked around.

"What is this, the United Nations?" he asked.

A ripple of polite but uneasy laughter went through the lift.

As I took my seat in the large briefing room, Commander Jenny Hilton went up to the front to address the group of around one hundred officers.

She looks uncomfortable. Maybe she already knows something we don't, I thought.

"In 1989, twenty-six out of thirty-five black and Asian recruits prematurely resigned from the Metropolitan Police," she said. "And these seminars have been designed to help us understand just why we are seeing such high levels of premature wastage among our black and Asian recruits. Members of the Metropolitan Police Management Resource Centre (MRC) will be present over the two days and will facilitate conversations among small groups of officers in break-out rooms."

I think most of us here know exactly why those officers prematurely resigned. But if you need to hear it first-hand from nearly three hundred officers, it's going to be painful for you, I thought.

While the briefing lacked any sense of passion or enthusiasm, it did the trick. Now we knew exactly why we were going to Bristol Polytechnic for two days. And most importantly, we knew when. While ticking off all the positives in my mind, I could not help but think of the extraordinary social and psychological benefits of meeting with black and Asian police officers in a friendly environment. And if nothing else, it would be fun. This was something our white colleagues took for granted whenever there was a conference or overnight meeting away from work.

A few days later I went back to New Scotland Yard to meet the coach arranged to transport us to Bristol. As I got in and took my seat, a white officer approached me.

"Hi, my name's Inspector Nick Lipscomb. Please call me Nick. I will be accompanying all of you to the seminar these next two days."

After we shook hands, he continued slowly moving down the coach aisle, shaking the hands of just about all the passengers.

Not long into our journey to Bristol the coach became filled with the sounds of laughter, shouting and joking as everyone enjoyed the company of their fellow passengers. By the time we reached the M4 motorway, the atmosphere on the bus was positively electric. I didn't want our journey to end. In my seven years as a uniformed police officer I had never felt so relaxed and at ease, knowing that everyone around me had experienced the same things I had experienced and survived. That is what we were, a coach full of happy and joyous survivors.

After we arrived at Bristol Polytechnic, we were ushered into a dining area for refreshments and then it was down to business. We were divided into groups of twelve and told we would remain in our groups for the next two days. We were then sent to our designated syndicate rooms, where we introduced ourselves to one another. Everyone looked at each other warily, not quite knowing what to expect.

The facilitator, a member of the Metropolitan Police Management Resource Centre, was the only white person in the room. He went up to the front and addressed us.

"I want us to discuss and understand a number of challenges facing the Met. I invite you to be part of that process. Let me assure you that while the comments will be notated, the source of each comment will remain anonymous," he said.

I could sense the suspicion; it was almost tangible. I was the only Sergeant in my syndicate while the remainder were constables. That was not the reason for the suspicion, though. It was the white facilitator. No one quite knew what the hidden agenda was or if there even was one. Only one thing was clear. He was going to have to work extremely hard to get people to open up and express their true feelings.

After we took our next break, we came back to find our seats carefully arranged in a horseshoe, with the facilitator in front.

"Let's talk about some things that are going well for you," he said.

People began to offer various comments, without any sense of urgency or passion.

"Plenty of overtime."

"Just got my driving course."

"Money is good."

"Ok, that's good. Now, let's discuss what's not going so well," the facilitator said.

"Not enough overtime," someone said.

"Still can't get a driving course," another added, laughing.

We all laughed. These responses were typical of the police humour that we all understood and were so well-versed in.

The facilitator looked frustrated. We all knew the reason why we were here, and he probably wanted to delve into that, yet here we were acting like our problems were the same as our white colleagues. If no one else was going to throw the metaphorical hand grenade into this conversation, I would.

113

"I suspect racism in the workplace is the elephant in the room?" I said, glancing at the faces of my colleagues.

"Would you like to elaborate?" the facilitator asked.

"Well, I suspect that racism had probably been a regular feature in the everyday working life of everyone here. Probably not the overt stuff, but racism, nevertheless. I'll be incredibly surprised if this hasn't been an issue for all of us."

I hoped that by my speaking up, it would encourage a response from the rest of the group. It worked.

An African officer seated next to me turned and looked directly at me.

"I think being called a black bastard by my Inspector is probably overt racism," he said. His voice and his expression screamed *you have not felt my pain.*

That response unleashed an avalanche. Over the next day, everyone spoke passionately about their personal and painful experiences. Some would be in tears as they spoke, and some would become so overwhelmed they would have to get up and leave the room. The happy, smiling black faces I had seen on the bus were now gone.

As stories of racist abuse, personal lockers being broken into, personal vehicles vandalised, car tyres slashed, racist graffiti sprayed on items of police property and other criminal acts went around the room, the facilitator would lean forward and crane his neck, as if he could not believe what he was hearing.

As troubling as these stories were, the dichotomy was that police officers were effectively reporting that they had been the victims of criminal assaults and acts of criminal damage in the understanding that it would go no further. This was a particularly troubling aspect for me. I understood the cathartic value of speaking up and sharing experiences in a safe and supportive environment. However, we were all police officers who had sworn an oath to uphold fundamental human rights, act diligently and impartially. Yet here we were, parking the oath for two days and overlooking criminal acts committed by police colleagues to improve the Metropolitan Police Service's retention and recruitment of black and Asian police officers. It was a high price to pay, but everyone I spoke to over those two days agreed it to be a worthwhile one if it worked.

On the second day of the seminar, all the syndicate groups were asked to assemble in a large hall and choose one person to speak for each group. This speaker would be invited on the stage to address the main assembly, in the presence of Assistant Commissioner Wyn Jones. This opportunity was too good to pass up, so I volunteered to represent my syndicate.

I took a seat and awaited my turn to speak. Keith Mendoza, a former colleague at Croydon, sat next to me. He was a Trinidadian by birth with about fifteen years of service in the police. When it was my turn and I stood up and began making my way to the stage.

"Paul, you're not going up there, are you?" Keith asked.

I turned and looked at him. He looked slightly bewildered. "Yes," I said.

"It won't make any difference. You know that, right?" he said.

"We have to try, otherwise we'll never know," I replied.

I took my place on the podium and made a short, impassioned, and *off-the-cuff* plea for change. A change in the way colleagues treated officers from black and Asian backgrounds and a change in the way, we, the police treated black and minority ethnic members of the public. The two issues were intrinsically linked, I said.

As I spoke, Assistant Commissioner Jones nodded and took notes. After the final presentation, he walked onto the stage to give the closing remarks. He was an impressive figure of a man. Tall, smartly groomed, and charismatic. He thanked everyone for their participation and acknowledged that it had been difficult for some. Most importantly, he outlined the next steps. They would begin working now to identify the key issues that were raised during the seminar. Then, over the next few months they would work to begin drawing together a raft of measures tailored to address these key areas.

"You will be invited to get involved in that work," he said.

His words excited me, the prospect of getting involved in something this big. I left Bristol Polytechnic on a high that day.

The coach journey back to New Scotland Yard was noticeably different. The laughter and jokes that had previously filled the coach were subdued, yet there was a tangible increase in camaraderie and respect. People spoke in hushed conversations, and in some cases, couples sat huddled together, romances had blossomed in those two days.

The previous night, during drinks in the bar, some officers had expressed scepticism about the whole Bristol exercise. They questioned the true extent of the 'racism problem'. But after two days of conversation there was now a degree of acknowledgment that while casual and everyday racism in the workplace may not be personalised, it is nevertheless always intended to dehumanise people who look just like you. It is this daily experience of casual racism that is so often internalised as normal by so many.

A heightened sense of realisation and understanding during those two days, in the safety of friends, was now manifesting before my very eyes in an enhanced sense of brotherhood.

Surely things will never revert to 'normal' following the Bristol experience, I thought.

Chapter 25

Bristol Seminar Project Team

Following the Bristol Seminar, I returned to work and waited patiently for word about the measures Assistant Commissioner Jones had said would be implemented. I eagerly scoured the pages of Police Orders, an internal police notice published bi-weekly, that conveyed important announcements and job opportunities.

Finally, one day an announcement appeared in Police Order 19 dated 24th July 1990. Officers were invited to apply for posts that were being made available based on recommendations received during staff seminars at Bristol Polytechnic. These posts included occasional work on four groups that were being established:
- Grievance and Discipline
- Training
- Recruitment
- Support Mechanisms

There was also a full-time post available for a sergeant who would be responsible for coordinating the work undertaken by these working groups. I eagerly set about applying for the sergeant's post. My application dated 7th August 1990 was formally submitted having received the support of my immediate line manager, Mick Botting, and endorsed by Chief Inspector Stuart Carr.

A few days later I received notification from Mick Botting that I was to be interviewed for the Sergeant's post of full-time coordinator. The interview panel would consist of Chief Superintendent David Martin and Christine Gifford, a senior civil staff member from New Scotland Yard's Personnel and Training department.

On the day of my interview, I put on my best blue suit and took the train to New Scotland Yard, where I was shown into the interview room. I nervously sat down before the panel.

Both panel members were friendly as they asked me about my personal aspirations, what I had thought of the Bristol Seminars, and what I thought needed to happen now. I answered each question with a touch of enthusiasm and passion.

"Is there anything you'd like to ask us?" Christine Gifford asked.

"No, but I need to point out that I currently attend Croydon Business School once a week on a day release basis. I am studying administrative law, among other things," I explained.

"I don't see that being a problem, if you're successful," said Chief Superintendent David Martin.

My heart began to race at the suggestion that I just *might* be successful.

The next day I was working in the Custody Suite at Catford Police Station, when a member of my team approached me with a message that Superintendent Brian Crosbie wanted to see me in his office.

I completed what I was doing and asked a fellow sergeant to look after things until I returned. I anxiously made my way upstairs and knocked on the open door.

"Come in, Paul," said Superintendent Crosbie, smiling. "They want you."

"That's fantastic news, Sir," I said, hardly able to contain my absolute elation.

"Have a seat. I'll call Dave Martin and find out when you will be starting," he said, picking up his phone.

After a brief conversation, he hung up the phone and looked up.

"They want you as quickly as possible," he said.

After a little over 18 months in the rank of sergeant, on 17th September 1990 I was transferred from Catford Police Station to work on the Bristol Seminar project team under the auspices of New Scotland Yard's Personnel and Training Department (PT1). Our offices were in Tintagel House, a grimy 1960s HQ building owned by the Metropolitan Police, which overlooked the river Thames on the Albert Embankment. It was here during the 1960s that a team of detectives worked to bring down the notorious East End gangsters, The Krays.

Our small project team included police constable George Rhoden, who had also been recruited on a full-time basis. George and I had first met during my Law Clerk years when he attended boxing training at Cannon Row gym under the supervision of Johnny Banham. The project operations lead was Chief Inspector Chris Mikellides, another former boxer who was well known to George. He was the Met's most senior officer of Greek-Cypriot heritage. Inspector Nick Lipscomb who had been present in a supervisory capacity at the Bristol Seminar and Janet Alton who served as our Executive Officer with overall responsibility for ensuring that we had sufficient resources to be able to do our work. It was her job to ensure the smooth running of the office. George Rhoden and I were the only black officers on the project team.

But why on earth was Bristol chosen was a question I and many others had asked, given the City's historical and shameful links with the enslavement of African people. The answer was provided by Jan Alton who had also been involved in arrangement of the seminars,

"It was all about value for money, of all the Universities and Conference centre's approached, the fact is that Bristol Polytechnic offered us the most attractive rates," explained Janet in a matter-of-fact manner.

Shortly after we began setting up our systems at Tintagel House, our senior management lead, Chief Superintendent David Martin (or Action Man, as he was called out of earshot) introduced his deputy, newly promoted Superintendent Peter Brant. Peter was an odd choice, as he'd clearly made a name for himself as a career detective at New Scotland Yard. Working on a project of this nature was always going to raise a few eyebrows among his former colleagues and of course some black and Asian officers who were suspicious of the CID's notorious 'culture within a culture' that appeared to militate against the inclusion of anyone who was different.

A few days after arriving at Tintagel House, a copy of the Bristol Seminar report appeared in our office, as if by magic. We were advised to never remove it from the office as it was an extremely sensitive document.

"Where did this report come from, Nick?" I asked.

"Three police officers were tasked with making sense out of all the data collected from the Bristol Seminars. What you have on your desk is a revised version. The original had graphic accounts of racist behaviour and was considered too sensitive," he said.

"I don't find that hard to believe, but who were the three officers who put it all together?" I asked.

"Sergeant Sultan Taylor, Sergeant Nicola Ainsworth, and WPC Patricia Gallan. All university graduates who were given a 'pokey little office' at New Scotland Yard and provided with all the flip charts from the Bristol Seminars. They were left to their own devices in terms of making sense of an inordinate amount of written flip chart material," he said in a tone that suggested a great deal of admiration for the three officers.

I opened the restricted report and began to leaf through its pages. Some sections particularly captured my attention.

The Bristol Seminars were held with the intention of examining the reasons for black and Asian officers (prematurely) leaving the Service. The extremely skilled work of the MRC facilitators, however, brought forth a wealth of additional material on the subjective viewpoint black and Asian colleagues had, and the attitudes by which they found themselves surrounded. Many felt that the seminar was the first opportunity that they had to openly express their most personal thoughts and feelings, and they did with vigour and sincerity.

These thoughts and feelings have been examined by detailed analysis of the notes made by the officers themselves as they discussed in syndicate the problems faced by black and Asian officers within the Service and the presentations which each syndicate gave to the seminar group as a whole. A great deal of that expressed indicated that far from being well within the service, most black and Asian officers had, at some time, been subject to racist attitudes from within the organisation and for some this was almost a daily occurrence.

The 'Canteen Culture' and the name calling and behaviour it gives rise to featured so prominently that it has been examined in detail. The aspects which are looked at include observations on the way police officers address their black and Asian colleagues, the ethnic minority public, women officers, and officers from other minority groups.

The sense of isolation to which so many black and Asian officers are subject was very clearly apparent in much of the material they presented. Detailed analysis shows that it is often present in their interaction with colleagues and with the organisation. It is also apparent in many transactions with the white public, the ethnic minority public and occasionally their own families (Page 4. Bristol Seminars Report)

There is no doubt that the Bristol Seminar has caused great debate and the disclosure of many unhealed deeply personal wounds. Black and Asian officers have opened up in part their soul to the organisation and have placed great trust in it. Specifically, expectations have risen and cynicism for the moment, has been pushed to one side. The Force now has a responsibility to ensure that these hopes are not dashed and that steps are initiated to bring about at least a process of enlightenment if not change of racial attitudes and awareness.

As with any revolution in ideas when expectations have risen, practically, they cannot be fully fulfilled. However, Bristol had a realism; they did not expect Rome in a day. Rather, that in the long term there is genuine commitment to reaching a destination where the content of their character and not the colour of their skin is important. They asked for equal treatment, no more, no less. (Page 20. Bristol Seminars Report)

After thoroughly reading the report, I now understood the methodology applied across all the Bristol Seminar syndicates. Conversations about racial issues, recruitment, grievance procedure, support, and public relations were key points that were discussed in all the syndicates.

What I did not appreciate was the existence of a white control group. These white officer syndicates were canvassed in the same way as the black and Asian syndicates. They too gave presentations to Assistant Commissioner Wyn Jones at the conclusion of their two days.

What seemed to be of immediate concern to Chief Superintendent David Martin was not so much the white control group's absolute denial of any racial discrimination or issues likely to impact black colleagues negatively. No, it was the fact that after the first day's business had concluded, several officers retired to the bar, just as we had done. But unlike the black and Asian officers, this group of white officers drank excessively and became very rowdy.

It was in this inebriated state that some of them decided to visit the female accommodation block and attempted to enter the room of a female Inspector colleague. For thirty minutes they banged and kicked at the door and shouted at the woman.

"The matter was the subject of an ongoing and sensitive internal complaints and discipline inquiry," explained Chief Superintendent Martin

Chapter 26

Bristol Reunion

One day George Rhoden, whose desk was directly across from mine, leaned over to me and whispered.

"I'm organising a reunion at the London's Waldorf Hotel, for everyone that attended the Bristol Seminars. I want to keep that camaraderie alive."

"That is excellent George," I said, "I'll be there, looking forward to it".

Before the Bristol Seminars, the thought of George, or anyone else for that matter, organising functions that targeted black and Asian police officers would have been unthinkable. Now it was the way forward. Chief Superintendent David Martin, Christine Gifford, and Superintendent Peter Brant understood this. There was no hint of resistance, no red tape, and no questions that might be considered obstructive. This was something George was doing off his own back, with the blessing of all in the project team. As far as the Metropolitan Police were concerned, it was a private matter involving police officers acting in their private capacity. It was nevertheless unofficially condoned and supported, given its strategic support for an important police recruitment and retention issue.

The idea of a reunion was undoubtedly a piece of forward thinking on George's part. The whole office was behind the idea and excited at the prospect. It seemed like such a logical and simple next step to cement the friendships and the bonds that had formed during the Bristol Seminars, and keep the two-day experience on the agenda for black and Asian officers.

An important by-product of this social enterprise was the potential for enhanced support for black and Asian officers. Officers could have the assurance that they were not alone with their concerns, and they had someone they could turn to. This was a central issue for black and Asian officers and one that was identified in the Bristol Seminar report. Officers had reported feeling isolated, not having anyone to turn to, and not having anyone in the workplace who understood what they were experiencing. The Bristol conversations had helped raise an awareness, providing a deeper understanding of the nature of racism and how its toxicity was woven into the informal culture of the metropolitan police force.

In the full swing of the 1990 festive season, I attended the first Bristol Reunion at the historic Waldorf Hotel in London. Everyone was dressed to impress. Soul, reggae, and funk music blasted from the speakers in the main ballroom. Caribbean food was provided by the hotel. George had taken care to provide every conceivable comfort. Police officer numbers were matched by guests from the community, including a healthy number of young ladies who were undoubtedly interested in meeting a potential suitor. Despite the many issues the black community had with family members becoming police officers, many black women seemed willing to look beyond that and see a man in a stable, respected, profession who earned a good income and had an attractive pension to look forward to.

The atmosphere was informal and lively. There was no rank structure that evening. We all knew why we were there. Conversations about the Bristol experience flowed, as did the discussions, and jokes about the numerous romantic liaisons that had occurred between black and Asian officers over those two days. This was a natural by-product of the seminars that wasn't documented in the final report.

The music and dancing were the highlight of the evening. Prior to this it would have been difficult to imagine black and Asian officers dancing together in carefree abandon at any police function, yet here we were.

No one was swigging from a bottle of beer on the dance floor or fooling around. There were no silly dances or drunken behaviour and there was not a pair of jeans in sight. The unwritten code of conduct and etiquette at all the black night clubs, dances and social functions I had attended in the last fourteen years held firm in the magnificent Waldorf ballroom that night.

The following Monday morning, George came into the office looking tired but smiling. I stood up and clapped.

"Well done, George, brilliant night," I said.

"I'm still absolutely mashed," he replied as he slumped into his chair.

"Well, take it easy. You deserve it."

A couple of months later, things took a twist. George was not smiling when he walked in that morning. In fact, he looked quite upset.

"Is something wrong?" I asked.

George walked over to me and looked around to make sure no one was listening.

"We have a problem, Paul," he whispered. "I've done the accounts for the reunion and it turns out I still owe the Waldorf Hotel about two hundred and sixty pounds."

While that was a relatively small amount of money, in the bigger scheme of things it could potentially be very damaging. A disclosure such as that to senior management would probably bring up difficult questions about merging police resources (such as ticket and promotional leaflet printing) with a private event. This was a grey area that could be explained away but might lead to management oversight of the reunions and awkward conditions if the reunions were to continue.

After a brief discussion with Nick and Chris, it was decided that I would put together a memorandum (F728) to Superintendent Peter Brant. The Bristol Reunions had to be preserved at all costs, so it was necessary to get on the front foot.

In the report to Superintendent Brant, I requested the funds to cover the shortfall and highlighted some challenges faced by promoting the reunion in a busy Christmas period. This resulted in lower attendance than expected which when coupled with expensive ticket prices and an unexpected hotel room hire charge (introduced at a late stage when it became clear that ticket sales were lower than expected), resulted in a shortfall of two hundred twenty-seven pounds.

Furthermore, I explained that we accepted the fact that the staff workplace had suffered some disruption because of organising the event and laid out the strategies to be introduced before the next event. These strategies included the introduction of a special 'Operation Bristol' post box in New Scotland Yard's postal room to accommodate the receipt of cheques in payment for reunion tickets, I promised that, moving forward, officers organising further reunions would only do so in their personal time. Finally, proceeds from the next reunion would be used to reimburse the Commissioner's fund, with any remaining money to be paid to a known charity.

The report to Superintendent Brant did the job, and no awkward questions from senior managers were received. Shortly afterwards, George asked if I would officially help him organise future Bristol Reunions. I happily accepted.

Chapter 27

Assistant Commissioner Wyn Jones

Our team had barely finished setting up our systems when we were hit with a lightning bolt. A story came out in *The Sun* newspaper alleging that our sponsor, Assistant Commissioner Wyn Jones, was being investigated for misconduct. As soon as I read about it, I walked over to Nick's desk to talk about it with him.

"How does that work? Who investigates Assistant Commissioners? Isn't that unheard of? And how is it that *The Sun* publishes this information at a time when we are about to implement a number of much needed reforms?" I shouted. I wanted everyone in the office to hear how angry I was.

"You're right, it is unheard of. I have absolutely no idea what happens next," Nick said, throwing up his hands.

This was a huge blow for the Bristol Seminar project team. In the days that followed, Christine Gifford and Chief Superintendent Martin tried to put on a brave face and encouraged us to continue as though everything was normal. But as the days turned into weeks, it became noticeably clear that things were far from normal.

Without the leadership of Assistant Commissioner Wyn Jones, who remained suspended from duty, we tried our best to undertake the previously agreed upon work plan. I tried not to give it much thought, but it seemed to a few of us that our mission had been undermined in terms of importance, direction, strategic support, and achievement.

Gradually, rumours began circulating that some senior officers at New Scotland Yard were annoyed by Assistant Commissioner Jone's 'flamboyant manner', as well as his directorship of the whole Bristol Polytechnic exercise which placed New Scotland Yard's hitherto conservative approach to race equality at serious risk of change.

One morning, Christine Gifford came into our office and walked up to my desk.

"Paul, we want you to take the lead on revising and developing a new service Grievance Procedure," she said.

I stared at her in mild shock. It had been agreed at the beginning that the revision and development of a new police grievance procedure would be led by a small working group who would work through a series of meetings and discussions to help formulate the policy. But due to the recent events, all the working groups were in disarray, meeting on a haphazard basis and producing limited output.

"But I have no policy development background or experience," I protested, terrified at the thought.

"Now is a good time to get some," she said, turning on her heels and leaving the office.

Over the next few months, as I undertook the daunting task assigned to me, I pored over every sentence in the Race Relations Act of 1976 and the Sex Discrimination Act of 1975. Eventually, digesting an understanding of both pieces of legislation to the extent I felt equipped to embark on the not insignificant challenges facing me.

I began making tentative drafts of what a new Corporate Grievance Procedure might look like. The importance and centrality of my work was undoubtedly the result of a recent landmark Industrial Tribunal where, for the very first time, a black police officer used legislation in the Race Relations Act of 1976 to issue legal proceedings against the Commissioner of Police.

The Industrial Tribunal held that Police Constable William (Bill) Halliday had been unlawfully victimised by management following his complaint of racial abuse. While the tribunal did not find in favour of his allegations of racial abuse, it nevertheless held that transferring Halliday to another post was tantamount to victimising him for raising the allegation in the first instance.

The allegations of sickening racial abuse against Halliday, from his Inspector amongst others, was not the focus of senior officers. It was the ruling that the transfer of an individual against his wishes amounted to victimisation under both the Race and Sex legislation. Hence, my need to ensure that the Metropolitan Police adopted a fresh and more supportive approach to the handling of grievances.

Chief Superintendent Martin introduced me to Inspector Peter Strawbridge, one of the Met's highflyers. Peter would visit the office on occasion and sit down with me. He challenged my thinking, but more importantly, he showed real interest in my views about how we could progress matters. He came across to me as someone passionate about equality of opportunity.

Peter was a much-needed breath of fresh air. Feeling motivated and encouraged, I kept notes of our discussions. Within a few weeks we had a draft of a new Corporate Grievance Procedure. It was the Metropolitan Police's first staged procedure and placed a responsibility on the officer receiving the grievance to document it and try to resolve it. If it were unsuccessful, the process would be moved forward to the next stage, thereby taking the burden off the victim.

Chapter 28

Equal Opportunities Unit

When I learned that the Bristol Seminar Project team was to be amalgamated with the Equal Opportunities Unit (EOU), it seemed an eminently sensible development. The EOU operated under the Department of Personnel and Training (PT1) and was introduced in the late 1980s, probably because of a rise in complaints of discrimination. Its existence was previously largely unknown to many black police personnel, me included, because the primary focus of the EOU was gender discrimination. It effectively policed the Sex Discrimination Act of 1975, which protected both men and women from discrimination on the grounds of gender or marital status.

Before the Bristol Seminars, the full extent of the provisions of the Race Relations Act of 1976 were not fully embraced or actively promoted by the EOU. Positive Action was an alien concept. Staffed by police Inspector Tony Moore and Sergeant Tony Craighill, it was also responsible for coordinating the arrangement of equal opportunities training, a key component in the Metropolitan Police's strategy to help reduce the potential for sex and race discrimination litigation.

Because of the amalgamation, the Bristol Seminar project was relocated to room 1133 at New Scotland Yard in 1992. This gave us a new energy we did not have at our isolated Tintagel House location. We would now rub shoulders with influential departments such as the Directorate of Public Affairs (DPA) who were responsible for a large part of the Met's publicity and communications work.

Networking and socialising with our new neighbours helped build our profile and sense of importance, and of course we gained considerably more attention within the echelons of New Scotland Yard's senior officers.

As we had anticipated from the beginning, the Bristol Reunions had created a useful network and offered a degree of support. When George departed the Bristol Seminar project team and I planned to depart just a few months later, I began to think of the reunion in other terms. I saw it developing into an advocacy platform to mobilise significant numbers of black and Asian officers to lobby and advance the changes advocated in the Bristol Seminar report.

In 1992 Superintendent Tom Kelly was recruited to replace Peter Brant, who was to continue his career as a New Scotland Yard detective. We all wondered how much impact that would have on progress, or the lack of it. Kelly had an old school, hands-on, 'get things done' approach. He was a systems man. All informal meetings and practices within the EOU were suddenly being formalised leading to a growth in office files, ensuring clear audit trails and accountability. Work began to gather momentum under his guardianship, and it was a breath of fresh air.

While the Bristol Seminars had been very much a London initiative, it seemed to me that black and Asian colleagues across the country probably shared many of the experiences faced by their London counterparts.

With that in mind I began drafting a letter that I would address to the heads of personnel in large police forces across the country, such as West Midlands,   Leicestershire, South Yorkshire, Nottinghamshire, and Greater Manchester. Under the auspices of New Scotland Yard's Equal Opportunities Unit, I set out the reason for the Bristol Seminars, the resultant Project Team and its work to date. But most importantly, I emphasised how the introduction of the Bristol Reunion social function served as a useful and supportive by-product.

In September 1992 I sent out letters to heads of personnel across the country, to extend an offer to their black and Asian officers to contact New Scotland Yard's Equal Opportunities Unit to discuss our work in greater detail, including the hugely successful Bristol Reunion functions. I showed a copy to Superintendent Kelly, who nodded while he read.

"You're quite intent on creating a little empire, aren't you?" he laughed "But it's a good idea, nevertheless."

A couple of weeks later Superintendent Kelly came into the office with a young, black woman I had never seen before.

"It's you! You're the one!" she said loudly when she saw me. She then began laughing hysterically and Superintendent Kelly joined in her laughter.

I gave her a blank stare. What was happening?

She stepped towards my desk and held out her hand.

"Sergeant Robyn Williams, Notts Police. You must be Paul. You sent a letter to our Head of Personnel," she said.

I stood up and shook her hand. It was good to meet a fellow Sergeant from Nottingham. This was to the beginning of a firm and lasting friendship.

As 1992 progressed it became increasingly apparent that the usefulness of the four ad-hoc Bristol Working Groups, comprised of officers that had attended the Seminars, were now receiving less direction and minimal support. At least, that is how it appeared to me. A great deal had been achieved on paper, but the huge raft of policy documents that emanated from the months of Working Group deliberation were continuously subjected to what appeared to be a dilution process, whereby groups of senior officers sitting on numerous central committees would offer views and recommendations effectively toning down the intention of what had been developed over the previous eighteen months.

The feeling that Bristol had been a hastily arranged and ill-conceived social experiment that somehow backfired was made more believable by the unprecedented nature of its architect's suspension.

With the work of the Bristol Project team drawing to a close, it was decided by Personnel and Training senior management that the introduction and revitalisation of the old Equal Opportunities Committee was the way forward. This committee, comprised of police and civil staff, and union and police federation representatives, was a means of monitoring the continued implementation of a new equalities policy.

At the outset this appeared a logical development, particularly as the new Grievance Procedure, one of the more successful outcomes of the post-Bristol work, had significant ramifications for all police personnel who were both victims and perpetrators of unlawful discrimination.

Chapter 29

Equal Opportunities Committee

When talk of the newly constituted Equal Opportunities Committee appeared to start taking place behind closed doors, this piqued my interest. But as a mere Sergeant, I did not expect to be included in policy discussions of a strategic nature. Nevertheless, I enjoyed an enhanced profile in the Equal Opportunities Unit because of leading on the development of a lauded Grievance Procedure that was now being presented as good practice to police forces across England and Wales.

My expanded role as the Met's voice on all matters involving grievances and 'race', championing the promised new dawn of race equality throughout the metropolitan police, took me the length and breadth of the Metropolitan Police District. It was here that I would conduct presentations on the mechanics of the Grievance Procedure and the requirement for officers to be aware of the relevance of both the Race Relations and Sex Discrimination Acts.

In addition to my roving brief, I would regularly be called upon to partake in numerous Equal Opportunities' training sessions. These were led by Dianna Yach, a formidable South African lawyer. Often in the middle of her training session she would invite me to come up to the front and give the EOU's perspective on the high-profile nature of the Industrial Tribunals, increasingly causing concern for New Scotland Yard's senior management. Yet, despite all of this, I was clearly not privy to any decisions around the new Equal Opportunities Committee - who would be sitting on the Committee?

Since Superintendent Tom Kelly had an 'open door' policy, I went into his office one afternoon when he was away and rummaged around his neatly ordered desk. I found the file setting out the rationale for the new Equal

Opportunities Committee. A quick read confirmed my suspicion. There wasn't a single black, Asian or minority ethnic committee member. Despite the high-profile nature of my work to date and my close working relationship with Superintendent Kelly, I felt that any protestations from a mere Sergeant would fall on deaf ears. Aside from sharing my simmering anger and sense of betrayal with my Bristol Reunion friends, what else could be done?

Since the next Bristol Reunion at The Strand Palace Hotel was taking place on 20th November 1992, a few days away, that seemed like the perfect opportunity to do something as I would have access to many black and Asian officers on the night. The day before the reunion I drafted a statement which in a few lines set out in the strongest of terms the 'betrayal'.

'Despite being included for two years we are now apparently excluded from the newly constituted Equal Opportunities Committee...........'

Below the statement were numerous boxes for signatures. The Equal Opportunities Committee protest petition had been prepared.

As one of the organisers of the Bristol Reunion, I stood alongside my co-organiser, George Rhoden, at the door of the prestigious Strand Palace Hotel and greeted guests, all the time rehearsing in my mind how I would present the petition to them. I believed it would be helpful if a senior officer signed it first, as this would give credibility and confidence to the junior officers.

Dalton McConney, an Inspector of Barbadian origin, had a demeanour and authority that seemed to demand attention. However, I had doubts that he would support the petition as it could be construed as a radical move and he was very much from the Bajan old school of conservatism and tonight he was wearing a navy-blue blazer, formal shirt, and tie.

I later spotted Dalton's wife by standing by herself.

"BRISTOL REUNION"
presents
a

★ ★ ★ ★ ★ ★

PARTY NITE

★ ★ ★ ★ ★ ★

at
The prestigious
STRAND PALACE HOTEL
STRAND, WC2
(Nearest tubes, Charing Cross/Covent Garden)
on

FRIDAY 20th NOVEMBER 1992
8 p.m. - 2 a.m.

★ Renew old acquaintances - make new ones!
★ The best in Soul/Funk/Reggae
★ Food
★ Late Bar
★ Admission : £8.50 (payable on door)
★ Dress : to impress!

Organisers : George Rhoden and Paul Wilson

"Hi Stella, hope you're enjoying things. Do you think Dalton will support this petition, demanding the inclusion of black and Asian officers on the new Equal Opportunities Committee?" I asked, holding up the petition.

"Paul, Dalton will want to be the first one to sign," she said.

A couple minutes later Dalton walked up, and I briefly explained the situation to him.

"Let me be the first. They can't get away with this," he said, snatching the petition out of my hand.

With Dalton's signature now leading the way, armed with the petition I spent a large part of the evening approaching guests and asking them to sign if they agreed that this development was a scurrilous and reckless oversight in our equal opportunities' journey, one that had held so much promise at

Bristol. By the end of the night, we had 80 signatures. Most of these signatures were from members of the metropolitan police, both black and white.

There was never going to be a good time to present the petition to Superintendent Tom Kelly. I decided it would be best to wait until he was doing his usual early morning walkabout, during which times he would speak with staff and find out how things were progressing. That morning he headed straight for me since he knew that there had been a Bristol Reunion social function over the weekend. I stood up and greeted him, then handed him the petition.

"By the way, this is something that came out of Saturday night's reunion," I said.

As he read the petition, his face became flushed.

"Please come talk to me in my office," he said.

I followed him into his office, and he closed the door. He appeared shaken.

"Look, we don't need this," he said, placing the petition on a pile of files on his desk. "I'll get you to say a few words at the first meeting of the Committee where you can make a case for representation from the Bristol Reunion network."

And with that the petition was filed away in Superintendent Kelly's office, never to see the light of day again. It had however served its purpose in giving a voice to a collective body of disappointed police personnel from all backgrounds.

A few days later I attended the inaugural meeting of the new Equal Opportunities Committee. It was during the pre-meeting conversation and refreshments that I noticed Superintendent Kelly informing members of a small addition to the agenda. I happened to be nearby as he was talking in hushed tones to a small group that included Helen Grant, a senior representative from one of the Unions representing civil staff colleagues. She turned away from Superintendent Kelly and said to no-one in particular, *"But we represent the views of our ethnics,"*

What Helen said was technically correct. Her Union represented all of its members, including those from minority ethnic groups. It was not so much what she said as it was the way she said it. It invoked memories of the Empire when the colonists ensured that local 'ethnics' had little or no say on matters of importance.

Regardless, I got my five minutes during the meeting to make a case for black and Asian representation on the Committee. I was supported by Superintendent Kelly, who explained the history and importance of the Bristol Reunion network and suggested that someone from that network should serve as a representative on the committee.

I looked across the white faces of the inaugural committee and each one was devoid of expression. This was not a welcome development; they were being asked to allow someone to join the Committee based on their attendance at a social function. Nevertheless, the proposal was agreed, albeit begrudgingly with inaudible mutterings and looks of incredulity from some assembled delegates. Superintendent Kelly was a happy man. The petition had the potential to cause him and senior managers political embarrassment and now he had managed the issue in such a way as to reduce any possibility of potential for backlash from the Bristol Reunion network.

The question remained. Who would represent the Bristol Reunion network on the Equal Opportunities Committee? After giving the matter some thought, I decided to approach Inspector Dalton McConney, given his enthusiasm in signing the petition and since he was one of the few black senior officers who was well known and respected by many.

Dalton agreed to attend future meetings of the Equal Opportunities Committee to represent the views of the Bristol Reunion network. However, a few weeks later when I spoke with him, he appeared very disillusioned about the way in which discussions at the Equal Opportunities' Committee had progressed, suggesting that it had been little more than a talking shop. This was indeed a worrying development, particularly as my time in the Equal Opportunities Unit was soon to come to an end. After my departure, there would be no black or Asian representation in the EOU, and I could see how things might well be allowed to slip back into a comfortable regime of training sessions with little actual change taking place.

Chapter 30

Call to Action

In February 1993, prompted by recent developments, I circulated a memorandum to colleagues and friends from the Bristol Reunion Network (see next page) setting out a proposal. In my mind and that of a few others in the Network, the time had come to move on from the purely social networking aspect of the Bristol Reunion Network to a more defined representative body of officers, a consultative group, able to offer views on a range of issues affecting black and Asian police officers.

Superintendent Kelly had always appeared keen, during our informal conversations, for the Bristol Reunion Network to become a more formal entity, but I had always steered clear of such an arrangement as I was suspicious of the powers that be, their intentions and the role senior officers might play in managing such a group. But now, with the recent Equal Opportunities Committee fiasco and my impending departure from the Equal Opportunities Unit, with our options diminishing, it seemed the right time to promote a discussion around a more formal structure.

February 1993

Sergeant Paul Wilson
Room 1133
New Scotland Yard

Dear David

As you know, myself and George Rhoden have, for the past two years, organised the Bristol reunion socials. Being in the Equal Opportunities Unit enabled us to establish all the necessary contacts with all the resources and support at our fingertips. George left the Unit some time ago, however, we have still managed the reunions with little difficulty. With my forthcoming departure from the Unit, George and I will find it increasingly difficult to co-ordinate the functions. I know the Equal Opportunities Unit views the reunions/networking as an important 'support mechanism' and is keen that they should continue in some format. However, it is essential that any initiatives are driven by individuals and not 'The Job'.

With this in mind, I am seeking the views of yourself and some other officers, on establishing some form of group/committee to organise/oversee and share responsibility for social/networking type functions, and perhaps act as a consultative body in respect of specific equal opportunity issues. Superintendent Kelly, Equal Opportunities Unit, is supportive of the idea and has promised administrative assistance, should it be required, eg photocopying, telephone facilities, postal collection etc. The possibility is a real one but healthy debate is needed to establish terms of reference. If this sounds interesting to you and it is something you would like to be involved with, please contact me on CO extension 6-3893 between 9am-5pm.

I look forward to hearing from you.

Yours sincerely

Paul Wilson

I loved my work and enjoyed the profile and recognition I had attained, so departing the Equal Opportunities Unit was a wrench. I always knew that it would be. For two years I had worked tirelessly to develop a new corporate

Grievance Procedure and had seen it formally accepted and introduced into metropolitan police policy. I would definitely miss the informal social advantages of working and networking within New Scotland Yard. Going back to work at a police station would be a culture shock, but it was necessary if I were to progress up the slippery promotion ladder. Specialist postings at New Scotland Yard were traditionally sought after by many of my colleagues, but it was the coal face experience of working at a police station that helped amass the experience needed to get through the police promotion system.

Since many police stations had vacancies for uniformed Sergeants at the time, my Personnel Department offered me a choice. I chose Battersea Police Station because it was still in my favoured South London but within spitting distance of New Scotland Yard and my gym on Monck Street in Westminster. I was given a start date and an appointment to meet my new boss, Chief Inspector Keith Gausden, beforehand. This would also give me the chance to look around the station that would be my home for the next few years.

A few days later I was driving my white Mercedes 190E along Battersea Bridge Road. As I turned into the slip road that services the police station, a Battersea marked response vehicle (known in police circles as the Area Car) approached me. Since it was a small road, I slowed down to a snail's pace to enable the police vehicle to safely pass my car. As the police car edged level, the female driver looked at me sternly and gestured for me to wind down my window.

"What the fuck do you think you're doing? Can't you see that this road is for entry to the police station only?" she yelled.

I was stunned. I was out of touch with the harsh police culture that existed outside of New Scotland Yard. I had worked in a closeted environment for two-and-a-half years, so it came as a shock for me to encounter this level of aggression, before I had even stepped foot into the station.

The Area Car sped off before I had a chance to respond or show my warrant card. I drove into the Station yard, parked my car, and went inside to the main control room. I showed the Control Room Sergeant my warrant card.

"The female driver on your Area Car just gave me a mouthful. Who is she?" I asked.

"Really?" he asked. "She can be a bit like that. Maybe it's her time of the month. You know how they are," he laughed.

A few minutes later I was shown into the office of Chief Inspector Keith Gausden for my induction interview. It went well, but I could tell he was a little mystified that I had selected Battersea after such a high profile posting at New Scotland Yard.

"You'll be working with Inspector Gary Kitching on the Battersea Village sector. Gary is one of our best Inspectors and he's progressive. I'm sure you'll get on well," he said at the conclusion of the interview.

I left Battersea that day feeling a lot more hopeful than I had when I arrived. Within days my transfer was complete, and I officially began work at my new station home.

My reintroduction to frontline policing in Battersea went well. I was tasked with establishing a Business Watch on Plantation Wharf, a relatively new business development on the banks of the Thames. I found getting out, meeting people and organising meetings to be rewarding work.

My sergeant colleague Noel Craggs seemed friendly enough. He had just passed his Inspector's exam and was waiting for a posting to another station.

"Do you want to know the first thing I thought about you when you arrived?" he asked me one day.

"I can't think what that might be, Noel. Put me out of my misery," I said.

"Your Malcolm X watch," he said.

I smiled. The Malcolm X movie had been released recently, and the X on my swatch watch resembled the one from the film's promotional material. I was proud to be associated with such an iconic figure.

Chapter 31

'Is There A Need For A Black/Asian Support Group?'

As the days passed into weeks, I found myself continuously thinking about the next step for the Bristol Reunion network. I had been at Battersea police station for about a month when I made some enquiries at New Scotland Yard regarding the use of a meeting room and was advised of an availability in Drummond Gate, a police headquarters building in Pimlico, near to the London Underground station. I circulated a further memorandum to the same small group of officers in the Bristol Reunion network.

PS Paul Wilson
Battersea Police Station
(WA)

26th March 1993

Dear David

You will recall the letter I recently sent you regarding the suggestion of forming some kind of support group/network.

The date arranged for the inaugural meeting is Wednesday 21st April 1993, at 5.30pm in Room 202. Drummond Gate. (Next to Pimlico LT)

I must emphasise this is to be an informal 'brain-storming' meeting, however, to facilitate matters I shall circulate an agenda prior to the meeting.

If you have any suggestions/issues you wish to raise, please send them to me in order that they may be included on the agenda.

Yours sincerely

Paul Wilson

It was a Monday night, I was working the night duty shift in the custody suite at Battersea police station and during the course of a quiet night, I mulled over the feedback, or rather the lack of feedback, from my two memoranda. David Michael had visited me in the Equal Opportunities Unit in response to the first memorandum however, despite informal conversations and assurances from several members of the Bristol Reunion inner circle, I was not surprised at the minimal response to my second memorandum. It just seemed to be the nature of things. As the date for the meeting approached and in the absence of any constructive feedback, using the Custody Office typewriter with a less than functional ribbon, I bashed out what I considered an agenda for the 21st of April should look like.

INAUGURAL MEETING TO DISCUSS AND DEVELOP THE BRISTOL REUNION NETWORK
ROOM B202 CONFERENCE ROOM, DRUMMOND GATE (BESSBOROUGH ST. ENTRANCE)
WEDNESDAY 21ST APRIL 1993, 5:30PM

AGENDA

1. PERSONAL INTRODUCTIONS
2. IS THERE A NECESSITY FOR A FORMAL NETWORK/SUPPORT GROUP?
3. BY WHAT PROCESS SHOULD SUCH A GROUP MAKE ITSELF HEARD?
4. BY WHAT MEANS SHOULD THE GROUP ADVERTISE ITS EXISTENCE?
5.CONSIDER ELECTING A SUB-COMMITTEE TO OVERSEE AND ORGANISE SOCIAL FUNCTIONS
6. WHAT STRUCTURE SHOULD THE GROUP TAKE?
7. CONSIDER APPOINTING PERMANENT CHAIR AND OTHER NECESSARY POSTS.
8. ANY OTHER BUSINESS
9. DATE FOR NEXT MEETING (if applicable)

It was not so much an agenda as it was a series of directives and prompts. Anyone looking closely enough would have noticed that item two was the central issue. If we couldn't agree on this one point, then all other items would be immaterial.

Just prior to my posting to the Bristol project team, one of my first actions was to make an appointment with Chief Inspector Ron Hope, who was now at Streatham police station in South London and remained the most senior black officer in the Metropolitan Police. I was interested in getting his take on the Bristol Seminars as well as discussing my new role with him.

We met in Streatham and I was pleased to discover he was very positive about the Bristol Seminar, in fact he confided in me that some of his colleagues had been taken aback by his stance regarding the rationale for and outcome of the Seminars. Ron had become a central figure in the Bristol Reunion network and now I wanted his commitment to the proposed meeting on 21st April. A chance meeting in a South London supermarket provided me with the opportunity to get Ron on board.

"We'll get Mike Fuller to Chair it. I've seen him in action at Bramshill police college. He's an exceptionally good Chair," Ron said.

Pimlico was only a few minutes' drive from Battersea, so on the 21st April I arrived at the meeting venue in Bessborough Street nice and early, equipped with a large white 'flip chart' with stand and black marker pen, all borrowed from the Battersea police training unit.

I placed the flip chart on its stand and positioned it strategically at the front of the room, in full view of arriving guests. With the black marker pen, I wrote in large capital letters the words:

'IS THERE A NEED FOR A BLACK/ASIAN SUPPORT GROUP?'

I then sat back and waited, and watched the invited group members slowly arrive, ticking them off my list as they walked through the door.

Among them were Detective Chief Inspector Mike Fuller, Chief Inspector Ron Hope, Winston Baird (Higher Executive Officer), Cleo Sandiford (Administrative Officer), Inspector George Lee, Detective Inspector David Michael, Inspector Paul Ramsay, Inspector Chula Rupasinha, Sergeant Pam Hardcastle, Sergeant Leroy Logan, Constable Dele Bolude, Constable Chris Donaldson, Constable Jennifer Donaldson, Constable Manjit Johal, Constable George Rhoden, Juliette McLean (Executive Officer) with apologies received from Chief Inspector Dalton McConney, Inspector Sultan Taylor, and Chief Inspector Jeff Braithwaite.

The Chair, Mike Fuller, called everyone to order and formally opened the meeting, introduced himself and explained that he had been invited to chair the meeting. No-one asked why or by whom. After inviting everyone to introduce themselves, Mike handed the floor to me, for my presentation on post Bristol Seminar developments.

This was my opportunity to set the tone for the remainder of the meeting, so I was well prepared. I began by giving the group an in-depth report on the thinking behind the Bristol Seminars, the subsequent establishment of the project team, and the work streams flowing from the project.

I also shared research undertaken by Inspector Peter French for his Master's dissertation on voluntary resignations in the metropolitan police. Peter would visit us in the Equal Opportunities Unit on a regular basis and update us on the progress of his work. I summarised the outcome of his dissertation which concluded that:

There is racism in the Metropolitan Police Service. It does have an impact on black police officers. It does contribute significantly in their decision to resign.'

I explained to the assembled group that while French's findings were consistent with the Bristol Seminar report, they were not publicised or acknowledged by the Met as being relevant, given the small size of the sample used. I was able to update the group on the number and type of grievances recorded by the Equal Opportunities Unit which found that race related complaints were significantly higher than complaints of sexism.

I set out in some detail the contentious issue of the recent inaugural meeting of the joint police and civil staff Equal Opportunities committee, where the Met's clumsy decision not to include black or Asian representation was met with looks of frustration and anger from the assembled group. By adding the incendiary comment made by Helen Grant, (*'we represent our ethnics'*) the touch paper had been well and truly lit. Further explanation that I had secured the inclusion of Dalton McConney on the Committee only to discover that Dalton had recently resigned his position. This decision, he informed me, was due to both the intransigent nature of discussions at his first meeting, and Committee papers arriving in his in-tray the day after the second meeting had taken place. Dalton's withdrawal from the Equal Opportunities Committee served to impress upon my disenchanted audience the hopelessness of trying to comply with the rules as set out by our parent organisation.

I then spoke about the initiatives shaped by the Bristol Project team to address the key concerns from black and Asian officers present at Bristol. The Mentor Approach was something that George Rhoden and Jan Alton had worked on and while the idea of appointing a mentor to support black and Asian recruits was well intentioned, the insensitivity and inconsistency of policy implementation when presented to police colleagues meant it was always doomed to fail.

A further well-intentioned piece of work to flow from the Bristol Project team was a 'postings policy' for officers from black and Asian backgrounds to ensure that these officers were not posted to a station where they were likely to be the sole minority ethnic officer. That initiative had been diluted to the extent it was now applicable to all new recruits, regardless of ethnicity, and the ensuing workload created in police personnel departments across London saw the policy fall by the wayside.

There was unanimous agreement among the group that the Bristol Reunions, an unofficial by-product of the Seminars, had been an enormous success and were viewed favourably by the Met's Senior management as a support for black and Asian officers.

Following my truthful but bleak portrayal of the situation post-Bristol, the assembled group excitedly discussed on the many topics and issues that had flowed from my presentation. The loud chatter continued for some time until the Chair brought the meeting back to attention and expertly summarised the key points for consideration going forward. Not pausing for a break, the Chair moved to the next item on the Agenda and invited a simple show of hands from those in support.

"Is there a need for a Black and Asian Support Network?" he asked.

I looked across the group as hands and fists punched the air, the vote was unanimously carried.

Moving onto Agenda item three, the Chair asked, "Should that network be a formal constituted body, or should it remain informal?"

I looked on in interest as I knew that one or two members present were suspicious of going down a formal route. Nevertheless, the group voted by a majority to adopt a formal structure. I was both relieved and quietly elated at the outcome. As we moved down the agenda, the structure and organisation of the Lesbian and Gay Police Association (LAGPA), established some three years previously, became an intense topic of conversation. It was agreed that the LAGPA model and constitution was certainly something that we should consider using as a template.

The Chair went on to echo the sentiments of the assembled by decreeing the group, in its infancy, should not disclose our existence to any of the managerial channels in the Metropolitan Police. It was, he emphasised, critically important that we remained under the radar until such time as our constitution was agreed.

Furthermore, the Chair tasked individual members to approach similar black support groups. These groups included the Society of Black Lawyers, Black Social Workers, Black Prison officers and Sergeant Bruce Harris. While working in the EOU, I had discovered Bruce was leading a black police support network in Leicestershire Constabulary.

As the meeting concluded, a buzz of excitement filled the room as it dawned on all present the monumental nature of the decisions taken that evening. Everyone present agreed that they wished to remain involved with the fledgling group. We left the meeting on a high, knowing that a great deal had been achieved but we were in no doubt that if we were to sustain impetus, we needed to identify our aim and objectives to ensure we remained focused.

On my return to the workplace, I immediately started thinking about how we might add value to the commitment shown by attendees at the first meeting. I recalled a conversation I had with Janet Alton a few months previously, where Janet shared with me that a handful of black metropolitan police civil staff members had recently participated in a Civil Service staff development initiative, at the Civil Service College in Sunningdale Park. A management course specifically designed for underrepresented black and minority ethnic Civil Servants, under the auspices of *positive action*. According to Janet, following their attendance, the metropolitan police participants had displayed similar emotions to those officers that attended the Bristol Seminar.

After making some enquiries, I discovered the names and phone numbers of two participants of the Civil Service Initiative and contacted them. Keith Smith, a Higher Executive Officer in the Department of Technology and Nana Amoa Buahin, an Executive Officer in the Met's Personnel department were both brimming with positivity and enthusiasm when asked about their experience at Sunningdale Park. When I disclosed the nature of what our Bristol Reunion Network was about, they both expressed an interest in getting involved, so I invited them to the second meeting of the fledgling group to take place on 24th May 1993.

The Bristol Reunion network would embrace both police officers and our civil staff colleagues who provided a range of essential support services within the Metropolitan Police Force.

Any concern I had that participants at the first meeting might be considering a slightly more conservative approach was dissipated within seconds of the second meeting. Members showed up, brimming with enthusiasm. Inspector Ramsay had spoken with Bruce Harris in Leicester and reported his findings on the nature of the support offered by Bruce's group. This was followed by Sergeant Hardcastle's detailed presentation on the birth and development of the Lesbian and Gay Police Association (LAGPA). Initially, starting out as an informal network, LAGPA had grown into a constituted organisation with a significant profile. This interested the meeting participants a great deal, to the extent it was agreed that the committee should consult with LAGPA to both learn from their experiences in developing their constitution and equally as important, avoid making the same mistakes.

Detective Inspector Michael gave an account of his meeting with Peter Herbert, President of the Society of Black Lawyers (SBL). Their willingness to assist us in drafting our constitution was an important development as the SBL was well established and enjoyed a considerable profile. PC Johal spoke about his research into the Association of Black Probation Officers and the difficulties they faced in gaining acceptance from their senior management. Finally, Keith Smith concluded the meeting by providing an overview of the Positive Action training offered by the Civil Service College for minority ethnic managers.

I was particularly interested in the Committee's decision to allow our Chair to consult with senior management at the Equal Opportunities Unit prior to disclosing our existence to the senior echelons of the Metropolitan Police. My concern was that we were attaching too much importance to my old boss. It was always my view that while we should embrace resources offered by the police establishment, we should take our own responsibility for decisions made and that process should remain within our group.

Chapter 32

Birth of the Black and Asian Police Association

On 5th July 1993, the third meeting of the Bristol Reunion Network convened in the usual place, Room B202, Drummond Gate, Pimlico. The Chair, Mike Fuller, introduced Inspector Sultan Taylor and Tracey Deal an Executive Officer at Chelsea police station as our two newest members. Sultan had been involved in the writing and development of the Bristol Seminar report on behalf of the management. Our Chairman recapped recent developments and informed the committee that he'd spoken with Superintendent Tom Kelly from the Equal Opportunities Unit, who was positive and encouraging and expressed a willingness to attend any of our meetings.

Deciding on a name for our group was another sticky issue and one that promoted considerable emotion among the members. This task was delegated to a sub-committee comprised of Inspector Ramsay, Inspector Rupasinha, Nana Amoa Buahin, and Keith Smith. I sat and waited in eager anticipation as the Chair invited the sub-committee to present their findings. After some excited discussion during which Chris Donaldson quipped *'What about NWA?'*, a remark that was met with silence - after all this tongue in cheek suggestion was an acronym associated with the popular American hip hop band NWA (Niggaz Wit Attitude). As the animated chatter subsided, the Chair summarised the previous few minutes discussion and decreed that the propal put forward by the sub-committee, *The Black and Asian Police Association* (BAPA), would from now on be our official name.

The fourth meeting of the Black and Asian Police Association convened on 26th July 1993 with most of the meeting being taken up with discussion around the Aim and Objectives of the draft constitution that was now before the Committee. It was finally agreed.

The Association seeks to improve the working environment of Black and Asian Personnel within the Metropolitan Police Service, with a view to enhancing the quality of service to the public. This aim would be achieved by the provision of a support network working towards equality of opportunity, working towards improved relationships between Police and the Minority Ethnic Community. Working towards improving recruitment and reducing wastage and providing a social network.

I listened with interest. No-one was broaching the issue of membership but discussions outside of our meetings regarding this potentially controversial issue were heating up and I envisaged it being one issue that could possibly cause a chasm in the BAPA Committee once it was tabled for debate.

A small number of us were already expressing disquiet at the possibility of Superintendent Kelly or indeed any other senior police manager not only attending our meetings but joining the Association as a member with all the rights and benefits that conferred. There was, I and others believed, a real possibility of BAPA being taken over by white senior officers wishing to demonstrate their commitment to equalities issues. However well-intentioned, that was not something I could ever countenance. If the majority were minded to adopt an all-inclusive route, then I would quietly retire my services. But for now, while issues of membership had been discussed in hushed circles outside of the meeting, it remained in the draft constitution as *'…. open to all serving police personnel, police officers, special constables of any rank or grade and civil staff directly employed by the Metropolitan Police Service.'*

The meeting of the Black and Asian Police Association dated 11th April 1994 was essentially a coming of age where personal friendships and the camaraderie built over the previous few months were put to one side in the interests of the future health and viability of the BAPA.

I volunteered to take notes, even though I disliked doing so since it tended to limit my involvement in the meeting. I figured this would help expedite a difficult conversation. Chief Inspector Hope was the acting Chairman. Following usual formalities and revisiting the notes of the previous meeting we were into the proposed amendments to the draft constitution, tabled by Sergeant Leroy Logan.

Sergeant Pam Hardcastle was noticeably missing from the meeting. While this was not surprising, it gave me a twinge of sadness and guilt. I had been the one responsible for inviting her into the group in the first place. I did this because she was a proficient equal opportunities trainer and able to advocate on equality issues. She had shown considerable interest in the work of the Bristol Seminar project team during her numerous visits to our office.

This finally persuaded me that she should be included at the inaugural meeting. It seemed to me at the time to be the right thing to do and the fact that she was a white officer did not enter my thought process.

From the very beginning Pam demonstrated her enthusiasm in much the same way as others, volunteering to become involved in several important projects. But our development and understanding of the journey on which we were embarking had now grown exponentially. I was now among a large contingent of BAPA committee members that believed to truly determine our own existence then we must limit membership of the BAPA to those of African or Asian heritage. Sergeant Hardcastle had obviously heard about the proposed membership amendment and had absented herself from this meeting to save any embarrassment.

As the debate on membership heated up, PC Chris Donaldson slammed the desk and emotively accused the BAPA of *behaving like Apartheid South Africa*.

Nevertheless, once the explanations and alternatives had been exhausted, it became clear that while we were prohibited under the Race Relations Act legislation to discriminate based on colour, to make a generic requirement premised on geographic and historical criteria, while pushing the boundaries of the Act, advice received suggested it did not contravene the Act.

And so, it was that the majority on the BAPA committee elected for a change in the constitution, thereby ensuring that all members of the BAPA must meet the new membership criteria.

The BAPA had in making this decision lost two valuable members and possibly more would follow. But, if anyone had challenged us with the case that all humankind originated in Africa, I believe they would have been permitted to join.

Chapter 33

Executive Post Holders elected

The meeting of the Black and Asian Police Association scheduled for 11th May 1994 was undoubtedly one of extra importance given that much of the evening involved the first open election of Executive post holders who would then take responsibility for the impending and much discussed public launch of BAPA.

Not everyone attached the same degree of importance as four members tendered apologies and the remainder were late in attending, causing the Chair to defer the election of an Executive Committee and post holders until later in the meeting. This allowed agenda items such as the production of our first newsletter to be discussed at length. Leroy Logan produced two newsletter formats for consideration and several logos which he urged the committee to consider as we were still without a corporate BAPA logo. We were able to agree on a traditional design for our newsletter but the calibre of logos on offer was such that the decision was deferred.

Keith Smith was proving to be a useful addition to our Committee in so many ways, particularly given his work and extensive contacts in the technical and Information Technology arena meant that he was able to circumvent the usual red-tape and access the diary for the prestigious fifth floor auditorium at New Scotland Yard, where it had been agreed we would hold the launch of the BAPA.

The election of postholders eventually took place with the following appointments.

For the post of Chair (Ron Hope thoughtfully announced prior to the election process that I had not expressed an interest in standing for the post of Chair), three nominations were received, Ron Hope, David Michael, and Winston Baird. David Michael and Winston Baird both withdrew, and Ron

Hope was then unanimously elected as Chair of the Black and Asian Police Association.

A vote followed for deputy Chair which was won, 9 votes to 4 by, Winston Baird. For the post of General Secretary, there were four nominations. Paul Wilson, Paul Ramsay, David Michael, and Leroy Logan. I was duly elected as General Secretary with 9 votes to David Michael's 4 votes.

The post of Treasurer had one nomination, Nana Amoa-Buahin who was duly elected.

For the post of Membership Secretary, two nominations had been received, Juliette McLean and Jennifer Donaldson. The votes were 7-3 in favour of Jennifer Donaldson with Juliette McLean taking on the deputy role.

For the post of Social Secretary, there were three nominations, George Rhoden, Deli Bolude and Leroy Logan. George Rhoden received the unanimous vote and a second vote for deputy resulted in 7 to 4 in favour of Leroy Logan.

For the post of Social Treasurer, Dele Bolude was unanimously voted into the post. The following were nominated for the remaining Executive Committee posts; Keith Smith, Mike Fuller, Dalton McConney, Rob Jones, David Michael, Paul Ramsay, Sultan Taylor and Jeff Braithwaite.

At the meeting of the Black and Asian Police Association on 4th July 1994, the Chair introduced two guests, Ronald Hampton, Director of the National Black Police Association in the United States of America, and Sabra Desai, a visiting South African lecturer specialising in anti-racist studies. I had made contact, via the new Internet technology, with Ron Hampton shortly after the initial meeting of the Bristol Reunion network and we had spoken at length about the National Black Police Association (NBPA), its constitution, membership, relationship with police unions, how it had been received in the United States and some of the key considerations we should take on board if we were to develop a similar organisation in London, so I was so pleased to at long last be able to meet him in the flesh.

The day before, I had met Ron Hampton with his friend, Sabra Desai, at Heathrow airport and taken them to their respective central London hotels. When they were given the opportunity to speak during the meeting, they both praised the efforts of the BAPA. Ron Hampton promised continued support from the National Black Police Association in the United States.

The Chair recounted our current position regarding the official launch of the BAPA. It seemed that a promised phone call from the Director of Personnel, Helen Maslen, was to have raised the issue with the Commissioner, Paul Condon, however at present there was no indication that this has been done. In the absence of any response from the

Commissioner, we heard that the Chair, utilising his contacts, had entered the BAPA launch into the Commissioner's diary for 26th September 1994. Furthermore, said Ron, the Met's publicity machine will assist with the launch should the Commissioner's support be forthcoming.

We all agreed that the disclosure of a letter inviting Herman Ousely, Chair of the Commission for Racial Equality (CRE), to the launch would place the Commissioner under pressure to attend. Furthermore, the meeting agreed that communication with the Commissioner's office must be maintained if we were to make progress with plans for the launch. Mike Fuller emphasised the importance of a contingency plan if the Commissioner's support is not forthcoming.

During the meeting, it was decided that we would contact Trevor Hall, Principal Race Relations Officer at the Home Office and meet with Jerome Mack from Equality Associates, Turvey in Bedfordshire who it was provisionally agreed should be invited to host the launch.

Before everyone departed the meeting and with permission from the Chair, I made an announcement, "I will be holding a barbecue at my home in Manor Way, Mitcham on Sunday, August 7th, commencing at 2pm. Partner's welcome!"

Chapter 34

A Change of Name

In the days following my barbecue, to prepare for September's launch of the Black and Asian Police Association, a few of us were engaged in placing printed and embossed invitations into addressed envelopes. Committee members agreed that our guests at the launch were to be opinion formers and other influential members of London's black community. Many Caribbean and Asian High Commissioners were on the invitation list.

As General Secretary, I had lived and breathed the issues leading up to the launch of our Association, often to the detriment of personal and professional matters. I had over the past weeks engaged in tough conversations with the Police Federation and met with many friendly and supportive organisations and agencies. But our busy BAPA schedule had clouded my thinking and that of my colleagues. We had overlooked the especially important fact that the hundreds of invitations we stuffed into envelopes with enthusiasm may just as well have been mini press release statements, announcing our existence to the outside world. With no media strategy in place, no prepared press release agreed, no key talking points, the media headlines caught us off-guard and unprepared.

12th August 1994 started out like any other Friday until the very first news broadcast hit the airwaves. All of London's radio stations seemed to read from the same script; 'the impending launch of the Black and Asian Police Association signals an important milestone in the history of police and black community relations....'

Nervous perspiration collected on my forehead and trickled down my face as the bulletin was broadcast over the airwaves of my car radio at 7am on my drive to work. I pulled over, switched off the engine and unhooked the vibrating pager clipped into my trouser belt. Scrolling through the messages, I could see they were all from various media outlets seeking a statement and further information. Turning off my pager, I started my car and continued my journey to work, my head spinning with what had just happened. How could we have been so naïve? On reaching work, I ran across the road to a news stand and leafed through the papers. The radio news source was apparent.

Black and Asian police to form a US-style police association - The Times,
Black police officers form ethnic force to fight for equal rights - The Guardian.
Ethnic officers find a voice after years of suffering in isolation - The Guardian.

Fortunately, the following day was a Saturday, which gave us a breathing space in which to plan a much-needed media strategy, but by now the cat was well out of the bag.

A few days later I entered the small Battersea Village Sector office, my usual place of work that I shared with Inspector Gary Kitching, my line manager. Gary was sitting in his usual position, rocking back on the hind legs of his chair with legs extended and feet pushed against the edge of his desk. In his lap was a piece of paper on which he appeared to be doodling with a pencil.

"Morning, guv," I said.

"Morning, Paul. You still don't have a logo, so I'm helping you with that."

Gary and I had discussed the formation of the BAPA on numerous occasions, and he appeared fascinated and genuinely interested in its development. I can honestly say that I would not have dreamed of confiding in other colleagues for fear of causing upset or worse. I walked across the office to look at what Gary was doing with his pencil.

"Only one small snag with that guv," I said. "You have used BAPA in your design when the name of the Association will tomorrow night change and become the Black Police Association, or BPA".

Gary stopped rocking in his chair and looked at me.

"After all your recent media attention, this seems like a strange time to change your name," he said. "What about your launch coming up in a few days?"

"Oh, we're still planning to launch, but I expect there to be a vote at tomorrow night's meeting in favour of a name change," I said.

Gary shook his head, laughed, and continued with his sketch.

The Black and Asian Police Association meeting of 7th September 1994 convened at the usual time of 5:30pm in the Conference Room, Bessborough Street, Pimlico. It pleased me to inform the meeting that I had contacted Jerome Mack and confirmed that he would attend the launch of the Association as host and facilitator.

Jerome was a charismatic man and had that rare ability to grab everyone's attention. The Cabinet Office had selected him to review Equal Opportunities within the Civil Service. His company, Equalities Associates, was chosen to run the Home Office Specialist Support Unit for Community and Race Relations. This he did from premises in the tiny village of Turvey, Bedfordshire. They would often invite myself and other black officers from around the country to take part and contribute to Turvey training sessions and to speak about our experiences in the police. Those police officers who progressed through the six-week course became known as Turvey graduates, many of whom became the most enlightened police officers you could wish to meet.

As in previous meetings and with worrying consistency, not all Committee members were present to discuss what was a critical constitutional amendment. Keith Smith filled in time with an important update from the Directorate of Public Affairs (DPA) at New Scotland Yard. We had agreed at a recent meeting that publicity material, overseen by Keith Smith and the DPA, would prepare for the launch.

We would make a corporate folder available to all guests attending the launch, containing photos of the Executive post holders, a collage of press articles, a history and precis of our work programme and some statistical data. The Chair, Ron Hope, advised us he had drafted a letter for the Commissioner's office outlining the evening's events. We discussed as a Committee the Commissioner's presence at the launch ceremony's question-and-answer session, but no-one knew for sure how long the Commissioner would remain at the launch.

The Chair clarified that members of the Executive must be present at New Scotland Yard, on the 5th floor by 3pm. Keith Smith would be on hand to instruct everyone as to their role, ensuring that we received guests smoothly and professionally. The Chair advised Police officers on the Executive to wear uniform and personal name badges. No detail was being left to chance. I was excited and felt a special vibe at the meeting that had not been present before. I had a sense that history was being made.

Keith Smith, who by now was at the forefront of our communications strategy, presented to the meeting a new logo prepared by external designers, sourced by the Directorate of Public Affairs. I winced at the sight of two chain links. If there was ever proof needed that we must do everything to keep control of our destiny, then this was it. After a brief and direct discussion among Committee members, we agreed that the chain link concept was unacceptable. We tasked Keith with returning to the DPA for further consultation regarding our logo design.

And while we seemed to address some fundamental communication issues, all very necessary for a professional launch, the sensitive issue of our relationship with the media was not, I felt, given sufficient attention. Our strategy, as directed by the Chair, was not to discuss any Association matters with the media at this stage. All media enquiries would be forwarded to the Chair or Leroy Logan, who was acting as Press Liaison.

Further on in the meeting, once we brought all members up to speed, we invited Leroy Logan to table the proposed constitutional amendments. This is the moment that I and many of the others had been awaiting. The thorny issue of changing the name of the Black and Asian Police Association had been brought up at Committee but had always been filed into the 'too difficult' tray. But this evening was different, I was confident that we would now see a consensus in favour of renaming our Association, the Black Police Association.

The persuasive argument for change, presented to us by the Association of Black Probation Officers (ABPO), had been circulating for a few weeks. It had been passionately reinforced to the extent that if the name BAPA continued, we would lose the respect of ABPO and similar groups.

The central point of ABPO's argument was that by retaining 'and Asian' in our title, we were decreeing that Asian peoples were not welcome under the black umbrella. An alternate viewpoint, presented by some Asian members, was that many in their communities were uncomfortable with the term 'black' for lots of social and historical reasons. It filled the room with passionate, loud voices, all vying for attention in this most volatile of conversations. Catching the Chair's attention, I used the Southall Black Sisters, a high-profile advocacy group composed of Asian women, to support my argument.

"By continuing with 'and Asian' in our title we would send out a powerful message to this and similar groups that Asian people cannot co-exist under the black political umbrella,' I argued.

But the clincher was a letter, circulated to all Committee members, from the influential West Indian Standing Conference, (an umbrella organisation formed in 1958 to promote the interests of the African Caribbean community in Britain), setting out a powerful argument, not dissimilar to ABPO's, for bringing people of colour together under one powerful and united black umbrella.

Both the Roman and much later the British empire had played small tribes and groups against one another to control their lands and territories. The Romans used these same tactics when they occupied Britain, as did the British Empire when they colonised India, but tonight's decision by the Committee, a majority of 9 for and 2 against, with 1 abstention, ensured that for now *divide et impera,* used to such devastating effect by European colonists, was not something the establishment could exploit.

We were now the *Black Police Association.*

Chapter 35

The Launch of the Black Police Association

On Sunday 25th September at New Scotland Yard, I met with the Chair, Ron Hope, and Keith Smith to discuss and fine tune the agreed upon launch programme.

Launch of the Black Police Association at New Scotland Yard
Monday, September 26, 1994
16:30-17:00 Guests Arrive.
17:00 Welcome by Jerome Mack, Director of Equalities Associates
17:05 Presentation by Chief Inspector Ron Hope, Chairman of the Black Police Association
17:35 Address by Sir Paul Condon, Commissioner of the Metropolitan Police Service
17:45 Address by Herman Ouseley, Chairman of the Commission for Racial Equality
17:55 Questions and Answers
18:15 Closing address by Winston Baird, Deputy Chairman of the Black Police Association
18:25 Refreshments

On Monday afternoon, 26th September 1994, I made my way to New Scotland Yard, dressed in full uniform but with a casual jacket hiding my tunic. Getting off the underground train at St James' Park, I walked along the platform and thought about the number of times I had made this journey since arriving in London in the summer of 1979.

Leaving St James Park Station, I crossed the road and entered the glass walled foyer of New Scotland Yard. Nodding to the two black security officers as I walked by, I took the lift to the 5th floor auditorium.

Keith Smith was in the control room at the back, surrounded by banks of impressive IT equipment and various controls for lighting and sound. Soon, all members of the Executive and post holders had assembled in the function room opposite the auditorium. We all knew our role was to facilitate the smooth reception and seating of our one hundred and fifty guests, whose names had been lodged with security at the front desk earlier that day.

Our volunteers were now awaiting the guests' arrival at the front desk, after which they would be given a security name badge and from there, they would be brought to the fifth-floor auditorium. My heart beat fast as I awaited the guests' arrival. How many would show up? A small turn out would be embarrassing. I need not have worried as the guests filled all the seats with late attendees having to stand off to the side.

With Jerome Mack at the helm, the launch got underway with the introduction of Chief Inspector Ron Hope. The BPA Chair's speech presented a historical overview of racism suffered by the UK black community at large and the modern-day plight of black and Asian people within the police force. Chief Inspector Hope recounted a time when an unofficial colour bar during the 1960s had prevented the recruitment of black police officers. This passage was something the Directorate of Public Affairs had found unpalatable when presented with Ron Hope's speech but following an intervention from the Commissioner who supported the BPA's right to recount history, the colour bar reference remained, to the obvious delight of the assembled guests. It was after all their shared experience and was not to be expunged by faceless public relations experts.

"We are professional in our approach to our work, and proud to be a member of the Metropolitan Police Service. But most of all, we are proud to be black members of the Metropolitan Police Service. The Association's maintained its major thrust of working for fair treatment and support for black colleagues together with a desire to contribute towards improvements in police and community relations."

Ron Hope's speech was met with a standing ovation. Following an introduction from our Chair, the Metropolitan Police Commissioner was invited to the lectern. With more than a nod to his indecisiveness on attending our launch, he began.

"Sitting on the fence is a painful place to be, so I got off. I would like to offer my support to the launch of the Black Police Association…."

For the next fifteen minutes the Commissioner spoke in supportive and congratulatory tones, to the obvious enjoyment of all present. After his speech, I watched as he made his way out of the auditorium.

No question-and-answer session for the Commissioner, I thought.

Later in the ceremony one of our guests, Robyn Williams, a uniformed Police Sergeant from Nottinghamshire Constabulary, rose to her feet and gave a brief but well said statement to the assembled audience.

'...the Black Police Association should be encouraged and introduced in all police forces and not just London...'

Leaving New Scotland Yard that evening, with joyous friends and colleagues seeking a local hostelry where we might exchange accounts of what we had just witnessed, I purchased a late edition copy of the London Evening Standard newspaper from the news stand outside of St James' Park Underground Station. On the front page my eyes became transfixed on an article in which Crime Reporter Barbara McMahon ensured our launch was to be forever enshrined in the annals of policing history.

'Black and Asian Police officers made clear today that they would no longer tolerate racism within the Metropolitan Police Force as they launched their own association in a ceremony attended by Commissioner Sir Paul Condon.'

Chapter 36

Balls Pond Road

One Saturday evening in 1994 I was personally introduced to a scenario that black friends in my social circle were all too familiar with.

It was my night off, so I decided to visit La Prison night club in Stoke Newington, North London, to indulge in some much-needed escapism.

In my white Mercedes with sparkling new alloy wheels I drove across the river Thames into North London and headed north on Kingsland High Road and then, by mistake, I turned left onto the Balls Pond Road.

Damn! Why did I do that? I thought.

Then I remembered that I used to have a girlfriend who lived in Palmers Green, and I would use this route to go visit her. I had been on autopilot.

I need to turn around and head towards Stoke. I'll just do a quick U-turn, I thought, glancing in my rear-view mirror.

As I drove back to Kingsland High Road, an all too familiar wailing noise came up behind me. From my rear-view mirror, the lights of a police vehicle flashed. I pulled over, wound down my window, turned the car off and waited.

Two white police officers stepped out of the vehicle and walked towards me, carrying flashlights.

"Hello mate. We saw you do a U-turn back there," one of them said when they reached my window.

"Yes, officer. It's quiet and there's no one around so I thought I'd save a bit of time," I said.

"Where are you going?" he asked, shining his flashlight on the front footwell of my car.

"Stoke," I said.

By this point the second officer was walking around the car shining his flashlight into the backseat.

"Your car is it?" the first officer asked.

"Yeah," I replied.

"Okay. We're just going to do a vehicle check. We won't keep you long."

The second officer called his station for a Police National Computer check on my registration plate.

"No trace," he shouted to his colleague.

"Okay, mate. Can you step out of the car so we can have a look around?" the first officer said.

I quietly opened my door and stepped out of the car. The cool night air went right through the light jacket and shirt I was wearing. I sat down on a low wall and folded my arms in front of me to keep in as much warmth I could.

In the meantime, the two officers opened all four doors of my car, searched the glove compartment, rear seat pockets and looked under the floor mats.

"Okay, mate. Can you open the boot for us?" one of them asked.

"Is that really necessary?" I asked.

I better just open it and put them out of their misery, I thought.

Before I could do so, the second officer climbed out of the back seat and shined his flashlight in my face.

"Yeah, it is!" he barked.

Okay, let's just see where this goes, I thought.

I walked over to the rear of the car and unlocked the boot.

The first officer opened the boot lid and began searching inside.

"When you two super sleuths are finished, we need to have a chat," I said as I watched the search.

"Is that right?" said the second officer, standing up and shining his flashlight in my face again.

"All clean," confirmed the first officer, closing the boot lid. He turned and shined his light on me as well.

"Right, mate. You carrying anything in your pockets that you shouldn't have?" he asked.

I reached into my back pocket and pulled out my warrant card holder. I stretched out my hand and flicked it open with my thumb. My photograph and shiny, silver metropolitan police crest glistened in the light.

"Sergeant Paul Wilson," I said, staring at them.

"Shit. Don't tell me you work for Complaints," said the first officer.

"No. I'm at Whisky Alpha (Battersea)," I said.

"We're so sorry, Sarge," said the second officer.

"The stop was going well until the unlawful search on the car and then me…on what grounds?" I asked, my voice raised in authority.

Discomfort spread across their faces, they looked like two schoolboys caught stealing sweets from a corner shop. Heads bowed, they turned their flashlights off and took a rigid stance with arms straight down by their sides.

"Right!" I said. "Now, I want you to get on your PR (personal radio) and ask the night duty inspector to join us. When he gets here, I'll relate the facts to him and you'll both get stuck on…"

I paused. That would mean I would have to attend Islington station and write out a statement. *It will ruin my evening*, I thought.

"Sorry, Sarge. I can't say it enough," said the first officer.

"Or I could give you both a verbal warning and you can get back on the streets and do something useful and lawful. How does that sound?" I asked.

"Sounds perfect, Sarge," said the first officer, smiling.

"Okay, lads. I've got your numbers. When I get into work, I'll make a pocket book entry that I've issued you both a verbal warning for an unlawful vehicle search. It will go no further," I said.

"Much appreciated, Sarge," said the second officer.

"By the way, I've got a friend who works at your nick. Leroy Logan. Do you know him?" I asked.

Leroy had been a few weeks ahead of me at Hendon Police College which is where we first met. Following Hendon, we became good friends often visiting each other's home. But it was our late-night partying and clubbing together that occasionally saw me bearing the brunt of Mrs Gretel Logan's wrath. The nightclubs we tended to frequent were far removed from my usual East End haunts as Leroy favoured swanky West End night spots such as Stringfellows, The Hippodrome, and Limelight. Two black guys entering these venues together was not the norm but, undoubtedly facilitated by Leroy's close friendship with Leee John, frontman with the band Imagination, it was never a problem. A social butterfly maybe, but Leroy was never short of ideas and enthusiasm when it came to helping resolve the toxic work environment our chosen careers had presented us with.

"Yes. Sergeant Logan is our night duty Custody Officer."

"Is he really? Right, when you see him you tell him that you pulled me over and I got out my pram and gave you loads of verbal abuse," I laughed.

"Will do, Sarge. You have a good night," The first officer said as the two of them walked back to their vehicle.

A few days later I bumped into Leroy Logan.

"I met a couple of your PCs during night duty. Did they mention the stop?" I asked, smiling.

"Yeah, they came into the custody suite and asked me if I knew Paul

Wilson. They said they pulled you over and you lost your temper," he said.

I laughed, "And what did you say to them?"

"I said, I don't understand. That's not like him at all. He's usually mild mannered and easy going," he said.

We both laughed.

Chapter 37

BPA Logo

The mid-nineties presented Battersea police station with a new and expensive stand-alone computer system. This system, we were informed, would considerably alleviate the insurmountable stress of managing an awkward shift system for hundreds of police officers.

My work entailed ensuring all the various roles on my Battersea Village sector were filled by relevant police personnel. I would spend hours each day juggling various bits of paper and completing a rather messy grid with a ballpoint pen. However, the new computer system remained upstairs and out of sight; an expensive toy for a select few and I was certainly not one of them. I knew nothing about computers. That worried me because I could see that computers were gaining in popularity. My thoughts on the matter had been reinforced by a recent visit to my police station by a successful local businessman, who when being shown our state-of-the-art Computer Aided Dispatch control room, the hub of the station where all nature of information is received, recorded and actioned, had remarked, 'this antiquated system,' was in need of an upgrade. He even suggested his personal computer was far more efficient. On departure, he left us with his business card. Looking at it, our Chief Superintendent, Stephen Pilkington, pointed out to me the strange wording in the top corner of the card was an electronic mail address. I had never seen such a thing.

My appetite whetted, I made up my mind, I did not want to be left behind in what I foresaw as a new computer age. Later in the week, I opened my copy of the free ads newspaper LOOT and scoured the section where computers were being offered for sale. I had little or no knowledge of what I was looking for, but the second-hand personal computer with a hard drive of 400MB had an attractive fifty-pound price tag. I telephoned the number at the bottom of the advert.

Poplar was somewhere in East London, so with help of my A-Z, the following evening, I jumped into my car and made the cross London journey to examine and hopefully buy my first computer. Living in South London, but socialising mainly in East and North London, I was familiar with the main routes, but never had I been to Poplar, an area that on my arrival appeared to have received little attention and investment since the second World War. I parked my car outside the address in a street reminiscent of an *EastEnders* TV series set. I quickly looked up and down the street expecting to see the Queen Vic pub on the corner.

My door knock was answered by a young man of Asian appearance.

"Hi, I called about your computer advertised in Loot," I said.

"Yes, come in, I'll show it to you."

I followed the young man into his living room where he showed me the computer. Although I had never examined one before so he could have shown me anything, I examined it with absolutely no understanding of what to look for.

My vendor plunged straight into a demonstration, with lightning speed, he pointed out several things that I guessed would have meant something to someone familiar with computers. Finishing his demonstration, he looked up at me and said,

"So, what do you think, you interested?"

Looking blankly at him, I said, "So what happens when I turn it on?"

He patiently took me through the demonstration once more; this time at a snail's pace, ensuring that he doubly explained each feature.

With the personal computer and keyboard on the back seat of my car and having memorised the location of its on/off button, I happily made my way home to South London, leaving behind the Poplar East End grime.

Each day I would turn on my computer, now housed on a purpose-built computer desk with a slide-out shelf for the keyboard; equipped with the assistance of a subscription to a computer magazine, I slowly began to realise its potential. Disappointingly, it was a car without wheels, for I had no means of 'dialing up' the internet and that, I had read in my magazine, was the future of computing.

Out came 'Loot' once more, I scanned the by now familiar computer section and quickly found myself a brand new 28.8 bits/s modem; this time, from a local South London vendor.

Excitedly, I connected it to the phone line in my house, switched it on and watched the lights across the front of the plastic modem blink as I dialed up on my computer, a sure sign that something was happening.

Loading and installing the Netscape web browser was not easy but waiting for a website to download onto my computer screen was akin to watching paint dry. Nevertheless, I was hooked, and, over the next few weeks, I spent every waking hour trying something new on my computer. I would read all the major PC magazines and taught myself the rudiments of HTML, the web design language. Within six weeks of buying the modem, I had designed and launched my first website. The launch also coincided with my first through-the-night computer session. I had been so determined to get the thing done I had lost all track of time and as my website slowly downloaded onto my screen, I noticed the birds singing; it was getting light outside.

Knowing that I had uploaded the files to a server somewhere in California added to my excitement and achievement. It was an exhilarating experience.

But the real purpose of embracing this new Internet technology was to give the Black Police Association an advantage in the world of communications. At every opportunity I would seek to introduce the internet and its capabilities at meetings of our Executive Committee, I was often met with glazed expressions.

On one occasion I offered to design a BPA website, but the Executive was unconvinced and declined my offer.

Undeterred and anxious to show off my skills, I approached Norwell Roberts and suggested to him that I would like to devote a website to his remarkable achievement as London's first black police officer. Norwell agreed and using a published interview that my BPA colleague Keith Smith had undertaken with Norwell, I launched the Norwell Roberts tribute website.

Not only was I General Secretary, but I was also now Chief Geek! Of the many frustrating issues confronting the BPA Executive, the absence of a corporate logo was probably near the top of our list. We had managed to launch the BPA without a logo, despite well-intentioned efforts by some colleagues.

I had taken a keen interest in the logo debate, as I felt it reflected poorly upon the BPA as a professional organisation. Following one such debate among the Executive, myself and Winston Baird visited a young man in Catford, South London. He was a graphic designer, who had come highly recommended by a friend of a friend. As Winston and I sat in the young man's flat I was struck by the fact that he had managed to fix a chair onto the wall of his apartment, about five feet from the floor, not something I had ever seen before. Surely, designing the BPA a logo was within his skill set.

Sadly, this was not to be the case. His logo designs for the BPA were a disaster and most other designs we considered over the weeks and months were not much better. I was frustrated and I knew various colleagues on the Executive shared my frustration. Leafing through a copy of Micro-Mart magazine, I spied a small advert placed by a graphic designer, someone who specialised in logo designs.

I logged onto my computer and within a few minutes, I was scrolling through the site of New York based designer, Ari Weinstein. He specialised in logo design and many examples of his work were made available in his website gallery. I was immediately impressed with the clean uncomplicated lines and imaginative design. The logos were of such a high standard, I assumed they must surely carry a hefty price tag.

The more I looked at Weinstein's site the bolder I became; I had to approach him. So, late one night, I penned a lengthy email to Ari, explaining who we were, what we were trying to achieve, the fact that we did not have a logo and that I loved his work, but did not have any money.

I anxiously waited for a response and received one within about 48 hours. Ari expressed his admiration for what we were trying to achieve and congratulated us for taking a stance. Most importantly, he offered to design the BPA a logo for free! I was absolutely elated and could not wait to share the news with BPA Executive colleagues. However, my presentation to the Executive was met with silence, perhaps a murmur here and there.

Maybe they were so fed-up discussing logos because it always caused disagreement among the Executive, to the extent they were probably resigned to the fact that we were destined not to have a logo. It also crossed my mind that my exuberant presentation was thought of as yet another opportunity for Chief Geek to relate his adventures on the internet.

Of course, I did not relay any of this indifference to Ari. No, I thanked him profusely and asked him to kindly go ahead with a design, which he did. We co-operated over the internet and within about a week he had completed the logo.

Trying to get the logo onto the BPA agenda was a frustrating task. After a few months of trying, I decided to give the matter a rest.

Then, during an Executive meeting, completely out of the blue, the issue of a logo arose and our communications officer, Keith Smith said he had found a particular logo in his emails and quite liked it. I waited with bated breath hardly able to keep quiet, but I knew any intervention on my part at this delicate stage might plunge the Executive into a heated debate. Keith, a senior member of the civil staff had gained the attention of the Executive. I would wait to see what he was referring to, await the response and then weigh in with my views. Keith pushed a piece of paper into the centre of the table. It was the Ari Weinstein design. I had completely forgotten that I had emailed Keith a copy. I looked around the table and within a few seconds and with minimal discussion, the Executive agreed to adopt the logo. After months of disagreement, we were united!

I went back to Ari with the news that the BPA wished to adopt his design, but his attitude had changed somewhat slightly. He had after all been kept waiting for about nine months. Ari explained to me in an email that yes, he had offered to design the logo for free, but that was some months ago and that now we would have to pay a (discounted) fee for his work. 30 US dollars, which, at the time, I considered to be an absolute steal. I paid him the money and took possession of the proofs via email. The BPA had its logo.

Chapter 38

Toronto

By 1995 it had become apparent to me and others on the Executive that gaining recognition or help from our parent organisation, the Metropolitan Police, would be a challenge following the successful and high-profile launch of the Black Police Association.

Despite this setback, we were gradually able to make things happen through contacts and friends who were sympathetic to our cause. One notable example of this is BPA Deputy Chair, Winston Baird. Because of his seniority and network of civil staff contacts, he was able to secure a small office for BPA in the basement of 105 Regency Street, close to where my initial job interview had taken place in 1979.

While we were all grateful for the accommodation, it was like a crumb of comfort from an estranged parent. BPA Executives offered a range of voluntary support to black police officers and civil staff suffering racial discrimination, but the Metropolitan Police seemed oblivious to the toll the ever-increasing workload was having on us.

At its outset, the dank and dark months of 1995 held little in the way of promise. Nevertheless, it transformed into a busy and steep learning curve after two memorable events that stretched my understanding and role within the Black Police Association.

It all started with a phone call from our Chair, Ron Hope, "Paul, I just received an interesting letter from a Canadian organisation called The Association of Black Law Enforcers. They have invited me to give the keynote speech at their upcoming Awards Ball in Toronto, Canada."

"That's excellent news, Ron. It's nice to know that we're being recognised abroad even if the Met is dragging its heels," I replied.

As General Secretary my job was to support the Chair, so I began making enquiries about this Canadian organisation. I discovered they shared similar experiences of organisational indifference and racism, which led to a group of disenchanted black law enforcement professionals making a stand.

The Association of Black Law Enforcers (ABLE) was born three years before the BPA, with a focus on improving black community relations with Canada's law enforcement agencies. This was achieved through many community-based projects and social activities.

Since a significant number of our members had joined the BPA to take advantage of our support network, I felt that ABLE's support for those suffering from racism in the workplace would particularly interest the BPA Executive team.

A couple of weeks later I received another unexpected call from our Chair, "As you know, I am taking a temporary Superintendent post with the Home Office programme at Turvey in Bedfordshire. Jerome Mack has informed me I need to start right away, so I cannot attend the ABLE Awards Ball in Canada," he said.

"That's a real shame, Ron!"

"Would you be interested in going in my place?" he asked.

"What about your deputy, Winston?"

"I had considered Winston, but it seems our Canadian friends expect a police officer to deliver the keynote speech," he said.

"In that case, I would be honoured to attend in your place."

I was absolutely delighted that Ron recognised me as someone able to represent the BPA at the highest level.

"Good, we'll get it endorsed at the next meeting of the BPA Executive," he said.

At the next Executive committee meeting it was confirmed that I would be going to Canada with my colleague, Sultan Taylor. This decision was made to ensure the BPA would be accurately represented, should I become unavailable for whatever reason.

I was elated to visit Canada, even if it was as second choice to Ron. It was a great deal of responsibility on my relatively inexperienced shoulders. I was, after all, a sergeant whereby Ron was a seasoned and highly respected Chief Inspector.

On 19th May 1995, Sultan Taylor and I were greeted at the Toronto Airport by David Mitchell, President of ABLE and a senior officer with the Canadian Department of Corrections. David was a young man of black African heritage with an impressive physical frame and infectious laugh. Within minutes of our meeting his larger-than-life personality had become apparent. This was someone who exuded confidence from every pore.

Or is this just typical North American swagger? I thought.

During our drive into Toronto, Sultan and I struck up a rapport with David as we talked.

"How many ABLE meetings have you missed since it was formed?" I asked David. I felt certain he had missed none. In the short time I had been in his company, his commitment and enthusiasm for ABLE was evident in every breath.

"None," he said, tilting his head. I hoped I hadn't offended him.

"I didn't think so. Me neither," I replied.

We laughed and continued our journey to David's home, where we would stay for the duration of our visit. After we got settled, he shared with us our terribly busy itinerary for the next seven days. That afternoon we would meet with members of ABLE and visit a medium security prison at Brampton, then in the evening stroll down Toronto's Yonge Street to get insight into the best and worst of Toronto's street life. I was especially excited that our hosts had included a visit to Niagara Falls in our itinerary.

Outside of the breath-taking experience of Niagara, every minute of our stay involved either meeting with Departmental Directors and Superintendents, giving presentations to ABLE members, or shuttling back and forth between police stations, firearms training units and a high security prison. Each day was enjoyable but left us truly exhausted by the end.

When I managed to catch a little downtime, I would study the keynote speech that Ron Hope had prepared. I had scribbled copious notes in the margins, introducing changes to give it personal flavour. I rehearsed key lines to improve my confidence because I was nervous at the prospect of standing before what I imagined to be a large audience that included senior people from the world of law enforcement. While our Canadian cousins' behaviour was more in line with the British, I was expecting the glitz and glamour of a truly North American Awards Ball.

On May 27th, 1995, I walked into the International Plaza Hotel in Toronto with Sultan and David Mitchell. As I walked through the lobby, looking chic in my black tie and patent leather shoes, my heart raced as I watched the guests filing into the ballroom.

Hundreds of tables decorated with flowers and gold embossed name plates sat underneath a large shimmering chandelier in the center of the ceiling, I weaved my way through the tables and chairs, trying to maintain a sense of decorum as I climbed the steps of the stage leading to the top table. Just as my feet touched the stage, there was a tug on the back of my jacket.

"Commissioner of the Royal Canadian Mounted Police straight ahead, buddy," a voice with a Canadian accent whispered.

A distinguished-looking gentleman rose to his feet as I approached. "Good evening, Commissioner, a pleasure to meet you," I said, extending my hand.

He gripped my outstretched hand and shook it rapidly. "Welcome, Paul. I've heard so much about what you guys in England have achieved."

"That's very kind of you, Sir. Our aim is to become as famous as your organisation," I replied.

I found my nameplate, which also showed I was from London, England. I sat down and sipped on my glass of water as David Mitchell walked to the lectern and gave the welcome remarks. I was in awe of his natural, confident, and charismatic style.

"Without further ado, it gives me enormous pleasure to introduce tonight's keynote speaker, all the way from London, England. Please welcome Paul Wilson, General Secretary of the Black Police Association."

Polite applause rippled through the seated audience.

I stood up and walked to the lectern with my speech notes gripped in my perspiring palms. Photographers moved towards the stage and began taking pictures. Momentarily blinded by the flashes, I composed myself and held onto the lectern with both hands.

Hundreds of faces looked at me expectantly as I placed my notes neatly on the lectern shelf. I took a deep breath and relaxed. My inner coping mechanism had signaled my brain to remain calm as there was no way my key organs could accommodate this level of stress.

"Good evening Commissioner, President of ABLE, distinguished guests, ladies and gentlemen. It is with great pleasure that I address you on this auspicious occasion," I said.

For the next twenty minutes I navigated effortlessly through my speech, pausing, and smiling when appropriate. I alternated my eye contact between three or four tables spread across the ballroom. My concluding remarks were met with great applause. I had successfully completed my very first international speech for the Black Police Association.

My return to England was as anti-climactic as I expected it to be. However, only a few days after settling back into my routine, another unexpected opportunity arose.

Chapter 39

Race for Justice '95

As I entered the swish Thai restaurant situated just off High Street Kensington, a smartly dressed, middle-aged Thai gentleman approached me.

"Do you have a reservation, Sir?" he asked politely.

"Yes, I'm with a large group. Our reservation is under the name *Race for Justice '95,*" I said, looking at the tables for any familiar faces.

The Maître d looked down at his reservation list. "Ah yes. You are early, but that's not a problem. Follow me."

I had intentionally arrived early to secure a seat in the middle of the long table we had reserved. I ordered a chilled glass of chardonnay and sat quietly to wait for the others and reflect on all that had taken place over the last few months.

It all started with an invitation from our friends at the Association of Black Probation Officers (ABPO) to assist in the organisation and development of a high-profile conference to highlight the disparities and injustice suffered by black communities in the criminal justice system.

News of the ABPO invitation had been met with muted interest when presented to the BPA Executive Committee meeting. Most felt that this might be a step too far and too early. We were still a fledgling organisation with executive members who often had to make personal sacrifices and substantial time commitments just to stay afloat.

We were rapidly gaining experience as advocates on issues faced by black police and civil staff, yet we were still inexperienced in assessing the bigger picture presented by the criminal justice system. On the other hand, the conference could improve our standing in the community and the theme blended nicely with our constitution.

Once the potential benefits of the conference were understood, the mood among the committee members changed. A show of hands confirmed our involvement in supporting the conference, I volunteered to represent the BPA on the conference planning steering committee.

The first of many planning committee meetings took place in the chambers of barrister Peter Herbert, President of the Society of Black Lawyers (SBL). Next to Peter sat Lloyd Larose Jones, Chair of the Association of Black Probation Officers (ABPO) and staunch friend of the BPA.

Both Peter and Lloyd had offered invaluable assistance and practical guidance to the BPA in our formative days. Other members included ABPO members Jennifer Douglas and Octavia Findlay. Khami Alexander and Caroline Newman represented the Society of Black Lawyers, and Yvette Williams from the National Black Caucus who diligently took notes at every meeting.

Peter and Lloyd took turns in chairing the planning committee when we met at alternating venues every two weeks, usually in the evening after work. I did not feel comfortable with the idea of chairing the group myself, certainly not in the presence of these stalwart campaigners. I felt privileged just to be there representing the BPA as best I could. And if that meant securing a meeting venue for the planning group on police premises, then that is what I would do.

The meetings provided me an invaluable insight into how seasoned race equality campaigners think and work. I picked up many useful pointers. Unfortunately, as with the BPA meetings, conflicts and arguments soon arose. Peter and Lloyd were two assertive individuals with vastly different management styles, and that would often cause them to bump heads. Sometimes the arguments became heated and personal, but by the end we usually agreed to focus on the business of getting the conference off the ground.

Finally, after weeks of discussion, presentations, disagreements and frustrations, the Commonwealth Institute in London was confirmed as the conference venue. Even then there continued to be contentious discussions centered on guest speakers, workshop leads, and themes.

But it was the committee's agreement to broaden the scope of the conference to include international speakers and representatives that excited me. This presented the BPA with the unique opportunity to reciprocate the camaraderie extended to me and Sultan Taylor on our recent visit to Toronto and strengthened our relationship with the National Black Police Association.

With little disagreement, the committee accepted my proposal to invite two speakers to the conference. Leslie Seymour, the Chair of the National Black Police Association in the United States, and David Mitchell the

President of the Association of Black Law Enforcers in Canada. Professor Stephen Small, from the University of California in Berkeley, was to facilitate the conference.

A further development took me by complete surprise as Peter Herbert proposed that we invite two extremely high profile African American lawyers to the conference. Johnnie L. Cochran Jr., lead defence lawyer in the O.J Simpson trial and Milton Grimes, lead counsel for Rodney King, the Los Angeles taxi driver who was covertly filmed being savagely beaten by Los Angeles police officers. The two recent controversial trials had attracted massive media attention worldwide. The committee agreed unanimously to extend invitations to the two prominent lawyers.

One key issue that caused considerable frustration for the steering committee was the matter of raising sufficient funds for conference related costs. The news that Johnnie Cochran accepted our invitation to speak at the conference eased this tension. As soon as this information was released to the media, offers for interviews and media appearances flooded in. Several high paying interviews were scheduled with popular breakfast time TV shows. The amounts were staggering, but we were soon disappointed to discover that these were personal payments to Cochran and not for the conference administration coffers.

Besides appearing at the conference, our committee also arranged for several international guests to speak at other events in London, Brixton, Liverpool, and Birmingham. But it was the impending arrival of Johnny Cochran at Heathrow Airport that caused considerable debate among the committee members. Both Lloyd and Peter felt that they should personally represent the planning committee and greet Cochran on his arrival. Tempers flared as both men raised arguments for why they should meet Cochran at the airport. Neither one would budge, and the issue remained unresolved. During the next meeting, prominent black community activist Lee Jasper addressed the planning committee meeting.

"Hi, I'm Lee Jasper. I think everyone here knows me. I'm Chair of the National Black Caucus and as such I represent all member groups, including SBL and ABPO. So, since that means I'm essentially your Chair, I'll decide who greets Johnnie Cochran when he arrives at Heathrow."

The National Black Caucus does not represent the BPA, but I'm not interested in meeting Cochran at Heathrow anyway, so I'm staying out of this, I thought.

I looked over at Peter and Lloyd, who did not look pleased with the proposed solution but remained silent.

"Look, I'm going to meet Cochran at the airport. If you guys want to join me, please do," Lee said, sitting back down with a mischievous grin on his face.

Lee Jasper had in a few seconds diffused a volatile situation that had threatened to splinter the committee and undermine weeks of work.

Now here I was a few months later, on the eve of our *Race for Justice '95* conference, sitting alone at a long table, sipping my Chardonnay and reflecting on these events as I waited for the other guests to arrive.

A voice jolted me out of my contemplation.

"You're early, Paul. Must be your police discipline."

Yvette Williams stood at the end of the table, smiling at me.

"Hi, Yvette. Is everything okay for tomorrow? No last-minute panics I hope," I said.

"No, everything is going as planned. We had a few teething problems with security personnel, but that's all been smoothed out," she replied.

"Great. I'm looking forward to it. Hopefully, tomorrow all our hard work will pay off."

As soon as I had finished speaking to Yvette, I saw a familiar figure being escorted to our table by the maître d' and Peter Herbert. Along with millions around the world, I had followed last year's trial of American football legend, O.J Simpson, for the murder of his ex-wife, Nicole Brown Simpson, and her friend Ron Goldman.

A key character in the high-profile trial was Simpson's talented and charismatic lawyer, Johnnie Cochran. That individual now approached our table and pulled out a chair directly across from me. Before he could sit down, I stood up and held out my hand.

"Pleased to meet you, Mr. Cochran. Paul Wilson, Black Police Association and member of the conference planning group."

Mr. Cochran smiled and shook my hand. "Hey Paul, good to meet you. Thanks for all the work you guys have put into this."

The rest of the conference planning members soon arrived and walked over to greet our international guest. The queue was so long that the poor man was barely able to look at the menu. As the evening progressed, things settled down and we enjoyed a good meal and conversation.

I was just about to take a bite of my Pad Thai when someone shouted, "Hey, Spike!"

I looked up as the maître d escorted an unexpected guest to the table, actor and film director Spike Lee.

"A friend of yours, Johnnie?" I asked.

Spike Lee walked over and sat next to Cochran, avoiding eye contact with everyone else. From their initial greeting, it appeared they were the best of friends. I tried not to stare at our new celebrity guest, but I found it hard to conceal my excitement. Perhaps it was my fork full of noodles suspended in mid-air that caught his attention as he placed a napkin on his knee.

"Hey man, you good?" he asked.

"Yeah, I'm good. Pleased to see you," I said, shoveling the hanging noodles into my mouth.

Spike nodded and moved closer to Cochran. They exchanged whispers for what seemed like ages.

My thoughts turned to 1986 when I had toured the southern part of the United States on a Greyhound bus. One of my stops was Atlanta, Georgia, where I paid my respects at the memorial to black civil rights icon, Dr. Martin Luther King. During my time in Atlanta, some newfound friends took me on a tour of the historical Morehouse College. It was here that we discussed attending the film premiere of 'She's Gotta Have It', directed by a local guy and Morehouse student named Spike Lee.

Since one of my new friends worked as a projectionist at the Atlanta cinema where the film was to premiere, I was able to watch the film from the projection room. The mostly black and white film set in Brooklyn, New York, featured a black cast (including Spike Lee) but was not a film about being black in Brooklyn.

With its beautifully arranged jazz soundtrack and exploration of black sexuality, the film made a huge impression on me. I immediately fell in love with the lead character, sexually liberated Nola Darling, played by actress Tracy Camilla Johns. At the film premiere after-party I was introduced to some of the cast (except Tracy) and was presented with a signed film poster that hung in my South London flat for many years. From the moment I walked out of that film premiere, I was a Spike Lee fan and had closely followed his progress over the years.

Should I regale Spike with my in-depth knowledge of his first feature film? I thought.

I suddenly remembered reading that 'She's Gotta Have It' was not one of his favourites, so I thought better of it. I just sat back and other than the occasional glance and nod allowed Johnnie Cochran to monopolise Spike Lee for the rest of the evening.

The following day, I made my way to the Commonwealth Institute in Kensington nice and early for our *Race for Justice '95* conference.

As I walked along Kensington High Street, I reflected on the totality of my planning committee experience. It had been a steep learning curve for me and the BPA Executive when, in the final planning stages, I applied for a substantial sum of money to underwrite unforeseen conference costs.

This was a wake-up call for the BPA Executive committee who, for the most part, silently nodded at my regular updates and expressed little interest in the importance of this partnership. Fortunately, this was recognised by Ron Hope, who, in discussing my application for a financial contribution, admitted that the BPA Executive had allowed matters to coast and had not paid enough attention to my involvement on the conference planning committee. Sufficient funds were eventually released by the BPA, enabling the conference arrangements to continue.

As I approached the Commonwealth Institute, I stopped suddenly. Hordes of camera toting journalists congregated outside the main entrance.

If it's like this now, what will it be like when Cochran takes the stage at the conference? I thought, squeezing through the crowd to get to the building entrance.

Once inside, I looked around for members of the planning committee and spotted Jennifer Douglas.

"Good morning, Jennifer. This is our big day, but the size of that media crowd outside is frightening. Do we have space for everyone?"

Jennifer shook her head. "You haven't been inside the auditorium yet. It is already almost full. This was an outcome we never considered. I'm worried that our afternoon programme will suffer as a result."

I went into the auditorium, and as Jennifer said, it was almost full as people continued to stream through the doors and rapidly fill the empty seats.

I took my seat upstairs, where I was able to look down on the conference floor as Professor Small got things underway. An uneasiness filled the pit of my stomach. We were running almost an hour behind schedule. What if we were not able to make up for the lost time?

Michael Mansfield QC stood and presented his perspective on race and the Criminal Justice System. Ordinarily the media would have hung on his every word, but from my position there appeared to be constant chatter around the auditorium in anticipation of the keynote speaker, Johnnie L. Cochran, Jr.

My pager vibrated. I unhooked it from my belt and looked at the message screen.

"Milton Grimes has not yet arrived. His plane is late. It's not known if he will make it."

Damn, I thought.

Milton was another headline speaker. His appearance on our programme had created considerable interest from the media and grass-roots activists alike. I was just about to get up to go make some enquiries about how we were going to make up for lost time, when our keynote speaker walked onto the stage. Almost everyone in the auditorium rose to their feet. The applause and cheers were deafening as photojournalists scrambled for a position in front of the stage.

I sat back down and listened for the next hour as Johnnie Cochran laid bare some of the more contentious issues of the trial, including the infamous moment when O.J Simpson put on those now iconic gloves. To the obvious delight of the mesmerised conference audience, Cochran repeated his famous line.

"If it doesn't fit, you must acquit."

My pager vibrated again. "Milton Grimes has just arrived."

I breathed a sigh of relief and looked at my watch. We were due to break for lunch very shortly. As I turned to leave my seat, an unshaven and casually dressed Milton Grimes stood a few feet away, watching and listening to Cochran's speech. I approached him and held out my hand.

"Hi Milton. Paul Wilson from the conference planning committee. It's really great to see you. I understand your flight was delayed?"

"Hi Paul. Yes, I came straight here from Heathrow. I haven't even been to my hotel yet."

"I'm sorry to hear that. What do you want to do? Do you feel up to going on stage to speak?" I asked.

"Hell yeah. I just flew halfway around the world. I have no intention of sitting in a hotel room while you are all having fun."

"That's good to hear. Let's get you downstairs and see what we can do to get you on after Johnny Cochran," I said.

By the time Grimes took the stage, he informed the audience that he "had not flown all this way just to speak for the remaining moments before lunch,".

"What do you want to do, listen to me tell you about the Rodney King trial, or should I say injustice, and the ensuing riots that gripped Los Angeles, or attend some workshops?"

From the audience's response, it became clear that there would be no afternoon workshops that day.

The 'Race for Justice '95' conference took place on November 18th, 1995, at the Commonwealth Institute in London. It was the first large-scale event planned by the recently launched Black Police Association in cooperation with other black criminal justice groups to highlight injustices to the black community. The conference programme for the event included a foreword by Tottenham MP Bernie Grant that served to remind us of the stark realities of racial injustice during the nineties.

It was no surprise that the mainstream media's reporting of the event focused on the flamboyant Johnnie Cochran and his defence of O.J. Simpson. Little mention was made of the Black Police Association's involvement in planning the event.

Regardless of this, significant coverage was given to all the black criminal justice groups involved from the black media at the time. From a racial justice perspective, this was perhaps the most high-profile conference of the nineties.

Paul with Johnny Cochran Jr and Milton Grimes (Race for Justice 95)

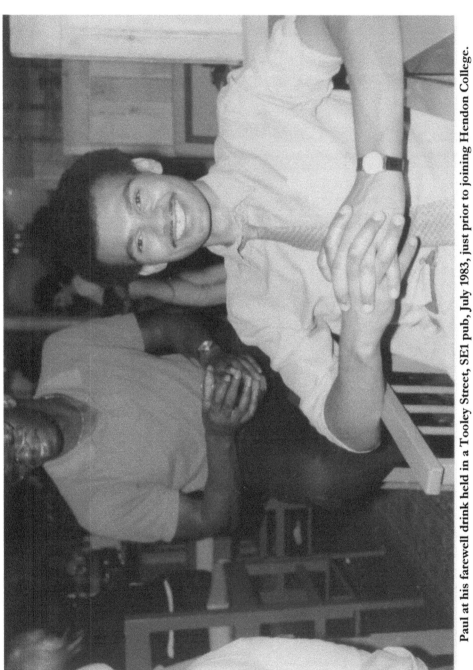

Paul at his farewell drink held in a Tooley Street, SE1 pub, July 1983, just prior to joining Hendon College.

Paul in uniform, Police College, Hendon, 1983.

Meeting Jesse Jackson at Congressional Black Caucus, Washington DC, 1989.

Paul presents keynote speech at ABLE Awards Ball, Toronto, 1995.

Paul with Sultan Taylor, ABLE Awards Ball, Toronto, 1995.

Paul and Executive members of the first National Black Police Association, Preston, Lancs, 1999.

Paul 2002. Neighbourhood Warden Unit.

Paul with George Rhoden and Metropolitan Police Commissioner, Sir Peter Imbert, presenting a Bristol Reunion donation to representatives from Great Ormond Street Hospital and a London sickle cell charity.- 1992

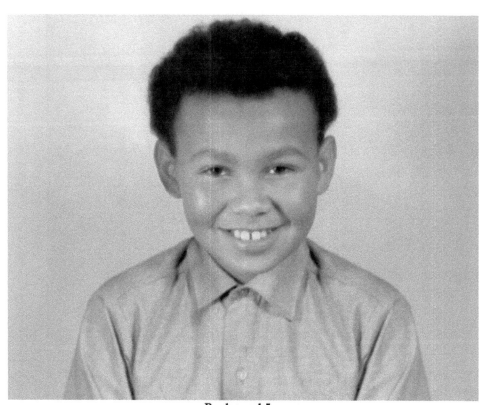

Paul, aged 5.

Paul, aged 20.

Paul, aged 13 outside Carrington village home.

Policing Notting Hill Carnival, 1999

Paul and Winnie Mandela, Soweto, South Africa, 2000

Paul Wilson, Brixton Police Station, circa 2008. Photograph by Andy Martinez

Channel 4 News still from the 1998 BPA AGM, with Jack Straw

Chapter 40

The OSPRE incident

In 1995, I had recently been promoted to the rank of Inspector and posted to Kennington police station in Lambeth, South London. Looking for ways to diversify my CV, I spied an internal memorandum inviting Inspectors to apply for 'National Police Exam Assessor training'. Further investigation revealed that to complete the training meant spending a week at a training centre in the leafy surrounds of Harrogate, North Yorkshire.

A week in Harrogate sounds appealing, I thought to myself.

I completed the brief application, had it endorsed by my line manager and, a few months later, I was driving my faithful Mercedes 190E in the northbound carriageway of the A1 motorway, on my way to Harrogate.

The Monday morning introduction to our training course reminded me that the nature of police examinations had certainly changed since I took my sergeant's exam. With a great deal of focus now on the necessary skills required to perform in the rank, the exam process was divided into two parts, the first a purely written exercise. Mainly, my fellow trainee assessor colleagues and I were interested in Part 2 of the Objective Structured Performance Related Exam, or OSPRE as it was commonly known. During this part, the candidates would undertake several exercises in small rooms or stations, where they encounter a role actor and over the next five minutes the candidate must attempt to solve the problem or issue presented by the role actor. These scenarios were specially designed by a team at Harrogate to test a candidate's ability to deal with 'real-life' situations.

As one of two assessors in the station, my role was to either observe the candidate's performance and, using a score sheet, score their performance appropriately or undertake a role play designed to test the candidate's understanding of a problem or issue.

The week's training, set in the dreamy surrounds of Harrogate, was interesting if not intense. It was here that I met Dean Charles, the brother of actor Craig Charles; someone who had recently been arrested on my patch in South London for a serious sexual assault but was subsequently acquitted by the Crown Court jury of all charges. Dean was an Inspector with Merseyside Police but had taken time out to join the team at Harrogate to help train Assessors.

A few days following the successful completion of my training at Harrogate, I received a letter, dated 29th May 1996, from Superintendent Bolton in the Examinations Department, congratulating me for successfully completing the OSPRE Assessors' Course and that I was now eligible to both assess, and role play in the Constable to Sergeants' examination.

A few months later I was asked to attend the PC to Sgt's Examination site in Bristol, where I was to be paired with Dean Charles for the duration of the examination period. We shared one small station where our candidates would enter and the two of us would take turns at role acting and assessing. We operated well with one another. This is probably because of our similar backgrounds. We had both joined the police in 1983 and Dean had a black father and white mother. What I found particularly endearing about Dean was his refreshing positivity when speaking of his African heritage and despite his noticeably light complexion, he was never in any doubt - he was black. He had confided in me that when he began policing as a young probationary constable on the streets of Liverpool, members of the black community would shout, as he walked by in full uniform, "Is he or isn't he?" We both laughed, finding it both funny and a relief from the insults often hurled at black police constables.

As our week together progressed in the small confines of our room, we spent our downtime exchanging stories about our personal and professional lives. It was during these conversations that I picked up that Dean was enormously proud of his high-profile brother's achievements; additionally, Craig's arrest and three-month imprisonment awaiting trial had taken a huge emotional toll on him. Following our days of discussion, it eventually became apparent to me that Dean had effectively curtailed his career with Merseyside Police because, of his disenchantment with the criminal justice system and, as he saw it, the way his brother had been treated by police colleagues in South London. This, I felt, was tragic for Dean was absolutely brimming with spirit and intelligence, hugely charismatic and funny. He was someone that would, in my estimation, effortlessly rise in the police ranks and achieve a very senior level.

However, in July of 1997, my enjoyment as an OSPRE assessor was brought to an abrupt end.

Paul Wilson

Training Support, Harrogate
Yew Tree Lane, Pannal Ash, Harrogate, North Yorkshire, HG2 9JZ
Tel: 01423-859-_____ (Direct) or 01423-871201 (Switchboard)
Fax: 01423-859132

National Police Training

Mr P Wilson

GH/EH

17 July 1997

Dear Mr Wilson

SERGEANTS OSPRE PART II 1997

I considered it was important to write to you personally to explain why we would not be using you as an assessor/role actor in this year's Sergeants examination.

I am sure you are aware that the policy which the PPEU had adopted for the Sergeants' Part II examination in 1996 and thereafter was to take no account of gender or visible ethnic minority in the allocation of assessors/role actors to any of the stations. The outcome of introducing this policy was that at the marking process, which is conducted by an occupational psychologist employed by the LGMB, it was ascertained that there were significant differences in performance where candidates had been presented with visible ethnic minority role actors and white role actors across the same exercise. The hypothesis postulated by the 'marker' was that candidates had been given different stimuli as a result of which the exercise has not been 'fair' to all candidates undertaking those exercises.

At the Police Promotion Examination Board which was held following the examination it was decided that until the findings of the OSPRE Review were published the PPEU would adopt a practice of standardised exercises. This means that where visible ethnic minority assessors/role actors are used in an exercise, ALL candidates will be presented with a visible ethnic minority role actor. Because of this decision and the fact that we have insufficient visible ethnic minority assessors/role actors this has determined that at the next examination no visible ethnic minority assessors/role actors will be used.

The PPEB and the PPEU have taken this step very reluctantly and we are hopeful that the Review will determine an outcome whereby the indiscriminate use of visible ethnic minority role actors in any exercise is an acceptable practice. In the meantime the PPEU are actively pursuing to recruit additional visible ethnic minority assessors/role actors to ensure their proportionate representation within the examination irrespective of the final findings of the Review.

I should add that the standardisation of exercises is a common practice across assessment centres and we have been at the 'cutting edge' of changing such practices in consultation with the Equal Opportunities Commission.

I hope the above goes some way to explaining the current situation and to assure you that we are as aggrieved by the constraints as you must be. We sincerely hope that you will still remain available for future examinations and support an important process in the development of both the individual and organisation.

Should you wish to discuss this matter further please contact me direct (01423 859122) or speak with Chief Inspector Fraser Sampson (01423 859204).

Yours sincerely

Glenn Hutton
Superintendent
Head of Police Promotion Examinations Unit.

I read and re-read the letter with absolute incredulity. The more I read it the more incensed I became. I picked up the phone and spoke with my BPA colleague David Michael.

"David, I'm so upset I can hardly speak; I've just received a letter from the Police Promotion Examination Unit informing me that black OSPRE Assessors will not be required in future examinations…."

"Ok, Paul just calm down. What do you mean by 'not required', why?" said David in his usual measured tone.

"I'm to be excluded from future examinations on the basis that the colour of my skin presented some candidates with a 'different stimulus'."

"Is that what it says in the letter, I mean the exact words?"

"Yes David, I have it in front of me!"

"Ok, bring the letter with you on your next visit to the BPA office and we'll consider what we can do," suggested David.

In the meantime, the following day I reported for my early shift as Duty Officer. During that morning, I decided to approach Superintendent Johnson, my line manager at Kennington Police Station. I knocked on his open office door and entered.

"Yes, Paul. How are things this morning, all quiet?" asked Superintendent Johnson.

"Thankfully, yes, but something has cropped up and I'd just like to run it by you to get an objective viewpoint."

"Fire away, Paul."

I read the offending letter to Superintendent Johnson and as I concluded the final sentence, I looked closely at his facial expression. He smiled.

"Well, you can see why they've done it can't you? One of those things; there is not much that can be done. Never mind, I'm sure there'll be similar opportunities in the future."

Superintendent Johnson's viewpoint was not unique. Indeed, it was shared by every colleague of Inspector rank and above that, I approached in the following days and weeks. That was the problem; by and large police officers did not see a problem with the directive issued by the Police Promotion Examination Board. Even some black assessor colleagues I telephoned seemed to accept what was being said as 'inevitable'.

Obtaining the agreement of the BPA Chair and colleagues on the BPA Executive, I made a phone call to a journalist at *The Voice* newspaper, *'Britain's favourite black newspaper'*. The conversation led to a meeting where I showed the journalist my letter from the police examination unit and expressed in the strongest terms the BPA's viewpoint that this new policy of excluding black assessors was both discriminatory, unethical, and potentially unlawful.

I waited anxiously for the next copy of 'The Voice' to appear in the newsagents. When the publication day arrived, I jogged the short distance from my house to the local newsagents. I entered the shop and scanned the shelves until I found a copy. I quickly picked it up and opened the newspaper, looking fervently at the various articles until, on page two, I found a banner headline.

'Black Cops Excluded from Exams'

The article underneath the headline was a verbatim account of my conversation with the journalist. I was incredibly pleased as I knew from experience that *The Voice* was widely read by senior police and politicians because of its considerable reputation of being a useful barometer by which to measure and monitor historically fraught tensions between a predominantly white police force and black communities.

Two weeks following 'The Voice' coverage, I received the following letter at my home address.

Training Support, Harrogate
Yew Tree Lane, Pannal Ash, Harrogate, North Yorkshire, HG2 9JZ
Tel: 01423-859- *(Direct) or 01423-871201 (Switchboard)*
Fax: 01423-859132

National Police Training

Mr P Wilson

5 August 1997

Dear Mr Wilson

SERGEANTS OSPRE PART II 1997

Further to my letter of the 16 July 1997, you may well be aware by now of the Home Office decision to revert to the original policy of the indiscriminate use of role actors irrespective of their gender or ethnicity.

This decision has been welcomed by the PPEU and we are currently in the process of establishing your availability for the subject examination. I have been made aware of some of the reactions to the suspension of the policy pending the ongoing OSPRE Review but would encourage your continued support of the examination process.

I look forward to seeing you during the next or future examinations.

Yours sincerely

Glenn Hutton
Superintendent
Head of Police Promotion Examinations Unit

Days later, I received a telephone call from a colleague with connections at the

Home Office who informed me that the Home Office Minister for Policing had picked up a copy of 'The Voice' newspaper as he walked through the reception area on the way to his office; had read the *Black Cops Excluded from Exams'* article. As a result, he had taken immediate steps to ensure the directive from the Police Promotions Examination Board was rescinded with immediate effect.

Although I received further personal correspondence inviting me to return to the fold as an Assessor/role actor, I politely declined the offer; my small protest at the unwillingness of the police establishment to take seriously issues of racial equality.

Chapter 41

Consultant to TV and Film Industry

During 1998, despite the increased demands made on my role as Chair of the Black Police Association, I managed to hold down my duties as a Police Inspector at Vauxhall in South London. As the year progressed, I was offered a role in charge of a neighbourhood policing team at Cavendish Road Police Station in Clapham. I gratefully accepted the position because it offered me a little more time to fulfil my responsibility as BPA Chair.

"There's a call for you, pick up your desk phone," shouted Andrea, my front office clerk at Cavendish Road.

"Inspector Wilson, how can I help?"

"Morning Paul. Ian Blair, Chief Constable of Surrey here."

"Yes, Sir."

"Paul, I would appreciate it if I could come over for a chat with you on Wednesday."

"Sorry, Sir, I am busy on Wednesday."

"How about Thursday?"

"Thursday is not good either."

"When are you free?!", bellowed Chief Constable Blair.

The Chief Constable's sudden change of tone jolted me out of my laid-back manner. His deepened tone coupled with rumours I had heard that he may well be the next Metropolitan Police Commissioner made me quick to turn the conversation around.

"I can do Thursday, Sir; what time suits you?" I responded.

"I can do Thursday afternoon at Cavendish Road police station. Please keep it to yourself and don't make a fuss."

The following Thursday, I was in my office with the door wide open when Andrea walked in.

"There's a bloke sitting in an old open-top sports car at the back gate. Says he's got an appointment with you."

"Yes, Andrea, that will be the Chief Constable of Surrey. Let him in please."

A few minutes later a very relaxed and informally dressed Ian Blair was seated in my office.

"Paul, I have applied for the Met Commissioner's job and if by some chance they give it to me, I need to be up to speed with what's happening from the Black Police Association's perspective."

For the next forty-five minutes, we discussed a range of topics including race and police service delivery issues that were of interest to the BPA and, it seemed, to the Chief Constable.

I was not surprised at Chief Constable Blair's approach. The forthcoming public inquiry into the murder of black student, Stephen Lawrence, had propelled the Black Police Association and its Chair into the media spotlight. This very act brought my attention to individuals and organisations with a keen interest in racism and the future of policing.

Nevertheless, there was no amount of real-world circumstances that could have prepared me for the conversation I would soon have that would introduce me to the world of television drama and movies.

One afternoon, just as I was about to leave my Cavendish Road office, I received a phone call from former Detective Chief Inspector, Jackie Malton. Jackie was well known during her time in the metropolitan police as a tough, no-nonsense detective, who had managed to attain a senior rank in the less than female-friendly, testosterone-fueled Criminal Investigation Department (CID). Jackie's role as a 'Flying Squad' detective had caught the attention of author and screenwriter Lynda La Plante, who based Helen Mirren's character in Prime Suspect on Jackie.

"Paul, you know I do some work advising the TV drama series, The Bill?"

"Yes, Jackie, I heard a rumour that your post-retirement work involved The Bill," I said

"Well, I think the writers of The Bill would really benefit from speaking with you, to get a black perspective of policing from the inside."

"OK, sounds interesting but what does it involve?" I replied curiously.

"We can arrange for you to meet with the scriptwriters at the Sun Hill police station set in Wimbledon."

Two weeks later I parked my car on an industrial estate in Merton, South London and walked up to the front door of the well-known, fictional police station, Sun Hill. As I entered the building, I was struck by the authentic notice board and display cabinets in the front office. I had visited numerous police stations during my career and had I walked into this without knowing it was a TV set, I would not have believed otherwise.

Introductions made, I was shown into a room where a small number of casually dressed men and women, predominantly white, were seated in a semi-circle with notebooks rested on their knees. I was invited to sit out front, facing the group.

My sixty minutes with members of The Bill writing team were insightful and reminded me of the time, about eight years previous, where I had been invited to address a Senior Command Course at Bramshill, the National Police College. The course students on that occasion were all white, male Chief Superintendents from England and Wales. Most of them were destined to be future Chief Officers. The purpose of my invitation, by the course director, had been to help these future Chief Officers understand the experiences and challenges faced by officers from black and minority ethnic backgrounds. As discussions and questions progressed, I was bemused at the fact many of the senior officers denied knowing or even suspecting that black officers in their command might have lived through different experiences than their white counterparts.

However, I had ceased giving such presentations in police training environments as I began to question their worth and was uncomfortable with the voyeuristic dimension that I perceived to be particularly unhealthy. Furthermore, little, if any, thought was ever given to the presenter reliving what were, in some cases, very traumatic experiences. I had concluded that we were cheap and very authentic training props to help future Chief Constables understand what it was to be black in the police with no discernible reward for the black officer, who often recounted very personal and disturbing stories of racist behaviour.

But the writers from The Bill were not senior police officers. They were members of the public with an extremely limited understanding of the nature of racism in the metropolitan police. That had changed at the conclusion of our sixty minutes: their naive rose-tinted view of life in the police had been injected with a large dose of realism.

I had used my experiences at the Bristol Seminar coupled with my time in the Equal Opportunities Unit, where I had encountered and helped mediate and resolve several race-related grievances, to illustrate a Metropolitan Police Service that struggled to acknowledge it had a serious problem accepting the sheer extent of racism that pervaded everyday life for many black officers. My audience of scriptwriters seemed genuinely fascinated by my stories of everyday discrimination and racist language. Unlike some police colleagues, who would try and rationalise or explain away such behaviour as harmless banter not to be taken seriously, the writers from The Bill brought with them their everyday experience of life that substantially did not involve racial banter. I had explained, always a difficult issue for a white audience to grasp, the raft of advantages, often termed 'white privilege', bestowed upon white police colleagues purely because of their racial heritage. Consequently, these officers had little to no understanding or interest in the everyday challenges faced by black police personnel. After all, "everyone was treated the same," a mantra often trotted out by those employed to defend the reputation of the police service. The writers, some visibly moved by our discussion, thanked me profusely for my time and insight and promised to incorporate many of the issues I had raised into their writing.

Satisfied that they had all left Sun Hill police station with a much healthier appreciation of how skin colour adversely impacts so many areas of the police service, both internally as well as externally, I made the short drive back to my home in nearby Wallington.

A few weeks later, I received a telephone call from one of the producers at The Bill.

"Paul, we are planning to introduce our first black detective into the series; a young actor by the name of Karl Collins. Would you mind having a chat with him?"

"Sure, but can he attend Cavendish Road Police Station? My time is a bit limited and he also needs to get acquainted with a real police station."

"Sure, we can arrange that."

A few days later, Andrea popped her head around my office door.

"There's a rather nice young man here to see you - Karl Collins."

"Thanks, Andrea, show him through."

Karl entered my office, and we shook hands and exchanged pleasantries. Karl took a seat in front of my desk. He was a young black guy, in his twenties, dressed in a loose denim top and denim flared jeans. He most certainly did not follow the current fashion trends seen in South London and elsewhere. His large Afro hairstyle only served to confirm this. My first impression of him was that he had just escaped from the stage production of the rock musical 'Hair'.

"This is not an interview Karl, by all accounts you have the job and start work soon," I joked.

"Thanks," he laughed,

"So, how did you, a young black guy get into acting?" I asked.

Karl recounted his early life, growing up on the sprawling Clifton council estate in Nottingham. He recalled the hardships and his entry into Central Junior Television Workshop, which was set up as a casting pool for youngsters based in Nottingham.

"That is some journey and a very inspirational one, given your humble beginnings," I complimented, slowly warming to Karl's quiet personality.

"Thanks, but you know my character in The Bill is a Metropolitan Police detective, quite different to what I've done before. What I'm really interested in is how a black person might be perceived both within the CID and by the public."

"Ok, Karl, I'm pleased you asked that. I will take you into an operational CID office shortly, introduce you to a few colleagues, but before we do that let me give you my perspective of the CID, as a black-uniformed inspector with fifteen years of police service."

Karl listened intently as I recounted my time on the crime squad and my various interactions with CID officers over the years. I tried to give a balanced viewpoint, the good with the not so good. At the Bristol Seminar, I had heard stories from a few black detectives. One detective shared that when seated at his desk on his first morning in the office, he had the logbook used by the office cleaner, someone of African heritage, thrown at him. There was no doubt in my mind that fitting into the CID for a black person was doubly hard and required a raft of additional skills and effort. You would have to perform with perfection while on the job, for you were likely to be subjected to much greater scrutiny than white officers.

Despite being disadvantaged, success was still possible, as we had a few, probably a handful, of seasoned black detectives. This shortlist included my BPA colleague Detective Inspector David Michael, who suffered serious racism from work colleagues following his appointment as Chair of the BPA when he was known as the "civil rights spy in the camp" and a "troublemaker". His health had gradually deteriorated to the extent he had to take a year off work because of the stress. I had personally written to the Assistant Commissioner, Ian Johnson, in my capacity as Chair of the BPA, to bring David's extraordinary circumstances to his attention. Detective Inspector Michael had, earlier this year, reached an out-of-court settlement with the Metropolitan Police after a four-year race discrimination action that nearly destroyed his health.

"Ok, Inspector Wilson, I think I've grasped everything you've said. It's been enormously helpful, but there remains one critical question," Karl said, and then pointed to his hair, "Will my hairstyle be acceptable in the CID?"

"In a moment we will find out because I am going to introduce you to the CID office, and we'll ask the question."

I led Karl out of my office to a building across the yard, where I knew Clapham's Detective Chief Inspector Keith Gausden currently worked. I knew Keith to be very approachable as we had worked together at Battersea police station when he was a uniformed Chief Inspector.

I knocked on Keith's office door and pushed it open. Karl stood behind me.

"Come in," Keith answered from behind his desk.

"Guv, this is Karl Collins; he is an actor with The Bill and is shortly to become a detective constable in the series."

Detective Chief Inspector Gausden and Karl shook hands.

"One particularly important question for you, Guv, would you have Karl working for you in the main office - with his current hairstyle?"

DCI Gausden looked directly at Karl and grinned.

"Absolutely – no problem at all."

I caught the large smile across Karl's face. It was obvious he had just heard the answer he had hoped for.

I walked Karl around the main office where most CID officers worked and introduced him to a couple of colleagues. Afterwards, we made our way out and into the station yard.
I shook Karl's hand.

"Looking forward to seeing you on The Bill, I'm sure you will be great."

"Thank you so much, Inspector Wilson. I now feel better prepared for my new role and look forward to making a start."

Karl Collins' character, DC Danny Glaze, was introduced to The Bill viewers in 1999, complete with Afro hairstyle.

I was interested to get feedback on Karl's first appearance in The Bill. Fortunately, I did not have to wait for long. Geoff Schumann, comedian, and Saturday morning presenter on urban black radio station Choice FM, was quick off the mark.

"Where does the brother think he is going with that hair?"

"Someone, tell him the date."

Schumann's caustic comments on Karl Collin's "unfashionable" hair were to continue and helped build a significant wall of opinion; most of it opposed to Karl's hairstyle. Whether Karl was made aware of this ongoing debate, he kept his hairstyle for months, until at last DC Danny Glaze suddenly, without warning, appeared on screen with short hair. This new style was considered familiar and acceptable to most black radio listeners at that time.

In early 2000 I received another phone call from Jackie Malton.

"Hi Paul, you did such a great job with The Bill. How would you feel about advising on a film that is due to start shooting very soon?"

"I might be interested as long as it is something I can do in my spare time as I have recently been appointed as Police advisor in the Government's Neighbourhood Renewal Unit."

"OK Paul, I'll ask the producers to speak with you and you can make some arrangement regarding your availability."

The following day I received a phone call from a lady who explained that she was one of the film's producers.

"Paul, we have spoken with Jackie and we think you are the right person to help us with our film script for a new production that starts shortly."

It was, she explained, a modern-language version of Othello, with the Moor of Venice, reimagined as the first black Metropolitan Police Commissioner. The film would have a Stephen Lawrence-influenced subplot about police racism and brutality that substitutes for the war between Venice and Turkey.

"What do you think Paul, does it interest you?"

"I love the idea. Just a little concerned about time and, how I can fit it in."

"What we can do is email you the script as we go along. Nothing is set in stone and we'd love to get your viewpoint and input on a regular basis. Something you can do in the evenings; I would have thought."

I was already hooked by the originality of the concept and asked for more detail regarding cast members.

"OK, we have an all-British cast. Playing Othello, we have Eamon Walker, an actor of Grenadian parentage, but someone who has made a name in the United States as "the conflicted Muslim Kareem", in HBO's harrowing prison drama Oz. Playing Jago, we have Christopher Eccleston and Desdemona is played by Keeley Hawes."

My interest was piqued, but I decided not to give an answer there and then.

"Can I call you back tomorrow? I need to establish my availability, given that I have recently started a new role and I'm unsure of my schedule over the next few months."

I slumped back in my chair, stared into space, and allowed the gravity of what had just been said to sink in. I was not familiar with Eamon Walker but had long admired Eccleston's work. Along with Timothy Spall, another favourite, Christopher Eccleston had that apparently effortless ability to portray gritty working-class characters with ease. I also felt that his previous roles probably resonated with me given my own working-class background and chosen profession. As a former Croydon police officer, I had admired his role in the film 'Let Him Have It', based on the true story of Derek Bentley. The main character, played by Eccleston, is a young man hanged for the 1952 murder of PC Sidney Miles, a Croydon police officer. Bentley was convicted as a party to murder, by the English law principle of "joint enterprise". The case became a cause célèbre and, following a forty-five-year campaign, Bentley was granted a posthumous pardon and a couple of years ago the conviction was quashed by the Court. Too late for Derek Bentley but for his family and campaigner's justice, at last, was seen to have been done. Ecclestone had also caught my attention in another drama involving police; 'Hillsborough', where he played the part of Trevor Hicks—a man who lost both of his daughters in the 1989 Hillsborough disaster where it had been alleged a catalogue of police failures had contributed to the death of ninety-six football supporters. But it was his role in 'Our Friends in the North', a BBC drama series that tackled police corruption and the 1980's UK miner's strike among other things, that was to indelibly etch his name in my psyche and that of the British TV viewer.

How could I not get involved? I pondered.

The next day I made the call to the Othello production team.

"Ok, I'm in, I'll do it. When do we start?"

"Well, first, we'd like to introduce you to Eamon Walker. He is the principal actor and plays Othello."

The following week, we met for a cup of coffee. Eamon Walker was a formidable black guy in his early thirties and someone who looked like he spent much time at the gym and was very affable and humble. We talked about his early life and I shared with him stories about my time in the police force and how his forthcoming role would undoubtedly be featured in the mainstream press given that we had never had a black Metropolitan Police Commissioner.

"The likelihood of seeing a black person at the helm of the Metropolitan Police in my lifetime is negligible; so, you are probably the closest to a black Commissioner I will ever see," I laughed.

"That's a very sad state of affairs, Paul, are you sure?" said Eamonn.

"I can't be certain, but unless there is some major cultural turnaround, the Met is likely to remain predominantly white. I do envisage more black officers being recruited, but, for the most part, experience tells me they will remain at the bottom, like a snow-capped mountain."

We both shook our heads in silence.

"Paul, is there any possibility of me getting into New Scotland Yard and perhaps meeting the Commissioner? It would help to bring some reality to the role," said Eamon, with a mischievous grin.

I laughed, "That's a big ask Eamon, but let me see what I can do."

Commissioner Sir John Stevens was now in office and I enjoyed a reasonable relationship with him. In fact, he was very approachable, but as Commissioner his diary was closely guarded. Perhaps the Deputy Commissioner, Ian Blair, former Chief Constable of Surrey, would indulge me.

A short phone call to the Deputy Commissioner's office at New Scotland Yard was enough to secure me an appointment with Deputy Commissioner Ian Blair, who had expressed his willingness to meet with the actor.

I arranged to meet with Eamonn outside of New Scotland Yard, next to the famous revolving sign; a favourite point of reference for many in the news media.

"Hi Eamonn, excellent timekeeping. You really are getting into your new role," I joked as Eamonn walked toward me.

"Ok, the plan is this, we go into New Scotland Yard; I've already arranged your security clearance. Then we will take the lift to the fifth floor, where we will find the Deputy Commissioner's office. Once we are introduced, we just go with the flow. It might be an idea to explain the plot to the Deputy as I am sure he will be familiar with the Shakespeare play. Just take any and every opportunity to ask him questions along the way."

"OK", nodded Eamon, displaying the slightest trace of nervousness.

Surely not, I thought to myself, as we walked into the lobby area at New Scotland Yard, *this man has made a career out of acting on the big screen and TV, yet here he is anxious at the prospect of meeting the Deputy Commissioner of Police.*

We entered the lift, which was already occupied by Bob Cox, Director of

News at New Scotland Yard. He looked surprised to see me. Perhaps it was the sight of two large black men in his lift.

"Hi, Bob, this is actor Eamon Walker; we have an appointment to see the Deputy,"

Bob's surprised look increased.

"I didn't know about that." said Bob.

I remained silent, not wishing to be drawn into a conversation with someone who, a few years earlier, had invited me for a Sunday night drink at a South London pub in a blatant, but clumsy, attempt to establish why I was such an outspoken critic of the Metropolitan Police's numerous attempts to portray itself as an organisation on top of its racism problem.

A bell signaled that we had reached the fifth floor and both me and Eamon walked out.

Our meeting with Deputy Commissioner Ian Blair lasted about thirty minutes. During that, time Eamonn's questions about protocol, dress uniform and other trivia issues were graciously answered in full by the Deputy Commissioner. He showed obvious signs of intrigue by the actor's forthcoming role.

"I thought that went well," I surmised as we made our way to the lift.

"Definitely, a really nice guy," said Eamonn.

"Yes, he has a reputation as a progressive thinker. Although, I'm not convinced that is necessarily a good thing in this line of work," I said.

Over the next weekend, I received my first email from the production team at Othello.

The script involved police officers who had executed a search warrant at the address of a black man who, it was claimed, had wielded a knife at officers. As officers tried to arrest the suspect, he sustained serious injuries and was now hospitalised. News of the police search and brutalisation of a black man had spread through the local community, sparking sporadic outbreaks of disorder that culminated in a violent protest outside a local police station.

Paul, we want Othello to address and quell the rioters while standing on the steps of the police station. What might he say to gathered protesters on the brink of a full-scale riot?

I gave thought to what I expected a black senior police officer would say and crafted a speech.

Brothers and sisters, you know who I am…born here, grew up on these streets, went to school here…what are we to do now, burn down the police station, torch cars, loot shops…is that what you want?

Before you go ahead, stop and take a second because the world is watching tonight…Is that the way you want the world to see us? What will the world call us then, ignorant fools? You know they will. So, my friends, I promise you this, if Billy Coates was unlawfully killed there will be no escape for his killers, no place for him to hide, that is a promise…

We have our dignity…people want justice but justice under the law, justice under the law…

I read and re-read, hitting the send button when I felt satisfied with my work.

Chapter 42

On the Set

A few days later I received a further email, this time inviting me to attend the film set as an observer.

I had to be in Pall Mall, in central London, by 10.30 am to make it on time to see them begin filming at 11.00 am at the address of a renowned Gentlemen's club. I arrived promptly at 10.30 am and made myself known to the receptionist, who summoned one of the film production crew.

"Follow me, Inspector Wilson; I'll take you to Mr. Walker's caravan."

We walked out of the club and around the corner to where a large silver caravan was parked. The film crew member knocked on the door. It was opened and a smartly dressed Eamonn Walker stepped out onto the pavement.

"Hi, Paul, good to see you. Come in."

I stepped into the caravan, looked around and saw that the well-appointed van was equipped to serve as Eamonn Walker's retreat and office. It had all the trappings of home comfort, bar, TV and computer console.

"So, the scene we are shooting today is a discussion; a chat between myself and Jago. We'll both be seated for the duration of our conversation."

Not remarkably interesting, I thought to myself, *but not to worry, I am sure it will be educational if nothing else.* I was disappointed though; I'd rather hoped I might see a fight scene.

"First thing we need to do is to introduce you to Christopher Eccleston and his team. They should know who you are and the role you have; it's a matter of courtesy."

"Sure, I understand," I said.

I followed Eamonn up the steps of the Gentlemen's club and passed the reception into a grand hall, where I saw numerous people milling around with various large pieces of camera equipment positioned around the perimeter. Two large, sumptuous looking, leather chairs had been positioned in the centre of the hall.

I looked around and instantly recognised Christopher Eccleston, who was seated on the far side of the hall, surrounded by four or five people who busily adjusted his clothes and dabbed his face with what I assumed was make-up. Eamonn walked toward him and I followed.

"Chris, this is Paul Wilson; he's an Inspector with the Met Police and he's advising us on a number of scenes."

Christopher Eccleston looked up in my direction, smiled and immediately stood up, stepped toward me, and shook my hand.

"Good to meet you, Paul, hope you enjoy today."

At that moment, my recent musings about Christopher Ecclestone's star-spangled career flashed through my mind. *Should I take the opportunity to impress him with my encyclopedic knowledge of his previous work, or would I appear to be a fawning sycophant and embarrass him and me?* My conservative automatic pilot took over in such moments of indecision.

"Good to meet you too and yes, I'm looking forward to it."

We retreated to Eamonn's caravan where his female assistant was waiting with last-minute instructions.

At precisely 11 am, I followed Eamonn and his assistant onto the film set and was given a seat against the perimeter wall, from where I had an excellent view of the proceedings. However, after an hour or so it dawned on me that this was going to be a long day. This realisation came to me as I witnessed the filming start only for it to stop and be repeated from a different camera angle. Close up shots, followed by intermediate shots followed by distance shots. This was a repetitive cycle for each piece of dialogue. To film a short conversation took hours with constant breaks for refreshments and touch-up from the makeup artists. It was during the breaks that I noted something unusual. Christopher Eccleston retreated to his corner and conversed with his entourage, and Eamonn Walker did likewise. There did not appear to be any friendly chatter between the two once the camera had ceased filming. I approached one of the film crew and asked why this was.

"Eccleston is considered the bigger star, but in this movie, he's playing second fiddle to a lesser-known actor and I guess that might explain what's going on."

At each break, I peered over at the noisy exaggerated behaviour that emanated from the small area occupied by Eccleston's entourage. The mannerisms, glances, false laughter, and a copious amount of backslapping and high fiving suggested to me that they were trying to outdo or belittle Walker's people. I put this to Eamonn, and he would neither confirm nor deny my suspicions. Later in the afternoon, bored beyond belief, I had left the film set with a changed perception of acting and movie making. Although I had witnessed a seated conversation between two actors that on-screen would last five minutes, it had taken the best part of the day to film. In addition, I had witnessed diva-like behaviour that I might have expected from a teenager, but certainly not from a mature film star of working-class origins.

In the following days, I received further emailed scripts to read and comment upon. This entailed me applying my experience and common sense to what the scriptwriters wished to portray. I was given a free rein by the scriptwriters and used a red font to highlight my displeasure, ideas or deletions. There was of course no guarantee that my input would be taken seriously by the writing team.

The recent script in my email inbox detailed a new twist in the police evidence. Now, it seemed that the black suspect had not wielded a knife but had "got his penis out and waved it at a male police officer". These actions enraged the police officer causing him to lose his temper, which led to a brutal assault of the suspect, causing him serious injury, hospitalisation and death. I felt compelled to emphasise my displeasure at the extraordinary, and, in my view, unbelievable nature of what was being presented,

I know of no black man that would get out his penis and wave it at a male police officer, I think we have white female fantasy at play in this scene and I would suggest it is rewritten, is the view I expressed to the white female scriptwriters. The following day a further email arrived with absolutely no reference to my protestations, but this was the nature of my relationship with the script production team. Weeks of email exchange elapsed until I was finally advised that all filming of Othello had been completed. A few months later, I received an invitation from Othello production staff to attend a special event at the headquarters of The British Academy of Film and Television Arts (BAFTA) Piccadilly, in London's Mayfair.

I was excited to have been invited to this prestigious venue, but with little background information provided I assumed the invitation had been extended to all staff involved in making Othello, by way of a thank you. As I walked through the doors into the sumptuous surrounds of the BAFTA building, I was still under the impression that Othello had been a low budget made for television film. After all, this is what I had been led to believe by the production team. This assumption was dispelled once I was seated in the grandiose hall with a copy of the evening's programme in my lap. As I leafed through the glossy brochure, I noted that Othello was financed by LWT Productions and Canadian Broadcasting and had won twelve awards including the BAFTA TV Award, International Critics Prize, Broadcasting Press Guild Award, Best Single Drama and Royal TV Society UK, along with a clutch of nominations.

As I sat, engrossed in the programme notes, I felt a tap on my shoulder. I looked up to see a young lady I recognised from the production team, accompanied by an older gentleman.

"Paul, this is Andrew Davies, creator of Othello; Andrew, Paul is our police adviser."

I sprang to my feet and Andrew Davies profusely shook my extended hand.

"Thanks for all your work Paul; it's greatly appreciated, I hope you enjoy the evening."

Later in the evening, with copious amounts of food and bubbly consumed, I settled back to watch speeches from those involved in the film's production. Andrew Davies was called onto the stage and was presented with one of the many awards I had just read about. His acceptance speech mentioned his colleagues, actors, and others whom he thanked profusely for making the film possible.

"I'd just like to mention our editing and special effects department for their sterling work, in particular the scene involving a naked Chris Eccleston crouched on the edge of the bath; I'm sure you all recall it. Well, Chris's bollocks were hanging down so low that we had to laser them out of the final production."

The assembled audience exploded into loud laughter and rapturous applause.

I later watched the film in its entirety and gleefully made a mental note of my contributions to the script. My powerful speech delivered by Othello on the steps of the police station as he faced the angry baying mob had survived mostly unedited. My reference to a positive action recruitment initiative for black police officers had been edited but remained an early and powerful statement for the outgoing Commissioner of Police.   However, I was disappointed to see that my protestations regarding the 'penis waving scene' had fallen on deaf ears; it had remained. But my interest piqued as the final credits rolled down the screen, prompting some people to get up and collect their belongings. But not me, I remained in my chair, eyes fixated on the big screen. I nudged my neighbour. "There it is!", I exclaimed, pointing at the rolling credits.

Police Adviser – Paul Wilson

Chapter 43

Institutional Racism

December 1997 was cold; a dark month and like many I was looking forward to the holiday season. However, on the 16th that all changed.

Sitting in my office reading the morning newspaper it quickly became apparent that the media were once again focused on the tragic events surrounding the racist murder of a black student, Stephen Lawrence. As I read the article, I reflected on the four years that had passed since that fateful evening in Eltham, South East London, when eighteen-year-old Stephen and his friend were standing at a bus stop where they were approached by a group of white youths who were shouting racial slurs. Stephen's friend made good his escape, but Stephen was surrounded by the youths and stabbed twice. He attempted to run away but collapsed and bled to death near to the scene of the attack.

The police investigation into the murder of Stephen Lawrence just beggared belief. The Metropolitan Police was world renowned for its professionalism and competence in bringing the perpetrators of many infamous and serious crimes to justice. Yet the Stephen Lawrence murder investigation was riven with such gross incompetence and negligence that some police officers I knew, black and white, believed corruption and/or racism must have been a contributory factor in the quite astonishing investigative oversights that had occurred.

Following what was yet another shameful milestone in the Metropolitan Police's checkered relationship with London's black community, the BPA had not hesitated in supporting Stephen's parents, Doreen, and Neville, in their campaign for justice. The Lawrence's 'thank you' letter remained proudly affixed to the BPA's office noticeboard.

It was common knowledge that Stephen's parents shared serious misgivings about the incompetent nature of their son's murder investigation and had made an official complaint to the Police Complaints Authority (PCA). The neighbouring police force of Kent was commissioned by the PCA to enquire into the nature of the complaint and their findings had now been published. My newspaper, *The Independent*, probably encapsulated the mood of many newspapers and broadcasters, with its headline:

'Stephen Lawrence police weren't racists, just staggeringly incompetent.'

The 'Kent Police report' had disclosed an astonishing catalogue of errors on the part of the Metropolitan Police murder investigation team but found there to be 'no evidence of racism', *that's not really surprising,* I thought to myself, *they wouldn't recognise it if it was apparent.*

The morning after the newspaper coverage of the Kent Police revelation, I received a telephone call from Trevor Hall, who was now an adviser to Home Secretary Jack Straw.

"Paul, can you pop over to see me? I need to have a chat with you," said Trevor in his lilting Barbadian accent.

That same day, in the afternoon, I walked to the Home Office in Queen Anne's gate, across the street from St James' Park London Underground Station and just around the corner from New Scotland Yard.

"I've got an appointment to see Trevor Hall," I informed the lady receptionist, holding open my police warrant card.

With the necessary security pass hanging around my neck, I made my way upstairs. Standing outside Trevor Hall's open office door, I knocked and stepped inside. Trevor was seated behind a large paper filled desk. He beckoned me into his spacious office with its corner window view over St James' Park.

"Take a seat, Paul."

As I sat down, Trevor stood up and began slowly pacing around the office. "You've seen the newspaper reports about Kent Constabulary's findings?"

"Oh, yes. Nothing of surprise. 'The Metropolitan Police bungled the murder investigation but none of the investigating officers were racist at any stage,'" I recited with more than a hint of sarcasm.

"That's the one," responded Trevor, now pacing back and forth, and wringing his hands as if giving a lecture on a heartfelt subject.

"But what they failed to understand is just how racism works," he remarked. "Even here in the Home Office, they're in denial. They do not understand or accept that institutional racism presents a significant challenge for the police."

I nodded my head, but in my mind, I was thinking back to my attendance at a black history evening class in Norbury, South London during the early eighties. There, our knowledgeable Rastafarian tutor had introduced me to the concept of institutional racism. I had then found it a slippery issue to get my head around.

Trevor paused in his pacing and turned to look at me. His stern expression told me that he expected me to comment on his pronouncement. "There's a tendency not to talk about institutional racism in the police. After all, didn't Lord Scarman's report into the 1981 Brixton riots make it very clear that the Metropolitan Police was not institutionally racist?" I voiced in a tone that suggested I wanted to believe Trevor, but the Lord Scarman ruling was giving me second thoughts. "Well, you can choose to believe Lord Scarman's view of the world, but I'm here to tell you that institutional racism is a problem for the police," at which point Trevor sat down in his chair and rocked backwards with arms folded across his chest, looking at me directly in the face.

His body language said it all, *what are you going to do about it?*

As I left Trevor's office, his words still echoing in my ears. I recounted our conversation, asking myself, *what just happened in there?*

The Home Secretary's close adviser had summoned the Chair of the Black Police Association, not for a cosy fireside chat but to emphasise the importance of a matter he undoubtedly believed to be a crucial element of the investigation into the murder of Stephen Lawrence.

I walked down Victoria Street, oblivious to the chilly London air, too busy thinking of my next step. I was not well-versed with the concept of institutional racism and before I could support or dismiss it, I needed to better understand it.

That evening was spent at my home computer where I trawled the world wide web. My search engine had taken me to the seminal work of Stokely Carmichael and Charles V Hamilton, authors of *Black Power: The Politics of Liberation.*

After spending what seemed like an eternity glaring closely at my antiquated computer screen, reading and re-reading, the penny finally dropped. Pushing back my chair, I stood up and began excitedly walking around the room. Of course, now it all made sense. *My damascene moment had arrived!*

But I'm guessing those Kent police officers had never been exposed to Stokely Carmichael and Charles Hamilton, I thought to myself.

Feeling confident in the belief that I now had the same understanding of institutional racism as Trevor Hall, I sat at my computer and began typing a letter addressed to 'The Voice', *Britain's Best-Read Black Newspaper.* After hitting *send,* I just sat there, and furthermore wondered whether they would print it.

Walking into my local newspaper shop at the end of the week, I saw just two copies of *The Voice* on the bottom shelf. This was the price I paid for living in leafy suburbia as local newsagents, in the belief that black people only lived in the inner cities, generally did not bother stocking many copies of *The Voice.* I turned the pages until I found the prominently placed article.

Britain's Black cops have joined the family of murdered teenager Stephen Lawrence in slamming the report into the police investigation of his murder. By Paul Macey

"The Police Complaints Authority (PCA) report cleared the investigating police officers of racist conduct. But Paul Wilson of the Black Police Association (BPA) which looks after the interests of Black officers in the force, told The Voice, "We remain unconvinced that those conducting the PCA inquiry possess the appropriate skills and understanding to determine whether institutionalised racism had any effect on the decisions made by those responsible for the murder investigation."

I purchased a copy and took it home where I read and re-read the article. I felt pleased that I had taken a stand on this issue but, a little concerned that I had not discussed it at length with members of the BPA Executive. Later in the day, I received a message from one of my colleagues in the BPA office.

"Assistant Commissioner O'Connor has been in touch. He wants the Chair, and all members of the BPA Executive to meet with him this afternoon, at New Scotland Yard."

What does he want? I thought to myself, *he has not been in the Metropolitan Police that long; probably wants to introduce himself to the BPA Executive.*

All the members of my Executive Committee assembled at New Scotland Yard, on the appointed floor at the given time.

Within two minutes we were joined by Assistant Commissioner O'Connor. He was a middle-aged white man in a dark grey suit *who for the first time in his sparkling policing career was about to occupy the same office space as eight black British police personnel,* I theorised to myself.

"Thanks for coming guys; just let me find us an empty office," he said, darting along the corridor trying each of the locked door handles.

He seems friendly enough, I observed, as I looked at the pensive expressions on the faces of my colleagues. Some of them were junior in grade and rank and certainly not used to meeting with Assistant Commissioners.

"Here we are, come in," said O'Connor, who had finally found an unlocked office.

"Not your office, I'm guessing?" I spoke, hoping to break the ice.

"No, these are for the use of Commanders," apprised O'Connor, ignoring the invitation for a friendly riposte.

Once inside, us members of the BPA Executive sat on chairs backed against the wood-paneled wall of the office while O'Connor sat, with legs crossed, in front of the large wooden desk.

"So, what's this nonsense about institutional racism?", questioned O'Connor in his unmistakably Irish accent.

So that is why we were summoned, I thought to myself.

I knew from my time at New Scotland Yard that each morning the Directorate of Public Affairs (DPA) would circulate a briefing pack: a collection of police-related newspaper clippings from the major newspapers. Included in this pack was *The Voice* newspaper, given its prominence in the Black community. These press clippings, I guessed, would be a standing item at the Police Commissioner's morning get-together with his Management Board, a meeting colloquially referred to as *morning prayers*.

I imagined the scenario: each member of Management Board would have finished reading my article and collectively agreed that these misfits 'need to be spoken to.'

As Chairman of the BPA and author of the letter in *The Voice*, I felt an overwhelming sense of responsibility to shield my colleagues by fielding the Assistant Commissioner's increasingly biting questions; particularly because I had not yet had the opportunity to adequately discuss our stance on the issue of institutional racism. This alone probably explained why many of the Executive remained quiet and expressionless during the Assistant Commissioner's questions and assertions about institutional racism, or rather, the absence of it. We had been ambushed by a well-prepared Assistant Commissioner and I felt complicit because, of my failure to sufficiently brief my colleagues on what I had meant in my letter to *The Voice*.

"You know what Lord Scarman said about institutional racism?" inquired O'Connor[3], looking directly at me.

"He preferred the rotten apples theory," I answered.

"He didn't say anything about rotten apples; I suggest you read what he did say," said O'Connor.

Within the space of a few days, I was again on the receiving end of a lecture on the issue of institutional racism.

This was not going well; despite my reading of Carmichael and

---

[3] I later discovered that a young Chief Inspector O'Connor had been seconded to the '81 Lord Scarman Inquiry and had travelled to the United States where he met with members of the National Organisation of Black Law Enforcement Executives (NOBLE). His mission; to gain experience of maintaining law and order sensitively in a multi-ethnic society.

Hamilton's seminal work, I was unable to sufficiently challenge the Lord Scarman viewpoint so expertly expressed and supported by the Assistant Commissioner. There was also another powerful element to our discussion, that of rank and one that by tradition promoted subservience in interactions. Although I was Chair of the BPA, I was also an Inspector, someone significantly junior in rank to an Assistant Commissioner. I could not help but think, *there comes a point when sticking to your guns by mounting a vociferous argument is construed as insubordination.*

O'Connor eventually got to his feet, a signal surely that he was about to put us out of our misery.

"He's still around you know, Lord Scarman. Lovely old gentleman," stated O'Connor as he walked to the door and held it open to allow a glum Executive to file out like some funeral procession. As she passed me, the expression on my colleague Deborah Thomas's face said it all. It screamed at me, *You idiot, what have you done?*
O'Connor turned to face me as I reached the office door,

"Institutional racism is an outdated, unproven '60s American concept that has no place in today's society."

"We'll see," I remarked smiling, as I left the office to join my colleagues.

We gathered at the lift lobby and I explained to the still sullen faces that I would put things right and that they had nothing to worry about. This was part and parcel of being a BPA Executive member after all.

Deep down, I was angry with myself for not putting together a cogent argument to counter O'Connor's strident viewpoint. Most of all, I felt a sense of guilt for putting the Executive through what had been a friendly enough ordeal, but nevertheless a dressing down from one of the Metropolitan Police's most senior officers. I had to keep my word to the Executive and put things right.

As far as I was concerned, O'Connor's parting comment was a metaphorical gauntlet and I had picked it up!

That evening, I took Assistant Commissioner O'Connor's advice and, logged onto my home computer, where I found a copy of Lord Scarman's Report into the 1981 Brixton disorders.

Many consider Scarman's following observation to be central in rebutting any argument suggesting the police to be infected with institutional racism. This was certainly the conclusion obliquely referred to by Assistant Commissioner O'Connor in our earlier meeting.

'The direction and policies of the Metropolitan Police are not racist. I totally and unequivocally reject the attack made upon the integrity and impartiality of the senior direction of the force. The criticisms lie elsewhere - in errors of judgment, in a lack of imagination and flexibility, but not in deliberate bias or prejudice.' (Para 4.62, p 64).

Interestingly, a common thread throughout Lord Scarman's pronouncements on suggestions of racism within the police was his protection of senior police officers in the Force, while apparently happy to throw junior officers under the proverbial bus.

'...*some police officers, particularly those below the level of the senior direction of the force were guilty of ill-considered immature and racially prejudiced actions .... in their dealings on the streets with young black people.*' (Para 4.63, p 64).

This view that some or a few police officers were responsible for racist acts against black people was picked up by the media and others and termed the 'few rotten apples', a metaphor that had failed to impress Assistant Commissioner O'Connor.

If the Black Police Association was to prove Lord Scarman mistaken in his diagnosis, then we would need to enlist some big guns.

Trevor Hall immediately sprang to mind as someone to help counter the O'Connor/Scarman viewpoint. As a civil servant, Hall would not be able to express his privately held views in public. I had to find someone else to help fight in our corner. Luckily, it was not long before someone came to mind.

I had first met Dr. Robin Oakley during my posting to the Bristol Seminar project. Subsequently, I had encountered him again when he was a specialist adviser to the Home Office. Dr. Oakley was an impressive and widely respected academic devoted to human rights and racial equality issues. What also spoke in his favour was Dr. Oakley's background; for a white, male, Oxbridge graduate would hold great sway with the white, male, senior police fraternity. After all, Commissioner Sir Paul Condon was himself an Oxbridge alumnus.

The irony that we might employ *white privilege* to further the goals of the Black Police Association was not lost on me as I sat hunched over my desk with one pressing thought on my mind, *how might I approach Dr. Oakley and what I should say to him?*

I bit the bullet and phoned Dr. Robin Oakley the following day. "Hi Robin, Paul Wilson here. Yesterday, the BPA had a difficult meeting with a senior police officer, who rubbished the notion that institutional racism has any place in modern society and is definitely unwilling to accept it exists in policing."

"I'm afraid it's not acknowledged or understood in police circles and any mention of it will have been red rag to a bull," said Robin in a calm, measured tone of voice.

"But what can we do Robin; is there something you could help us present to the Commissioner?"

"You're right Paul; something has to be done. The Macpherson Inquiry might be the place to air the subject in a rational manner. Let me draft something and I'll get back to you," offered Robin in an excited tone of voice.

I knew only a little about the terms of reference for the recently established public inquiry into matters surrounding the murder of Stephen Lawrence. The BPA had certainly not considered the Inquiry to be a vehicle for airing major issues in the way Dr. Oakley had suggested.

Within about one hour I received an email from Dr. Oakley. I eagerly opened the attachment and began to read.

When I finished, I dabbed my moist eyes, slumped back in my seat, and stared silently at the ceiling, allowing what I had just read to percolate through my senses. A massive surge of euphoric relief gradually flooded my being, for Dr. Oakley's note[4] had for the first time crystalised in academic terms an experience that I had lived through. This was a monumental development in the short history of the BPA, as a renowned academic had just presented a powerful and eloquent argument that outlined why institutional racism was an issue for the metropolitan police in such a way that the Met[5], or indeed anyone else, would find exceedingly difficult to refute. (see annex A, page 363)

My lengthy discussions with Dr. Oakley about institutional racism in policing had given me the clarity and confidence to enable me to place my thoughts on paper.

Time was pressing; we had now received two requests from the Stephen Lawrence Inquiry administration office inviting the BPA to produce a paper. The BPA submission was briefly discussed at our Executive meeting, but I knew the task fell to me. It was very apparent to everyone that my recent deliberations with Dr. Oakley had energised me to discuss the subject of institutional racism, to the extent it became a central tenet of any discussion about the BPA submission.

The written BPA submission to the Stephen Lawrence Inquiry would provide examples of what we considered to be institutional racism. After giving the matter much thought, I decided to include three persuasive

---

[4] Dr. Robin Oakley's note on *Institutional Racism* was submitted to the Stephen Lawrence Inquiry in April 1998. The content was publicised and ignited considerable discourse within policing circles and the wider general public around the issue of institutional racism and the police.

[5] "Following a series of dialogues with Dr Oakley, some of them quite heated, it became apparent to me just how far the debate regarding institutional racism had progressed since the days of Lord Scarman" - Deputy Assistant Commissioner John Grieve - p.11 Institutional Racism and the Police: Fact or Fiction? (2000) Institute for the Study of Civil Society

examples.

'In October 1997, the Police Promotions Examination Board decided that the presence of minority ethnic role players in the national police assessment examination presented most candidates with a "different stimuli" and as a result all minority ethnic role actors/assessors were advised that their services would no longer be required for future examinations'.

This was an issue that had personally affected me but that aside it was one of the most powerful examples of institutional racism that I could recall in my policing career.

'In April 1998, a serious crime occurred in North London. The suspects were black males who made their getaway in a vehicle. The Detective Chief Inspector in charge of the investigation transmitted a message to each control room in the metropolitan police. Included within the text of the message was the following: "all vehicles containing IC3 (black) males should be approached with caution."'

On investigating the source and reaction to the message I discovered that only one person officially challenged the content of the message, a member of the BPA. Such was the routine stereotyping of black people within the metropolitan police, when a message of this nature was brought to the attention of thousands of police personnel it was not only deemed acceptable, but served to reinforce existing stereotype. A stereotype that in my view had continually resulted in the disproportionate stop and search of black people during my policing career.

The final example was 'low hanging fruit' but nevertheless an important illustration of institutional racism.

'Cursory analysis of the latest metropolitan police personnel demographic illustrates the significant under-representation of black and minority ethnic personnel in senior police ranks. An almost identical profile is mirrored within the civil support staff grade structure. The ethnic profiles graphically illustrate the lack of progression of both police and civil staff of African and African Caribbean origin. The figures beg the question - why has the Metropolitan Police not taken remedial action allowed for within the Race Relations Act, 1976?'

With my draft paper circulated to the Executive, I asked members for feedback. A couple of typos were apparent and must be rectified before submission to the Stephen Lawrence Inquiry offices in Elephant and Castle. However, with literally days before the submission deadline, my role as Duty Inspector at Kennington Police Station proved to be the busiest night duty that I had known. So much so, that the deadline for submission approached and passed. Still determined to get the papers to the Inquiry Office as close to the deadline as possible, at about 4am I climbed into my police car and made the short drive to Hannibal House, Elephant and Castle. I parked outside the Elephant and Castle shopping centre. Equipped with the BPA submission stuffed inside my jacket, I walked up to the front entrance, expecting to see a post box of some description. There was none. Even more discouraging, security grilles prevented access to the inner building.

I walked around the complex to the rear of the Centre. It was dark but the glow from adjacent streetlights faintly illuminated a dingy yard used as storage for vegetable market stalls. I carefully picked my way through various stacks of wooden pallets and half-empty crates of rotting vegetables, before reaching the rear perimeter of the building. I had seen a staircase, most probably a fire escape, and began climbing. At the top of the stairs was a highly polished wooden door. Thinking that this door most probably provided access to the suites of offices, I removed the neatly addressed brown envelope from my tunic jacket and carefully slid it under the door.

My concern that the envelope would not be found was allayed the following afternoon when the BPA office was notified of its receipt and of our invitation to appear before the Stephen Lawrence Inquiry panel.

The invitation was gladly accepted.

On the second day of the Inquiry, myself, along with my BPA colleagues, Bevan Powell and Leroy Logan attended Hannibal House.

We entered the cavernous Inquiry room, which was packed with public and press galleries. Our Metropolitan Police colleagues, clustered in an area on the far side of the Inquiry room, turned and acknowledged our presence. I nodded, smiled, reciprocating their gesture, but decided to remain a healthy distance from our police colleagues.

The physical distance between black police personnel and white police personnel, giving quite different testimony about matters of racism in the metropolitan police at a high-profile public inquiry, was not only unprecedented in the history of The Met but would be a powerful image for observers to behold.

I was anxious to get underway. My usual stress coping mechanism had already kicked in and I was ready and raring to present my version of life inside the police. One most definitely at odds with the Lord Scarman/O'Connor viewpoint. The following is an excerpt from The Stephen Lawrence Inquiry report.

6.28 The oral evidence of the three representatives of the MPS Black Police Association was illuminating. It should be read in full, but we highlight two passages from Inspector Paul Wilson's evidence:

(Part 2, Day 2, p 209): "The term institutional racism should be understood to refer to the way the institution or the organisation may systematically or repeatedly treat, or tend to treat, people differentially because of their race. So, in effect, we are not talking about the individuals within the service who may be unconscious as to the nature of what they are doing, but it is the net effect of what they do."

(Part 2, Day 2, p 211): "A second source of institutional racism is our culture, our culture within the police service. Much has been said about our culture, the canteen culture, the occupational culture. How and why does that impact on individuals, black individuals on the street? Well, we would say the occupational culture within the police service, given the fact that the majority of police officers are white, tends to be the white experience, the white beliefs, the white values. Given the fact that these predominantly white officers only meet members of the black community in confrontational situations, they tend to stereotype black people in general. This can lead to all sorts of negative views and assumptions about black people, so we should not underestimate the occupational culture within the police service as being a primary source of institutional racism in the way that we differentially treat black people. Interestingly I say 'we' because there is no marked difference between black and white in the force essentially. We are all consumed by this occupational culture. Some of us may think we rise above it on some occasions, but, generally speaking, we tend to conform to the norms of this occupational culture, which we say is all powerful in shaping our views and perceptions of a particular community."

"We believe that it is essential that the views of these officers should be closely heeded and respected."

With our testimony concluded me, Bevan and Leroy filed past the Inquiry bench on our way to the exit and as we did so the Bishop of Stepney, the Right Rev Dr John Sentamu leaned forward and said, "Chairman, there is but one human race, yet you seem to believe in the concept of many different races."

I was momentarily taken aback. What was the point he was making and why now? And then it dawned on me. The Bishop was making an oblique reference to the title of the BPA written submission, *'Identifying and addressing the issues around the failure of a police occupational culture to embrace the importance and needs of a multi-racial community.'* My use of the term *multi-racial* denoted the existence of different races. Emotionally drained and physically exhausted from giving testimony I had no energy or inclination for an exchange of views with the Bishop. I smiled and continued walking toward the exit. The 350-page Stephen Lawrence Inquiry report concluded that the investigation into the killing of Stephen Lawrence had been 'marred by a combination of professional incompetence, institutional racism and a failure of leadership'.

The Inquiry upheld our argument that Institutional Racism exists within the police service;

"6.39 Given the central nature of the issue we feel that it is important at once to state our conclusion that institutional racism, within the terms of its description set out in Paragraph 6.34 above, exists both in the Metropolitan Police Service and in other Police Services and other institutions countrywide."

The Inquiry defined institutional racism as:

"6.34 [...] the collective failure of an organisation to provide an appropriate and professional service to people because of their colour, culture, or ethnic origin. It can be seen or detected in processes, attitudes, and behaviour which amount to discrimination through unwitting prejudice, ignorance thoughtlessness, and racist stereotyping which disadvantage minority ethnic people."

On the issue of the Kent Police Report, the Stephen Lawrence Inquiry agreed with the content of my letter to *The Voice'* newspaper,

"44.11 insofar as [the Kent Police Report] suggests that regard was paid to the allegation that institutional racism may have influenced officers in the case, we cannot accept the conclusion [...] that there was "no evidence to support the allegation of racist conduct." No overt racism, other than perhaps the use of inappropriate language, was evident. But the conclusion that there was a 'collective failure' to provide an appropriate and professional service to the Lawrence family because of their colour, culture, and ethnic origin is in our view inescapable."

Banner headlines appeared in all major newspapers following publication of the Inquiry's report;

Watershed for a fairer Britain' (Evening Standard);

'An historic race relations revolution' (Daily Mail)';

'Dossier of shame that will change the face of Britain's race relations' (Daily Mirror);

'Racists won't win' (The Sun);

'Never ever again' (Express);

'Findings should open all our eyes' (Daily Telegraph).

Chapter 44

The Home Secretary

On Monday, January 12th, 1998, I was the Duty Inspector at Kennington Police Station in South London when Home Secretary, Jack Straw walked into the front office of the station with his son, William. It was a pre-arranged visit; William was to receive a police caution for supplying a controlled drug to a newspaper reporter a few weeks previous. *This was a moment dreaded by many parents; having to haul your son into a police station,* I thought to myself as I followed the Home Secretary and his son into a very crowded Custody Office to complete the necessary procedures.

I liked Jack Straw, he lived just down the road from Kennington Police Station, his modest home made all the more visible by the twenty-four-hour protection afforded him by officers from the Diplomatic Protection Group. Perhaps it was his humble Essex Council estate upbringing that endeared him to so many working-class people across the political divide.

A few weeks following that incident I received a telephone call from the Home Office, "Inspector Wilson, in your role as Chair of the Black Police Association, would you be available to meet with the Home Secretary?"

"Yes, of course, when?" I responded in an instant

We are thinking the end of March, would that be suitable?

"Yes," I replied, trying to sound cool, calm and collected.

"Good, we will confirm the time and date in writing, by the end of next week."

"Thank you, look forward to it," I said.

I reported my conversation back to the BPA Executive Committee and the question on everyone's lips was, 'What does the Home Secretary want with the Black Police Association?'

This was not an unusual question given that four years had elapsed since our launch but during this time the BPA had experienced minimal support and recognition from the Met, or indeed anyone in the wider policing family. We had to continually make a case for basic resources and only because of our internal contacts had we managed to secure a small basement office with phone line and fax machine. However, since the Home Secretary's announcement of a Public Inquiry into the murder of Stephen Lawrence, we had noticed an improvement of late as senior officers gradually included BPA Executive members in meetings and began to involve us in a range of consultation, but an audience with the Home Secretary was beyond our wildest expectations.

Mindful that Black Police Associations had now emerged in a number of police forces across the country, many of whom were seeking recognition and an advocacy platform, I contacted Ravi Chand from the Bedfordshire Police Black and Asian Staff Support Group (BASS) to confirm whether he would be interested in accompanying myself and members of the Metropolitan Police BPA at the meeting with the Home Secretary. However, inquiries of the Home Office to establish the numbers I was able to invite, revealed that my invitations should be limited to the Metropolitan BPA. This advice did not sit well with me and I decided to ignore it, as Chair I would choose whom to invite.

On Monday 30th March 1998, myself and BPA Executive colleagues, Bevan Powell and Leroy Logan, accompanied by Ravi Chand, made our way to the Home Office to meet with the Home Secretary. It was a warm sunny day and I think I can speak for everyone by saying we were more than a little apprehensive. As we entered the Home Office in Queen Anne's Gate, we were approached by two ladies who assisted with our security passes and escorted us to the lift. On leaving the lift we walked down the corridor to where one of the ladies was holding open a door. I entered the room first and was immediately taken aback by the sheer number of people seated around an awfully long table. Naively perhaps, I had expected a cozy armchair chat with the Home Secretary in a small office with perhaps one or two aides. I scanned the seated guests and recognised Jack Straw seated halfway down the table, jacket off and sleeves rolled up he looked very cool and comfortable. I on the other hand felt extremely uncomfortable. The meeting room was very warm and stuffy, the sun was shining in through the numerous windows and lack of air, and high temperature was exacerbated by the numbers crowded into the room. Perspiration, caused by the nature of the occasion, excessive heat and lack of fresh air, rolled freely down my face as I took a place at the table. Jack Straw, noticed my discomfort and asked for the windows to be opened. The fresh air that entered the stuffy meeting room was a life saver. I began to regain composure as I looked around the table at the luminaries from the world of policing, including Sir David O'Dowd, Her Majesty's Inspector of Constabulary, Paul Pugh, Head of the Operational Policing Policy Unit, and Mike O'Brien QC, Under Secretary Minister of State and numerous civil servants that I failed to recognise. All had one thing in common, they stared in my direction.

The Home Secretary opened the meeting and introductions were made. Initially overwhelmed by the occasion, me and colleagues soon got into our stride and began relating a number of concerns raised at a recent National Communication Network Seminar organised for black police personnel from around the country. The Home Secretary listened intently while those around him took copious notes. And then, without warning, the Home Secretary leaned forward, "Chair, does your Association have an annual general meeting?"

"Yes, Sir, it does," I replied.

"Would it help if I was to speak at your AGM?" said the Home Secretary.

"It would indeed, Sir," I replied, unable to stifle a broad grin.

"Good, please liaise with my staff and we'll arrange something."

At that point Ravi Chand raised his hand and cheekily said, "Home Secretary, the Bedfordshire Black and Asian Staff Support Group also has an annual general meeting."

The Home Secretary gave a little chuckle and continued discussions but whatever else was said after that, 'the need for improving minority ethnic recruitment', 'key objectives for Community and Race Relations', was important but secondary to the stunning offer just made by the Home Secretary to speak at the AGM of the Black Police Association.

The Black Police Association was about to emerge from the shadows and take a seat at the top table, usually reserved for those that did not look like us. I sensed that this was the moment when we had arrived.

Nevertheless, Monday 19th October 1998 was a date that I thought would never arrive. Lambeth Police Support HQ, near to Lambeth Palace, was an ideal venue for the BPA AGM, just across the river from the Houses of Parliament it afforded easy access to our visiting dignitary, the Home Secretary. Unlike previous AGM's this one had attracted significant interest from the Met hierarchy with the Commissioner, Sir Paul Condon and Assistant Commissioner Denis O'Connor confirming attendance. Another special guest, Sir Herman Ouseley, Chairman of the Commission for Racial Equality, ensured that this AGM would be like no other. We expected a full house. Unexpectedly, Channel 4 news arrived just prior to the commencement of the conference. They wanted access to all the day's proceedings. Their correspondent, Simon Israel, presented a persuasive case for allowing cameras to film the historic events about to unfold. Nevertheless, in a joint decision taken by the BPA Executive, access to the media was to be limited to the opening few minutes of the conference.

My conference speech crafted, the considerable time and effort taken for its preparation reflected the gravity and importance I bestowed on the occasion. The once in a lifetime opportunity to speak in the presence of a Home Secretary, the Met's Commissioner and the Chair of The CRE was not lost on me. There could be no room for mistakes.

I awaited in a side room, away from the main conference room and was soon joined by the Met Commissioner, the Chair of the CRE and lastly, a very relaxed Home Secretary. Our entrance into the main conference hall was to be carefully choreographed to ensure that I was in line with and not following the Commissioner and the Home Secretary. As we waited the signal to move off, I looked across and down at Jack Straw's open leather-bound folder that appeared to hold various papers all neatly tagged with different coloured stickers.

"Mustn't get the Black Police Association mixed up with the Police Federation speech," laughed the Home Secretary as he thumbed through the papers.

"God forbid," I whispered.

The Home Secretary laughed.

As my time had arrived, I walked to the lectern and looked out at the expanse of smiling expectant black faces, all willing me well. I would try not to let them down.

Home Secretary, Commissioner, distinguished guests, ladies and gentlemen, I have been approached on a number of occasions just recently and asked 'what do I feel about my photograph plastered all over the London underground system as part of an Evening Standard advertising campaign?' Well, I'd just like to say, for the record, that I have in fact complained to the Evening Standard. Yes, - I've found two Stations in South London that they've obviously missed!

The last twelve months has seen the credibility and reputation of the BPA reach almost unimaginable heights. Given that just four years ago we were viewed by many as a divisive group with no sense of loyalty to the police service. We cannot fail to recognise that a new government has been instrumental in moving the issue of race to 'centre stage'. We have enjoyed a productive relationship with the Home Office, contributing in a number of important forums. We have also welcomed a more positive approach from our own organisation, the MPS. And I am also pleased to be able to say that we have regular contact with very senior officers, providing our perspective on a whole range of issues. This consultative relationship is particularly important to the BPA for the communality of our experiences as black police officers and civil staff mirrors the reality of life for many in the black communities. I believe the greatest challenge we face, is also our greatest opportunity. Of all the questions of discrimination and prejudice that still exist in our society, the most perplexing one is the oldest, and in some ways today, the newest: the problem of race. Can we fulfill the promise of fairness and equality of opportunity by embracing citizens of all races? In short, can we become a police service with a multi-cultural outlook in the 21st century?

I've been in the MPS for fifteen years in total. It is true that during that time I have seen significant change, mostly for the good. In fact, when I joined the MPS in 1983 I recall walking into the police college at Hendon and seeing row upon row of smartly dressed young police officers. I remember scanning the rows until my eyes finally rested upon the one black face. That was indeed an eerie sensation. Fifteen years later, last Monday in fact, I again visited the police college, this time as a student on a 'management development course'. Once again, I surveyed the rows of young police officers standing smartly to attention. I am able to say that the number of black faces had improved by 100%. There were two. I no longer felt an eerie sensation because I have become accustomed to the reality of the situation. A situation ladies and gentlemen that we must all become accustomed to for some time to come. For within the current race relations legislation, budgetary constraints, general decline in overall police recruitment, it will take us many, many years before we can hope to reflect the communities we serve.

I'd like to speak a little about the 'management development course' I attended, essentially a series of presentations from representatives of numerous departments within the MPS. The first was a powerful presentation, providing an insight into the implications, ramifications of our failures in the Stephen Lawrence investigation. This was followed by an equally powerful presentation from Mr Grieves's 'Race and Violent Crime Task Force'. We were shown where we are now in terms of investigating racially motivated crime and then shown a number of impressive measures and systems that will take us, as an organisation, to where we want to be. The two presentations had a considerable impact upon the seventy or so Inspectors present. I should add that there was one other black Inspector present who just coincidentally is the highest ranking black female officer in the uniform branch of the service. During the course of the week, we heard from a number of speakers all eager to tell us about the latest 'cutting edge' initiatives, policy etc. Occupational Health and how we might manage and reduce sickness. New measures and initiatives from our complaints investigation dept. A risk analysis assessment procedure designed to help us assess the potential risk associated with the possible outcomes of our decisions. A Business Excellence Model designed to assess how we deliver our service and how best to continually enhance that service through assessment and managed change. Leadership principles designed to help us become effective, accountable leaders. All good stuff, I'm sure you will agree. However, I can almost detect that some of you are thinking 'yeah, but so what!!' Well, allow me to look at this 'course' from a slightly different perspective. On the Monday, the issue of 'race' was mentioned. There was no mention of race during the remainder of the week. The context in which race was mentioned was arguably a negative one in that it wasn't 'good news' for the service. For the duration of the week, all the speakers, bar one white female, were white males. It is unfair of me to single out this particular course or any other course for that matter. However, some of you might have detected that I'm using the course to illustrate the day-to-day reality of life for many of us in the Metropolitan Police. I call it the 'drip, drip effect'. Let me explain in more detail what I have just said. Again, using the course as a micro example of life in the police. Did the course designer consider that only raising the issue of race in a negative context might contribute to the existence of any subconscious, low level resentment already present in the students. Did he consider that the usage of white speakers throughout the week just might reinforce the myth that we have no suitably qualified black personnel within the MPS? Did he check the ethnic composition of the group when designing the course? Did he consider the possible negative cumulative effect his ethnocentric perspective might have on the black officers? What I'm really asking is why didn't the course designer consider the outcomes of his actions in the context of race relations? The answer is simple: we do not, as an organisation, critically consider the outcome of our actions in terms of how we deliver our service to an increasingly multi-cultural community, be it internal or external. It has been said that we cannot find examples of good practice in terms of developing an 'anti-racist police service' However, you have heard me speak about a number of 'cutting edge' initiatives designed to take this organisation forward into the next century. It would seem we have considerable expertise and creativity when addressing issues which we consider vital to the future health of the Met. The key to moving the Met forward, enabling us to meet the expectations of an increasingly multi-cultural community, enabling us to effortlessly recruit from the multi-cultural community, enabling the development of a multi-cultural workforce, is the application of this expertise and creativity to dismantle these subtle but powerful institutional barriers. We've heard about a Business Excellence Model as a means of mobilising organisational change. We need a similar Excellence in Diversity model, equally as stringent and thorough, which we must apply to everything we do in this service. The challenge is simple; we have to move from a 'mono-cultural' organisation serving a 'multi-cultural' society to an organisation that embraces and respects ethnic diversity. I'm not advocating that the Commissioner should hang a poster of Bob Marley in his office… We laugh, but those of you that work in police buildings, how many pictures of black people do you see on a daily basis…without the words 'suspect' or 'wanted' underneath. What does the absence of any positive black images convey to the majority…it's the 'drip, drip effect' However it is important to point out that prejudiced attitudes are not the essence of this subtle form of institutional racism. Racism is unfortunately too often equated with intense prejudice and hatred of the racially different- thus with men of evil intent. This kind of racial extremism is not necessary for the maintenance of a racist institutional structure. For the most part the individuals that fail to analyse the outcome of their actions are not intentionally prejudiced and may well have positive attitudes towards black people. However, we have to rigorously challenge the seemingly harmless Institutional practices that have existed for years, practices that exclude the participation of racial groups by procedures

235

that have become conventional, part of the bureaucratic systems of rules and regulations. In short, our Association wants one thing: A true multicultural working environment. Who benefits? We all do.

Racists who are not able to accept the full humanity of other people are themselves badly damaged - morally stunted - people. The principal product of a racist society is damaged people and institutions - victims and victimisers alike. When we reform these institutions, we give ourselves a better, more able, more just society. So, although I am speaking today as the chair of the Black Police Association, about our own workplace, I want to invite you to think about every other workplace in Britain. I would like you to recollect the "canteen culture" of the organisations you have known. Recollect the moments that may have given you most pause, or a twinge of hindsight guilt. It is in the subtleties that we read the temperature. And it is not always a comforting reading. From all that I have said today, you might imagine that I am bitter or discouraged. I am neither. The Metropolitan Police has been placed under tremendous scrutiny during the Stephen Lawrence inquiry. The results have been difficult to deal with. But I believe that good can come from this, if we are prepared to make the changes. And we need to remind ourselves of this: what would we find if we held other public bodies and organisations up to such scrutiny? Can we really imagine that the only organisation in Britain with these problems of institutional racism is the Met? So, let's not bog ourselves down in apportioning blame. Far better that we look for the answers. But in all of them we should be starting from the same premise: you can't make a rainbow with just one colour.

To summarise then: The BPA advocates the introduction of procedures and measures to ensure that we systematically and critically consider the outcome of everything we do in terms of how we are likely to impact on a multicultural community.

Dr. Martin Luther King had this to say about racism: Men hate each other because they fear each other, and they fear each other because they don't know each other, and they don't know each other because they are often separated from each other. A tragedy has left us with some clear lessons. We will be guilty of a much greater failure if we fail to heed them.

Thank you.

I looked up, the assembled audience, including the Home Secretary and Police Commissioner rose to their feet, tumultuous applause followed while many BPA members loudly cheered. I was momentarily stunned and then overcome with emotion as I gathered my speech papers from the shelf of the lectern, head bowed, trying hard to hold back tears that now welled up and threatened to roll down my cheeks, I returned to my seat.

The BPA AGM was a resounding success, the Home Secretary's participation and supportive comments made sure of that. His willingness to answer questions during our plenary session, alongside a metropolitan police commissioner who had refused such an opportunity at the launch of the

BPA, was testament to the importance now attached to the issue of *race and policing*.

Chapter 45

BBC Newsnight

On the 17th of July 1998, the producers of BBC's *Newsnight* had arranged a car to pick me up from my home in Wallington, South London and ferry me to their Shepherd's Bush studios, where I would feature as a guest on that evening's *Newsnight*. The car pulled up outside the BBC studios and before I unbuckled my seat belt, my driver in one smooth motion climbed out and opened my door. I stepped out and headed for the entrance door. Once inside a young lady holding a clipboard approached me.

"Inspector Wilson?" she asked.

"Yes," I answered.

"Great, thanks so much for coming. We're so looking forward to hearing what you have to say. Please follow me; we'll visit make-up first."

With my face powdered, I was led to the green room. I entered and quickly scanned the occupants. My heart sank, for one of the two men I instantly recognised was Mike Bennett, Chair of the Metropolitan Police Federation: a quasi-Union type body representing all police officers up to and including the rank of Chief Inspector. I knew Mike from my time at Croydon police station, where he worked as a Sergeant. Memories of him holding court in Croydon police canteen, his chair pushed back from the table, slightly reclined with arms folded majestically across his chest, legs crossed and surrounded by worshipful police constables eager to hang onto every word uttered by the new Federation Chair were indelibly etched in my psyche.

However, our paths had crossed over the past few years, most notably in the printed word, as I published letters and responded to articles that challenged the Metropolitan Police Federation. Most particularly, its Chair's outspoken and thinly veiled racist rhetoric. Mike's persona was blunt, arrogant, and often insensitive. His demeanor, to me, characterised an era in the 1960s when policing and any notion of community consultation was tantamount to heresy. It was very much about them and us. An era where black faces were actively discouraged from joining the Met, an era that saw a Conservative MP win a parliamentary seat with the slogan; "If you want a nigger for a neighbour, vote Labour." An era where the Met reflected white working-class and largely racist views and values that would remain intrinsically embedded in the police occupational culture for decades to come. Mike had joined four years before the advent of the first Race Relations Act in 1965. It was an era where police constable pay was on a par with a London shop assistant; corruption was endemic in all ranks. The white working-class views espoused by the Met presented front line officers with an uncomfortable dichotomy when faced with alien black faces, unprepared to accept second class citizenship, who sought to challenge the very views and values that formed the bedrock of the police occupational culture. Resentment and frustration gave rise to "nigger hunting"[6], an unofficial pastime practiced by some metropolitan police officers, on and off duty. An unethical practice, where police officers would scour the darkened streets to seek out a black face to brutalise for the offence of being a "nigger." Yet, during my time as a police constable, I often heard the *old sweats* wax nostalgically over coffee in the police canteen as they recalled the job's 'good old days'. Unfortunately, there is absolutely no evidence, anecdotal or otherwise, to support any notion that the Windrush generation ever enjoyed this rosy retrospection.

I nodded at Mike to acknowledge his presence as we made our way into the Newsnight studio. Jeremy Paxman, the fiery interviewer, was already seated. As I walked to my chair, I exchanged a few words with another guest, Neville Lawrence, father of murdered black London teenager, Stephen Lawrence. Five years of campaigning for justice had taken its toll on Neville; the hardship, heartache, and disappointment were etched into his face. A forlorn figure, he sat hunched in his seat. Across the table was a dreadlocked young black man, Barry Munsden, a member of the Lawrence family campaign group. My chief concern, aside from Paxman's caustic interview style, was Mike Bennett and his approach to the Met's cataclysmic failures during the Stephen Lawrence murder inquiry. Would he act with appropriate humility, as a key representative of an organisation that had failed the

---

[6] It has been confirmed from reliable sources that sergeants and constables do leave stations with the express purpose of going "nigger hunting", that is to say, they do not get orders from superiors to act in this way, but among themselves they decide to "bring in a coloured person at all cost". NIGGER HUNTING IN ENGLAND (1966) - Joseph A. Hunte B.A. Published by West Indian Standing Conference (London Region)

Lawrence family in so many unprecedented ways or would we witness his favoured attack dog mentality?

My concerns unfolded before my very eyes, on national TV in front of millions, as Jeremy Paxman turned to Mike Bennett for a response to Neville Lawrence's belief that the police officers investigating his son's murder were both corrupt and racist.

Bennett began by deflecting the blame to police officers at the 'top-end of the rank structure', thereby protecting those he was elected to represent.

"It's not surprising to me that the only officer facing disciplinary action is a Detective Inspector...we'd like to see more accountability at the top."

"Do you believe, had the victim been white, there still would not have been a conviction for the killing?" asked Paxman.

"From my knowledge, I do; for there to be a conviction in a murder inquiry there needs to be evidence. The names of suspects are not evidence and to this day no evidence has come to light," responded Bennet.

I looked on in disbelief. *Evidence? What about the police surveillance team that on consecutive days watched and did nothing as potential murder suspects carried out black plastic bags filled with who knows what, from their address,* I thought to myself.

"Inspector Wilson, you are obviously black; you speak for the Black Police Association. Do you believe the police to be institutionally racist?" asked Jeremy Paxman with his piercing gaze.

I was not about to allow Mike Bennet to get away with his insulting rhetoric. "What the Black Police Association hopes is that this inquiry, which we support, we also support the Lawrence family, in fact, we would dissociate ourselves with the views of Mike Bennett and the Police Federation in this matter. What the Black Police Association hopes is that this inquiry will serve to elevate people's understanding of what we mean by institutional racism."

"Inspector Wilson, what is institutional racism?" asked Jeremy Paxman.

"During the Scarman inquiry the notion of racist conduct revolved around a few rotten apples; the racist acts or conduct of a few people. Now we are beginning to see that institutional racism underpins the organisation and what we mean by institutional racism is, as police officers, we tend to get involved with a very skewed cross-section of society and that has the potential for creating several stereotypes around groups. Now, unfortunately, those stereotypes become a common culture, common currency within the police occupational culture, so if predominantly white police officers have no interactions with minority ethnic groups other than those negative interactions at work, then those negative stereotypes can take on a formidable meaning."

"Do you recognise that picture of your trade?" asked Paxman, leaning back, and looking directly at Mike Bennett.

"I didn't understand a word of that; it sounded like a script," responded Bennett, who then pulled out a copy of the London Evening Standard newspaper and rambled on about a story where police had come to the assistance of a black man. "I would have hoped that after tonight, Mr Lawrence, to try and heal the wounds, because it's going to take both sides, would accept that we are not endemically racist. We have racists within our ranks… and he must take away that stain where he said that police officers did not want to get the blood of a black man on their hands. That is the worst defamation I have heard in my 37 years as a police officer," snarled Bennett staring directly at Neville Lawrence.

"Would you like to detract that comment?" said Paxman turning to Neville Lawrence.

"I didn't make it," responded Neville Lawrence.

"If he didn't say it then he can't retract it.", said Paxman, dismissively.

I took the opportunity to again illustrate an example of institutional racism, "How do we account for the differential treatment of black people up and down the country, not just in London? Black people are more likely to be stopped and more likely to be treated differently by the police; now that cannot be because of the actions of a few *rotten apples* and I go back to the institutional racism prevalent in the police," I explained.

The discussions later disintegrated into near chaos when Paxman held up a copy of a Police Review magazine that included a letter, signed by Mike Bennett, in which he had 'questioned whether the Lawrence Inquiry should have taken place at all.'

Mike Bennett's response was typically ferocious. "No, I didn't!"

"Yes, you did; you sent a letter to Police Review magazine," responded Paxman.

"I didn't write a letter, I wrote an article which the Police Review edited into a letter," said Mike Bennett, with a look of discomfort now increasingly visible under the studio lights.

"But it's on the letters page of Police Review, signed by you!", responded an increasingly animated Paxman, holding up the offending page of the Police Review magazine.

Mike Bennet leaned forward into Paxman's personal space and with his finger-wagging tried to defend the indefensible.

The content of the Police Review letter undermined any glimmer of understanding or empathy that Bennett may have sought to attach to the plight of the Lawrence family.

The following morning, I attended my workplace at Clapham Police station for the early shift. Seated in my office, I heard a knock at the door. It was

Kevin Hyder, one of my team Sergeants.

"Come in, Kevin. How are things?"

"Not good, Sir," stated my crimson-faced sergeant. "Some of the team saw your appearance on last night's *Newsnight* and are very upset at the words you used. They feel you accused them of being racist."

The *Newsnight* programme more than any other media appearance catapulted my views on institutional racism into the wider public and of course police domain. It signaled the beginning of a difficult and uncomfortable episode in my police career; one that was to last until my retirement. My cards had been marked, a consequence of my utterances, I had done the unforgivable by describing, on a popular national TV news programme, how I believed institutional racism to be a key ingredient of the police occupational culture. Carefully engineered, the discomfort afforded me over the next eleven years was often subtle in nature, discreet, never obviously linked to my race or views, but was omnipresent. It was not unlike a debilitating disease, I learned to live with it by carefully managing my career in such a way as to distance myself from areas of vulnerability.

Chapter 46

London Evening Standard interview

Despite the hostility displayed by some junior members of my team, matters took a twist a few days later when I was afforded welcome shelter and protection from an unexpected quarter.

I stood in the foyer at New Scotland Yard conversing with Eddie, who now worked as a security guard following the closure of *The Tank* by the new Commissioner, Sir Paul Condon. Apparently, our new Commissioner disliked the smell of alcohol and the raucous laughter that permeated New Scotland Yard's foyer most evenings; expressing his view that it was not in keeping with the Met's professional image or values. The Tank had been replaced with a fitness centre. The end of an era.

"Hi, Paul."

I turned; it was my partner, Sonia Campbell, also a police officer.

"Am I late?" she asked.

"Not at all, two minutes early in fact," I replied.

"I dropped everything as instructed and made my way here from Kensington. What's going on?"

"Well, it's to do with the article in today's Evening Standard…"

"Yeah, been reading it on the way over, very good too."

"Yeah, I gave an interview to journalist Andrew Billen a couple of days after the *Newsnight* appearance and as you've seen, it's splashed all over today's Standard. It seems the Met's senior hierarchy likes what I had to say, on this occasion. So much so, I've been telephoned by a jubilant Deputy Assistant Commissioner John Grieve and invited for lunchtime drinks. He specifically asked that I bring you along."

"Really? And that's who we are waiting for, is it?" asked Sonia, with a look of disbelief on her face.

As if on cue, out of the corner of my eye, Deputy Assistant Commissioner Grieve approached.

"Hello, you two, thanks for coming; let's take a walk down the road. I know a little bar where we can have a quiet drink."

Grieve turned to me and patted my back. "I've got to say Paul, there's nothing in today's article that we don't like, it's all good."

"Thanks, Sir, I always try to strike a balance, as difficult as that sometimes is."

Grieve smiled and ushered myself and Sonia through the exit door.

As we slowly walked and chatted, the Deputy Assistant Commissioner disclosed some information that made me rather nervous.

"It makes a pleasant change walking the streets of London," commented Grieve.

"Why is that, boss, you office-bound these days?" I asked.

"No, not at all. You remember when I was Commander Anti-Terrorism? Well, I never walked anywhere; I was the only Commander to have a car at my beck and call twenty-four hours a day. I still don't make a habit of walking," he laughed.

So, the mother of my two children might at any second get caught up in a spray of machine-gun fire, from a passing vehicle, meant for the once arch-nemesis of the IRA, I thought, allowing my fertile imagination to get the better of me. Nevertheless, as we continued our walk, I closely scanned the occupants of passing vehicles, only relieved once we had stepped off the pavement and descended into the bowels and relative safety of the Caxton Street wine bar.

Chapter 47

South Africa

Post Stephen Lawrence Inquiry, Black Police Associations became a recognised catalyst for change within the criminal justice sector. As a result, I received many invitations to speak at conferences around the country to share information and experiences to help motivate others to adopt the same strategies the Black Police Association used.

One such speaking invitation I received was to a black workers conference in Southport, north of Liverpool. I accepted and made the journey by train from London to make a speech in front of the assembled delegates. Afterwards, I was approached by a young black man.

"Hi, my name is Alfred Tshabalala. I work for the Police and Prisons Civil Rights Union (known as POPCRU) in South Africa. I think they would be extremely interested in hearing you speak," he said.

"That sounds great. Just call me when you want to set that in motion," I said, handing him my card.

As Alfred and I continued to talk, he told me the fascinating story about his work with POPCRU, which had emerged as the largest police union on the African continent. It was established during the Apartheid regime when one *coloured* police officer's reluctance and defiance to carry out orders to brutalise his own people triggered a whole movement.

It's the stuff Hollywood films are made of, I thought.

However, once the excitement of our meeting subsided and Alfred returned home to Johannesburg, I did not expect any follow up beyond maybe an email expressing his pleasure in meeting me.

When the email arrived a couple weeks after the conference, it was far more than just the friendly pleasantries I had expected.

Dear Paul,

... the Executive leadership of POPCRU would like to invite you to speak at our forthcoming National conference taking place in Pretoria...

Whatever elation I felt about this invitation was short-lived. Ruwan was a friend and someone recently elected as General Secretary of the National Black Police Association at the same time as my election as Chairman.

"I've taken some soundings Paul, the small clique that didn't vote for you in the national elections are not impressed with your invitation to visit South Africa," said Ruwan

"Why am I not surprised, Ruwan, what's their gripe?"

"If I can sum it up, they basically feel that the South African experience has little or no relevance to Britain or the struggle of the Black Police Associations."

"Ok, that's a minority viewpoint among the BPA's across the country but has it percolated into our National Executive committee?"

"I think it safe to say the minority has been vigorous in their briefing against you on this one," said Ruwan shaking his head.

"So, Ruwan, what you're telling me is that I stand little chance of obtaining funding to travel to South Africa from the National Executive?"

"Sorry, Paul, but that's about it, we need to keep this noisy clique onside and manage them as best as possible," said Ruwan

This was very frustrating for me. I was being denied an opportunity to extend friendship to our brothers and sisters in South Africa by people of colour in Britain who refused to recognise the hugely significant and historical connections between our two countries.

But as with previous occasions where I had been denied the opportunity to travel because it did not meet a particular agenda, I began to consider alternatives.

I was still a member of the Metropolitan Black Police Association and discussed the situation with Leroy Logan, Chair of the London Black Police Association, and former chair of the interim National Black Police Association. After our conversation, I could submit a formal business case to the Metropolitan BPA Executive members for funds to support my travel to South Africa. Hotel and ancillary costs would be supported by POPCRU.

Informal soundings had been positive with several of the executive citing the complicity of some prominent British politicians and business leaders in supporting and therefore prolonging apartheid in South Africa. Among those in favour was BPA Treasurer Keith Smith.

I attended the next BPA Executive meeting and recused myself prior to the discussion of my proposed visit to South Africa. I anxiously waited outside the door for five minutes until the door opened and Paul Ramsay appeared.

"We've finished, Paul. You may re-join us now," he said.

I sat back down at the table as Leroy Logan explained the decision arrived at by members of the executive committee.

"Paul, the executive has agreed to provide financing for your visit to the POPCRU conference in Pretoria, South Africa," he said. "The BPA is firmly in favour of establishing a relationship with South Africa's police and prison officers."

A huge wave of relief and excitement washed over me at the prospect of forging relations on the African continent. I quickly addressed my colleagues.

"I wish to thank the Chair and members of the Executive for this forward-thinking decision. During my time in South Africa, I promise to do my utmost to represent the values of the BPA. Upon my return, I will of course prepare a report detailing my activities and experiences."

"And don't forget to bring us some biltong," said Keith Smith.

We all laughed.

~~~~

Weeks later I arrived in Johannesburg after an eleven-hour flight, where I was met by several members of POPCRU. My introduction to the harsh realities of post-apartheid South Africa began immediately after we drove away from the Johannesburg International Airport.

"See those small, corrugated iron shacks strewn across that hillside?" one of my hosts asked, pointing out the window.

"Yes," I said.

"Those were homes for blacks and coloureds," he said.

We rode in silence for several minutes until we began approaching a city. Tall buildings towered over city streets congested with traffic.

"Paul, this is Johannesburg–or Egoli as we Africans call it," someone said.

This looks the same as any large American or British city I've seen, I thought. *In fact, this bumper-to- bumper traffic reminds of me of Central London.*

However, upon closer inspection the differences became obvious. Most people on the streets were black, while only a handful of the white or minority ethnic community scurried about their daily business.

The driver pointed to one of the large downtown buildings. "That was a five-star hotel during apartheid, but it closed all operations and has been sitting empty ever since the criminals moved into the area," he said. "The dismantling of apartheid left many in the white community feeling vulnerable. With poor black people now free to live in Johannesburg, many squatted in vacant properties. With the oppressive tentacles of apartheid no more, crime inevitably escalated, and as a result businesses closed and moved to white suburbs."

The next morning, POPCRU officials picked me up from my hotel and took me to their national headquarters, on several floors of an impressive office block in the

Braamfontein district. As we pulled up outside, my attention was drawn to a group of disheveled black kids gathered across the street.

"Those kids there are homeless," my host said. "They run a makeshift but effective car wash and car security business. I give them my car to wash," he added with a laugh.

Once inside the building, I was taken to a suite of administration offices and introduced to the busy staff.

A tall, slender Dutchman smiled and extended his hand.

"Paul, this is Fons Geerlings from The Netherlands. He's one of your European Comrades," my host said.

"Pleased to meet you, Paul. I hear you're speaking at the conference, looking forward to it."

"Thank you. Pleased to meet you as well," I said, shaking his hand.

"Fons here is one of the architects of POPCRU in its early formative years when he was Secretary of the ANC in Holland," my host said.

Numerous cardboard boxes sat stacked against the walls of Fon's office, each filled with condoms to be dispersed at the conference. It was a sobering reminder that South Africa was gripped in an HIV/AIDS pandemic.

Later that evening, my escorts from POPCRU gave me a tour of the city. As we cruised through Hillbrow, the area of Jo'burg that attracts the most negative publicity, ladies of the night huddled together on street corners, hoping to gain the attention of passing motorists. It was an area renowned for poor quality government housing, high crime, and few local amenities, all hallmarks of a depressed neighbourhood.

However, when we visited a local bar, I learned from various conversations that the area is an attraction for the liberal academic community and others who feel comfortable in the classless and non-racial environment.

By the end of the city tour I was reminded of the words from the classic "Johannesburg" by African American singer/poet, Gil Scott-Heron.

"Detroit like Johannesburg, freedom ain't nothing but a word,"

~~~~

I have travelled through many large American cities with substantial black communities and they display depressingly similar characteristics as the Hillbrow neighbourhood. And why shouldn't they? America also had its apartheid system and now reaps the same legacy of racial segregation, high crime, and inequality.

Because of my profession, I could not help but notice the absence of police officers on the streets of Jo'burg. This was particularly relevant in the evening when Jo'burg resembled a ghost town.

Crime, I was informed by my hosts, had curtailed the public transport system. This in turn adversely impacted the poorer black workers who still lived in the same townships created under the apartheid system. From the comfort of the car, I watched as we drove past long queues of tired workers lining the pavement as they waited in quiet desperation for one of the many taxi buses to take them home to the townships.

In striking similarity to many of the large American cities I had visited over the years, there was little in the way of social entertainment that was of interest to black people in the centre of Johannesburg. In fact, it was difficult to find anything open after 9pm.

"A visit to Johannesburg is incomplete without experiencing the vast sprawling Townships of Soweto, the country's largest Black urban complex and a symbol of the long struggle against apartheid," said Alfred.

The thirty-minute drive from Jo'burg to Soweto gave my hosts an opportunity to give me insight into South Africa's unique history and the strategic social and racial engineering of the apartheid system.

"African and 'colored' people were not allowed to occupy areas reserved for the white European. We are going to see these places called townships, which were built far enough away from the white community to not annoy or contaminate yet close enough to enable the African workforce to travel into the city to provide that all-important source of cheap labour. Your people, the British, effectively introduced this system of forced removal and segregation. While despising the African people, they recognised the importance of having a ready resource of labour."

My people? As far as they were concerned, I was British, and maybe that was true, but I still felt more than a little hurt by that remark.

As we drove through a myriad of streets, I couldn't help but be impressed by the quality of housing, until I was informed that Diepkloof the area we were in was an affluent section of Soweto.

"Paul, despite what you might hear on BBC, Soweto is a collection of different Townships. This area is favoured by artists, politicians, and celebrities. Some homes here sell for a million rand."

As we continued navigating the dusty streets, we came upon an area where the standard of housing appeared to be on the other end of the Sowetan spectrum compared to Deipkloof.

This is the colored section, I thought as I looked at the scores of dejected people standing outside ramshackle properties.

People classified as "colored" by the apartheid system, but black in Europe and the United States, inhabited street after street and row after row of sub-standard housing.

"Next on our itinerary is a visit to Winnie Mandela's marital home, which is now a museum," said Alfred.

As the vehicle slowed to a stop in Vilakazi Street, our driver shouted something in his African tongue.

Alfred pointed at a large black limousine parked across the road. "I think that's Ma'am Winnie's car," he said calmly.

"Really?!" I said, raising my voice. I looked around eagerly for any signs that might confirm this exciting news.

A few seconds later, the limo driver got out and walked to the rear door. He opened it and Winnie Mandela stepped out. Just at that moment a large coach passed by and hissed to a stop 100 yards away. The door opened and a crowd of white tourists stepped out onto the pavement and began walking excitedly towards Ma'am Winnie.

Without a word I flung open the rear door of our vehicle, jumped out, glanced both ways and sprinted across the road to meet the lady herself. Looking resplendently chic, her youthful appearance failed to betray the years of hardship and struggle when she alone kept the Mandela name in the public spotlight.

"Hello Ma'am, my name is Paul Wilson. I'm a police officer visiting from London, England. I'm here to speak at the POPCRU conference in Pretoria. May I take a photograph with you?" I asked breathlessly.

"Yes, of course," Winnie said, moving close and placing her arm around my waist.

I handed my camera to Alfred as the surrounding crowd drew in closer, waiting for their own chance to meet Winnie.

"Take about ten, Alfred, just in case."

Winnie looked at me and gave me a smile that has been transmitted into every living room in the world over the years. My day had been made.

~~~~

Bright and early the next morning, POPCRU sent a driver to collect me from my hotel. We were going to the policy conference in Pretoria, much to the amusement of my driver and other members it seemed.

"Pretoria is the capital and the seat of the old National government responsible for introducing the apartheid regime and therefore remains a fiercely conservative area. You will see that for yourself," he said, chuckling.

After a forty-five-minute drive on a four-lane highway that reminded me of the ones in England, we arrived at the conference venue located in a suburb of Pretoria. We still had plenty of time to kill before the doors opened, so I asked my hosts to show me the shopping area so I could find some gifts to bring home.

Walking the streets of this wealthy suburb of Pretoria, with well-heeled white residents gazing into designer-shop windows, I momentarily forgot I was on the continent of Africa. With its European styled shopping malls and ambience there was little or no indication that the majority population was black African.

The restaurants I noted did not compare with the multicultural diversity of London fare. Fish and chips, beef burger bars and steak restaurants were commonplace here. If I thought I might be able to purchase gifts reflecting the rich, cultural traditions of Africa, I was mistaken.

We got back in the car and made our way over to the Wonder Waters leisure complex on the outskirts of Pretoria. A line of coaches came off the highway and entered the car park. Delegates in African cultural dress milled around the entrance to the Leisure Centre. Many of them had driven through the night, some as much as fourteen hours, from as far away as Port Elizabeth and Cape Town, I was told.

We parked the car and went inside the building, where I was escorted into a huge conference centre. Staff members stood behind rows of desks, assisting with registration. I walked up to one of them and gave the lady my name. I was immediately escorted to meet with a man standing nearby,

"Hello, Paul. I'm Abbi Witbooi, General Secretary of POPCRU," he said, handing me my VIP name badge. "I trust we are looking after you?"

"Yes, it's going great," I replied.

Abbi handed me a list of workshops and began talking quickly as he outlined the business of the conference. This was very much a working conference where I was expected to participate in discussions.

"It's a pleasure and I look forward to being able to participate in the conference workshops," I said.

Abbi smiled and walked away. He was clearly a terribly busy man.

It was the middle of winter in South Africa, but the weather was still warm enough that a number of workshops could take place in the open air, under palm trees. It was not exactly the kind of workshop environment I was used to. But before that could happen, there was still the matter of my conference speech.

Alfred and I walked into the huge, exquisitely decorated auditorium. On the large stage in the front sat a long table with people seated around it.

"That's where the post holders of POPCRU are seated," Alfred whispered. "As our guest you will need to take your place at the table."

A few minutes later I climbed the platform steps and walked across the stage. Hundreds of delegates in colourful tribal costumes looked up from where they were seated. An eerie silence descended across the hall as I took my seat. I was not sure who was more nervous, them or me.

After what felt like ages, the President of POPCRU stood up and addressed the audience. This was followed by Abbi Witbooi who spent an inordinate amount of time setting out the conference itinerary (he sure wasn't in a hurry this time).

Finally, the moment I had been waiting for arrived.

"And now comrades, I want to welcome our international guest, Paul Wilson. He's an Inspector with London's Metropolitan Police and the Chair of the National Black Police Association," Abbi said.

The delegates rose to their feet and following a series of chants began to dance.

"Quiet Comrades, please allow Paul to speak," pleaded Abbi.

A hush fell over the auditorium.

I gripped my notes in sweaty palms as I slowly walked over to the podium.

After thanking my hosts and greeting everyone, I discussed my own African roots.

"And I just want to add, after the enforced exile of my forefathers, I'm glad to be back home again," I said.

To my surprise a huge round of applause filled the auditorium as row after row of delegates stood up and began singing and dancing. Overcome with emotion, I fought back tears. This was like nothing I'd ever experienced in my life. But then again, this was my first business engagement on the continent of Africa.

After my speech, I returned to my seat. The General Secretary went to the microphone and gave the order of the day's business to the delegates, in a manner leaving no room for misunderstanding. I was struck by his disciplined approach. In many ways it echoed the formality of a bygone age when Trade Unions in Britain during the 70's would observe similar rigid business management protocols at their meetings.

~~~~

As the business of the day got underway, I walked around the various workshops before deciding on the Communications workshop as my first port of call. As the Chair opened the meeting, I listened intently as he expressed his frustration at the unwillingness of appointed liaison officers to communicate with the Centre or submit articles for publication in POPCRU's newsletter.

These issues seemed all too familiar to me as I remembered the many BPA meetings where the exact same matters had been discussed with grinding monotony. We went over the draft communications policy document in detail and I made several contributions, based on my experiences with the BPA and in particular the use of the internet, which was still in its infancy. I left the workshop with the impression that my ideas had been received well.

Later, I visited a workshop that had a much more emotional style of debate. The "sexual harassment" policy workshop was trying to reach an agreement on appropriate wording. During my time with the Equal

Opportunities Unit, I had become familiar with principles of sex discrimination legislation. I thought this experience would provide the debate with a different perspective.

My initial input appeared to be greeted with interest and aligned with the views expressed by several of the ladies' present. However, as the debate progressed, I became uncomfortable. Was I not doing what the British and others have so successfully done over the years? I was providing African people with a Eurocentric solution to a problem without fully understanding the impact of my views on the historical and cultural environment in which these issues take place.

I decided to tailor my contribution by actively listening to all aspects of the debate. This was difficult for me because the collective male viewpoint in the room favoured the status quo. While they gave the impression of accepting there was a problem, their body language, verbal quips, and occasional laughter did little to suggest that measures on the scale advocated by female members of the group would be forthcoming.

I left the workshop believing that South African women can and do face sexual harassment in the workplace, but the policy that was being proposed (apparently lifted from an American equality manual) did not cater to nor recognise the cultural nuances of what was a profoundly serious issue in South African society.

The sexual harassment debate was later brought up again during the full conference. Following some emotional discussion, I became more confident that many male executive members, with some guidance from the General Secretary, were committed to rigorously addressing the status quo.

A visit to the debate in the main conference hall acquainted me with several cultural nuances not usually seen in conferences I had previously visited. After a particularly difficult debate or an impressive speech, a delegate would shout "Amandla!" meaning "Power". In response, hundreds of delegates would shout "Awethu", completing an old ANC rally cry of 'Power to the People'. This would be followed by all delegates breaking into African song and dance, like the ones used by South African anti-apartheid protestors seen on BBC news in the 70s and 80s. Many of what were known as freedom songs played a prominent role in the struggle against the oppressors during the apartheid era.

I was pleased to visit and participate in several other policy workshops on a variety of issues, ranging from HIV/AIDS to *positive action* measures. In each one I was impressed with the level of commitment shown by attendees and gained the impression following conversations around the conference hall that my contributions had been well received and noted.

After the business of the day was concluded, I persuaded the Executive

Committee members that there was a need to socialise together to celebrate a job well done. There were benefits to bonding after a day of occasionally heated debate. I suggested a bar named "Cool Runnings" that I had spotted on the way to the conference. It had caught my attention with its Rastafarian colours and Jamaican flag, and I thought it would be a good place to relax in an African setting.

With the Executive Committee in agreement, we set off for the venue. Determined to be the first to buy everyone a drink (South African prices were low compared to London) I rushed towards the brightly coloured entrance door. As our group of one 'colored', thirty Africans and two whites entered the building, heads turned and talking ceased. It reminded me of old Western movies where the bad guy walks into a saloon and the pianist stops playing.

If my African friends noticed anything unusual, they were too polite to mention it. Personally, I was embarrassed, uncomfortable, and annoyed for the first time since arriving in South Africa. POPCRU members bunched together in a corner while groups of white people huddled around tables, stared at us, and whispered to each other while reggae music played in the background.

I was incensed at the rudeness so blatantly on display. I rarely lose my temper, but when I do personal safety is usually not at the forefront of my mind. My blood boiled when a table of young white men at the rear of the bar began laughing and nudging one another as my friends came through the door.

"I'll be back in a moment. I'm just going to have a word with those guys," I said to Alfred.

I slowly walked through the mass of seated punters, now staring at me, and over to the group of white guys. They stopped and looked up at me, their white cheeks-tinged crimson. I crouched down.

"Hi guys. You enjoying this *black* music?" I asked.

They looked at each other in confusion and didn't respond.

"I said, are you boys enjoying this reggae music? Do you not understand English?"

Each one looked at me and nodded their heads.

"Good. I'm not from here. I'm from England, and back there we don't like people who lack good manners. Do you understand what I'm saying?"

They stared into their drinks and nodded while mumbling under their breath.

"Good, now that we understand each other I'll go re-join my friends. Have a nice evening," I said, standing up and walking away.

When I came back to our table, I suggested to my friends that we stand next to the bar. They looked at me like I'd lost the plot.

"Come on guys, if you want me to buy you drinks, we're going to stand over by that bar," I shouted.

I walked over to the barman and ordered beers for everyone in my group. The barman appeared friendly enough, so I asked why black people did not frequent this place.

He explained that the bar was a West Indian themed bar named after the movie "Cool Runnings", which is a comedy about the exploits of a Jamaican bobsleigh team. He went on to explain, rather matter-of-factly, that it was not intended to cater to nor attract black people.

~~~~

Later in the evening, I was introduced to Gregory Rockman, Chief Executive for POPCRU Investment Holdings, a business arm of the Union, a practice developed during apartheid when the regime tried to control the growth in Unions and strictly regulate their ability to raise funds.

Well groomed, intelligent, square jawed with greying hair, Rockman had the appearance of an ambassador or attaché. As a *colored* from Cape Town, as well as the founding father of the Police and Prison Officers Civil Rights Union, discussions of race inevitably made him emotionally charged.

In 1989 he was a twenty-four-year-old senior officer with the South African police service. As an academic with all the trappings afforded by his rank, his future was bright, even during apartheid.

He leaned across the table and began passionately sharing a story about how his life was changed forever one September day. He spoke as if it had just happened last week.

A peaceful demonstration by the colored population was to be 'disrupted' by police who considered the march to be 'politically subversive'. Rockman argued that the demonstration was peaceful, and the demonstrators were advocating a legitimate point of view. However, his protests were not heeded by senior officers nor by junior officers who refused to take orders from a 'colored'.

Rockman dug in his heels and refused to undertake orders from senior officers. The issue escalated. Rockman was ostracised and victimised. His stance attracted considerable media attention in South Africa, where police were the main instruments of apartheid and such radical action was unheard of.

The pressure upon Rockman to stand down from his position of 'non co-operation' must have been enormous. He looked to fellow police officers for support and found it in Port Elizabeth amongst African and coloured officers. He had been held in high esteem in the coloured community even before his stand, but almost overnight he became the role model for African and coloured officers who were unhappy with the system.

Around that same time, African prison officers had begun withdrawing their services due to their unhappiness with the inhumane treatment that African prisoners were receiving. Rockman joined forces with these officers and the dispute attracted attention in Europe. With the help and advice of European Police Unions, an embryo Police and Prison Union, was formed in 1989. Prison and police officers were sent to Denmark for training in Union, police management, and Human Rights issues. Financed by Dutch police unions, Rockman embarked on a European tour to publicise the plight of his police and prison colleagues.

Rockman further explained how his arrival in England was enthusiastically received by the Prison Officers Association in 1991. It was a complete contrast to his meeting with the Police Federation, which represented rank-and-file police officers. I listened with interest as Rockman expressed his utter disbelief at the 'frosty' reception from Federation officials.

"I had been on the receiving end of a number of similar receptions from the London Police Federation. During one such meeting to appraise them of our plans for a black police association, John Barnie, the General Secretary, tried to convince me that using the term "police" in our title was in contravention of some ancient piece of legislation enacted to prevent its misuse," I said, laughing loudly.

"They just couldn't seem to accept that police officers had the right to withdraw their services in such circumstances. They were definitely not in support of what I was doing," Rockman said.

"I'm afraid to say, that comes as no surprise to me," I said, shaking my head.

Further discussion with Rockman revealed that he entered politics in 1994, in the new dispensation, as a member of the ANC parliament. His years spent in government undoubtedly honed his political skills and awareness. In the space of a few minutes, he was to give me a political assessment of how the British establishment might respond to a Black Police Association.

"Your liberal establishment will appear to greet you, they will not wish to be associated with a bygone age, not so long ago, when people of colour were not welcomed into mainstream society. However, that welcome should be met with caution as you must understand the establishment will always wish to dictate the pace of progress around matters of equality and justice," Rockman said.

"So, what might politicians do to control us?" I asked.

"Well, it's not difficult. One tried and tested method is to single out a leader, someone outspoken that has the ear of the community, give them a job and an impressive title, a nice salary, all on the condition that they work to further an agenda set by the establishment," Rockman said.

I sat upright in my chair, thinking of the occasions when I had potentially been approached to work on behalf of the establishment. In 1997 I'd been invited into the Home Office by Mike O'Brien, Minister responsible for race relations, for a friendly chat that seemed at the time to be all about getting me 'onside' and exploiting my network of contacts.

Similarly, a year later Bob Cox, Director of News at New Scotland Yard and not someone who would normally pass the time of day, invited me for a quiet Sunday night drink at a pub in Sutton. I always thought the whole episode a rather clumsy attempt to calm down my public facing rhetoric and persuade me to adopt a 'more measured approach'. It did not work.

Rockman continued, "Furthermore, the issue of resources. Campaigning groups never have sufficient funds, they're always seeking that little bit extra just to do the basics. This is where the establishment steps in with an offer you can't refuse. And once you are comfortable with your new-found resources, your leadership will have little appetite to go back to how things were.

"There's no such thing as a free lunch in politics, so you'll gradually be asked to 'participate' in the Government's agenda. You will start to feel uncomfortable biting the hand that feeds you. Your strident advocacy and blistering rhetoric are neutered!" he added with a laugh.

As depressing as his analysis sounded, I had to accept that it resonated on many levels. I particularly reflected upon the National Black Police Association's willingness to accept office accommodation within the Home Office, which was something that I had argued against. Now, as the Chair of the National BPA I had felt it necessary to take a desk in that very office, if only to exert an element of control over the powers that be conveniently located just down the corridor and who would regularly pop in to *make sure everything was ok.*

By the end of our discussion, I realised just what a master stroke it had been when the Union urged Rockman to relinquish his political career and once again join them as a Chief Executive.

My friend Alfred Tshaba, who was an exceptional host, had been very protective in the early stages of my visit. I repeatedly reminded him that this was greatly appreciated, but my time on the streets of Southeast Washington DC had been far more foreboding than my Johannesburg experience. Finally relenting, he and a couple of other POPCRU staff members agreed to escort me into Soweto for a Friday night 'out on the town'. Something that 'Westerners' do not do, I was told.

"We'll take you to a typical Soweto tavern," said Alfred as I climbed into our people carrier for what was to be my last night in South Africa.

As usual, my ride turned into a tour like experience with my hosts chipping in with information about Soweto, "The languages spoken in Soweto include, isiZulu, isiXhosa, siSwati, Tshivenda, Setswana, Sepedi, Sesotho, isiNdebele and Shangaan , so you might be in for a lonely night my friend."

The people carrier erupted with laughter.

"About 3.5 million people live in Soweto and drinking beer is a favourite pastime, we have 2, 500 shebeens and 220 taverns."

A shebeen it was explained is an informal drinking establishment.

Much like Railton Road, Brixton at the end of the seventies, I thought.

Finally, the people carrier pulled up outside a nondescript building with none of the usual adornments to suggest it was a public house.

"Don't worry Paul, this is one of our better Taverns," Alfred said.

I followed my hosts through the entrance door and entered a dim and smoky room full of men and one solitary woman in the whole establishment.

That puts a bit of a damper on the whole evening, I thought.

I leaned over to my host. "Where are the women?" I whispered.

"Oh, they tend not to come into places like this. The men will be drunk later, and women generally feel unsafe when that happens."

I sat on one of the wooden benches next to a long wooden table. A young waiter came over and spoke to my hosts in one of the African languages.

"Guys let me buy the drinks, you just order them. I'll have a Castle beer," I shouted, trying to make myself heard over the loud chatter of perhaps fifty patrons.

After about an hour of drinks and conversation about my visit, I began to think of food.

"Does this place sell food? I'm getting hungry?" I shouted.

"No, it doesn't. But there's a van down the road that sells chicken."

"Great, I'll get some. Don't worry, I won't take long," I said assertively, making it clear to my hosts that I wasn't afraid to go alone.

For around five minutes I walked along the darkened streets following the directions I had been given. Finally, I spotted an old white caravan on the side of the road with what appeared to be a serving hatch. As I got closer, I noticed that a man and woman were inside.

"You sell chicken?" I asked, trying to disguise my English accent.

The man nodded, "You want leg or breasts?"

"Give me six legs and eight breasts," I said, thinking that my hosts were probably hungry too.

With the warm parcel of food tucked under my arm, I retraced my steps back to the Tavern. On entering, I instantly noticed an increase in punters. I edged myself through the crowd, now standing shoulder to shoulder, until I reached my hosts still occupying the same table.

I unwrapped the paper and opened the large polystyrene container, pushing the exposed chicken towards my hosts.

"Help yourself, guys. I got plenty for all of us."

Without warning, the whole Tavern seemed to descend on the open tray of chicken. Scores of fingers eagerly tore the chicken into small pieces as hands shoved meat into open mouths. I sat back and watched, not bothering to compete in the feeding frenzy. Within less than two minutes, the tray was empty.

My host leaned over "And that Paul is a very important lesson in African culture. Food is always shared," he shouted.

"So I see," I said, smiling.

The next morning, I stood in my hotel room packing my belongings into my suitcase in preparation for the evening flight back to London. I reflected on what had been a truly memorable experience. The argument from some National BPA colleagues that 'the South African experience has little to no relevance to Britain or the struggle of the Black Police Association' had been well and truly defeated by several revelations. Not least among them were the actions of some South African police officers, in defiance of a white establishment's intolerance of black people. This served to establish and mobilise South Africa's first representative body for black police officers. In so many ways, the black South African police experience in 1989 mirrored the beginnings of the Black Police Association in 1993.

Chapter 48

National Black Police Association

Saying goodbye to my South African hosts, I boarded my plane, certainly not expecting the bumpy landing that would await me.

After nearly eleven hours in the air, I was so grateful to hear the 'fasten seat-belts, we have started the descent into London Heathrow'.

Switching on my cell phone it vibrated and flashed furiously as messages downloaded. I was not surprised as I had been incommunicado for such a long period. Resisting the temptation to look at my messages, I collected my cabin luggage and disembarked from the plane. As I walked into the Immigration reception area, my cell phone rang. I turned it off because telephone conversation was prohibited. Having passed through Immigration, I turned my phone on and within seconds it began to ring again.

It was Sonia, my ex-partner.

"Hi, I've literally just landed at Heathrow. How are the kids?" I asked.

Sonia replied, "Shani and Lewis are fine. Have you seen the messages on your phone?"

"No, not had the chance. Why what's happened?"

"Journalists have been camped outside the house all week, but I refused to talk to them."

"What the hell for; what did they want?"

"I'm afraid you need to look at today's *Mail on Sunday*. They put together a story about our break-up. Nothing to do with me. Someone leaked bits of the story to them and the rest they've made up."

"Shit!" I shouted, causing heads to turn as I awaited my luggage to appear on the conveyor belt.

With my suitcase collected, my heartbeat raced; I pushed my luggage trolley through the *nothing to declare* exit. *Please, don't anyone stop me because I'm not sure how I'd react,* I thought to myself.

I walked into the lobby area to be met by a crowd of people congregated to receive friends and relatives. I was not expecting anyone to meet me and looked around for a newspaper stand. WH Smith answered my call. I entered the shop and quickly found the *Mail on Sunday* newspaper. I nervously leafed through the pages and there it was, on page eight. My photograph headed the article.

'WPC wife has black officers' leader barred from home after 'fight'
'Naomi's aunt takes police chief husband to court.'

The article included a photograph of Sonia and of her supermodel niece, Naomi Campbell. It was all designed to gain maximum attention. I eagerly read the article; elements of which rang true but there were undoubtedly some falsehoods here that tried to portray me as a bully.

How I wished I'd never agreed to take on the role of the National Black Police Association (NBPA) Chair, I thought as I finished reading the article. It was never my intention to stand for the office as the London Black Police Association had effectively taken over my personal and professional life for the past six years. During that time, not once had I missed a BPA meeting. In recent years my children's grandfather, Mr. Campbell, would often at a moment's notice agree to childcare responsibilities; looking after Shani and Lewis at his Brixton address so that I might attend yet another *critical* meeting. In fact, without Grandad Campbell's unconditional assistance, the BPA I was convinced, would not have evolved in the way it did. Nevertheless, it was fair to say my relationship breakdown with the mother of my two children was for the most part directly attributed to my blinkered determination in establishing and developing the BPA movement; during which time, I had not given sufficient attention to my family.

In addition to looking after my personal affairs, my intention, in standing down at the end of my BPA Chairmanship in 1999, was to help revive a police career that I felt had stagnated. Furthermore, and most importantly, it would also enable others to take on the leadership mantle of the BPA as I was very conscious of the fact that I had reigned in a manner that was arguably appropriate for the Stephen Lawrence Inquiry, but now fresh blood was needed to take the BPA to the next stage.

However, my plans for retirement from the BPA movement was not shared by two officers from Bedfordshire police, Ravi Chand and Jack Mahli, for they both had very different ideas for my future. Each would take turns to telephone me, most evenings it seemed when they would embark upon a series of extraordinarily lengthy and very persuasive reasons as to why I should contest the post of National Chair. I resisted for I was only too aware of the politics at play. My old friend and BPA colleague, Leroy Logan, had a few months ago been appointed to lead an interim committee of regionally based black/Asian officers keen to gain a national advocacy platform, a position the London Black Police Association occupied by default. Neither I nor any other colleagues on the London Black Police Association Executive were particularly enamoured by Leroy's unilateral move that helped establish a national body. He was, after all, a member of the London BPA Executive. Leroy knew of my feelings but, nevertheless, some members of the interim national representative body, impatient for a democratic structure, had forced the campaign for open elections and I unwittingly became a central actor in that drive.

Jack and Ravi's eloquent arguments won the day and I agreed to stand for the post of Chair of the National Black Police Association. Sides were polarised within the interim group; those in favour of allowing things to continue an informal basis and those in favour of an open democratic election process. It had been a thoroughly uncomfortable and messy affair as I had friends on both sides of the divide.

The election for National Chairman had taken place at the Lancashire Police HQ in Preston, between two candidates, me and Derbyshire police Inspector, Kul Mahay. I gained the most votes and was declared the first democratically elected Chair of the UK's National Black Police Association.

A few months later, I sat on the train into central London, as I mulled over the *Mail on Sunday* article. I cast my mind back to my election campaign for the post of National Chair, where I had created a private campaign website and shared the domain name with those colleagues eligible to vote at the election. I had uploaded a detailed biography and shared a great deal of career information not previously in the public domain. These very same snippets of my career history had been published in the *Mail on Sunday* article.

That information had to have come from one of the colleagues with access to my website, I thought. I felt sick at the thought of someone from the BPA movement going to the trouble of contacting the offices of the *Daily Mail*, while I was out of the country, to try and rubbish my reputation.

The next morning, I drove to my solicitor's office on London Road, in Mitcham, South London.

"Angela, did you see yesterday's *Mail on Sunday* article?"

"No Paul; I get *The Observer*. Why?"

"They published a sensationalised account of my break-up with Sonia and I want to publish a statement rebutting the fictitious and damaging elements."

I showed the newspaper article to my solicitor, who looked it over very carefully before looking up at me.

"If we publish such a statement it will draw attention to this article and those people, like me, who didn't see it will look for it. Is that what you want?"

I slumped into a chair. The realisation of what my solicitor had said took the wind out of my sails. She was right. We would not issue a statement.

Following the visit to my solicitors I caught a train into central London although the mere though of travelling on the train had my stomach in knots.

The significant media profile that I considered to be a huge plus at the time was now haunting me by exacerbating feelings of nausea as I travelled by train into central London. Slightly paranoid, I looked down the packed carriage and imagined passengers discreetly looking at me while asking their neighbour, *isn't that the police inspector in yesterday's Mail on Sunday?* My stomach felt queasy throughout the journey into London Victoria station.

When the train reached its destination, I climbed out of the carriage and walked to my office at the Home Office, in Queen Anne's Gate; not because I wanted to but because, the thought of a hundred gawking faces had dissuaded me from taking the short train journey between Victoria and St James' Park.

I entered the familiar revolving doors at the Home Office and walked past the security officer. As I did so, out the corner of my eye, I caught the two ladies on the main reception desk staring in my direction. I felt sick.

My two police colleagues in the office were all too polite and gracious to mention the Sunday tabloid squalor. As the day progressed, I became a little more confident; although, I avoided straying too far from my office at lunchtime.

Ruwan Pererra, General Secretary of the NBPA, had the ear of the various factions within the National BPA and would monitor rumblings of discontent; often prefacing it with 'there's trouble at mill' whenever we met. He called my office phone.

"Some people are unhappy with yesterday's newspaper article, Paul; they're saying it reflects badly on the National."

This was Ruwan's way of saying the usual mischief-makers were having a dig at the Chairman.

By the end of the week, I'd read the newspaper article it seemed a thousand times, and considered very carefully the various elements, down to the choice of the Kensington based tabloid newspaper. As I read, I became even more convinced that the newspaper's source *was* from within the BPA movement. I had made my mind up to challenge the suspected mole but, after careful thought, I decided against igniting an argument that had the potential to destabilise the National BPA movement.

As my tenure at the helm of the National BPA progressed, the divisive nature of internal politics became increasingly difficult to manage or avoid.

Post- Stephen Lawrence Inquiry, the Home Secretary, Jack Straw, established a steering committee to oversee the recommendations from the MacPherson Report. On that steering committee was Robyn Williams, a Nottinghamshire officer and a friend. Robyn had been a leading member of the interim National Committee when she was appointed to the Home office steering committee.

'Robyn must be removed from the Lawrence Steering Committee and replaced with the Chair of the NBPA' was a murmuring from certain sections of the National BPA.

"They see it as a weakness of the Chair if Robyn remains on that Committee," confided Ruwan.

With some reluctance, I sent a letter to the Secretary of the Stephen Lawrence Steering Committee and made it clear, in my capacity as Chair of the NBPA, that I would be replacing Robyn Williams at the next meeting.

Not having received a formal response, I attended the next meeting of the Stephen Lawrence steering committee; it had taken place two floors above my office. I was met at the door to the meeting by two Home Office officials.

"Inspector Wilson, we received your letter but as the invitation had already gone out to Sergeant Williams, there wasn't an opportunity to discuss it with the Home Secretary."

"So, Robyn remains a member of the Group?" I asked.

"Yes, you will replace her at the next meeting."

It was a very tense discussion. Clearly, the Home Office staff were embarrassed at the potential for some form of confrontation, in the presence of the Home Secretary.

There was not and I withdrew, clearly to the annoyance of some NBPA colleagues. It was a particularly low point in my tenure as Chair. I was formally appointed to the Stephen Lawrence Steering Committee at the following meeting and remained a member until the conclusion of my Chairmanship.

In the knowledge that I would not be occupying the NBPA Chairman post for a further term, I eagerly looked through *Police Orders* each week to plan for my next posting.

Chapter 49

Neighbourhood Wardens

While keen to move on, I was also interested in extending my voluntary absence from the Metropolitan Police during its post- Stephen Lawrence Inquiry introspection. The ongoing internal police debate around the validity of the Stephen Lawrence Inquiry finding of institutional racism had generated considerable hostility to those supporting such views. With my high-profile media pronouncements along with my oral testimony at the Inquiry and subsequent media coverage during and after, I felt under a degree of suspicion and resentment. A level of discomfort that I had not previously experienced. The Metropolitan Police, I had concluded, offered me a less than comfortable and welcoming work environment at this moment in time but, on a positive note, it encouraged me to seek lateral development opportunities I probably would not have otherwise found.

It was not too long before I unearthed a gem innocuously placed within *Police Orders* at the bottom of the last page.

'Inspectors are invited to apply for a two-year placement as police advisor to the recently established Neighbourhood Warden Unit, currently placed in the Department of Environment, Transport and the Regions, (DETR) Victoria Street, SW1…'

My interest was piqued, *that appears half interesting,* I thought to myself, but what is a Neighbourhood Warden?

I made an appointment to meet with Susan King, Head of the Neighbourhood Warden Unit, in her Victoria Street office, a few minutes' walk from the Home Office.

"Hi Susan, I'm interested in applying for the recently advertised police advisor role but admit I know nothing about Neighbourhood Wardens."

Susan explained her background; she had been head-hunted from her previous community safety role with Safer Merthyr Tydfil, where she had some success in introducing Neighbourhood Wardens, to head up this new Government programme.

"Basically, Paul, Neighbourhood Wardens aim to improve the quality of life in under-resourced communities by providing a uniformed presence in residential areas. They can help deliver local crime and disorder reduction targets. They are the 'eyes and ears' of the police, local authority, and community," explained Sue.

"This all sounds interesting, if not a bit radical Susan. How are these Wardens viewed by the Police?"

Susan smiled, "That's part of your role if you are successful. We expect some pushback from the police and will have to work hard to educate your colleagues on how the Neighbourhood Warden can add value to policing."

"Obviously, the Met is onside otherwise the post wouldn't have been advertised in our internal newsletter," I mentioned.

"Oh, yes, very much so. The police post is sponsored by your Deputy Commissioner, Ian Blair, he's incredibly supportive of our agenda."

"Ok, that's good to know. So, what will the police role entail?"

"Many things, including management of 'bids' received from Local Authorities."

I looked blankly at Susan, "What's a 'bid' Susan?"

Susan smiled once more, "The government has made funding available in order to roll out Neighbourhood Wardens in certain less-resourced Boroughs, our Unit will invite Local Authorities to apply for these funds to enable them to introduce Wardens at a Borough level, these applications are called 'bids.'"

"And what else do you see the police advisor involved in?" I asked.

"Well, we have top-sliced our budget to allow us to deliver extensive training and education for Local Authority Warden managers. This will involve looking at good practice in other countries where Wardens have proved to be successful, namely the United States and Holland."

I uncrossed my legs and leaned forward in my chair. Susan had my complete attention.

"If successful you would be involved in managing some of our tours of the United States and Holland. Would this be a problem?" smiled Sue.

"Not at all," I replied.

Two weeks later, I attended the selection interview panel consisting of Susan King and John Curtis, a career Civil Servant attached to the Neighbourhood Warden Unit. I felt confident. I had done my homework; the Neighbourhood Warden idea came from the Government's Social Exclusion Unit (SEU), set up in 1997. Prime Minister Tony Blair had asked the SEU, "how to develop integrated and sustainable approaches to the problems of the worst housing estates, including crime, drugs, unemployment, community breakdown, and bad schools etc."

My preparation revealed that the implementation of Neighbourhood Wardens into under-resourced communities was premised on communitarian philosophy; thought to enhance local governance and build civic society.

"Will you please wait outside Paul; we'll notify you of our decision shortly," informed John.

A few minutes later, Sue King emerged from the interview room.

"We'd like to offer you the post, Paul. Congratulations!"

On the inside I was ecstatic. The sheer relief in knowing that I would very shortly embark on this new and exciting chapter in my career was overwhelming. Contrastingly, externally I continued to project the same calm demeanor I had so expertly projected throughout the interview.

"Thanks, Susan; I'm really looking forward to working with you and John."

Within a few months of my move into the Neighbourhood Warden Unit details of the Met's internal promotion procedure for Inspectors seeking promotion to Chief Inspector was announced. I began my preparation.

The day of my promotion interview process was announced. Following what I considered to be an exceedingly difficult interview panel, I waited for the outcome. Some days later, seated behind my computer, Susan King shouted across the office.

"Paul, there's a call for you. I think you might want to take it in my office."

"Ok, Sue," I responded, kicking back my chair, and making the short walk across the office while thinking that such a sensitive call was either the Deputy Commissioner ordering my return to the Met, or the result of my promotion board.

I picked up Sue's phone, "Yes, Paul Wilson speaking."

"Paul, this is your Human Resources office at the Met; please give me your warrant number, including the prefix."

I rattled off the unique number assigned to me at the beginning of my police career.

"Paul, I'm pleased to inform you that you have been successful in the Chief Inspector selection process."

"Thank you!" I said, "Will I be promoted while on this current placement as I understand this post's job description was initially written for a Superintendent?"

"Paul, please put your request in writing and a decision will be made shortly."

I was eventually promoted to the rank of Chief Inspector while serving my placement with DETR.

With the Neighbourhood Warden Unit now subsumed into the huge Neighbourhood Renewal Unit and relocated to Eland House at the Victoria Station end of Victoria Street, my job description took an unexpected turn.

"Paul, Jon would like to see you in his office. He's got some new work that he wants you to be involved with," explained Sue.

Jon Bright was Sue's boss and someone I guessed had been instrumental in securing Sue's position as Head of the Neighbourhood Warden Unit. Jon, a published author on the topic of crime prevention and previously Operations Director for the quango, Crime Concern, wasn't the usual career civil servant, nor did he portray a blandness sometimes associated with Oxbridge alumni. He had an almost mischievous sense of humour, once telling me that, *Paul, there does not exist any grave situation that cannot be made considerably worse with the introduction of a police officer.*

I knocked and entered Jon's office.

"Thanks for coming, Paul. Are you aware of the rapidly deteriorating situation in northern England culminating in serious disturbances in Oldham last weekend?"

"Yes, Jon, I read that a number of police officers were injured."

Jon looked pensive and peered over his spectacles.

"Yes, well there are a small number of northern towns that look particularly vulnerable to further and even more serious outbreaks of disorder. They all share strikingly similar characteristics, former centres of the textile industry stricken with unemployment since the 1980s and with a substantial British South Asian population."

"'Systemic racism, poor housing, unemployment, no job prospects; a perfect cocktail for large scale disorder', is how one of the Sunday broadsheets described it," I said.

"And I wouldn't disagree with that, Paul, and these areas are very much on the Neighbourhood Renewal radar given their position on the social deprivation index."

"So, what is the plan, Jon?"

"Well, we have been given the green light to divert significant Neighbourhood Renewal Unit resources to these affected areas and what I want to establish is a Public Order and Community Cohesion (POCC) task force to help us direct assistance in a smart way."

"And my role?" I inquired anxiously.

"We need you to link into the police intelligence gathering in order to equip us with the bigger picture and of course, ensure that any activities promoted by the NRU do not conflict with operational policing and vice versa."

"What type of activities do you foresee the NRU sponsoring?"

"We need to help strengthen these communities Paul; over this summer we will have lots of young people on the streets. We need to engage them in some worthwhile activities and to that end, we will be funding numerous third sector organisations to run programmes across the north of England on our behalf."

For the next few months my attention was directed away from Neighbourhood Warden implementation and onto my POCC role, where, with others, I was involved in helping stabilise the tinderbox environment in towns, such as Burnley, Oldham and Bradford that experienced significant outbreaks of public disorder during the summer of 2001. At the conclusion of my role, I was summoned by Jon Bright.

"Paul, your work on the POCC initiative during this summer is really appreciated and went far beyond that expected in your job description. The powers that be feel you should be rewarded with a special 'one off' payment, a small token of our gratitude."

"That's very kind, Jon, thanks."

"Another challenge for you to negotiate is just how we make this payment to you as the Met's HR department informs us that police officers cannot receive such additional payment?"

I rose to my feet and walked to the door. Turning, I said, "Don't worry about that Jon, as you know problem solving is within the police officer DNA."

Jon smiled.

Chapter 50

President of the United States

I had settled back into my usual role when Sue King called me into her office.

"Paul, while you were on the POCC initiative we organised a visit to Washington DC in the United States for a number of our new Warden managers. Would you be interested in going last week in July?"

"Yes, Sue, but why Washington DC?"

"They have an interesting and by all accounts hugely successful Warden scheme managed by a Business Improvement District. We've contacted one of their Directors, a retired police chief," explained Sue.

"That sounds interesting," I replied.

"Yes, I thought it would be of particular interest to you as the programme works closely with the local police department; many of the supervisors are retired police officers," communicated Sue.

I returned to my desk, logged onto my computer, and opened my personal email. A few weeks previous, I had received an invitation from the National Organisation of Black Law Enforcement Executives (NOBLE) to attend their 25th annual conference to be held in Washington DC. I had not paid it that much attention as I did not expect to be able to attend.

Upon opening the email, I saw the date of the NOBLE conference; it coincided with our Warden visit to the DC Business Improvement District. In addition, on a closer reading of the conference itinerary I noticed that the President of the United States, George W Bush would be addressing the conference. I wondered, *would there be time in our schedule for me to attend the conference.*

"Yes, that's fine Paul. We have some downtime scheduled during that period, so no problem."

A few weeks later, along with Sue and twenty Neighbourhood Warden managers from Local Authorities across England, we arrived at Washington's Dulles airport, and then checked into our hotel. The following day, pre-arranged transportation ferried our group to offices on K Street in the heart of Washington DC, home of the Downtown DC Business Improvement District (BID). It was here that we were introduced to the Deputy Executive Director of Downtown DC.

"Hi, welcome to Washington DC, the nation's capital. My name is Frank Russo, a former Police Major in the city of Baltimore, where I served for twenty-five years. Following retirement, I spent six years at Downtown Baltimore Partnership and moved here to Downtown DC in 1999. Later this morning, we'll take you out onto the streets of DC, where you will see our red and blue uniformed Safety, Hospitality and Maintenance Ambassadors (SAMs) going about their business of making people feel safe."

With introductions finished, Sue walked over to me.

"Very impressive isn't he, as a former senior police officer who founded, developed, and implemented wardens in both Baltimore and Washington DC, I think he would be a great asset as a speaker at one or more of our regional conferences."

"Regional conferences?" I asked with a puzzled look on my face.

"Oh, I haven't mentioned it? We're going to organise a conference in each of the government regions to promote the roll-out of Neighbourhood Wardens. Or rather, you are going to organise the conferences," Sue laughed.

On Monday, July 30th, 2001, I made my way to the Marriot Wardman Park Hotel in Washington D.C. for the NOBLE conference, where I planned to spend the day and return to my hotel in the evening. It had been three years since I had attended the NOBLE conference in New Orleans; so, I was interested to see what had developed since then and of course to catch up with old friends. I entered the hotel and followed signs to the NOBLE conference room. Following registration, I was given a seat on the second row from the stage, directly opposite where an empty lectern was placed. I took my seat and watched as what I assumed were plain clothed Secret Service agents thoroughly inspected the lectern. A few minutes later one of the agents approached the lectern and affixed to the front, the Seal of the President of the United States.

Seems as though the President's arrival is imminent, I thought to myself as I scanned the mostly filled seats in the conference hall. Many of the delegates were wearing the uniforms of police forces from across the United States. I had rarely seen this many black uniformed police officers congregated under one roof and then only in the United States. A deep voice boomed across the public announcement system.

"Ladies and gentlemen, please rise for the 43rd President of the United States of America, George W Bush."

A silence fell over the auditorium followed by the sound of hundreds of delegates rising to their feet. I followed suit.

President George W Bush walked onto the stage and addressed assembled members of NOBLE literally thirty feet from my seat. Looking considerably younger and somewhat taller than his TV appearances, he launched into his address. I thought to myself, *I'm definitely not a fan of this President's policies but I can't help but admire his delivery style and the content of his speech, much of what seems to be ad-libbed.*

As President Bush completed his speech, once again the delegates, me included, stood up and this time applauded. What happened next was most unexpected and as I looked at the panic-stricken faces of the Secret Service agents strategically placed around the lectern, I guessed it was something that had not been planned. The 43rd President of the United States stepped down from the stage, did a left turn and approached assembled NOBLE delegates seated on the front row.

If the President isn't safe in the company of hundreds of police officers, where is he safe? I thought to myself as I remained standing to get a better view of what was taking place. I looked at the large gathering that surrounded the President. Many of them were Secret Service agents, although it seemed a fair number of mainly female police officers, were standing chatting with a very relaxed looking President Bush. As I watched, it appeared that very slowly the President was moving down the line of delegates in my direction.

I'm sure his entourage of advisors and security staff will pull him away any second, I thought to myself. Shockingly, that did not happen, and the leader of the free world edged gradually closer to where I was standing.

I can't believe what's happening, because on his present trajectory he will be standing by my side in about 3-4 minutes, I thought to myself. Those were the longest 4 minutes I had ever known, until it happened. President George W Bush was standing opposite me and looked directly into my eyes. Without hesitation I held out my hand.

"Pleased to meet you, Mr. President. I'm Paul Wilson, a Chief Inspector with the Metropolitan Police, London, England and a former Chair of both the Black Police Association and National Black Police Association,", I said, in record speed.

"Paul, pleased to meet you, from London England you say?"

"Yes, Sir."

"Well, welcome to the United States of America. I hope we are treating you well?"

"Been here many times, Sir; I always enjoy myself."

During this time, the President continued to grip my hand, shaking it slowly as he spoke about his delight in being asked to address a NOBLE conference and all the while the gathered crowd gently buffeted both myself and the President, but he remained calm; his eyes fixed mine as we conversed. I was the only person in the room that mattered it seemed as out of the corner of my eye I could see many others vying to gain his attention.

"You know, I visited your Queen just recently, to try and get a piece of legislation passed."

But you refused to sign the Kyoto[7] *legislation and that's what we wanted,* I thought to myself

"Really, Sir, that's interesting," I replied, not wishing to prematurely curtail my only opportunity to chat with an American President.

"Yes, a lovely lady; a real pleasure."

Wow, I thought, *the leader of the free world really does not appreciate that our Queen has no executive power to persuade British politicians to enact legislation.*

"Paul, I'm getting signals from my staff, I need to move on, enjoy your stay in the United States."

"Yes, Sir, a pleasure to meet you."

As the entourage moved slowly toward the exit, I looked around anxiously, *surely someone photographed what just happened?* I thought to myself. I was wrong.

---

[7] In March 2001, President George W. Bush announced the U.S. would not implement the 1997 Kyoto Protocol. The Protocol was aimed at curbing greenhouse gas emissions and countering global warming.

Chapter 51

Prime Minister of the UK

On return to London and life within the Neighbourhood Renewal Unit, Sue asked me to come into her office for a chat.

"Paul, you know the Neighbourhood Renewal Strategy is very much a personal concern of the Prime Minister, Tony Blair?"

"Yes, Sue, I did read his foreword for the National Action Plan, where he said his vision is of a Britain where no-one is seriously disadvantaged by where they live, where power, wealth and opportunity are in the hands of the many not the few," I recited.

"Impressive, Paul; well, he's paying a visit to the Neighbourhood Renewal Unit this afternoon and you have been selected to meet him, as a representative of the Neighbourhood Warden programme."

A couple of hours later myself and several other chosen representatives from the Neighbourhood Renewal Unit lined up in the Eland House atrium to await our turn to meet the Prime Minister.

We were not kept waiting for long as a commotion at the entrance to the atrium signaled the entry of Tony Blair's entourage. Senior members of the NRU chatted with Blair. There were I guessed about ten individuals in line before he got to me and as I waited my mind began to wander back to the date of the General Election on the 1st of May 1997. On that date I was deployed as ground commander on London's South Bank where, later that evening, and into the early hours of May 2nd a huge celebratory election party was planned by the Labour Party at the Royal Festival Hall. A few hours before the commencement of the party when it was clear that the Labour Party had won the General Election, I was approached by one of my sergeants, he had clearly been running and breathlessly relayed his message to me.

"Guv, we've just received what the Yard is calling a credible bomb threat to the Royal Festival Hall."

I had dealt with several bomb threats in my career, but given the attendant circumstances, this one took on a level of considerable and urgent importance. The decisions I made in the next few minutes had career ending potential but more importantly, the potential for a legacy of carnage and mayhem had I made the wrong judgement. The IRA bombing of the Conservative Party conference in Brighton, early in my police career, flashed through my mind.

"Sarge, please find me the Festival Hall manager and bring him or her here please."

A few minutes later I was approached by the manager of the Royal Festival Hall, his face betrayed a level of stress he had probably never experienced in his professional life. I explained the information we had just received.

"At this moment in time we are faced with the distinct possibility of evacuating everyone from the Festival Hall and cordoning the whole area off," I said, as calmly as possible.

The manager stared at and through me. The stress I assumed had frozen his facial expression.

"Or we can await the arrival of our dogs and do a systematic search of the Festival Hall; obviously, that will be less disruptive. What is your view?"

"I would be happier if we were to follow the less disruptive course but that carries serious risk, I understand that."

"It does, but the buck stops with me," I said.

Within a short space of time several specialist police assets had arrived on the South Bank and following discussions I decided to take the less disruptive course of action. The Labour Party celebratory party was able to take place and concluded without incident.

Probably not a story appropriate for today, I thought as Tony Blair chatted away to the person next to me. I waited patiently.

"Prime Minister, this is Chief Inspector Paul Wilson, currently attached to the Neighbourhood Renewal Unit working on the roll out of Neighbourhood Wardens."

An unshaven Tony Blair shook my extended hand.

"You're with the Met I understand?"

"Yes, Prime Minister, this is my second year working on the Warden programme."

"I am very interested in the Neighbourhood Warden as a deterrent to street crime," said the Prime Minister.

"Absolutely, the Wardens' presence on the street sends a strong signal that the locality is cared for and that alone can improve the quality of life for residents by reducing the level of anti-social behaviour and the fear of crime."

"That's great, can they tackle these street corner drug dealers; get them off our streets?"

That's not the job of the Neighbourhood Warden, I thought to myself. They can be the eyes and ears of the police but confronting street dealers is not in their remit as they have no power of arrest.

"They will certainly be of assistance to the police in such localities," I said diplomatically.

"Thank you so much for all your work, Chief Inspector."

The Prime Minister moved onto the next colleague.

Within a few weeks of the Prime Minister's visit, Downing Street allocated the NRU thirty-five million pounds to pump prime a Street Wardens Programme (SWP). In a significant departure from the original Neighbourhood Warden concept, Street Wardens would have powers to issue fixed penalty notices for a raft of anti-social behaviour offences.

Chapter 52

Fulbright Police Fellowship Award

In 2002, nearing completion of my attachment to the government's Neighbourhood Renewal Unit I received a phone call from Clive Johnson, a friend and colleague, who worked as a lecturer at the National Police College, Bramshill. Clive had sent me an email with attachment a few days previously but now he had emailed again to say that he would call on Wednesday with some important information that might be of interest to me.

"Hi Clive, thanks for your email, I have just been so busy that I really haven't had time to fully digest it."

"Yes, I can imagine. Your recent visit to the States with representatives from ACPO, Superintendents Association and the Federation was the talk of the College, how was it?"

"It was good, I actually took someone from the NBPA too."

"Where did you go?"

"Baltimore, there's a successful warden scheme there that we like to show people, that's my third visit in two years."

Clive laughed, "You trying to get your face on that new tv series, 'The Wire'?"

"What's 'The Wire'?" I asked.

"Really? Never mind, I phoned to urge you to look at the email I sent you as I think it's something that you should apply for," said Clive.

I paused momentarily.

"Ok, why do you think it will benefit me, I'm really enjoying life in the Neighbourhood Renewal Unit."

"Yes, I know that, but the Fulbright Police Fellowship Award takes you to the United States for three months, to undertake research of your choice."

"Really?!" I exclaimed.

Clive really knew how to get my attention; as over the past fifteen years, I had enjoyed numerous visits to the United States, in both a personal and professional capacity. In addition to recent visits with the Neighbourhood Wardens Programme, last year I had been invited to Chicago by the Midwest Coalition of African American Police Officers, where I had been presented with the President Award, *for having the fortitude to address the various issues that plague the relationship between police officers and their community and for establishing an international network'.*

"So, why have I not heard of this Fulbright Fellowship before, but before you answer, is it available to people of colour?" I laughed.

"To be honest with you, Paul, I cannot recollect any black police officer being awarded the Fulbright Police Fellowship, but there has to be a first time for everything," said Clive.

"And this is the problem Clive, your work at the National Police Training College means you get to hear about these super opportunities but the rest of us get passed by, so only the select few get a look-in."

"Look, Paul, I wouldn't disagree with anything you've said, I think the Fulbright institution would be the first to admit it has problems connecting with racially diverse groups within the police service and elsewhere, but that shouldn't discourage you from applying."

My thoughts on the matter deepened.

"I know you are a good mate, Clive but why me and why now?"

"You've just completed your master's degree in Community Safety, and I think that, along with your anti-racism profile within the police service, will enhance your application enormously."

"Ok, Clive, you have me interested, I'm definitely going to look in some detail at the attachments you have sent me."

At the conclusion of my day in the office, I returned to Clive's email and looked through the attachments.

Fulbright Police Research Fellowship

Created in the aftermath of the Second World War through the vision of Senator J. William Fulbright, the US-UK Fulbright Commission promotes peace and understanding through educational exchange. It is part of the global Fulbright Program—one of the world's most prestigious awards programs, operating in over 150 countries with nearly 300,000 alumni worldwide. Of these, more have won Nobel Prizes than those of any other academic program.

The Fulbright Police Research Fellowship is one of several awards aimed at encouraging and supporting the exchange of information between the US and the UK and is highly regarded in both countries. Police officers can apply to carry out research in any matter relating to policing. It is extremely competitive and in order to be successful, participants must demonstrate that their research is an urgent and current matter, and a high priority for UK policing. They must also provide personal evidence of their ability to conduct themselves academically and with ambassadorial capacity so that they can represent the UK police and build an ongoing long-term relationship with US counterparts.

I was interested and excited at the prospect as there was nothing that I had seen in the literature's small print to discourage me. I had been absorbed in my master's degree for the past year or so and felt more than equipped to present my case for consideration. Before I submitted anything, I had to comply with the guidance Clive had forwarded. My compliance included the daunting task of identifying an educational institution in the United States willing to host me for three months or more. This task led me to the assumption that well-connected officers might have a strong advantage, which adversely, might be a discouraging hurdle.

I decided to sleep on it and the next morning I looked through some of my Community Safety course notes for inspiration. I needed a theme, something topical and pressing in order to convince the Fulbright Commission to choose me above the many applicants I suspected would apply for this prestigious award. Once I had identified the policing issue to underpin my application, I would be better placed to find a base to host me.

My master's degree study into the policing of disenfranchised communities had revealed an approach undertaken by the Chicago Police in the United States. The Chicago Alternative Policing Strategy or CAPs, as it was commonly known, sought to solve neighbourhood crime problems, rather than merely to react to their symptomatic consequences. This was an approach that had fueled considerable interest in the international policing family as it encouraged police and the public to work in partnership in order to solve local problems.

Then it clicked, I had read about Professor Wesley Skogan from Northwestern University in Chicago, someone who had evaluated the CAPS programme over a period of years to the extent that he was considered a valuable resource by Chicago police. Admiringly, I kept a copy of his book, 'Community Policing, Chicago Style' (1999), in my reading collection.

It crossed my mind that if I could base my interest around the Chicago Alternative Policing Strategy then that would surely be a basis on which to approach Professor Skogan to ask for his assistance with meeting the requirements of academic affiliation required for Fulbright applicants.

Not long after, an email expressing my intention to apply for the Fulbright Police Fellowship with a research interest in the Chicago Alternative Police strategy was sent to Professor Skogan. This opportunity was contingent upon whether he/Northwestern University would consider hosting me for the duration of my visit.

On the twenty-first of March 2003 I received an email reply from

Professor Skogan.

I received your message this morning. We would be happy to host you at Northwestern University, in our Institute of Policy Research. Chicago would be an excellent base for getting in touch with policing trends around the country.

I punched the air in triumph.

Yes! Part 1 in the bag, I thought to myself.

Being provided with Professor Skogan's office and home phone numbers at the conclusion of his email, I decided to call.

"Hi, Professor Skogan, Paul Wilson here, thank you so much for agreeing to host my Fulbright visit, that is if I am successful with my application."

"Hello, Paul, a pleasure. Be sure to get that application in as soon as possible but what I wanted to say to you is, do not confine your visit to Chicago; make the most of your three months and visit other American cities where there are some very innovative practices here that complement community policing."

That was the motivation I needed to hear and that evening I put together my Fulbright Police Fellowship Award application along with my Statement of Purpose with the project title, **Policing the socially excluded – an alternative policing strategy.**

Policing in the UK has for the past decade been largely reactive in its ability and desire to address issues of crime and disorder. There is little doubt that modernisation or the reform of the police, through Audit Commission inspired performance management, intelligence-led policing and other statistical and quantitative means of measuring police effectiveness and efficiency has caused a narrowing of the police approach and focus.

Without strong ties to the community, the police may not have access to pertinent information from citizens that could help or deter crime or indeed the support and authority police depend upon to police with the 'consent of the public'. There is a growing academic consensus in the UK to support the view that public confidence in policing is at an all-time low. Recent statements by the Deputy Commissioner of the Metropolitan Police advocating that policing must change and that more of the same is unacceptable, suggesting that officers must return to neighbourhoods, heralds the dawning of a new era for policing in the UK. An era that can undoubtedly learn a great deal from the US community policing experience of the past few years and in particular the Chicago Alternative Policing Strategy (CAPS), evaluated over the past seven years by Professor Wesley Skogan.

The Chicago experience suggests that officers 'returning' to neighbourhoods will not happen overnight, particularly in those communities often termed the socially excluded where years of neglect and an enforcement policing experience has generated substantial mistrust of the police, regardless of well-meaning intentions.

Among the many questions that persist in the UK are how to create communities out of neighbourhoods that must battle against such forces as poverty, hopelessness, powerlessness and debilitating levels of crime. Accepting the essential value of participation in a democracy, one must address how these neighbourhoods can be mobilised to promote greater community safety and what role the police can truly play in this mobilisation.

My US research would specifically focus on practical approaches that might usefully be employed in the UK to engage and mobilise communities that might appear reluctant or disinterested in dialogue with the police. Particular attention will be given to the largely unexplored issue of 'equity' and the consequence for police managers charged with making decisions regarding the resourcing of community or neighbourhood policing.

The application now submitted for consideration I contacted Clive.

"I need to thank you, Clive. I hadn't appreciated the meaning of the Fulbright Police Fellowship until I read the attachments you sent. I've now submitted my application and have a base at Northwestern University under the supervision of community policing guru, Professor Wesley Skogan if by some fluke I am successful."

"That's what I like about you, Paul; you don't hang around. It only seems like yesterday that I was encouraging you to go for it," he laughed.

"Yes, I have been terribly busy and recently spoke to Professor Skogan who suggests I should visit other American cities, in addition to Chicago. What do you think?"

"You know the Fulbright grant is quite modest and many police authorities will not subsidise the Fulbright Fellowship, but I happen to know that Norfolk, Essex, and West Yorkshire constabulary have recently made additional funds available to enable their Fulbright Fellows to both extend their study tour and meet travelling and living expenses."

"Clive, you are a mine of information, but I'm not going to get too excited about visiting other cities at this early stage of my application."

I had not discussed my application outside a small circle of people that I felt needed to know, which included my two references, Jon Bright Head of Programme Implementation at the Neighbourhood Renewal Unit, and Professor Simon Holdaway, Director of Criminological Research at the University of Sheffield. Because I was seconded to a work placement outside of the Metropolitan Police, my liaison person in Human Resources, John Green, was the only Metropolitan Police member of staff advised of my application.

About four weeks after I had submitted the application, I received a letter from the Fulbright Commission in London, inviting me to attend an interview at their premises on the first of May 2003.

I did a little dance around my kitchen, relieved that I'd got this far, *but what's with the interview*, I thought to myself.

I phoned Clive, "I've got to attend the Fulbright Commission for an interview. You didn't say anything about an interview!"

"Don't worry, Paul; that's really good news. It means you are virtually through the process. Providing you don't scare them off at the interview, it's yours I would have thought."

"I wish I could share your optimism; I was under the impression it was all decided on paper," I said.

Anyhow, I was determined not to allow myself to worry about the interview stage of the application. Hopefully, it was as Clive described, a formality introduced to ensure I was a fit and proper person to enter the United States.

Regardless, I prepared for the interview as though everything depended upon it. On the hour, every hour I snatched a little time to read my Statement of Purpose, critiquing every part and for the next hour I formulated numerous responses should I be asked.

Upon the first of May, I absolutely exuded confidence as I set out dressed in my grey suit, white shirt, and a conservative blue and red silk tie. Completely fitting for an officer prepared to walk into an important interview. My mind was just as sharp as my attire, ready for any question thrown at me.

I arrived at the Fulbright Commission's headquarters fifteen minutes early. *Time to read my Statement of Purpose another four or five times*, I thought to myself.

"Chief Inspector Wilson, the panel is ready. Would you please walk this way?" said the young lady from the Commission.

I followed her through the large double doors and my eyes immediately fixed upon the three interview panelists. With a facial expression that must have appeared as though I had just met up with three long lost friends, I took my seat in front of their table. Completely relaxed, my mind briefly dared to think that I would be flying out to Chicago in September.

Chairing the panel was Roger Graef, filmmaker, criminologist, and a committed member of the Howard League for penal reform. Roger had invited me to give a keynote address at the Howard League's Annual Conference at Oxford University a few years ago. We had both been members of the Metropolitan Police Independent Advisory Group on race. Next to Roger was Inspector Robyn Williams, someone who had been involved in the Black Police Association movement over the years. The third panelist was a Deputy Chief Constable, a lady whose name escaped me, but I recalled her from my visits to Bramshill, National Police Training College. All three panelists knew me well and what I had stood for over the past few years.

The questions were friendly and conversational. No-one was there to trip me up and all seemed genuinely interested in what I planned to do in the United States. As the interview concluded, all three panelists got to their feet and walked with me to the door. Roger Graef stepped forward and shook my hand.

"And when you get back, be sure to tell everyone all about it with that passionate delivery of yours."

No-one at the interview said I have got it, but Roger's parting comment was good enough for me.

The next day I received a letter at my home in Thornton Heath, South London. The envelope carried the Fulbright Commission stamp. I hastily opened it.

Dear Mr Wilson,

UK Fulbright Police Research Fellowship

Thank you for attending your interview on Thursday 1st May for the above award. I am pleased to advise you that you have been recommended for this award, which comprises a grant of £5,000 for a minimum of three months in the United States.

I did a little dance around the kitchen before flopping into a comfortable armchair where I put my feet up and allowed the news to sink in.

Teary-eyed, I reflected on my recent domestic upheavals as I had been through a very difficult time of late and was now separated from the mother of my two children and had moved out of the family home. This news served to give me a much-needed boost.

However, I was also concerned that my external placement with the Neighbourhood Renewal Unit was about to conclude. Where would I go, what would I do? I knew that my sponsor, Deputy Commissioner Ian Blair, was keen that I should transfer my skills and knowledge from the Neighbourhood Wardens' programme to the recently established Police and Community Support Officers (PCSO) Project, housed just off Trafalgar Square in central London.

The irony of my transfer to the PCSO project had not been lost on me. After all, my two year's posting to the Neighbourhood Wardens' Programme where our creation, development and funding to Local Authorities had enabled the roll-out of uniformed wardens in many London Boroughs. But the proliferation of these uniformed patrollers on the streets of London, all liveried in differing uniforms and answerable to various Local Authorities, was viewed by Deputy Commissioner, Ian Blair as an unforeseen and unwelcome development and one that prompted him to revisit his long-held belief that 'the police do not have a monopoly on keeping the streets safe'. In an about-turn and thinly veiled strategy to retain control of London's streets, Assistant Commissioner Tim Godwin had recently introduced the concept of a Police Community Support Officer (PCSO). Closely imitating the Neighbourhood Warden, the PCSO would not have powers above the ordinary citizen, but whose uniformed presence would serve to improve feelings of confidence and safety on our streets. But most importantly, for Deputy Commissioner Blair, they would be metropolitan police employees, directed, controlled, recruited, and deployed by the metropolitan police. This was a hugely significant development in ensuring the metropolitan police retained control of the uniformed community safety presence in London. It also served to undermine and replace the growth of Local Authority managed 'Neighbourhood Wardens'. And so it was to be, in the summer of 2003, my placement at the Neighbourhood Renewal Unit concluded, I moved from my Whitehall office into my new office at the PCSO Project office, just off Trafalgar Square.

About a month after my reintroduction into the Metropolitan Police Service, I attended a New Scotland Yard meeting that took me into the Deputy Commissioner's suite. As I left, I noticed Sir John Stephens, the Commissioner, speaking to a huddle of suited men in the corridor. He looked in my direction and immediately beckoned me over.

"What are you up to, Wilson, you've been gone forever?" said the Commissioner in his customary jovial manner.

He was particularly interested to hear about the programme I had worked on, but I quickly used the opportunity to tell him about my Fulbright Fellowship Award.

"I will be hosted by Professor Wes Skogan at Northwestern University, but he recommends that I should try and compare a number of American policing initiatives, complementary to community policing, by visiting other American cities besides Chicago," purposefully pausing, I carried on, "San Francisco and Miami police departments seem to be doing some sterling work. What do you think sir?"

"Absolutely, you must. I am also interested in the Chicago communication system 'Citizen Icam,' so please let me know what you find," said the Commissioner.

That short conversation was enough for me to put together my application file setting out my rationale for the additional visits to the American cities of Miami and San Francisco.

The application landed on the desks of various senior officers until, on the twenty-first of August 2003, Commander Brian Paddick supported and endorsed my application for additional funding to cover all air travel between London, Chicago, San Francisco, Miami, and New York, where I planned to write up my research notes over a nine-day period.

During my stay in Chicago, I arranged accommodation on the shores of

Lake Michigan, and while in San Francisco, an apartment on Market Street, a major thoroughfare. On the opposite side of the U.S., in Miami, I had booked an apartment two blocks from Miami beach in a relatively affluent Cuban neighbourhood. I was a little concerned by the fact that at each location I would be dipping into disadvantaged neighbourhoods to experience their way of life and in the evening return to the relatively affluent neighbourhoods. A commonplace experience in the academic community, I convinced myself, nevertheless, I could not help but feel a degree of discomfort.

The one city where I had not booked accommodation was New York, an area I was relatively familiar with, my father worked at Grand Central Station in Manhattan. Whenever I visited, being the young at heart father he was, together we would explore New York's nightlife. Occasionally, he would take me to Harlem's 125th Street where we would hang out and witness a side of New York not usually experienced by tourists. Although I had visited Harlem on several occasions, I had never actually stayed overnight there.

That was the answer to my dilemma, I thought to myself. Stay in Harlem for the New York visit. Tokenistic maybe, largely symbolic, of course, but maybe if I had a feeling, an experience of living in a poor underserved neighbourhood for ten days, the experience might provide a small insight to help me better understand the challenges faced by the community and the police in trying to implement community-based policing.

Renting an apartment in Harlem, the part where tourists do not venture, was not an easy task to perform from the depths of South London. My father was no help; he laughed at me down the phone when I broached the subject with him,

"Hanging out on Lenox and Martin Luther King Boulevard is a whole lot different to living in the 'hood, you gonna take your gun?" he asked, as in common with many Americans, he had difficulty believing that most of London's police are unarmed in their everyday duties.

I had exhausted the possibility of my dad helping me find somewhere to stay so I trawled the internet, looking for inspiration. I found it in *Craigslist*, a huge classified ads site with sections devoted to jobs, housing, for sale, items wanted, services, in fact, most services that you could think of were offered on Craigslist. *Not all legal*, I thought to myself, as I navigated through the websites many sections. I entered New York, housing wanted, apartment wanted, and drilled down until I found Harlem. To my surprise, listed on Craigslist were several rental apartments in Harlem. I researched the localities and finally decided on an apartment near City College, between Amsterdam Avenue and St Nicholas Terrace. The rent asked on a nightly basis was minimal. *Perfect*, I thought to myself. I emailed the name on the ad and received an immediate response.

'Yes, my apartment is available on the dates indicated. I will be out of the country, but I will arrange for a friend to give you access.'

With accommodation arranged, I sent numerous emails to police departments in the cities I intended to visit. I ensured that the Fulbright Fellowship was always mentioned upfront; for I had learned that Fulbright is widely renowned as a prestigious award in the United States.

As the weeks passed, I had received correspondence from the Chicago Police Department, extending an offer of visits and a contact name in the CAPs Division, but nothing received from San Francisco, New York, or Miami police departments. I was not overly concerned as I had several informal contacts through my association and friendship with the US National Black Police Association and the National Organisation of Black Law Enforcement Executives.

The Fulbright Commission in the UK was very thorough in their preparation for my visit. This included a visit to the United States Embassy in Grosvenor Square, central London, for various security talks and checks. Lastly, I was issued with a J1 cultural exchange visa, stamped into my passport.

A few days afterwards, as part of my preparation, I was invited to the US Ambassador's residence, which was an imposing thirty-five roomed mansion set in 12 acres of grounds north-west of London's Green Park, where all Fulbright Award recipients for 2003 had assembled in the palatial dining hall. As I mingled with my fellow alumni, it dawned on me that I was in the company of some of the brightest young academics in the country. Many I spoke to appeared fascinated and even envious of the fact that I was a police officer about to undertake a relatively short piece of research into "such an important and exciting area". An address by the US Ambassador followed our dinner. Of all the advice and instruction I had received in the recent past, it was the Ambassador's concluding comments that resonated with me the most.

"Work hard but ensure you enjoy your time, socialise at every opportunity and be sure to leave a little of yourselves in the United States and if you do that you will have fulfilled Senator Fulbright's dream."

Chapter 53

Policing, Chicago style

I arrived in Chicago, the first leg of my Fulbright visits on 30th of August 2003 and made my way to my residence where I would stay for a month. It was a luxurious, private house overlooking Lake Michigan, a massive freshwater lake spanning three hundred miles in each direction. Its beautiful sandy beachfront equally matched many that I had visited. I was warned by my host of its notorious riptides making it one of the dangerous lakes for swimming in the United States.

The next morning, I collected my rental car and drove to the Institute for Policy Research, Northwestern University, in Evanston, an affluent Chicago suburb. I had arranged to meet Professor Wesley Skogan at his office. I knocked on the door. Immediately entering, I recognised Chicago's community policing guru as his greying hair, beard, and bespectacled appearance accurately resembled the many photographs I had seen of him in various academic publications. Professor Skogan was seated behind his desk, drinking from a cup, and looked up at me as I entered the room. I looked on as he continued drinking, then very slowly he placed his cup very carefully down onto his paper-strewn desk.

With graceful athleticism, he leapt to his feet, walked around his desk and thrust out his hand, "Welcome to your home for the next few weeks, Paul. I have a desk sorted out for you where you may access our internet; so, just unpack your stuff and make yourself at home. Later, we need to introduce you to some colleagues, get your security clearance sorted out and familiarise you with the campus. Tomorrow we'll sit down and discuss exactly what it is you want to see and do."

Early in my visit, I took advantage of my enjoyment of walking by taking the opportunity to walk for miles as it offered a more accurate perspective of life on the streets. My observations were central to my research. As I talked to various community members, my British accent inevitably attracted interest and attention; a situation welcomed by all researchers. As a foreigner, I felt that local people seemed more willing than usual to open up and give their stories and opinions to me. One of my early observations was the homogeneous nature of the community in some localities and was reminded by residents that Chicago remained a sliced cake, each piece segregated from the next. The analogy was confirmed as I walked through many sprawling neighbourhoods. Contrastingly, when lurking about in London you would have seen black, white, and Asian residents simply going about their business, but not so in Chicago.

Errol, a veteran staff member with the City's Housing Department was keen to fill the gaps in my understanding of Chicago's history. "The neighbourhoods that you walked in struggled thirty years ago and are the neighbourhoods that struggle today. The legacy of racial segregation has made it difficult for poor black families to gain access to jobs in other parts of the city. This vicious cycle of segregation means that African Americans live near worse educational opportunities and fewer jobs than other people in Chicago."

Errol's colleague, James, interrupted, "You familiar with redlining?"

"No, I'm not," I answered.

"An old practice which made it impossible to get a federally backed loan for homes in majority-black neighbourhoods. This and other discriminatory practices successfully kept African Americans out of certain neighbourhoods. By the 1940s, half of Chicago's neighbourhoods were effectively off-limits to blacks. We are still suffering from this legacy."

Other staff members, keen to remain off the record, pointed to political leaders in Chicago who they say have compounded this problem over the years. With money being expended on lavish downtown projects, far from the poor neighbourhoods, reinforcing the walls around the ghetto.

The lack of opportunity with little prospect of upward mobility has devastated Chicago's African American communities. For generations, they have been confined to vastly under-resourced neighbourhoods, such as the South Side, where, on one of my ventures to see how real people live, I stopped for petrol in my rental car. The attendant on hearing my accent advised, "If you ain't got a big gun, turn back now."

William Townsel was my contact in the Chicago Alternative Policing Strategy (CAPS) head office. An African American young man working for the City, William ensured I attended several meetings in City Hall where I witnessed City employees and police working side by side to curtail the social decay and high levels of crime, a malaise grounded in a legacy of discriminatory practices. I had attended three Beat meetings where police and communities monthly get together to discuss crime trends and other related matters. Of particular interest was a meeting on Chicago's South Side. I was picked up by Lieutenant Richards, a generously proportioned African American veteran of the Chicago police department and someone the CAPs office had recommended I meet.

"Ok, Paul, this Beat meeting is in one of Chicago's poorest neighbourhoods, an African American community plagued by gangs, high crime, poor City services, and high unemployment, truly a community under siege. Tonight, you will witness their anger and frustration. We try to structure these meetings, but temper and emotions often dictate the order of the evening."

"I am interested to see how cooperative the community are and how problem-solving works," I said.

"I would suggest to you now that problem-solving and partnership working is a hallmark of middle-class wards on the Northwest and Southwest, where the community will participate in the Beat meeting agenda, but you're not going to see much of that tonight."

Lieutenant Richards parked his police cruiser near to the site of the Beat meeting, which to my surprise was held in the open air underneath a large concrete structure that seemed to be part of an overhead freeway. Many people had already gathered in small groups, and the conversation was loud and animated.

"You see that lady with a red top over there?" pointed Lieutenant Richards.

"Yes," I said.

"She always stands on that piece of concrete as it elevates her above everyone else and gives her a perfect speaker platform," he laughed.

I was surprised to see a white police officer bring the meeting to order as the crowd, now gathered, was predominantly African American.

"They don't mind the colour as long as police deliver results and tonight, we haven't got much in the way of good news."

Lieutenant Richards was at pains to point out, "What you researchers and other academics must appreciate is that the Chicago Police Department is currently understaffed by about 400 officers. Our usual complement is a little over 16,000, that is a sizable missing cohort of officers."

"Without a doubt," I agreed, "So, how are police numbers decided for this area and say an affluent area in the Northwest?"

"That's a good but very political point as our last Superintendent, Terry Hilliard and Mayor Daley wanted to redraw police boundaries in accordance with crime levels, meaning we shift more officers into high crime areas, but there is political pushback at the local level. Bottom line is no-one wants to lose police officers," said lieutenant Richards, shaking his head.

Lieutenant Richards' prediction proved to be correct as the imposed curfew dictated the agenda. I scanned the assembled community members, many appeared desperate to grab the Chair's attention but were unable to do so. The number in my view was unmanageable, and with no opportunity for structured conversations, problem solving was not going to happen. The police officer chairing the meeting did his best, occasionally assisted by various City representatives, but with the officialdom on the defensive for the whole evening, I had failed to see any glimpse of partnership working. Even though Chicago is generally perceived as one of the U.S.'s most prosperous cities, I gained the impression that it was going to be a long and difficult struggle for the authorities. I departed the City of Chicago after extending my gratitude and appreciation to Professor Skogan at Northwestern University and William Townsell with the CAPs office, as both had taken the time to ensure that my work encompassed a diversity of interesting and meaningful experiences.

Chapter 54

Policing, San Francisco style

I touched down at San Francisco's airport on 1st October, slightly anxious as I made my way by taxi to my accommodation on Market Street. I had not received any formal response to several communications I had sent to the San Francisco Police Department and that worried me as time was precious and I only had one month in the City. My apartment was small, but functional and offered easy access to downtown San Francisco. I unpacked my belongings and decided, despite San Francisco's notoriously hilly terrain, to explore my new neighbourhood on foot. After I had walked a few blocks my cell phone rang.

"Hello, is that Chief Inspector Wilson?" said the female voice.

"Yes," I replied

"This is Deputy Chief Heather Fong, when did you arrive?"

"About ninety minutes ago," I said.

"Good, we received your emails. Would you like to meet up this afternoon?"

"Yes, that would be great," I said, trying not to give away my feeling of relief and elation.

"Fine, I'll meet you by Pier 9 in an hour's time," said Deputy Chief Fong.

I could hardly believe that the Deputy police chief of the San Francisco Police Department (SFPD) was on her way to meet and greet me. I hailed a taxi as I had no clue as to the whereabouts of Pier 9 and did not want to be late for this golden opportunity.

Within minutes the taxi had delivered me to my meeting point on San Francisco's waterfront.

At the agreed time, I watched as a large black sports utility vehicle drove up to within feet of where I was standing. Its electric window slowly lowered.

"Paul Wilson?" said the lady driver.

"Deputy Chief Fong, I'm so pleased to meet you," I said.

"Please, call me Heather. Jump in, let's go for a coffee."

I opened the passenger door and climbed into the luxurious leather seat of the SUV. After a short drive down the road, Heather parked the car and pointed to Starbucks.

"Bruce, my partner, will meet us here. Let's go in and you can tell me all about London," she said.

Heather was a tall, willowy, bespectacled, middle-aged lady of Chinese heritage. She was soft-spoken, and someone who appeared to be extremely interested in my travels. After about ten minutes, Bruce joined us. Bruce, a sergeant with SFPD, was at the opposite end of the personality continuum; jovial, loud, brash with a rugby player physique and someone who I soon learned was not shy of using colourful language in Heather's presence.

We talked about my time with the Metropolitan Police and life in London, for what seemed to be an age. As I have found with many Americans, London proved to hold an enormous degree of fascination for both Bruce and Heather. Without warning, Bruce changed his jovial nature and adopted a serious expression as he sat upright and pushed his chair further under the table, he leaned toward me.

"Paul, you have arrived in San Francisco during an incredibly unique period in the history of our police department. Tomorrow you will meet Chief Alex Fagan, who, until very recently, was suspended from duty suspected of what you Brits call perverting the course of justice."

"Yes," interrupted Heather, "all very unsavoury and unfortunate…"

"Yeah, and this Chief's days are numbered," said Bruce, speaking over Heather who was shifting uneasily in her chair. "He needs to know, it's a mess and will probably contaminate his stay here. Especially as he will be one of your people," continued Bruce, raising his voice and nodding at Heather.

"You don't know that," said Heather, now raising her softly spoken voice very slightly.

"I work on the ground floor, Heather, and I know how divided this police department is. If you are for Heather Fong, you are against the Chief."

Heather looked at me and smiled, "Paul must be wondering what he's getting in to."

"Well, that's why we need to tell him," said Bruce.

"Can you tell Paul and not the rest of Starbucks?" said Heather, a reference to Bruce's loud voice.

Bruce appeared to ignore Heather's comment and proceeded to tell me about an incident that had shaken the foundations of the SFPD and local politics, known as 'Fajitagate'.

"It all began just over a year ago when the current Chief's rookie cop son and two of his rookie cop friends were outside a bar when they approached two guys carrying a bag of steak fajitas. Fagan junior and the other two officers demanded that the guys hand over their fajitas. A fight started, a beer bottle was thrown, and injuries were suffered by the two guys carrying the fajita. Anyhow, police get called and this is where it gets murky."

"So, what happened?" I inquired.

"The officers that arrived on the scene failed to arrest their off-duty colleagues," said Bruce.

"That is definitely murky," I commented, beginning to understand the gravity of what had taken place.

"Yeah," said Bruce, "But things rapidly slid downhill from there. Virtually, all of the Chiefs at SFPD *allegedly* covered up the whole incident, but it leaked out and a number of key senior officers, including the Police Chief, were indicted for 'obstructing justice'. The Chief resigned. Heather here was the only one on the top team untarnished by the whole sorry affair, and I know that is recognised by Mayor Gavin Newsom," said Bruce, in hushed tones as he leaned further across the table.

"What I don't understand is how Alex Fagan Senior is now Chief of Police," I said.

Bruce slumped back in his seat. "Because they dropped charges against him and because the Chief had resigned, Fagan Snr was next in line for the Chief's job," said Bruce, letting out a deep sigh.

"So, what happens now?" I said.

"Heather is liked by Mayor Newsom, who needs the political support of the large Chinese community in San Francisco; a community that loves Heather. Heather will be our next Chief," said Bruce.

"Nothing is guaranteed Paul, anything could happen," offered Heather in a feeble attempt to appear neutral in the conversation.

The following day I was taken to Chief Fagan's office as he "wanted to meet the Fulbright guy."

Fagan appeared to be in his early fifties or younger and his firm handshake suggested a gym membership.

"Welcome to San Francisco, Paul, I hear Deputy Fong has been taking care of you?"

"Yes, Chief, I'm looking forward to my stay with you guys."

"You are with the Met in London?" asked the Chief.

"Yes, twenty years now," I confirmed.

"Anything you want to see or do just let us know and we'll see what we can do to help," said the Chief, sitting back down in his chair; an indicator that his time with me was spent.

Had I not known about the Fajitagate scandal I would still have sensed that something was not quite right. Chief Fagan had said and done all the expected things to make me feel welcome. However, I picked up a vibe from the lack of eye contact and the forced unnatural smile, that suggested he did not really have time for me and was going through the motions. *Maybe it was because I was seen as a Deputy Chief Fong supporter*, I thought to myself.

The following day I received and immediately accepted an offer from the Chief's office to spend time with SFPD's firearms training unit. In the company of a small number of police officers, I sat in a classroom environment where two instructors engaged the officers in a discussion about various real-life firearms incidents, backed up with newsreel footage and/or newspaper clippings.

After being walked through a bank robbery incident that resulted in the fatal shooting of two suspects, I raised my hand, "I just find it extraordinary that the armed bank robbers were shot in the back as they fled the premises. In Britain that would not be acceptable. We cannot engage unless we, or members of the public, are under threat of being seriously injured and clearly that wasn't the case in the scenario you have just described."

Complete silence filled the air. The two instructors looked around the class at the expressionless faces. It was as though I had spoken out of turn.

One of the instructors responded. "Ok, if we let the perps go, what happens when they get down the street and kill a member of the public to aid their getaway? I'll tell you what happens, the police department is at fault and gets sued."

So, the rationale for shooting the suspects in the back was premised on protecting the image of the police department and presumably the City's budget, I had better not respond to that, I thought, *I will get into trouble.*

An invitation that seemed to be of more interest and relevance requested my attendance, at the graduation ceremony of the police department's Citizen's Academy. Eager to find out more, I accompanied Heather to the ceremony held in a large community hall. I looked on in interest as names of the graduates were read out and invited to walk to the stage to receive a certificate, handshake, and photograph with the Chief of San Francisco police department.

I leaned over to Heather. "What sort of things have the graduates done to earn the certificate?"

"They attend a ten-week program open to members of the community and designed to provide an overview of our police department's structure and activities. These graduates will have learned about a whole range of police procedures, each class teaches a different aspect of police work that ranges from the hiring of officers to the duties of our SWAT team. Included in the course is a ride-along with an officer," said Heather, in a tone and demeanour that suggested a great deal of pride in the nature of the programme.

"Very interesting, but what is the goal of the programme?" I asked.

"It is intended for community members to learn more about their policing and with that their own role and responsibility in the community. It's been shown to help build relationships with law enforcement personnel," said Heather.

As I caught my flight to Miami, I reflected on my time in San Francisco and concluded that their Citizen's Academy could, with a little tweak, travel well across the Atlantic.

Six weeks after my departure, Mayor Newsom appointed Heather Fong as San Francisco's first female police chief of Asian origin, a position she held for five years. Around the same time, an African American lady by the name of Kamala D. Harris was elected as San Francisco's first female District Attorney. Mayor Gavin Newsom is now Governor of California. Ex-Chief Alex Fagan died of a heart attack in London ten years ago while walking his dog.

Chapter 55

Policing, Miami style

On the 1st of November 2003, I arrived at Miami airport. I hailed a taxi to the Miami Beach area, where I had arranged accommodation in an apartment block about ten minutes' walk from the beachfront, and close to what my online research had indicated was an exceptionally good Cuban restaurant. I picked up my luggage from the conveyor belt and followed the exit signs to the taxi park. Once outside of the airport building, I was enveloped in a claustrophobic heat that I was not attired for. Compared to San Francisco's comfortable and warm climate, it was oppressive. I removed my jacket, rolled up my sleeves and headed for the taxi rank. Seated in the back of my taxi, I looked through my wallet until I found a tattered business card for Officer Linda Christie. She was someone I had met at the New Orleans cluster conference back in 1998. I punched her number into my cell phone. As it rang, I wondered whether she still worked in the same department after all this time.

"Hello, Juvenile Division, Officer Christie speaking."

"Linda, it's Paul Wilson, London police officer, we met at the New Orleans conference a few years back."

"Oh my God, Paul. So good to hear from you after all these years. What are you up too these days?"

"I'm in a taxi on my way to Miami Beach, where I'm staying for a month to do some research on community policing. I've written, emailed, and telephoned your Chief's office, but I've not had a response."

"I can't believe it; you are a few miles from my office! I'm busy right now but call me tomorrow and come over to my office and we'll talk."

I was so pleased to have contacted Officer Christie and was not surprised that she had remained with the Miami Police Juvenile Division for five years, as in my experience, American police officers moved far less frequently than their counterparts in London.

Safely checked into my apartment, I changed into shorts and t-shirt as the sun continued to beat down and made any venture outside of the apartment extremely uncomfortable. Now was not the time to explore the area, I decided, only mad dogs and Englishmen go out in the mid-day sun and I was not prepared to fit into either category.

Aided by a map purchased at the airport shop, I had located the Cuban restaurant and managed the one block walk from my apartment. Perspiration dripped off my forehead as I settled down and looked through the menu. By the time I tucked into a generous plate of black beans, rice with plantains, the air conditioning had provided much needed fresh cool air.

I pondered the lack of response from the Miami Police Department. It was most unusual not to have received some form of acknowledgement from police officials. I was anxious to get started with my work and now relied on Officer Christie to introduce the necessary contacts.

The next day I picked up my rental car and made the short drive to Miami Police Department headquarters. Once through the entrance doors, I approached the reception.

"Hi, Chief Inspector Wilson, Metropolitan Police, London, here to see Officer Christie in your Juvenile Division."

"Yes, Sir, we expected your arrival. Officer Christie provided us with your details and asked that you attend her office on the third floor."

As I entered the lift, it dawned on me that I had only been in Officer Christie's company for a twenty-minute conversation at the New Orleans conference, after which, we had exchanged business cards. I hoped that she had not changed her appearance dramatically, otherwise I would be embarrassed. I pushed open the double doors marked Juvenile Division. My fear became reality as I walked into the large open plan office with several police officers busily working at their desks. I quickly scanned the room but failed to see anyone that resembled my memory of Linda Christie.

"Paul, you made it!"

I turned around to see a police officer I instantly recognised. "Hi, Linda, you haven't changed one bit!" I said.

"Thank you, and likewise, walk this way, let's go to our cafeteria for a coffee, or do you Brits only drink tea?" she joked.

Seated in the Headquarters cafeteria, I fully briefed Linda on the purpose of my visit to Miami and explained my disappointment at not receiving any form of correspondence from the office of the Chief.

"Paul, I'm sorry to hear that. It's a long way for you to travel without some form of official welcome from the top team."

"So, do you think it's appropriate for me to visit the Chief's office and introduce myself?"

"Any other month I think Chief Timoney's office would have welcomed you and extended the appropriate assistance, but not this month."

"Why is that Linda, what's happened?" I said in a hushed voice, aware that we were surrounded by police officers.

"Have you not heard of the Free Trade Area of the Americas meeting due to take place in Miami later this month?"

"Sorry, that's escaped me. What is it?"

"All you need to know is it's an important political meeting designed to eliminate trade barriers with a number of countries, excluding Cuba of course."

"Ok, I've got that, but why should it impact the Chief's office?"

"You really need to watch local TV news channels, Paul. We expect thousands of protestors to visit Miami this month to demonstrate opposition to the meetings."

"Oh, I get it, Miami police are preparing to deal with the demonstrations?"

"Yes, Paul but that is an understatement. It appears as though we are getting ready for World War 3 around here!"

"You expect it to be violent?"

"You should start your research with a closer look at Chief Timoney's background and the militarisation of Miami police."

"Oh dear, this is not looking good for community policing."

Linda responded with a hollow laugh. "Look, I'm going to give you a contact that can bring you up to date with what's happening in Miami, both on the militarisation of the police and community policing."

I left Linda's office feeling dejected, as I had planned to use my Miami police's community engagement experience to contrast with findings in Chicago and San Francisco. Both of which had not met my expectations of what community policing in America would look like.

I guess there is always a gulf between academic research and on the ground reality, I thought to myself, as I drove back to my apartment for some desktop research.

The following day I received a call, "Hi Chief Inspector Wilson, Linda Christie gave me your number. My name is Robert Eccles; I understand you are undertaking some research on policing here in Miami?"

"Hi Robert, thanks for calling and yes, I am particularly interested in the community policing programme and underserved communities' engagement with police."

"Ok, Paul, sounds interesting and I think I can help you understand what's happening here in Miami. Can we meet?"

With arrangements made to meet for coffee the next day, I turned on my laptop and searched for Chief Timoney, head of Miami Police department as suggested by Linda.

'Born in Dublin, Ireland', *so he and Alex Fagan Chief of San Francisco Police both had Irish connections*, I thought to myself. I am certain that somewhere an academic paper exists explaining the reason why Ireland has historically provided the United States with so many police officers, but that was not my field of interest at this moment.

After I had browsed the internet for a couple of hours I sat back in my chair and mulled over my findings. Now I realised why I had not heard from Chief Timoney's office. He seemed to have a habit of spending time away from Miami. A number of online newspaper articles had, over the past few months, raised concerns about Chief Timoney's relaxed attitude to his new role.

'*Chief Timoney, appointed in January 2003 and exactly one week later he left Miami for three days for a policing conference in Washington, D.C. Additionally, two months later he was on the road again: this time to Orlando, Florida for a Law Enforcement Agencies meeting'.*

Last month, while I was in San Francisco it appears he was in Philadelphia for six days attending the International Association of Chiefs of Police annual meeting.

My own Force had made me aware that chief police officers loved to travel, as did I, but for a new Chief of Police, appointed in a week when eleven Miami police officers would stand trial for fabricated evidence in a highly publicised case of 'planting guns on arrested suspects', he was clearly unphased by the inevitable alarm bells his departure at this critical time would sound.

Further searches on the net revealed that protesters would descend on Miami because they objected to plans to create a free trade zone stretching from Alaska to Argentina. Doing so, they say will hurt poor workers, put downward pressure on wages and weaken environmental regulations.

'*Police in Miami were determined not to permit a repeat of the chaos that has marked other trade summits worldwide,'* screamed one website, boasting a large photograph of Chief Timoney.

My internet research had not assuaged my concerns about my visit and work in Miami. In fact, it had heightened my fears that this was a wasted journey. *Maybe I should have returned to New Orleans,* I thought, but then I remembered my research had disclosed several serious concerns about the legitimacy of policing in that city. A police department not yet fully recovered from the 1990s, when according to FBI investigators, it was infested with criminals.

The following day, I visited my Cuban restaurant for breakfast. Afterwards, I walked to my local launderette with a large bag of dirty clothes. I was pleased to see the elderly uniformed attendant as I had no desire to babysit laundry for the next hour or so.

"Excuse me can I leave my laundry with you and pick it up later, is that OK?" I asked.

The attendant looked at me. Her facial expression was one of annoyance. She responded to my question in Spanish.

"I'm sorry, I don't speak Spanish, only English," I said.

Her deeply wrinkled face failed to disguise her expression of deep disgust. If she had spat on the floor in front of me, I would not have been surprised. She again responded in Spanish and although I had no idea what was being said, it did not sound polite.

This time I used universal sign language and placed my laundry bag on the floor in front of her, stepped backwards and said, "Ok?"

She muttered something in Spanish, turned and entered a room that adjoined the launderette and slammed the door behind her.

With that, I looked at the instructions on the soap dispenser on the wall, resigned to the fact that I was stuck here for the next hour. I placed my money in the slot provided, obtained my cup of soap powder and emptied it into a washing machine, a weekly ritual I had despised as a young bachelor.

That afternoon I had phoned Robert. I was keen to meet with him in hopes he could rescue the purpose of my visit. We changed the venue and arranged a meet at my favourite Cuban restaurant.

I was about to down my café Cubano when I saw a young white guy, disheveled in appearance, with a laptop case slung over his shoulder, enter the restaurant. He had a slightly lost look on his face. *That must be Robert Eccles,* I thought to myself. I waved him over and as he approached, he held out his hand and greeted me in Spanish.

"Hi, Robert, why the Spanish?" I laughed.

He shrugged his shoulders, "Sorry, but now I've seen you, I assumed you had some Cuban heritage, you have an Afro-Cuban look about you."

"Really?" I said, and explained the recent reception I received in my local launderette.

He laughed loudly. "My girlfriend is of Afro-Cuban heritage and her older relatives' frown on her use of the English language when she is in their company; so, I can imagine that elderly launderette attendant thinking that you were being disrespectful to her."

We both laughed. "Linda tells me you are the guy to bring me up to speed with what's happening in Miami police department," I said, keen to understand what issues I might be facing during my stay.

"Definitely Paul. It can be summarised as follows: since the 9/11 attacks on the twin towers, the police in the United States have deployed a militarised response to what they accurately or inaccurately believe to be a threat to public order, private property, and their own safety. They have developed a policing culture in which protesters are often perceived as the enemy. Cops now think like soldiers and learn how to kill."

"Ok Robert, what exactly do you mean by the militarised response?"

"Paul, you need to visit the demonstrations later this month to see our cops wearing full military-style uniform, helmet, visor, masks, ammunition belts, the works."

I laughed, "Surely not, Robert."

Robert lowered his voice as he leaned forward and said excitedly, "People don't realise that a Federal programme now allows for the transfer of military equipment to police departments. And if that isn't enough, there is a Homeland Security grant programme to provide police departments funding to buy military-grade weapons and vehicles."

"And where is community-based policing in all of this?"

Robert shook his head very slowly, "A poor cousin, if that." He continued, "I'll give you some names of people in the Black and Hispanic communities that are trying to keep community and police engagement going, but it clearly has slipped way down the policing agenda."

I left Robert disappointed at what I had heard but likened it to the gradual acceptance of paramilitary-style uniform accessories in the UK. Long gone were the days when you would patrol the streets with a small wooden truncheon stuffed inside the lining of your uniform trousers. Nowadays, police uniforms bristled with heavy military style utility belts holding CS gas spray, metal extendable baton, heavy-duty Airwave radio, large rigid handcuffs, and other accessories usually associated with officer safety.

A couple of weeks after my meeting with Robert, on the day of the first scheduled meeting likely to attract protestors, I made my way on public transport to downtown Miami.

The streets were empty. Metal shutters guarded storefronts. Everything appeared to be closed. I had never witnessed anything like this. The streets were in total lockdown. Eerily quiet, like something out of a sci-fi movie, where inhabitants flee the city to escape the infection of a deadly virus. Randomly, I saw a group of cyclists, about six, cycling toward me. As they neared it was obvious that they were police officers. I felt like shouting out to ask what's going on in this great city but thought better of it. They passed me by; not one of them giving me more than a cursory glance. *I clearly did not fit the profile of a protestor*, I thought to myself.

I continued walking the empty streets when I spotted what appeared to be a large armoured personnel carrier parked on the pavement. As I neared it, I saw a man climb from the vehicle. He appeared to be a soldier dressed in a black uniform equipped with a large black metal helmet wearing a black ski type mask with holes for eyes, nose, and mouth. He leaned against the vehicle while he smoked a cigarette. His shiny black boots and reinforced knee protectors glistened in the sunshine as I walked up to the vehicle. From his belt hung about four large bulging pouches and my guess was that these were not full of sandwiches. I also recognised a CS type canister attached to his waistband under which appeared to be an ammunition belt.

"Hi, all quiet is it?" I said.

"Yep," he replied as he turned his back to me and appeared to kick the large rubber wheel of the carrier. It was then that I saw the word 'Police' emblazoned across the back of his heavy military body amour vest, the type usually worn by soldiers in combat zones. At that point, my attention was drawn to loud aircraft noise. I looked up to see a large helicopter hovering in the distance.

I used my judgement based on what I had witnessed and decided against attending the main area of protest. Instead, I would catch up with the day's outcome on the local cable news network.

The following evening, I turned on the news channel, which appeared to be dominated by footage of protesters and the tactics of the police in countering the demonstration. I watched in disbelief at the events as they unfolded before my eyes. Riot police wearing a paramilitary uniform, armed with what appeared to me to be Elephant guns, fought pitched battles with protestors while Chinook type helicopters hovered intimidatingly overhead. Armoured Personnel Carriers charged the demonstrators with apparent disregard for the safety of anyone unfortunate enough to be caught up in the commotion. Central to the news report that evening was a first-hand account of an incident whereby Miami Police Chief Timoney jumped off of his patrol bicycle and yelled at a protester: "Fuck you! You're bad!"

I had seen enough. I would visit two or three community groups to get their account of police and community engagement strategies before leaving Miami for New York, where I would write up my findings.

Chapter 56

Harlem

As I descended the aircraft steps at New York's Kennedy airport, I could hardly believe my eyes. Thick snowfall was piled on the edge of the runway. The temperature must have been just above freezing. I was hardly dressed for the sudden climate change; for it was only a few hours ago I had taken advantage of my last day in Miami by going to the beach where I had sweltered under the scorching sun. So much so that my skin was now a very dark brown in colour.

My familiarity with New York's train system helped me get to Harlem in a relatively short time. But as I walked toward 128th Street from 125th St it began snowing heavily and my canvas shoes were soon sodden. As I reached the apartment block, the snow was virtually knee-deep as I waded toward the entrance door that appeared to be wedged open despite the heavy snowfall. I looked up at the twelve-story block. I was on the 11th floor. It was clearly an old public housing block, but from the outside, it looked reasonable just a little grey, in need of paint with a few window repairs required. The people I had seen leaving the building, all black, wore large heavy coats and scarfs wrapped around their faces with sensible wellington boots on their feet. I looked down at my lightweight soaked jeans, sodden canvas shoes, and three-quarter length jacket that failed abysmally to keep out the wintry elements and with no hat on my closely shaved head, I was in desperate need of a hot drink, change of clothes, and a warm room.

I pulled my cell phone from my pocket; fingers numbed with cold, prodded the keypad. The number was ringing.

"Hi, Tom, it's Paul Wilson from London, as we arranged, I'm calling from the apartment block."

"Get yourself inside and I'll see you there in ten minutes," said Tom in a

London accent.

Sure enough, ten minutes later Tom appeared with the keys to let me into the apartment.

"You from London Tom?" I asked, curious as to know why a young white guy from London had the keys to an apartment in Harlem.

"Yeah, I am, been in New York for a few years now; I'm a musician. This is an ex-girlfriend's place; she's visiting relatives in Japan."

Normally such a response would have elicited numerous questions, but I was freezing cold and needed to get out of my wet clothes in a hurry before pneumonia set hold.

Tom unlocked the apartment and showed me the small, but comfortable space that included one bedroom and a small living area with cooking facilities. All that I needed. He handed over the keys, wished me well and disappeared. As the door closed, I pulled off my wet clothes and stood under the hot shower for what seemed an age.

The following day I scrolled through the contacts on my cell phone: Lieutenant Charlane Brown, New York Police Department was a Fulbright Police Fellowship alumna. I'd met her earlier in the year while she was spending her three months in the UK. She had visited London and the Fulbright institution had given Charlane my details. I had introduced her to our Black Police Association office and given her a tour of New Scotland Yard. She had been so grateful and had insisted that I contact her when I reached New York. I called her number.

"Hi Charlane, Paul Wilson here. I'm here in New York on the last leg of my Fulbright research assignment."

"Hey Paul, that's great, let's meet up. I'm currently working with Monique, you remember her. She's a police officer with Community Affairs and visited me while I was in London; you met her briefly. How about we all meet tomorrow evening for something to eat?"

"Absolutely, text me the time and venue and I'll be there."

About an hour later, my cell phone vibrated with a message from Charlane. 'Oceana, 55 E. 54St at 7 pm tomorrow'

The next evening, I walked into Oceana restaurant two minutes before 7 pm. I instantly spotted Charlane seated in the middle of the crowded restaurant. She looked in my direction, stood up and waved. As I walked over, I recognised Monique seated next to her. I gave each a big hug. We settled down and Charlane questioned me about my experience in Chicago, San Francisco, and Miami. We spoke for about three hours; the food and drink were incidental. I had so much to tell.

"Hey Paul, it's getting late and we both have an early start tomorrow but let us drop you home. I assume you haven't got a car?"

"No, I haven't got a car. I'm staying up in Harlem."

Charlane's smiling face suddenly changed to a more serious expression of concern.

"Whereabouts in Harlem?" she asked in the way a concerned parent might ask a young teenager about to attend their first party.

"128 St near City College," I said in a hushed tone of voice.

Charlane looked across the table at Monique. "You got your nine?" asked Charlane, "I got mine," and tapped her pocketbook placed on the seat by her side.

Monique nodded and tapped her jacket pocket.

Both ladies laughed, but I also recognised the serious nature by which Charlane asked and Monique responded to the question. The nine was a reference to the 9mm Glock service pistol issued to all New York Police Officers.

My residence in Harlem was noisy, particularly in the late evenings. The TV sets down my hallway seemed to compete with one another in terms of loudness. Neighbouring families would often raise their voices and argue; cussing was commonplace and very audible through the walls. The front door to the block was a worry in that it always seemed to be propped open, making the security pad useless. Aside from that everyone kept themselves to themselves. Unfortunately, the continued snowfall kept me indoors. I tried to engage a few residents in conversation, but little came of it, they seemed too intent on going about their business and disinterested in some questions from a guy with a strange accent. I used my time indoors to enter my research findings into my laptop. Saturday night soon came around and ever since my early teens I'd had this thing about going out on a Saturday evening. It was habitual; Saturday was a narcotic that I'd failed to shake after all these years and here I was in Harlem, New York City, home to so many of the musicians that I had grown to worship over the years. The pull was just too strong; I had to go out and explore, even in the snow. I closed the lid of my laptop and began to get ready. I showered, pressed my shirt and within forty-five minutes I was good to go. I placed the key in the lock of the apartment door, turned it and pulled the door; nothing happened. I tried once more, turned the key, pulled the handle. It remained locked.

Damn, I thought, *What the hell am I going to do now? Call Tom and ask him to come and get me out, I guess.* I pulled the cell phone from my pocket and looked despairingly at the black screen. I had been so busy on my laptop that I had forgotten to charge my phone and now it was completely flat. I knew that it took about 45 minutes to charge; time that I didn't have. I had to get out of here. I walked over to the window and opened it. It had stopped snowing. For the first time since I moved in, I looked carefully at the metal fire escape that snaked down the side of the apartment building. It was thick with snow. *That's my way out*, I thought, *down the fire escape.*

There's probably a short drop at the bottom but in this snow, I'd be cushioned. I had heard that narcotic users and those with an addiction were unable to process even simple tasks with any rational thought. Tonight, I was firmly in that category. My sensible inner self said, *you would be insane to step onto that fire escape, wait for an hour and get help*. But the addicted self-argued, *get out of here it's a Saturday night, don't be such a wimp!*

I climbed through the opened window and placed one foot out onto the fire escape, followed by a second foot. I stood up straight and looked down. It was dark; there was no lighting. So, I had no idea what was at the bottom. I gingerly kicked the snow off and began to climb down the metal steps. It was freezing cold; the steps were icy and slippery. I made my way down one flight. I was pleased with myself but a little concerned that the metal structure seemed to move and creak with each ultra-cautious step. The rail on the next flight was loose. Even in the dark, it seemed rusted through. *This building was old*, I thought to myself, this fire escape is probably poorly maintained too, but there was no turning back. *Only another eight storeys*, I told myself. I cautiously navigated to the next platform and as I reached it, I heard a window opening. I looked across and saw an elderly black lady with her head now poked out.

"Please, Sir, get back up to your apartment before you kill yourself."

"I'm locked in, I thought I'd use the fire escape to get out."

"Please, Sir, get back up to your apartment. I'll send my husband to help you. What floor you on?"

I gave my details to the lady and reluctantly returned to the safety of my apartment. Within minutes there was a knock on my door. It was my neighbour from downstairs. He tried with all his might, but he was unable to open the door.

"Thanks for trying, I really appreciate it. Would you call my friend? He can help."

I retrieved Tom Halpenny's number from my diary and gave it to my helpful neighbour and waited.

The door knocked.

"Hi Paul, it's Tom, sorry about this. I should have warned you that this occasionally happens."

The door opened and Tom entered. You just need to jiggle the key like this.

"Oh, is that all? So sorry, Tom. Hope I haven't ruined your Saturday evening."

"No it's fine. I was just rehearsing a set with Ron Carter; we'd nearly finished.'

I stared at Tom. "Tom, the only Ron Carter I know is a jazz legend, double bassist, who played with Miles Davis," I said with a smile.

"Yeah, that's him, a really nice guy," said Tom in a casual manner I personally would not have adopted when speaking of Jazz royalty.

"Oh-My-God," I breathed, "I had no idea, you said you were a musician but…what do you play?"

"It's OK," laughed Tom, "I'm a guitarist."

"Anyone else you have played with that I might know," I asked now extremely interested in this British Jazz musician standing in a Harlem apartment.

"Yeah, I've worked with George Benson, Curtis Mayfield, Rob Bargad, Jimmy Preacher Robins and a few others in my time…."

I looked at Tom. My jaw had dropped in admiration. "I'm impressed Tom, honestly, I had no idea. Really sorry to break up your session, too. Give my best wishes to Ron and extend my sincere apologies."

"Don't worry Paul, enjoy your Saturday night."

And enjoy my Saturday night I did, despite the heavy snowfall and freezing conditions that made the remainder of my stay in Harlem one to be enjoyed behind closed doors in front of an electric fire.

Chapter 57

Affirmative Action

In December 2003, I returned to London following my eventful three and a half months visit to the United States. After clearing immigration and collecting my suitcases at Heathrow Airport, I found a quiet place to sit and make an especially important phone call.

Although I had been in constant contact with New Scotland Yard's Human Resources Department over the months, I had received no news about potential vacancies or a placement. Now that I was back in the country, I decided this was a good time to see if we could make something happen.

"Hi, Chief Inspector Paul Wilson here. I just arrived back in the UK after spending a few months in the states. I'm keen to get back to work."

"Oh yes, Paul. We've received all your email updates. However, there doesn't appear to be any vacant posts for Chief Inspectors at this time."

"Really?" I asked, feeling annoyed.

"No, nothing, I'm afraid. You'll just have to do your garden until something's available."

Unbelievable! We'll see about that, I thought.

After I got home, I called up Pat Gallan, the Deputy Commissioner's Staff Officer, and an old friend.

"Hi Pat. I've just returned from my Fulbright in the States and I talked to Personnel about a job vacancy. They told me there isn't a job available and that I should do my gardening until something comes up," I said, matter-of-factly.

"Hi Paul, welcome back to The Met. We'll catch up later and you can tell me all about your adventures, but in the meantime let me see if I can help on the job front," she said.

"Thanks, Pat. Much appreciated."

The following morning, my house phone rang. It was Human Resources for New Scotland Yard.

"Chief Inspector Wilson, I understand you are seeking a post. We have an interesting opening in the Corporate Planning Unit at New Scotland Yard."

Corporate Planning? I know nothing about planning, I thought.

"What does that entail? I asked.

"You would develop and write the Policing Plan for London on behalf of the Metropolitan Police Authority. It's very high-profile work that you would conduct alongside some very senior people. This could prove helpful in the future, should you choose to seek promotion."

"Can I think about it and get back to you?" I asked.

"Sure, but I don't think you'll find a more prestigious position."

I spent the next day thinking it over. This posting would take me out of my comfort zone, but I also worried that I wouldn't have the required skill set. Then, a realisation dawned on me.

Am I creating barriers for myself?

This is a common mindset of minorities in the workplace. We prefer to remain in a role that is safe, does not attract attention, and will not stretch us too much. This is because we know that we are likely to be over-scrutinised. The HR guy said this might help me be promoted in the future, yet here I was thinking up excuses why I could not do the job. Would a white colleague have such thoughts? No, of course not. I called back the HR department.

"Hi. Chief Inspector Wilson here. I've thought about it and I'm happy to take the post in Corporate Planning. When do I start?"

"They'd like you to begin as soon as possible. Can you drop by and introduce yourself tomorrow?"

The next day I went to the New Scotland Yard's Corporate Planning Unit, where I was pleased to discover the Superintendent was Charles Bailey, who had been a Chief Inspector at Kennington. I settled into the role and my boss, John Zlotnicki, seemed impressed with my work.

"Paul, you have taken to this role much better than I ever expected," he said to me one day.

I enjoyed the work. Working with figures, charts and percentages appealed to my nerdy side, and I was able to brush shoulders with very senior people at various target setting meetings. These same people relied on my work to showcase their portfolio in a positive light, or at least that is what I thought.

Assistant Commissioner Tarique Ghaffur was the most senior minority ethnic officer in the country. I knew him from my time with the Black Police

Association. One day I bumped into him in a corridor near my office.

"Hello, Paul. What are you working on these days?" he asked.

"I'm developing the policing plan for London, on behalf of the Metropolitan Police Authority," I said with pride.

Tarique moved closer to me and smiled. "You realise we take very little notice of the targets set for us by these plans, don't you? That's the reality, Paul. Sorry to rain on your parade," he whispered, before walking away down the corridor.

I had been in the Corporate Planning Unit for a few weeks when one afternoon Leroy Logan and Bevan Powell, from the Black Police Association, paid me a visit. Leroy was now Chair of the BPA, and Bevan had spent years carving out a role as the BPA's strategic thinker. He would often call me at home in the evening to sound out his latest idea on improving police and black community relations. We would talk and bounce these ideas around, often until late into the night.

"We've got the Morris inquiry coming up and we want the Black Police Association to submit a thought-provoking paper to the Inquiry," Leroy said, as they stood in front of my desk.

"It's an independent inquiry into professional standards and employment matters in the Metropolitan Police Service, chaired by Bill Morris, the former TUC General Secretary," Bevan added.

"Yes, guys. I know," I said. "I heard they set up the inquiry after the Black Police Association announced a BME recruitment boycott of the force, claiming members were being disproportionately targeted for disciplinary investigations. How can I help?"

"We would like you to write a thought-provoking BPA paper for submission to The Morris Inquiry. We must be seen to be on the front foot with the Inquiry. We know you can knock a couple of such papers out, but we just need one," Leroy said, laughing.

This request did not surprise me. I had a track record for writing convincing reports for the BPA, not least of which was the BPA submission to the Stephen Lawrence Inquiry.

"Sounds right up my street. Give me a few days and I'll email the draft to you," I said.

That evening I sat down at my computer and began researching some issues I felt were pertinent to the Inquiry. I spent the entire weekend working on the paper and emailed what I felt was a decent draft to the BPA office on Monday morning.

Later that afternoon, Leroy and Bevan walked into my office, looking serious. Leroy walked over and tossed a paper onto my desk.

"What is this?" he asked, his voice tinged with anger.

"It looks like my draft report," I said lightly.

"Well, we can't use it, not like that. It's meaningless. We need something that will help move The Met forward," he said.

I picked up the report and glanced over it again. As much as I hated to admit it, I agreed with Leroy. I had written a position paper that relied on the work of W.E.B DuBois and other black academics, but that offered little in the way of suggestions for how to move forward.

"What about your Neighbourhood Renewal Unit visit to Northern Ireland?" Bevan asked, his conciliatory voice calmer. "Didn't you discover a recruitment strategy designed to improve the number of Catholic police officers in the police service for Northern Ireland?"

"Yes, of course. I just thought I bored you all to death talking about it," I laughed.

During my visit to Belfast on Neighbourhood Renewal Unit business, I heard about a U.S style affirmative action programme to improve the number of Catholics joining the Northern Ireland Police Service. Upon further investigation, I found that the British government had commissioned an inquiry into the entire issue of Catholic police officer under-representation.

"What about writing a paper advocating a Northern Ireland approach to BME recruitment? I would like to get involved too," Bevan said.

"Okay, let's do it," I said.

"Great! I think we should go to Northern Ireland. I'm sure the BPA will underwrite the cost. After all, this is an important BPA business," said Bevan.

"Okay. If you think you can swing it with the BPA Executive, we can use the contacts I made when I visited Belfast a few months ago. We only need to stay one day and fly back in the evening," I said, remembering my traumatic experience in the Belfast pub and not wanting to spend any more time there than necessary.

"Great, let me speak with Keith Smith and start the ball rolling," said Bevan.

Our excitement over our plans was tempered with the realisation that we would first need to get the BPA to agree to fund the visit. This was a significant hurdle, as BPA's Treasurer, Keith Smith, was known to keep a close eye on the purse strings. Nevertheless, Bevan's approach for funding was agreed as Keith felt the work in Northern Ireland would be in the best interests of both the BPA and The Met.

Within days Bevan and I were on a plane from London Heathrow to Belfast, Northern Ireland, to meet with representatives of the Northern Ireland Equalities Commission and Deloitte, the recruitment agency for the Police Service for Northern Ireland (PSNI).

While we had carefully structured our schedule to make maximum use of the short time we would be there, we found ourselves having numerous meetings with key people involved in the Police Service for Northern Ireland's recruitment strategy. After a very hectic and largely successful day's work, we returned to Belfast Airport for the return flight to London Heathrow.

Exhausted and excited, we boarded the plane and sat down to await take off.

"What are you two up to?" a familiar voice behind us said.

I turned my head as my old adversary, friend and mentor, Sir Denis O'Connor stood up in the aisle next to our seats. He was now the Chief Constable of Surrey, and his sudden presence made me feel like a schoolboy caught scrumping apples from the farmer's orchard.

"Just paid a visit to our colleagues in the PSNI," I said. The big smile on my face probably betrayed the fact that we were on a secret mission.

"That's good. I hope you learned something," he said. With a nod and a smile, he walked off towards the front of the aircraft.

"He must be making his way to first-class," Bevan jokingly said as O'Connor disappeared into the next section.

During the flight back to London, Bevan and I talked about the day's visits. It had confirmed everything I had previously shared with Bevan, who now had a first-hand account of what the PSNI recruitment programme entailed.

Bevan flipped through the documentation given to us by our hosts. "It was interesting to see that PSNI has outsourced all its recruitment and selection of suitable candidates to Deloitte, a private company but has kept the 1 Catholic and 1 Protestant selection process in house," he said.

"Yes, and that 1 for 1 or 50:50 procedure only occurs once a pool of candidates has met the required selection criteria. But the moment it's suggested we use the same process for the recruitment of BME police officers; just watch the popular press hammer home the under-qualified blacks' narrative," I said.

Bevan looked over at me and shook his head. "So, what we would say is that the number of BME candidates in the selection pool will dictate the number of white candidates entering the initial recruit training process, thereby over the longer-term ensuring that white candidates do not take all the available places," said Bevan excitedly.

"Exactly, the very same procedure that has seen the number of Catholics recruited to PSNI almost double over the past three years. Let's use the Morris Inquiry as a platform to bring attention to the simplicity of the Northern Ireland approach. Maybe this will generate enough media interest to cause the Government to give legislative change serious consideration," I said.

Bevan nodded.

In the days that followed, Bevan and I worked together to examine the PSNI recruitment policy in detail and decide what elements we thought should be included in the BPA report. We pored over the work of the Independent Commission on Policing for Northern Ireland, established in 1998 as part of the Belfast Agreement. The Commission had produced its report in 1999, entitled *A New Beginning: Policing in Northern Ireland*, popularly known as the *Patten Report*. This report contained 175 symbolic and practical recommendations, the key of which included a 50:50 recruitment policy for Protestant and Catholic police officers.

"This really is ground-breaking stuff, Bevan. To think, all of the Patten recommendations received the endorsement of the British government," I said one day while reading through the substantive report.

"Yes, but we are talking religion here. The Catholics and Protestants in Northern Ireland are white. It's less contentious than race," Bevan said.

"It is for now, Bevan. But there may come a day when it is seen through the same lens. The least the BPA can do is highlight the hypocrisy," I said.

The hypocrisy was a reference to a passage from the Equal Opportunities Commission in Northern Ireland.

It is not enough to have a few recruits from another gender (or religious background) entering the service. If they are less than 15 per cent, they can never have a substantial influence on the culture.

I continued, "This viewpoint was accepted by the British Government, hence their endorsement of affirmative action to improve the numbers of Roman Catholic officers entering the police service in Northern Ireland. They know that a trickle of black faces will not change the police culture in London and that plays into the hands of those not serious about a genuine change in policing."

"What do you mean, Paul?" Bevan asked.

"I once asked an Assistant Commissioner why he wanted more black people to join the police. His response was the usual "to improve representation, a police force that looks like London and will improve the confidence of all Londoners". See Bevan, just having more black faces in the police is not a solution by itself. We need a rapid recruitment process to get us into the numbers where black officers can influence the police occupational culture. Only when the culture is changed will we see a less confrontational style of policing afforded to the black community."

"I see, it's what's described as getting into "critical mass". It's ensuring that a minority doesn't find itself submerged in a majority organisational culture," Bevan said, reading aloud from the Patten Report.

"A powerful argument for the BPA to adopt as its own," I said.

Within a week I had completed *The Case for Affirmative Action* report and emailed it to the BPA office. Now all we had to do was wait for the discussion at the Morris Inquiry.

The day the Morris Inquiry got underway, I waited patiently until BPA Chair, Leroy Logan was called to testify before the Inquiry. I suspected Leroy's testimony would take some time, given his disproportionately harsh treatment at the hands of the Professional Standards Department when he was wrongly accused of dishonesty.

New Scotland Yard was just around the corner from where the Morris Inquiry was being held, so I awaited the message on my cell phone that the Affirmative Action discussion was imminent.

I received a message that there was to be a natural break in proceedings, followed by the Inquiry raising the issue of Affirmative Action. I walked over to the venue and took a seat in the room where the inquiry was being held. It reminded me of the Stephen Lawrence Inquiry setup.

On the raised bench at one end of the room were three members of the Inquiry Panel. The Chair, Sir Bill Morris, sat in the middle with Sir Anthony Burden, former Chief Constable of South Wales, to his right and Anesta Weekes QC to his left.

I was familiar with Sir Anthony as he had previously chaired the National Police College Equalities Forum that funded my visit to a conference in New Orleans. Anesta Weekes QC was a friend and had provided legal counsel to the Stephen Lawrence Inquiry.

The room was three-quarters full of mostly representatives from the press and those who had previously testified and those about to do so. I sat behind Bevan. Leroy Logan, Chair of the Metropolitan Black Police Association, sat at the front of the Inquiry panel.

A few minutes later, Sir Anthony Burden picked up the BPA's Affirmative Action report and held it up like a judge holding a scorecard. I recognised the distinctive cover and logo immediately. I leaned forward in anticipation.

"Chief Inspector Logan, do you support this?" he asked.

Leroy did not answer. He appeared to freeze.

"Do you support Affirmative Action?" Sir Anthony pressed again.

"No, we don't support positive discrimination," said Leroy, looking most uncomfortable.

Bevan gasped and turned around to look at me. His face looked like a lottery winner who had just been advised that his winning ticket was invalid.

Sir Anthony lowered the report and glanced at the expressionless faces of his two colleagues on the bench.

"So, you don't wish for us to take this into consideration?" he asked.

Leroy continued with his positive discrimination narrative and that black officers must be seen to achieve on merit alone.

Sir Anthony, looking deflated, slowly placed the report on the bench. "We'll read that later," he said softly.

I buried my head in my hands. The Affirmative Action paper was dead and buried. Without the vocal support of the Black Police Association Chair, it was consigned to the dustbin.

I anxiously waited for Leroy to finish his testimony so I could ask him to explain himself. Why the last-minute change of heart that appeared to take even his closest confidante, Bevan, by surprise?

A short time later I approached Leroy as he walked into the public gallery.

"What the hell happened out there, Leroy?" I asked firmly.

Leroy stared at me as if he did not understand my question.

Is he in a state of shock? I wondered.

"Well…" he began.

At that moment someone else walked up and he turned to begin speaking with them. He was not going to give me a clear answer.

I'd had enough. I turned on my heels and headed for the exit, kicking out at the door in frustration as I pushed it open.

I looked up at the blue sky as sorrow and disappointment engulfed me. The gems that Bevan and I had unearthed in the Patten Report, along with solid arguments for a change in legislation similar to that in Northern Ireland, would now remain hidden from the black community and media discourse. I felt we were destined for decades to come to replay the same storyboard: "How do we recruit and retain black police officers?"

Chapter 58

The Big Easy and Hate Crime

One summer evening in 1985, I stood in the middle of a crowded nightclub regretting the situation I had just found myself in. A band on the stage filled the air with jazzy saxophone riffs and frenetic drumbeats as the crowd swayed as one to the tempo. I tried to make my way to the bar for a drink, but it was impossible to move. I was wedged in the middle of what appeared to be a group of huge, white, muscular American football players with short blond hair.

I felt an uneasiness in the pit of my stomach. Not only was I bothered by the invasion of personal space, but this was New Orleans, a city whose history of slavery and racism now fed my furtive imagination with vivid recollections of the Civil Rights struggle and accompanying atrocities. Being surrounded by eight powerful looking white guys, with no room to move, was not a situation I preferred to be in.

"You wanna beer?" one of them asked me.

I turned around to see if he was talking to someone else. He was not.

"Yeah, that would be great," I said, feeling calmer.

"Laarm in the neck?" he shouted.

"I'm sorry. What?" I asked.

"Do you want laarm in the neck?" he asked again.

He sounded like the stereotypical southern boy I had seen on Sunday afternoon films, with a deep drawling accent and usually wearing a Stetson. Not only that, but his voice was competing with blaring jazz music and two hundred other people talking all at once.

"Yeah," I said, not knowing what the hell he was talking about.

He was keen to buy me a beer, so I thought it best to just agree with what was being asked.

I watched in awe as he forced his way to the bar, his huge shoulders brushing people aside like they were opposing players on a match day.

A couple of minutes later a bottle appeared and passed like a football down the line of people standing between the bar and me. Finally, someone thrust the bottle labelled Corona into my outstretched hand. And there wedged into the neck was a piece of lime. I later learned that Corona is a Mexican beer that is extremely popular across the southern states and is often served with a wedge of lime (or laarm) in the neck.

"You're not from here, are you?" someone shouted.

"No, I'm visiting from London," I said.

"London, England?" he asked.

"That's the one." I replied with a hint of sarcasm that went unnoticed.

"You want some oysters on the half shell?" the man leaned over and shouted in my ear.

Having grown up near the Lincolnshire coast, I was familiar with shellfish, but oysters were one thing I had never tried.

"Yeah, great," I said, taking a swig of my beer.

By this point word had apparently spread that I was from England, as the group formed a semi-circle to face me and ask questions or offer comments.

"You play ball?" (Because of my height and colour I was often asked this when I travelled through the states).

"Does it snow in London?"

"I like that accent, man."

"I didn't know they had black people in London."

"Do you watch Dr. Who?"

I responded to each question or statement in my best English accent. We laughed and joked around, overcoming language barriers and familiarising them with my English sense of humour.

Suddenly a man stepped forward and held out a large plate of raw oysters on the half-shell. I froze, not knowing how I should eat them. My momentary discomfort must have been picked up on by others in the group who stepped in to show me how it's done. One by one they picked up oysters, tipping their heads back and emptying them into their mouths.

Someone held out a small dish of what I later learned was cocktail sauce. "Try some of this."

With my left hand I picked up an oyster and with my right spooned sauce on top. Raising the shell to my mouth, I tipped my head back and slid the oyster into my mouth. I let the texture and slightly salty taste linger on my tongue for a moment before swallowing. A cheer went up from the group of onlookers. I was no longer an oyster virgin.

This was my first visit to New Orleans, or the Big Easy, as it is commonly referred to by Americans. The term Big Easy was first used by the extraordinarily talented Jazz musicians who were able to make an easy living performing in the many bars and restaurants throughout New Orleans. My encounter with the American football players stuck in my mind for years to come.

During my travels throughout the southern United States in 1985, I became aware through conversations with locals of the daily experiences of African Americans and the simmering racism that was still prevalent. In fact, I became convinced that my journey was made more enjoyable because of my English accent. It was a kind of British privilege that transcended the colour barrier. An English accent in the United States of America has powerful and historic connotations, particularly amongst the Southern Gentile class. As such, I found it to open doors to experiences and courtesy not usually afforded to African Americans.

During my time in New Orleans, I achieved one of my childhood dreams, a ride on the Natchez, one of the city's most famous flat-bottomed paddle steamer river boats. Immediately after boarding I made my way to a spot where I could watch the huge paddle wheels spring to life and propel the Natchez effortlessly across the expansive surface of the Mississippi river's calm, murky waters.

As we sailed upriver, childhood memories of stories by Mark Twain and others fueled my imagination. I joined a group of other passengers on a guided tour around the boat, imagining 19th century mustached gamblers wearing dandy suits, defending dubious sharp practice disputes with their tiny derringer pistols. On the upper deck, I broke away from the group to lean over the railings and watch the churning river below.

As I looked out across the great expanse of the Mississippi, the lyrics of Paul Robeson's *Ol' Man River* filled my mind, reminding me of the alternative life and harsh reality for enslaved Africans working on the Mississippi a little over one hundred years earlier.

I gits weary
An' sick of tryin'
I'm tired of livin'
An' scared of dyin'
But ol' man river
He jes' keeps rolling along

Colored folks work on de Mississippi
Colored folks work while de white folks play
Pullin' dose boats from de dawn to sunset

Gittin' no rest till de judgement day

But it was another visit to the jazz bars in New Orleans' famous French Quarter where my eyes were opened to an aspect of the city often overlooked by tourists.

~~~~

A young African American man stood against the bar enjoying the music. He was tall and slim with a distinctive pencil moustache. His jawbone was angular, almost European in appearance and his complexion was light. His features were like my own and it was probably this similarity that helped start up a conversation that gave me a fascinating insight into a unique aspect of Louisiana's history.

Louisiana was once French, and then Spanish, territory. France later reacquired it from Spain before selling it to the United States in 1803. Both the French and Spanish had a more relaxed disposition on 'race' and people like me with a combination of African and European ancestry enjoyed many of the privileges white people did.

Pierre proudly announced that he was Creole, a name originally used to describe the heritage and customs of the various people who settled Louisiana during the early French colonial times.

Creole people of mixed African and European heritage living in New Orleans enjoyed the privileges often given to people considered to be of a 'higher caste' than the dark-skinned slaves born in Africa.

Under French rule there were numerous ways for slaves to become free. As a result, New Orleans enjoyed a growing and prosperous population of color. In the years following the American acquisition of Louisiana, the division between black and white races became ever more widening. By 1850, the once thriving and free population of colour was economically decimated, diminished and segregated. Stripped of the privileges enjoyed under French and Spanish rule, the Creole community nevertheless continued to exist, passing on their unique skills as tradesmen and craftsmen to future generations. They often married into their own 'caste', thereby perpetuating the skin tone and physical features so apparent in the early Creole population.

Pierre seemed fascinated by my own racial heritage. As someone who had never travelled further than Atlanta, Georgia, he was eager to learn more about Black people in England. We discussed all aspects of life, but it was food that interested him the most.

"You had gumbo in Nawlins?" he asked.

"Not sure. What is it?" I replied.

Pierre laughed. "Let's meet up tomorrow. I'll take you to my grandma's house. She makes the best gumbo."

The next day I waited for Pierre on Canal Street at the agreed upon time and place. After he arrived, we jumped on a bus and rode two miles to a neighbourhood that differed greatly from what I had witnessed in my limited experience of New Orleans. The small, wooden houses needed fresh paint and basic repairs. The streets and pavement were littered with paper and plastic bags.

Pierre jumped up and walked to the front of the bus. I followed right behind him, taking notice of the other passengers for the first time. They were all African Americans of various complexions and for many of them their clothing suggested they were what Americans describe as 'low income'.

The bus doors opened, and we climbed down the steps onto the litter strewn pavement.

Pierre pointed to the right. "Grandma's house is over there. She's expecting us."

We walked along a row of small wooden homes in various degrees of disrepair yet unmistakably quaint. These were not the iconic and beautiful Creole houses with the brightly colored wooden shutters I had been shown on my guided tour of the French Quarter. These homes were inhabited by low-income families and not usually seen by average tourists. It was difficult to imagine this existed in the world's most affluent country.

When we reached Pierre's grandma's house, I waited outside on the small wooden veranda while he went inside. A few minutes later the door opened, and Pierre walked towards me. An elderly African American lady with grey hair and a light complexion walked behind him. She was carrying what appeared to be a bowl of soup in each hand.

"This is grandma, and this is gumbo," Pierre said, pointing at the bowls.

"Lovely to meet you," I replied.

Grandma smiled and greeted me in a deep southern accent, using words I didn't recognise or understand.

"Take one of the bowls," Pierre offered.

I took a bowl and placed it on the small, wooden table in the veranda.

"You like shrimp?" Pierre asked, setting a napkin and spoon on the table.

"I love all kinds of shellfish and seafood," I said.

"That's good, then you'll love gumbo."

Indeed, I did love the thick and hearty concoction of chicken, shrimp, crab legs and sauce. These were Creole people, and their gumbo recipe is famous in New Orleans and beyond. My love affair with New Orleans' unique history, people and architecture was finally cemented with gumbo.

~~~~

Thirteen years later I received an email that set in motion a series of events that led to the introduction of *'Hate Crime'* into the British criminal justice lexicon.

The email and colourful graphic attached had been sent to me by a friend in the National Organisation of Black Law Enforcement Officers (NOBLE), an African American association that I had reached out to following the launch of the Black Police Association.

NOBLE is a widely respected association in the United States that is generally composed of senior and middle-ranking officers. These officers represent federal, state, county, and municipal law enforcement agencies and criminal justice practitioners.

I received many such emails, which I usually deleted. But this one caught my attention in that it seemed to advertise a forthcoming and large multi-disciplinary conference to focus on and help address a cocktail of issues blighting the African American communities in the United States. That would normally pique my interest, but two words in the flyer heading had me riveted to the computer screen.

22ND ANNUAL TRAINING CONFERENCE AND EXHIBITION
NEW ORLEANS, LOUISIANA
JULY 18-23, 1998
A CLUSTER CONFERENCE FEATURING:
NATIONAL ORGANIZATION OF BLACK LAW ENFORCEMENT
EXECUTIVES (NOBLE)
NATIONAL BLACK POLICE ASSOCIATION (NBPA)
NATIONAL ASSOCIATION OF BLACK NARCOTIC AGENTS
(NABNA)
NATIONAL BLACK PROSECUTORS ASSOCIATION (NBPA)
UNITY OF PURPOSE: SETTING AN AGENDA FOR JUSTICE FOR
THE 21ST CENTURY.

I had made one other visit to my favourite American city since that first memorable trip in 1985. Now, I was being presented with the opportunity to return and to learn from the American experience in addressing similar issues facing law enforcement and people of colour in the UK.

Commissioner Sir Paul Condon had appointed Assistant Commissioner Denis O'Connor to lead New Scotland Yard's corporate response to the forthcoming *Stephen Lawrence Inquiry*, and as such O'Connor handled anything and everything having to do with issues of race and policing.

Assistant Commissioner O'Connor had taken a particular interest in the Black Police Association but a telephone conversation with his Staff Officer (military term for Executive Assistant) was less than welcoming and gave me the impression that the upper echelons were trying to find ways in which to challenge and undermine the BPA's growing popularity.

"Hello, this is Superintendent Green, Assistant Commissioner O'Connor's Staff Officer."

"Hello ma'am. This is Inspector Wilson. How can I help you?" I asked.

"Are you the Chairman of the BPA?"

"Yes, I am."

"Assistant Commissioner O'Connor would like for you to provide him the names of all members of the BPA."

"May I ask why?"

"No, you may not. How soon can you send me that information?"

"I can't give you a timeframe. I will need to discuss this request with my executive team. But I can tell you that the BPA is not likely to agree to release details about our members to the Met."

Superintendent Green let out a heavy sigh. "And why not?"

"Because we respect the privacy of our members, some of whom would not wish to have their identity disclosed to senior officers," I said.

"I see. So, your response to Assistant Commissioner O'Connor is that you refuse to disclose the information being requested?"

In only a few minutes her tone had changed from that of a friend enquiring about your health, to that of a senior manager demanding compliance with an unwritten policy.

"Yes, it is," I said, forgetting about any need to consult with executive colleagues.

The conversation ended. I heard no more on the subject.

Ever since that exchange with the Staff Officer I felt that my personal relationship with Assistant Commissioner O'Connor had blossomed into a mutually respectful one. His slight Irish brogue often came across paternal and assertive, yet friendly and reassuring. It might have been that once he saw his rather bullying strategy would not work, he adopted a more fatherly "hand on the shoulder" approach.

Assistant Commissioner O'Connor now stood between me, in my capacity as Chairman of the Black Police Association, and an official Met Police sanctioned and funded three-day conference in my beloved New Orleans. I immediately wrote up a file explaining the reasons why I should attend the conference and submitted it to Assistant Commissioner O'Connor's office.

A few days later I ran into Assistant Commissioner O'Connor in the corridor at New Scotland Yard. As usual he had an armful of files and an expression that said, "don't interrupt me, I'm about to save the world."

Nevertheless, he always seemed to have time for the Chair of the Black Police Association.

"Did you have the opportunity to consider my request to attend the conference in New Orleans?" I asked.

"No, we're not going to fund that. These conferences tend to rehash old arguments with no real result," he said.

"Okay, Sir, but I have to say I'm disappointed. I feel like it's a lost opportunity for the Met," I said. It was the best response I could muster off the top of my head.

He gave me a half smile and strode purposefully down the corridor. I shared my disappointment with just about anyone that would stand still long enough to listen, and I'm sure I often repeated myself. Then one day a Chief Inspector colleague brought something to my attention that offered a glimmer of hope.

"There's an Equalities group that meets at Bramshill, the Police Staff College in Hampshire," she said.

"That's interesting, but what does it have to do with attending the New Orleans conference?" I asked, slightly frustrated.

"Because they have funds and I happen to know they will soon be accepting applications for worthwhile projects that further the cause of race relations and equality of opportunity."

I found it difficult to contain my gratitude and plonked a kiss on her cheek. This public display of affection was not to be condoned between two uniformed Inspectors, but these were special circumstances.

My elation was short-lived. Shortly afterwards I made some enquiries about the composition and nature of this Equalities Group.

My heart sank. Their Chairperson was none other than Anthony Burden, Chief Constable of South Wales. There was a history between us.

In 1995 I had reached out to police colleagues in The Netherlands who had formed an organisation called PARAAT, which was similar in ideology to the Black Police Association. One morning the BPA office received a fax from PARAAT with details of a conference taking place in the Netherlands that day. The members of PARAAT were upset that their group was excluded, given that the nature of the conference was addressing issues of discrimination and exclusion of minority communities in the Netherlands. They also pointed out that no people of colour were on the list of guest speakers.

The more I thought about it, the more I shared their anger and frustration. The reason they had contacted the BPA was because a British senior police officer, Anthony Burden, was scheduled to be a guest speaker at the conference. After discussing it with my BPA colleagues in the office, I faxed a strongly worded letter to the organisers of the conference. I told them in no uncertain terms that this exclusionary behaviour was unacceptable and equated the conference with "the worst excesses of colonialism where black communities are excluded from decisions of importance."

Later that day I received a call from Chief Constable Anthony Burden. He informed me in a very conciliatory tone that he was not on the organisational committee and therefore had been unaware of the issue. It was not his intention to exclude the very communities at the centre of the conference discussions, he said.

I curtly accepted his explanation but made it clear that we and our colleagues in the Netherlands were disappointed at this ill thought through event and the detrimental repercussions for police and community relations in the Netherlands.

As Chair of the BPA, I was often in meetings and conversations with senior officers of Assistant Commissioner rank, the equivalent of a Chief Constable anywhere else in the UK. I had adopted a polite but firm and confident manner when discussing matters pertaining to race and equality of opportunity. However, I was unaware that it was still customary for police colleagues of my rank in provincial police forces to address their Chief Constables with an air of deference, regardless of the subject matter. After our phone conversation, a fleeting thought crossed my mind that maybe Chief Constable Burden found my tone and manner to be inappropriate for a police Inspector.

With these things in mind, I remained confident enough to revisit and revise my written application to Assistant Commissioner O'Connor's office, making several improvements and relevant alterations that I felt would help the Bramshill Equalities Group agree and accept my project proposal.

Days later I received a call from the administrator at the Police Staff College, Bramshill.

"Members of the Equalities Group would like you to attend their next meeting to discuss your recent application to attend a conference in New Orleans."

The day of the meeting I left early to make the one-hour drive from London to Bramshill with plenty of time to spare, as being late is unacceptable in the world of policing. I was in awe as I turned into the long, gravel drive leading to Bramshill House, the principal training establishment for British police.

The Grade 1 listed building, one of the largest and most important Jacobean mansions in England, was daunting in its imposing nature. Built in the early 17th Century, it majestically sits on 262 acres of grounds and includes an 18-acre lake. Several of the rooms have large tapestries depicting historical events on their wood-paneled walls.

After I parked and got out of the car, I turned to lock it. At that moment I noticed the driver of a nearby car also locking his door. It was a suited and booted Chief Constable Anthony Burden.

"Good morning, Sir," I said, stretching out my hand.

"Good morning, Paul," he said, shaking my hand. "I take it you're coming to see us?"

I smiled. "Yes."

We walked together to the reception area before parting ways as I signed in at the security desk. I sat down outside the meeting room where I was due to meet with members of the Equalities Group. I opened my briefcase and glanced at my proposal, refreshing my memory with the key points.

The door opened. "Inspector Wilson, please come in and take a seat." As I entered the room, Chief Constable Burden caught my eye and I nodded in his direction. He was flanked by two females and one male. After exchanging greetings, they invited me to present my proposal for funding. When I finished speaking, the panel members exchanged glances with one another before leaning over to whisper to the Chief Constable.

After all the murmuring stopped, Chief Constable Burden looked at me. "We're in favour of your visit to the conference in New Orleans. We see it as an important event, given the subject matter seeks to address the very issues that challenge many in our black and ethnic minority communities."

"Thank you, Sir," I said.

"Unfortunately, we are a small group, and our funds are scarce. While we will fund your airfare, we cannot fund your accommodations and food," The Chief Constable added.

"I understand, Sir. I'll sort something out. Thank you once again. I will of course provide you with a full report of my findings," I said.

After the meeting, I drove back to London full of excitement. There was only one problem. While I now had the air fare, I was still short of funds for hotel accommodations and the daily workshops. I remembered the historical dynamics between the Metropolitan Police, the UK's largest and best resourced Police Force, and the provincial constabularies. "The arrogant Met" was how one constabulary colleague put it.

"You guys think you know everything and look down on the rest of us," he said.

It was difficult to disagree with him.

With this history in mind, I decided to again approach Assistant Commissioner O'Connor, who had refused to grant funding for me to travel to New Orleans on official Met business. How would it be perceived at New Scotland Yard that a Met Inspector, the Chair of the Black Police Association, had been granted funding by a group of senior officers from the provincial constabularies who considered the nature of the New Orleans conference to be of considerable significance and pertinent to the contemporary and thorny issue of policing and minority ethnic relations.

I chose the moment carefully. During one of our regular meetings, I explained to Assistant Commissioner O'Connor that Chief Constable Burden as Chair of the Bramshill Equalities Committee had agreed with my proposal to attend the New Orleans conference. I asked if the Met would consider paying the conference workshop fees.

"We can do that," he said with a wry smile.

I am certain he realised that his agreement to fund my workshop fees put my visit to New Orleans firmly in the realm of official Met Police business. With that came a raft of requisite entitlements including a daily subsistence and expenses package to include hotel accommodation.

~~~~

I had mixed feelings when my plane landed at the New Orleans airport. My excitement about returning to this favourite American city was tempered with the pressure to prove to my backers, both at Bramshill and New Scotland Yard, that this visit was more than just a jolly. I was determined to work extra hard to take something worthwhile back home with me.

This same feeling had accompanied me throughout much of my police career. I felt I needed to be seen doing better than average to stave off any suggestion that I was getting an easy ride or was somehow less qualified to do the job. I was certain that visits to exotic locations by white police colleagues on official business did not invoke the same compulsion to excel.

Before leaving for New Orleans, I was summoned by Deputy Assistant John Grieve, Director of the Race and Violent Crime Task Force. This was a New Scotland Yard Unit devised to spearhead the Met's handling of racial attacks and incidents, and with some considerable success, pioneering an array of investigative approaches that would forever change the nature of criminal investigative techniques.

I felt extremely comfortable with DAC Grieve, a genial man who always seemed in touch with the ground floor. He had endeared himself to a diverse section of the policing family and public alike with his honest and open manner. Facilitated no doubt by his slightly disheveled appearance, unkempt hair that was longer than regulation requirements, and a voice that betrayed the slightest hint of a speech impediment.

I had known John Grieve when he was Commander in charge of Hendon Police College of Training during my time with New Scotland Yard's Equal Opportunities Unit. I would often take minutes at meetings chaired by Grieve, convened as part of a larger agenda designed to promote cultural change among police trainers.

DAC Grieve was a "big gun" in Commissioner Condon's arsenal of personnel assembled to defend the Met's credibility in anticipation of the exceedingly difficult public inquiry into the murder of Stephen Lawrence.

I have it on good authority that Grieve was literally on his way to Northern Ireland where he was due to be appointed Deputy Chief Constable (he was a friend of Northern Ireland's Secretary of State, Mo Mowlam) when he was ordered to return and meet with Metropolitan Police Commissioner Paul Condon who persuaded him to stay with the Metropolitan Police and head up a high-profile unit tackling racially motivated crimes.

The day I was summoned to meet with Grieve, our conversation was casual, as usual. "Paul, I want you to get us some contacts. Find people who are actually doing something and know what they're talking about," he said. That was about the totality of the instructions I received from him.

Upon my return from the New Orleans Conference, with DAC Grieves instruction etched in my psyche, I comprised a report. Here is an excerpt of that report.

To: Race and Violent Crime Task Force
From: Inspector Paul Wilson
Date: 21st September 1998
Subject: **HATE CRIME**

A collection of documents gathered from the National Black Police Association 'Cluster' conference, held in New Orleans, Louisiana, USA, July 19–26, 1998. These documents are designed to help assist in the understanding of the North American experience of issues around racial conflict or 'Hate Crime'. The documents provide not only an overview of current work being undertaken, but more importantly details of a number of key individuals with considerable experience and expertise in constructing strategies to reduce and address racial crime in the United States.

Key Players – A list of individuals with experience of dealing with racial conflict issues on a professional basis.

Judith Winston – Executive Director 'One America in the 21st century' – The President's Initiative on Race and personally appointed by President Clinton. Works with the President to educate agencies, government bodies etc. on issues of race. Ms. Winston has a responsibility to produce a report on the year-long initiative, which is more than likely to continue as an ongoing priority. Supervises a staff pool that includes 85 Attorney's.

Jesse Sligh – Executive Assistant District Attorney. Spoke authoritatively about the practices and procedures of New York Police Dept. in relation to the reporting of 'Hate Crimes'. Jesse promised to send some material on the issue of under reporting and steps taken by New York Police to address this problem.

Rose Ochi – Director, US Department of Justice – Community Relations Service. (CRS) The CRS seeks to prevent or resolve community conflicts and tension arising from actions, policies and practices perceived to be discriminatory on the basis of race, colour or national origin. It provides services including conciliation, mediation and technical assistance to people and their communities to help them resolve conflicts that tear at the fabric of an increasingly diverse American society.

Patrick Oliver – Chief of Police, Grandview Heights, Ohio. A member of the National Organisation of Black Law Enforcement Executives (NOBLE) Has a training portfolio within NOBLE and appeared particularly interested in current events in London, particularly in relation to training needs of Police Officers.

Lance Ogiste – Assistant District Attorney Bureau Chief, Civil Rights. Specialises in Civil Rights issues in New York. Gave every indication that he has a 'hands on' role within the wider community, working with several agencies, including New York Police Department, to resolve racial conflict issues.

William 'Billy' Johnson – An ex-police Supt. Of Irish American extraction has written a book on 'Hate Crime' and tours the lecture circuit and Police Colleges to highlight the importance of 'getting it right'. What makes 'Billy' Johnson so interesting in his background is that he never took 'Hate Crime' seriously, was one of the 'good ol' boys' and was always tremendously respected as a 'real' operational police officer. Until, one day, he happened to be in the wrong place at the wrong time, was mistaken for someone else and seriously assaulted as a result. 'Billy' Johnson was recommended to me by US District Judge for District of Columbia, Ricky Roberts.

At the time of the report's submission to DAC Grieve's office, I gave no thought to whether anything I had written would be acted upon. I did not know if the Racial and Violent Crime Task Force would even contact the individuals I had highlighted as useful contacts. I never received any feedback.

Nevertheless, I had fulfilled my job. I had made several valuable contacts and attended some fascinating and insightful workshops on a range of issues affecting black and minority communities during my four days in New Orleans.

I had also eaten my fair share of gumbo and made frequent visits to Café Du Monde, home of the Beignet, a heavenly and magical light as a feather rectangular doughnut, deep fried and generously covered in powdered sugar. The Beignet should probably be listed among those irresistibly addictive substances likely to speed up the onset of the dreaded middle-aged spread.

~~~~

This memorable period of my career was revisited on 28th January 2001 when the Scarman Centre at the University of Leicester planned to hold a conference entitled *Policing and Ethnic Minority Communities: What's Changed Since MacPherson?'*

I had a strong affection for the University of Leicester, as I had recently completed my Master of Science degree in community safety with the Scarman Centre. Jon Garland, one of the conference organisers and participants, was also the director of my degree course. He sent me an invitation to speak at the conference, which I gladly accepted.

I had purposefully chosen the thought-provoking title *'What are Black officers supposed to contribute to the Police Service?'* for my conference slot. I had become used to flirting with controversy in the last several years.

While looking at the conference agenda, I noticed that Deputy Assistant John Grieve was scheduled as the last speaker of the day. His slot was entitled, 'Critical Incidents, Hate and Anti-Racist Policing'. I was convinced he would walk into the conference hall five minutes before he was due to speak and leave immediately after. Such was his considerable profile and busy schedule.

I was wrong. He arrived before lunch. I was scheduled as the last speaker before lunch. This is the one of the least popular slots as everyone knows that conference attendees will see you as standing in the way of their food. I couldn't help but think that the Met felt the need to be on hand to ensure that their errant officer (me) could be reminded of corporate expectations (and this wasn't the first time either).

They need not have bothered. My presentation took a customary less than veiled swipe at the inability of the police to deal with racism within the organisation. At the same time, I recognised the success and welcomed cultural change to investigating racist crime *within communities*, largely promoted by DAC John Grieve's ground-breaking work.

When the time came for John Grieve to speak, there was hushed silence as he walked onto the stage. The audience somehow perceived that they were not only in the presence of an extraordinary police officer, but someone in the twilight of their career. As such, there might not be many more opportunities to hear from this man.

For many familiar with John Grieve's meandering style of humorous storytelling (almost Ronnie Corbetesque) his delivery was to the point, largely influenced I'm sure by the fact that he was the last speaker and the one standing in the way of the exit and for some a long journey home. As speakers everywhere will attest, it is an unpopular slot at any conference.

I sat in the front row; a privilege often afforded guest speakers.

"Paul Wilson said some nice things about us, so I'm going to say something about Paul," he said.

I slid down in my chair.

Surely a public bollocking isn't coming my way? I thought.

"Paul sent us a report some time ago in which he used the terminology 'Hate Crime' to describe a range of crimes motivated by prejudice. We liked that and used it in the title of *our guidance*," said DAC Grieve, staring directly at me.

I was stunned. I turned my head to look at the people around me. Several smiled politely. But I was sure they had no idea what DAC Grieve was referring to. What he was actually saying was that the subject matter in my 1998 New Orleans report influenced the introduction of the never previously used term 'Hate Crime' into the British criminal justice lexicon.

The Association of Chief Police Officers (ACPO) publication in 2000: *Guide to Identifying and Combating Hate Crime, (prepared on behalf of ACPO by Metropolitan Police Service, Racial and Violent Crime Task Force (CO24)* was subsequently promoted by ACPO and Her Majesty's Inspectorate of Constabulary (HMIC) as the basis upon which *all* local forces should deal with *Hate Crime*.

Although not privy to the mechanics of that publication process, an educated guess would suggest that it was the Met's Race and Violent Crime Task Force that developed the thinking and drafted a consultatory *Hate Crime guidance* document (referred to by DAC Grieve at the conference), subsequently agreeing for it to be published under the auspices of the Association of Chief Police Officers.

And nowhere in this or the subsequent 'Hate Crime' guidance issued by the Association of Chief Police Officers will you find any mention of Paul Wilson's fascination with the Big Easy.

Chapter 59

Kensington life

During my time in the Corporate Planning Unit, I received notification that I had failed to pass the Superintendent's promotion assessment. The fact that I was on holiday in Cuba when my superintendent colleague, Chas Bailey, called to break the news, did not soften the blow. I was absolutely gutted. It was a harsh wake-up call that jolted me out of my New Scotland Yard complacency. While many officers seemed to consider working at 'The Yard' to be an advantage in the promotion stakes, that was not necessarily the case as those working at the 'sharp end' of policing would often collate significantly more 'credible evidence' to bolster their all-important competency logs. Spurred on by the need to get some 'real police work' under by belt, I notified the staff in the Yard's Personnel office that I was anxious to leave for a new life on a Borough and was willing to consider anywhere within the Met's boundary, but preferably South or Central London.

Then out of the blue, I received a telephone call. "Would you be interested in working at Kensington & Chelsea as we have a position for a Chief Inspector? You come highly recommended."

Really, I thought, *by whom?* "Yes, definitely."

"Good, can you pop in to see the Borough Commander tomorrow?"

So, after that I arranged for an informal chat with the Kensington & Chelsea Borough Commander. Kensington police station was where the management team was located and for me was an easy commute with good rail links.

I arrived at Kensington for my introductory chat with Dominic Clout, the Borough Commander, who I felt bore a passing resemblance to a smaller version of Sean Penn, the Hollywood actor.

"Why do you want to work at Kensington?" he inquired.

"To be truthful, I need to get out of New Scotland Yard and experience police work on a Borough, such as Kensington and Chelsea," I answered.

"Not many people want to leave The Yard to come and work at a Borough Police Station," said the Borough Commander.

"Maybe, but I've just failed my superintendent's promotion assessment centre and I'm keen to get some new and credible experience under my belt," I said.

"That's what I thought, I just wanted to hear it from you," he commented with a wry smile.

Kensington and Chelsea was a small police Borough and each morning all of the Senior Management Team (SMT) would cram into Dominic's office, where we would discuss each overnight crime occurrence on the Borough. The SMT comprised of two other uniform Chief Inspectors, a Detective Chief Inspector, two Superintendents, Borough Forensic Manager and Head of Human Resources. My new Borough was the home to London's titled elite, with probably more aristocracy, Lords and Ladies living there than any other London Borough. It was also home to Harrod's, one of the world's most famous department stores.

Much of my work involved oversight of an office responsible for monitoring the Borough's overall performance against a range of performance indicators, in addition I had responsibility for Professional Standards and would occasionally receive transgressors in my office for a firm but friendly chat. My immediate boss, Mike Howard, was a pleasant enough guy and looked after the Borough's Criminal Justice Unit.

One day Mike entered my office and said, with a mischievous look on his face, "The Borough Commander wants you to lead on a little job that we both feel will be good for your personal development."

"That sounds ominous," I joked.

"Honestly, nothing to worry about, we want you to be the Borough's liaison for a forthcoming visit by Her Majesty, the Queen, at a private Chelsea residence."

"Okay, sounds quite straightforward; the Queen popping in for tea shouldn't prove too arduous. Why the fuss?" I said.

"Well, normally it wouldn't attract too much attention but the afternoon tea as you put it will be attended by the eighth President of Ireland, Mary McAleese."

I was obviously aware of the tumultuous history between Ireland and Britain and the ongoing political violence in Northern Ireland and reflected on my own recent experience when about three years ago I visited a Community Development conference in Belfast during my posting to the

Neighbourhood Renewal Unit.

On that occasion senior civil servants advised me to leave my police warrant card and any other police ID in London and not to mention any connection to the British government; if asked I worked for an NGO (Non-Government Organisation) and was interested in community development efforts in Belfast. After the conference had finished, I had wandered into a Belfast pub, attracted by the loud music. After a short time, I became embroiled in very pleasant conversation with a lady, who had introduced herself as Esther, a Shankhill Road businesswoman. She was fascinated by my visit to the conference and asked who the main conference speakers were. On hearing their names, she had joked that the English would learn nothing from such an event. I knew *The Shankhill* to be a devoutly Loyalist area and mistakenly believed that afforded me some form of protection. That deluded naivety was to abruptly change after about thirty minutes into our conversation when Esther leaned forward and placed a hand on my arm, "Stop, don't say anything else."

I watched as Esther slowly turned her head, looking first right and then left. My eyes followed hers. Then I saw them, twelve or more young men, all in their twenties and thirties, seated with folded arms, strategically around and facing our table. They had not been there when we sat down.

The demure, polite, well-spoken young lady that I had been speaking with suddenly erupted.

"What the fuck do you want, don't you know who I am?" she shouted in a heavy Northern Irish accent, quite different from the one used in our conversation.

The group of men that surrounded our table did not flinch and remained seated; their eyes seemed to flit from Esther to me. My heart began to race as I suspected these young men may belong to a paramilitary organisation. I knew only too well that the level of violence used by such groups tended to exceed anything I had ever experienced in any London pub brawl. I remained glued to my chair as my female companion slowly rose to her feet. She was of a slim build, in her late thirties and about five feet six inches tall. She kicked back her chair causing the maximum noise possible. The music continued playing from the pub speakers, but the conversation from the many customers in the bar was now hushed as she walked over to one of the seated men. He stood up as she approached.

"You know what's going to happen if my people hear about this?" she screamed into the face of the man standing only inches away.

I did not hear his response but clearly saw that he had nodded his head while looking in my direction. That nod and stare triggered a pool of perspiration on my forehead as I began to slowly scan the pub for possible exit routes, I even looked at tables for large bottles that I might arm myself with, but knowing full well that I would stand no chance against twelve men. *But why me, were they that racist in Belfast?* I pondered. I was the only black face in the pub but, from what I knew, had seen and heard from my short time in Northern Ireland, race hate was not an issue; it was religion that fiercely divided communities.

By now Esther, who moments earlier had listened with intent and polite curiosity as I described my community development work with a large London charity, was shouting all manner of obscenities, some I did not recognise; not just at the man standing close to her but had begun to share her venom with others, some of whom she appeared to be familiar with as their body language indicated a degree of reverence to her jabbing finger propelled rhetoric. This stand-off seemed to last forever, perspiration now freely flowed down my back, down my arms and ran like a small river from my forehead and into eyes that rapidly blinked away the globules of sweat to see what was happening. As I looked around the bar, it seemed that customers while pretending nothing unusual was happening, were in fact glued to the animated antics of my female companion. Then it happened, the seated expressionless group of young men slowly rose to their feet in unison and one by one shuffled toward the exit until the last had left. Esther turned, walked back to our table, and sat down.

"You need a drink?" she smiled, looking closely at my glistening face.

"The largest one they have," I replied. "Do you want to tell me what just happened?"

"Listen, Paul, people in Belfast are not stupid, you don't look like a charity worker, you look, behave, walk and talk like you have some kind of military background."

"But that's not true I…"

Esther held up her hand to silence me.

"Paul, if that is your real name, I do not want to know, it's over now."

"What did you say to them?" I asked.

"Put it like this my ex-husband is well known in the Shankhill community for his, let's say activism, and some of these young boys didn't make the connection between me and my ex, so I had to remind them of who he is."

"So, nothing to do with race?" I asked.

"Fuck no, they are convinced you are a British soldier or a member of Military Intelligence and were determined to take you outside for "a chat". When we've finished our drinks, I'll get you a driver to take you back to your hotel and please, do not come back in here," urged Esther.

A few minutes later, we were joined by two large guys who were obviously friends of Esther's. I said my goodbyes, thanked her for her help and was escorted from the pub and into the back of a waiting car and driven to my hotel.

Back to my Tea Party arrangements for HM The Queen…

Following the conversation with Mike I had decided to visit Crosby Hall, Cheyne Walk, Chelsea the private residence, where HM The Queen would dine and meet with President Mary McAleese in a few weeks' time.

I parked my police vehicle near to the address and got out of the car. My immediate thought was, *where is the house because all I see is a high wall and huge gates.* As I walked toward the gates, an elderly man appeared as if from nowhere.

"Can I help you?" he said.

"I'm Chief Inspector Wilson, from Kensington & Chelsea police, here to see Mr. Moran," I informed.

"Oh, you're expected, come this way," said the elderly gent as he beckoned me to follow him.

He opened a small door down the side of the walled premises; *probably for the trades people,* I thought.

I walked through the door, my jaw dropped as I looked at a sizeable and beautifully designed garden, complete with fountain; its lush green lawn bordered by small, manicured bushes at the end of which appeared to be a large, medieval mansion. My immediate impression was that we were in the grounds of an Oxford College.

As I stood in awe at the magnificent imposing structure, we were joined by a middle-aged man in a suit; he was small in stature with a full head of greying hair. He held out his hand.

"Christopher Moran, you must be Chief Inspector Wilson. What do you think so far?"

"Pretty damn impressive, never in a million years would I have believed this to be behind that exterior wall," I complimented.

"Yes, we've done a great deal of work to restore the mansion to its original splendour. This was once the City home of Tudor courtier Sir Thomas More, poor chap was executed by Henry VIII in 1535, and in 1910 his home was moved stone by stone to its present riverside location," said Moran as he pointed at the magnificent building overlooking the equally impressive garden.

"Follow me, I'll give you a quick tour; not all of its thirty bedrooms have been restored, still much to do," said Moran.

Once inside the mediaeval mansion, I was shown large ornate Tudor decorated halls with beautiful ceilings the like of which I had never seen before.

"I wouldn't like to pay your heating bill Mr. Moran," I said.

He laughed.

I had done my research and knew that heating bills were not a concern for Christopher Moran, a millionaire by the time he was twenty-one. His personal wealth was estimated to be in the hundreds of millions. However, he had enjoyed a colourful career, once arrested, and charged with conspiracy to defraud– but acquitted after a month-long trial at London's Central Criminal Court. In 1982, he was expelled from Lloyd's of London, for "discreditable conduct" and in 1992 fined $2m in New York for insider dealing.

His success in arranging for the President of Ireland and HM the Queen to attend his home was, I suspected, to do with his charity, Co-operation Ireland, and his proven ability to broker meetings between former IRA Commander Martin McGuinness and the British establishment.

"We have three weeks to prepare for our event. Will you be here on the evening Chief Inspector Wilson?" said Moran.

"Yes, I plan to be in the vicinity of the main entrance to ensure that our two VIPs' entry into your home is facilitated as smoothly as possible," I said.

The next morning, I entered Mike's office and debriefed him on my visit to Crosby Hall and my meeting with Christopher Moran.

"Quite a colourful past, Mr Moran, I'm guessing the Palace are aware of it?" I wondered.

"Don't concern yourself with that Paul, the Queen's diary is meticulously planned by Palace officials and every guest will be the subject of a Special Branch assessment, so please remember to obtain the guest list well in advance," said Mike.

"Speaking of the Palace, I have a meet tomorrow at Crosby Hall with a member of Buckingham Palace staff," I said.

The following day I attended Crosby Hall where I met with 'Cecil from the Palace'. In his mid-forties, hair trimmed immaculately with side parting, he was, I suspected, a Sandhurst military academy graduate, given the cut of the rather old-fashioned double-breasted suit, small, knotted tie coupled with his military bearing. We were joined by Christopher Moran.

"I am keen to see the private room where the Queen is to hold private conversation with the President of Ireland," said Cecil.

"Certainly, both of you just follow me," beckoned Moran and off we went.

I had already done my homework and checked out the Queen's intended route, including the private meeting room. I was therefore extremely interested to get Cecil's view of the room, with its beautiful period décor, Tudor artifacts, and furniture.   However, as in common with other areas of

Crosby Hall, restoration was in progress and the substitute laminated floor covering was not only out of character, but it also bounced when walked upon. While not an expert on Royal etiquette, I had a bet with myself that the Queen does not get to walk on springy laminated flooring.

Mr. Moran opened the door to the designated room and Cecil followed; I was last through the door. Cecil slowly marched across the room and as his highly polished heavy leather shoes hit the laminated floor, a gentle bounce was evident. I watched carefully as Cecil slowly turned to face Christopher Moran and politely uttered words that ended any prospect of the room being used for its intended purpose.

"Is there another venue we can use for the meeting?"

"Of course, follow me," said Christopher Moran.

Unfortunately, another suitable room was not found so arrangements were put in place for the private conversation to take place shielded by a large portable screen in one of the main rooms.

The big day finally approached. Every conceivable arrangement was in place. Special Branch had been furnished with the extensive guest list, especially trained police search teams discretely examined the areas where the Queen and President McAleese would frequent. Nothing had been left to chance. I was happy. All that remained was for the VIPs to safely enter the building and that would see my job done.

My personal radio crackled to life, President McAleese had arrived and was safely in the building. A few minutes later another radio message informed me that the Queen had just left the Palace and would be at the venue within ten minutes. I stood on the pavement close to the large front gates, police officers strategically placed around the building. All the while, members of the public walked by oblivious of the Queen's imminent arrival and the historical significance of what was about to occur behind these large oak doors. I watched as the Queen's vehicle approached Crosby Hall. I briskly stepped toward the vehicle as the car came to a halt. Walking swiftly across the pavement, a member of Moran's staff leaned forward with outstretched hand and opened the rear door of the Rolls Royce and, in one gracious movement, out stepped Her Majesty Queen Elizabeth II. In time honoured fashion and commensurate with my rank, I snapped to attention and saluted. As the Queen stood on the pavement she glanced in my direction and gave a gentle smile. Still saluting, I watched Christopher Moran approach and escort the Queen into the grounds of Crosby Hall. My job was complete.

Chapter 60

Promotion to Superintendent

After about twelve months into my posting at Kensington and Chelsea, the annual Superintendent's promotion assessment was announced.

My office door opened, and Dominic stuck his head in. "Will you be putting yourself forward for the Superintendents' promotion?"

"Yes boss," I replied.

"Just make sure you get the paperwork on my desk before the end of the week and that gives me the weekend to dream up reasons why I should endorse you lot," he laughed.

He might laugh but without Dominic's endorsement it would not be possible for me to progress to the assessment process. Having tasted the disappointment of failing my last attempt, I had begun early with my preparation and had spent hours working on a system that ensured I covered all relevant competency areas during my interview questions. Most evenings Carol, my wife to be, would patiently ask me pre-prepared questions in our kitchen and I would use my system to deliver a response. Never once did she admit to being bored senseless by a process that had taken over all my free time. The rank of Superintendent was hugely attractive and with only a handful, literally, of black Metropolitan Police officers having ever achieved the rank, it was, I felt, well within my grasp without having to sell my soul.

In Monday's meeting of the SMT, Dominic announced that he had endorsed all Chief Inspectors, for the superintendents' promotion assessment centre. There were grins and nudges all round.

Shortly afterwards, the Borough Commander offered to give a talk to all his superintendent promotion candidates and set aside a date when he was prepared to share his insight and knowledge of the process with the group. I eagerly pencilled the date in my diary, but gradually picked up from my colleagues that they perceived the offer to be a waste of their time as they clearly did not rate Dominic as someone with recent and contemporary experience of the promotion process. On the contrary, I had closely watched Dominic over the past months and had begun to mimic his personal delivery style and mannerisms in my kitchen presentations. I attended his talk and found it especially useful in that he unknowingly confirmed my personal approach to interview questions that I had been rehearsing over the past weeks.

The day of the assessment arrived, as usual my early nervousness quickly dissipated and was replaced by an urgent desire to get on with the interview. At the conclusion of my interview, I was happy with the way I had performed. I had stuck to my system, was clear and very loud and even paced up and down, much like my Borough Commander has a habit of doing when delivering talks to his officers. All that was left was the wait until results were announced.

A few days later the entirety of the Senior Management Team was to attend a half day workshop, away from Kensington police station, on Borough performance. It was a day heavily rumoured to coincide with the announcement of results from the recent superintendent promotion process.

As the assembled members of the SMT sat in the workshop, all that could be heard was the vibration of cell phones followed by quick glances and whispers as some of my connected colleagues repeated what was on their screen.

"They're out."

"Steve Roger's got it."

"Bill Smythe didn't."

My heartbeat now raced as I pretended to appear disinterested.

"Alright you lot, this workshop is pointless as you're clearly thinking of other things; so, what I'm going to do is ask Steve, my Personnel officer, to get our results from The Yard. I will then go into the room next door and one by one you will be invited in and given your result," said Dominic.

That sounded good to me. The last thing I wanted was to get my result from someone on my cell phone.

The first to be invited in to see the Borough Commander was Bert; he emerged after about a minute, his head hung low, his eyes red. He shook his head as he walked past his colleagues and left the room.

No-one said a thing.

"George, you're next," said Steve who was strategically placed next to the door leading into the Borough Commander's torture chamber.

A minute later George opened the door, his eyes said it all. He had failed. He went and sat in the corner to make the important phone call home.

"Jeremy, the Borough Commander's ready for you," said Steve.

Jeremy gave a big grin and theatrically waved to no-one as he disappeared into the room of gloom to establish his fate. He emerged a few moments later with head bowed and silently disappeared out of the room.

"Paul, it's your turn," said Steve.

I felt nauseous. The information I was about to receive would potentially have huge financial repercussions for myself and my family, not just in terms of a sizeable pay increase but a generous pension throughout my retirement. I slowly walked to the door.

"All the best, Paul," whispered Steve as I pressed the door handle and slowly entered the room.

Dominic was seated in the middle of the room; a wooden clipboard was nursed on his knee. His face failed to betray any emotion. His eyes stared down at the clipboard.

"Chief Inspector Wilson, I have to tell you that you…" he paused and lifted his head to look me in the eye, "passed the promotion process for Superintendent. Well done Paul," he exclaimed in a loud voice.

"Thank you, boss," I croaked, barely able to hold back the tears of joy. I purposely bit my lower lip; the pain curbed my emotions.

I turned, opened the door, and looked at Steve.

"Well done, Paul," he said before I could open my mouth. He had heard Dominic through the door or more likely had looked at the results list before handing it over.

"Thanks Steve, yeah I got it," I said in a quiet voice, but loud enough for colleagues in the room to hear.

My announcement was met by silence. My Chief Inspector colleagues sat there staring, it seemed just about anywhere to avoid eye contact with me.

I went and sat in the corner of the room, closed my eyes, thinking about all the months of preparation, the system I had devised, the input from my mentor Steve Dennis, the countless presentations I had attended and finally my Borough Commander's inspirational chat. I took out my cell phone and called Carol. We had recently announced our engagement and she was now living with me at my new home in Thornton Heath, South London. I knew she was at home today.

"I got it!" I said in a hushed tone to ensure I was not overheard sharing an unguarded moment of sheer elation.

"Congratulations darling, I knew you'd get it; you worked so hard, all those evenings practicing your system in the kitchen has paid off!"

"You are so right, but I couldn't have made it without your patience. I forced you to listen night after night and always keeping a straight face too," I laughed.

"How did your Chief Inspector colleagues get on?" said Carol.

"Unfortunately, none of them were successful and they're not exactly ecstatic that I've made it," I said.

"That's such a shame, I'm sure if things had been the other way around, you'd be shaking their hands and wishing them well."

"Yes, but you should know by now, it's the *Newsnight* affect."

"Yes; remind me when you can retire?" she laughed.

"Another four years, two months and thirteen days, not that I'm counting," I joked.

As I finished my conversation, I overheard Mike in conversation with Dominic. "I bet old Paul would like to hop around the room and scream his head off, but he can't of course."

Mike had hit the nail on the head. Out of respect for my colleagues, I had chosen to remain humbled and quiet while my emotions were doing a lap of honour with a huge trophy held aloft.

A few days following my promotion, I received a proforma from New Scotland Yard's central postings panel inviting me to choose the Borough to which I would prefer to be posted in my new rank. This was a welcome departure from a nepotistic system, where individual Borough Commanders got to appoint their mates from the list of newly promoted Superintendents, or those they felt would best 'fit in'. Without hesitation, I chose Lambeth. I had served in Lambeth as an Inspector and had grown fond of the community, its vibrancy, and the fact it was continually the focus of policing attention. In a recent report by Her Majesty's Inspector of Constabulary, Lambeth was described as 'one of the most challenging policing environments in the UK, and possibly Europe'. Lambeth was not for the faint-hearted, but it was somewhere where I felt my skills and attributes would prove to be of most use. I returned the completed proforma and within a couple of days I was notified that my first preference had been agreed by New Scotland Yard's central postings panel.

I knocked on my Borough Commander's open door and poked my head in.

"I'm going to Lambeth, boss."

"Well done, I know that's what you want, we need to get your leaving do sorted," he laughed.

The following day I made a phone call to Lambeth police headquarters at Frank O'Neil House in Kennington.

"Can I speak with the Lambeth Borough Commander please? Its Superintendent Wilson, I'm due to join you shortly."

"Hello sir, Ronnie Whelan here, I'm the Borough Commander's staff officer. He knows about your posting but is unavailable now. I have your number at Kensington, I'll get back to you."

At the end of the week, I received a letter from Commander Bob Broadhurst, the senior officer with overall operational responsibility for South London, congratulating me on my promotion success and impending appointment to Lambeth Borough. The letter also set out the Commander's expectations.

'...there will be no honeymoon period. I expect my new Superintendents to hit the ground running as there is much work to do...'

A couple of weeks passed, and I had still not heard back from the Lambeth Borough Commander's office. So, I made another phone call.

"Hello, Superintendent Wilson here. May I make an appointment to meet with the Borough Commander?"

"Hello, Mr. Wilson, Ronnie here. The Borough Commander will meet with you but is busy with some pressing operational matters. Can I get back to you?"

A few days later I decided to raise the issue with my Kensington Borough Commander.

"I've made a couple of calls to Lambeth to find out when they can receive me. I've also visited the outgoing Superintendent, who occupies an office in Lambeth Town Hall. All I get is a blank."

Dominic held up his hands and looked at the ceiling, shrugged his shoulders and didn't say anything in response to my thinly disguised plea for help. He was either helpless to intervene or reluctant to do so. I turned and left his office. To make matters worse, I had done some research and discovered that all of this year's newly promoted Superintendents were in post and of course would be receiving a Superintendent's salary whereas I, the lone black officer to achieve promotion, was not in post and not receiving the Superintendent's salary.

The next day I made another phone call to the Lambeth Borough Commander's office.

"Lambeth Borough Command, Sergeant Whelan speaking."

"Ronnie, it's Superintendent Wilson...again. I really need to get into the Borough Commander's diary, it's been a month now."

"Apologies, Mr Wilson, he is aware of your calls. I'll speak with him and get back to you."

The days passed and I had not heard anything from Lambeth. It was now becoming a huge embarrassment for me as work colleagues and friends were continually asking why I was not yet at Lambeth.

I was now consumed by what was a sensitive situation and one that could blow up in my face if I was perceived to be 'rocking the boat' this early in my new rank. Commander Bob Broadhurst, I discovered, was a close friend of the Lambeth Borough Commander, so rightly or wrongly I ruled him out and decided instead to approach my mentor, Superintendent Steve Dennis. Steve had been a Sergeant at Croydon when I was there as a PC and in those days was one of the few supervisors, I felt comfortable speaking with.

The following Monday I made my way to New Scotland Yard to meet with Steve, who was employed as Staff Officer to Assistant Commissioner, Tarique Ghaffur.

I walked out of the New Scotland Yard lift and headed for the Assistant Commissioner's suite of offices. I opened the door and saw Steve seated at a desk, reading a newspaper.

"Rushed off your feet I see,", I said jokingly.

Steve looked up, folded the newspaper, and jumped to his feet.

"Congratulations, Paul, really pleased for you!"

We shook hands.

"It's difficult to know what to do when your Principal is suspended from duty," said Steve.

"Yes, I've been following events in the media, along with millions of others; these are unprecedented times."

"That is an understatement," laughed Steve.

"Yeah, your boss alleges at a press conference while wearing full uniform, that the Commissioner of the Metropolitan Police, is racist. What is the Commissioner supposed to do...?"

"Well, he suspended him, didn't he?" interrupted Steve.

"Look, Steve, I know both men, Ian Blair has always been reasonable with me and has done much to move the Met into the 21st century. I also know Tarique and in common with many black colleagues with his length of service, over the years he's experienced racism in silence but there comes a point when you say to yourself 'enough is enough'. I believe Tarique has chosen his 'enough is enough' moment and unfortunately Commissioner Blair is on the receiving end."

"You might be right," said Steve.

"The Commissioner probably felt he had no alternative but to suspend Tarique, but I know from my days drafting the Grievance Procedure that TG's suspension will be viewed by any Tribunal as a contravention of the Race Relations Act."

"Doesn't help me, I still have a Principal suspended from duty. Anyhow Paul, how can I help? You mentioned you had a problem when we spoke on the phone."

"Well, since getting promoted, and thanks once again for all your advice and support in that process, I have been trying to get into my post at Lambeth, but the Borough Commander is blanking me."

"Really, I thought you had started. What explanation is being given?"

"He's busy and will call me back but of course he never does. It's a tricky one Steve, if I kick up a fuss I get branded as a troublemaker. You know how it works for people like me."

"Sure, but do you want me to intervene on your behalf? I'm still a staff officer to an Assistant Commissioner...even though he's suspended," said Steve in a purposefully loud voice, enough to turn the head of a passing senior officer.

I shook my head.

"I really want to keep this low profile. The tabloid press already claim the Met is engulfed in a 'race row' and what with the Black Police Association boycotting the recruitment of black police officers, if this gets out I can just see the headline now; 'top black cop denied promotion on the basis his Borough Commander's too busy to see him," I laughed.

Steve looked at me and shook his head.

"Look, Paul I'm more than happy to get involved, just say the word."

"Thanks Steve, I'm really grateful for the offer but I'll say no for now, but who knows what I will do in the future."

I left the Assistant Commissioner's suite. I had decided that this would not be my 'enough is enough' moment.

Approximately two months after my notification from the central posting panel that I was to be posted to Lambeth Borough, I received a phone call.

"Hello, Mr Wilson, Ronnie Whelan here; apologies for the delay but the Borough Commander will meet you at next week's senior team meeting to be held at Frank O'Neil House. I'll send you an official notification."

I put the phone down. *Hallelujah!* I thought to myself, but then wondered whether Superintendent Dennis had put in a phone call despite what I had said.

The following week, I attended Frank O'Neil House and met with my new colleagues, including Lambeth Borough Commander, Chief Superintendent Martin Bridger and arranged a start date in January 2006.

Armed with a start date sanctioned by the Borough Commander, I visited Brixton Police Station as the Borough Commander had advised in our meeting that I would be working from the Brixton Superintendent's office, and not the office within Lambeth Town Hall. I spoke to staff in the Lambeth Resources Unit, introducing myself as the new Superintendent and made enquiries about my office accommodation. I was informed that it was being prepared.

The next week I dropped into Brixton police station to confirm all was going to plan.

The Resources manager took me upstairs and pointed to my office door and said, "There it is, it's not quite ready yet but don't worry it will be."

Reassured, I left after a quick familiarisation tour of the station.

"Carol, I start at Lambeth on Monday; I'm going to drop off some personal stuff on Sunday night. Fancy coming with me?"

"Love to, I'm so excited for you," expressed Carol.

It was a dark and damp Sunday evening when I parked my car outside Brixton Police Station. This was a proud moment for me, and I wanted to share it with Carol, who had supported me in my quest to become a Superintendent and here we were at the end of that journey outside of my new home for the next few years.

Carrying a large cardboard box of personal effects to give my new office a personal touch, I walked through the station yard as Carol followed close behind. I punched the entry code into the security keypad on the back door, pulled the handle and entered the police station. As I walked up the stairs, I quickly reflected on my career to date, the highs, and the lows, but here I was, Lambeth's first black Superintendent in the 175-year history of the metropolitan police service.

"Here we are," I said pointing at my office door.

"Where's your name plate?" laughed Carol.

I pushed open the door; it was dark. I ran my left hand up and down until I found the light switch. I flicked it on. My eyes quickly scanned the illuminated office. I froze, a feeling of intense nausea shocked my system. Carol pushed past me.

"What the hell is this?" she shouted.

Stacks of dust laden cardboard files occupied the office floor. In the centre of the room was a heap of black plastic refuse sacks full of what appeared to be old cardboard files. Cardboard boxes were scattered around the room. The carpet was filthy. The sparse furniture, some of it clearly broken, was dated, and covered with dust. The windows were coated with dirt.

"I can't believe this is happening, Carol," I said, still in a state of shock.

Carol stood by my side and clutched my hand. I looked at her and saw that tears had welled in her eyes.

"OK, let's get this place cleaned up so you have somewhere decent to begin your new job," she suggested, trying to mask her sadness. She began opening desk drawers until she found a duster.

"I think there's a cleaner's cupboard on this floor; I'll see what I can find," I said, leaving the office.

Minutes later I returned with a dustpan and brush. Together we methodically worked around the office; dusting the furniture, cleaning the grime from the windowsills, lifting and moving the old files and sacks of rubbish into a corner until, after approximately two hours, we had managed to make the office semi-respectable.

"Shouldn't you have a computer or at least a telephone?" asked Carol.

"Of course, don't worry I'll get it sorted tomorrow," I said to play down my feelings.

The following morning, I arrived at my office early and immediately sought out the cleaning staff and tasked them with removing the sacks of refuse and broken furniture. I waited until the staff in the Resources office began work.

"Why wasn't my office prepared as promised?"

"It wasn't our responsibility, Sir; we asked your Inspectors to sort it out weeks ago."

I had no appetite for shouting at junior civil staff colleagues; clearly there was much more to this than met the eye. That evening I arrived home.

"How was your first day at work?" said Carol.

"Much of it was spent finding people to clean the carpet and do a proper job on the windows," I said.

"And your colleagues, how are they?"

"They seem friendly enough, interestingly a senior Detective stuck his head around my door, looked at my office and appeared surprised."

"Why was he surprised?" asked Carol.

"I guess he knew it was full of rubbish and now it looks half decent," I said.

"And your computer and telephone, sorted?"

"No, not yet; I made some enquiries with staff at the Resource office, but they seem to behave as though no one expected me to arrive," I responded.

On my third day in the office, I became so frustrated at not having a computer or telephone, I snapped.

I marched unannounced into the Chief Inspector's office across the corridor. "I need to use your phone as I don't have one," I said to the bemused Chief Inspector.

I picked up the telephone and punched in the Borough Commander's extension. "Hello, Ronnie, Superintendent Wilson, I can't do my job without a telephone and computer, but it seems all too difficult…"

"I'll get you a computer from my old office and bring you a telephone, be there in a bit," said Ronnie.

About two hours later Ronnie was in my office installing a personal computer and telephone. That evening I discussed the day's events with Carol.

"So, what is the Brixton Chief Inspector's office like?" she inquired.

"Spacious, overlooking the road, carpeted, nice modern furniture, en-suite toilet and shower," I vocalised in a matter-of-fact tone.

Carol laughed, "You are joking of course?"

"No, I'm not joking Carol. That's just how it is."

"But he's your junior?" emphasised Carol.

"Yes, Carol, but I'm not his line manager and how many times have we discussed *white privilege*, what part don't you understand?" I snapped.

The months passed during which I had kept my head down and through hard work and commitment established myself as a key player in the senior management team. Then one Saturday morning, quite out of the blue, I received an email from The University of California, Berkeley.

"Hey Carol, come and look at this email!" I shouted.

Carol walked over and peered over my shoulder at the computer screen and read aloud the open email.

"Dear Paul, An international, multidisciplinary round-table on the role of rank-and-file officers in police reform will take place 12th and 13th October 2006 at University of California, Berkeley…You are invited to submit a paper on the role of Black Police Associations in the wider police reform agenda…"

"I don't believe it, why is it that you never get invited to a conference in South London?" she laughed.

"Do you think I should attend? I mean, I'd like to, my old friend Professor Wes Skogan from Northwestern is one of the contributors," I said.

"Well, it does seem too good an opportunity to miss. Berkeley is next to San Francisco isn't it? But it says you must submit a paper," said Carol, continuing to read the email.

"Yes, that's how these round tables work, not really a conference, a meeting of peers for discussion and exchange of views."

"You have to go," said Carol.

"OK, that's settled, I'll get started on the paper and put in a request for assistance from the Met; four days should do it."

"I'm sure that will help endear you to your Lambeth colleagues," laughed Carol.

In due course, the Borough Commander finally asked me about the request for 'time off to attend a conference in California'.

"It's to do with Black Police Associations and the important role they play in the wider police reform agenda," I said.

He grinned and gave me a knowing look but as someone who had recently travelled to Pakistan to 'gain a better understanding of Islamic extremism' he was in no position to argue. My leave and travel were duly authorised.

Nevertheless, the delay in my posting to the Borough nor the state of my office on arrival were never discussed. I had decided not to raise it. I only had to survive another couple of years and then I would retire. For the sake of my mental health, I had planned to make my final few years in the job as stress free as possible.

The sudden unannounced departure of Lambeth's Borough Commander, Martin Bridger, caused considerable disquiet at the monthly Community Police Consultative Group's (CPCG) meeting with Lambeth's police command team. Members of the influential CPCG had on numerous occasions complained that Lambeth's top job was all too often seen by Borough Commanders as a steppingstone to bigger and better things. The arrival of a new Borough Commander was the opportunity to change that perception.

Chapter 61

Colour-blind Policing

With the new Lambeth Borough Commander in post, I was determined to carry on as usual and if that meant keeping my head down and saying nothing to disturb the status quo, then so be it. However, this coping strategy was to be challenged when the Borough Commander asked me to deputise for her at a large meeting of senior officers from across South London, to be held at the Lambeth Support HQ in north Lambeth, at the same venue as the Black Police Association AGM in 1998.

The meeting was due to commence at 10am. I arrived at 9.45am. As I entered the large room, I was confronted by a sea of about thirty white men wearing white shirts, that was my immediate impression. The visual was both powerful and surreal. The loud chatter and laughter of male voices filled the room. As usual, I was the only black face. I had been in this situation so many times in many meetings but of late, working in Lambeth had reinforced the obvious. London was a multi-cultural melting pot, but here I was yet again in the presence of senior decision makers that did not look like London and yet everyone continued to behave as if everything was absolutely normal.

We were shortly joined by Deputy Assistant Commissioner Alf Hitchcock, another white shirted white man; a hush fell over the room.

"Thanks for coming gents; we'll get down to business in a moment, but first I want quick introductions as we have some new faces amongst us."

When my turn came, I got to my feet. "My name is Paul Wilson, here representing the Lambeth Borough Commander and I want to take this opportunity to welcome you all to Lambeth, one of the most racially diverse Boroughs in the Met."

My pronouncement was met in silence, not a murmur, no witty response. It was a 'pin-drop' moment.

I sat down and the meeting continued. For the next two hours as crime and other policing concerns were addressed, not one mention was made of policing diverse communities and the inherent challenges presented. I got to my feet.

"What are we to do about the ongoing debate around stop and search and the disproportionality suffered by our black communities?"

There was a deathly silence until Deputy Assistant Commissioner Hitchcock rose to his feet and spoke in his drawled Lancashire accent.

"That's an interesting observation, Paul. The answer is complicated by a number of variables at play and not something we have time for today, let's move on, shall we?"

That evening, I arrived home feeling stressed and frustrated.

"What's the matter, Paul? You've hardly said a word since you got in," observed Carol.

"Work! It's getting me down. I have tried for the past year or so to keep a low profile, but it's no good. I can't help but speak out when all around pretend that everything is as it should be," I said.

"Did something happen today?" asked Carol.

"Nothing unusual, just the same stuff that's been happening for some time now. And that's the problem as I see it, we have a community suffering from overzealous policing and a police service that thinks it's business as usual."

"So, what are you going to do; what can you do?" said Carol in her concerned voice.

"I'm not sure, but I do know that doing nothing is not the solution," I said.

The opportunity to do something came after the Notting Hill Carnival. At 15.04 on 26th August 2008, when in a pique of frustration, I penned an email to Deputy Commissioner, Paul Stephenson.

Deputy Commissioner,
While the violence witnessed on the streets of Notting Hill following this year's Carnival is unforgivable; in terms of addressing the question as to 'why', I would offer my own unproven hypothesis:
'The outcome of Notting Hill Carnival can be linked to the recent collective experience of African Caribbean youth'.

In support of my hypothesis: over the past few months here in Lambeth and elsewhere, I have been involved in a number of discussions with members of the African Caribbean community regarding increased use of stop/search and associated policing tactics, while seeking to gain a better understanding of how we might tailor our local policing tactics to meet the needs and experiences of our communities. These discussions usually encompass the totality of the African Caribbean experience in London and inevitably touch upon wider societal issues, often resulting in the same interwoven themes; distrust, resentment, and racial discrimination. Nevertheless, the emerging concerns expressed regarding policing are sufficiently consistent to lead me to believe that police/African Caribbean relations are possibly at their lowest ebb for a number of years and any Management Board 'Carnival post mortem' should be mindful of what I would term a 'deteriorating relationship' that may well manifest in further and less obvious examples of African Caribbean community distrust and resentment. Such examples may well be the inability of the MPS to sufficiently recruit and retain BME officers along with a deterioration in the collective experience of serving BME police officers and staff; outcomes that I would argue are inextricably linked to my hypothesis.

That will most probably be filed in the too difficult tray, I thought to myself. I certainly did not expect a response, as in my experience matters of 'race' had taken a back seat in recent years with little if any proactive thinking coming from the Commissioner's Management Board, but just sending the email had given me a great deal of satisfaction. I wanted them to know that I knew what they had failed to see and act upon. But to my pleasant surprise I received a response from the Deputy Commissioner at 13.51 on 29th August 2008.

Paul,
Thank you for your note dated 26 August 2008.
By any standard, the policing operation for the Carnival was very successful. I, myself, attended and witnessed much of it. I was very impressed. Regrettably, the end of the carnival was tarnished by the actions of a small minority hell-bent on violence and disorder. But this should not detract from an otherwise successful event, in terms of policing.
I note your comments with some concern. I have copied your note - and my reply to DAC Alf Hitchcock - with a request that he sees you and you have an opportunity to expand on your comments.
I am interested in the outcome. But one thing on which I need to put you right is your views of our failure to recruit and retain BME Officers and staff. Your views here are just not in accordance with the data and progress that we have made over the last 2 or 3 years. As such, I am not sure that I could see this as 'inextricably linked' to your theory. But I look forward to hearing on Alf's meeting with you.

While pleased to receive a response from the Deputy Commissioner, I was nevertheless disappointed at his failure to grasp the correlation between general black community confidence in the police, and the well-being of black police personnel. To rely purely upon quantitative recruitment and retention data as a success indicator while overlooking invaluable qualitative data was, in my view, a failing of successive metropolitan police commissioners. In fact, not since the Bristol Seminar in 1990, some eighteen years previous, had the views and/or experiences of black and minority ethnic staff been recognised, and appropriate interventions introduced. However, the effectiveness of those interventions was never evaluated. Now, the email from the Deputy Commissioner was symptomatic of a school of thought within the upper echelons of policing all too willing to trot out the well-worn platitude, 'a great deal has been achieved where black and minority ethnic recruitment is concerned but much remains to be done.' For, unless real progress is made in shaping equitable police service delivery to black and minority ethnic communities, recruitment, retention and indeed progress through to the senior echelons of the Force will remain forever hindered.

I looked forward to my meeting with DAC Hitchcock. However, my enthusiasm was not shared by my new Borough Commander.

"Why is there a Deputy Assistant Commissioner coming here to visit you? We can do without that attention."

I totally understood where the Borough Commander was coming from as any close inspection of Lambeth Borough Command Unit at that time would have revealed an embarrassingly dysfunctional enterprise, not at all in keeping with the police inspectorate's good practice guidance. Nevertheless, I reassured the Borough Commander that the DAC would only be visiting my office to discuss the big picture and, I thought to myself, *not to question the Borough's top-heavy management structure overseeing three mini and disparate Commands.*

"I think I really pissed off my Borough Commander today," I said as I settled down for my customary glass of red in front of the TV.

"What have you done now?" asked Carol, glancing at me with a look of concern.

"I was at a meeting today with senior officers to de-brief the handling of the Notting Hill Carnival, and I raised the 'kettling' of a hundred plus black youth…"

"What's kettling, you're not at work now, speak English?" laughed Carol.

"Sorry, it's a police tactic used to contain large crowds, a cordon preventing their movement, but in this instance, it seems anyone that was young and black was caught up in a containment in Lambeth and transported miles away from their homes."

"Was it a gang thing?" asked Carol.

"It may well have been, but the complaints I've received suggest it was a colour thing in that if you were black in the vicinity then you were fair game."

"So, what happened at your meeting?" asked Carol.

"I challenged the senior officer responsible, Chief Superintendent, Mick Johnson, by asking him in open forum whether in implementing such a tactic he had considered the more strategic race issues and how they might be managed in light of criticism by the black community. He responded that race was not an issue and that every week he employed similar tactics when dealing with potential football hooligans," I said.

"Is he colour blind?" asked Carol with a broad grin.

"It's a stock answer that wouldn't have been given immediately after the Stephen Lawrence inquiry, but now things have reverted 'back to normal," I said, with more than a hint of cynicism.

Chapter 62

Lambeth BME report

It was not long afterwards that Lambeth's weekly senior management team (SMT) meeting presented a unique opportunity to address the issues raised in my email exchange with the Deputy Commissioner, for at the conclusion of our meeting my colleague, Diane McNulty, raised an important matter.

"There's so much negativity in the media at the moment, the recent Secret Policeman Returns Panorama programme, the BPA recruitment boycott, and the ongoing suspension of Assistant Commissioner Ghaffur and Commander Ali Dizaei, two of the Met's most senior BME officers; I just wonder if our BME colleagues on the Borough are adversely affected by it all?"

All eyes focused on me, as it always did, if ever the acronym BME was used during our meeting.

"The only way to find out is to ask them," I spoke up.

"We could circulate a questionnaire," another colleague offered.

"We could but we probably wouldn't get a rich picture," I retorted.

"What do you suggest Paul?"

"Leave it with me; I'll put something together," I said.

The meeting concluded with a general agreement that, in my capacity as Chair, I would take the matter to the Lambeth BCU's Equality and Diversity Forum and find a way forward.

The next day I spoke with Linda, my newly appointed Personal Assistant.

"We are going to seek the views and experiences of black and minority ethnic staff on the Borough. What do you think as a black woman?" I said.

"Me? That's easy, I've worked in the Met for a number of years. This is a racist organisation; I see it and feel it and if you plan to ask for the views of all black staff then you're going to get some uncomfortable answers," Linda replied in a matter-of-fact tone.

"Sometimes discomfort is what is required to get things changed," I responded.

Shortly afterwards, I visited Diane McNulty in her office at Frank O'Neill House. Diane was the senior Civil Staff member on the Borough and, as such, had overall responsibility for Human Resources, general resources and all matters pertaining to finance.

"I've consulted with members of the Diversity Forum and they are in agreement with my proposal that we write to all BME personnel on Lambeth BCU and invite them to attend a half day seminar, away from their place of work, where they can discuss recent events and related issues in a relaxed and safe environment."

"Oh, that sounds interesting, Paul; a really good idea," said Diane.

"I think so, but it's not new. Many years ago, Assistant Commissioner Wyn Jones used similar methodology for the Bristol Seminar."

"I remember Bristol and Assistant Commissioner Jones? Whatever happened to him?" asked Diane.

"He was suspended shortly after the Bristol Seminars and eventually sacked for misconduct, including the improper use of a police vehicle to attend rugby matches," I said cynically.

"Oh no, just make sure you don't use your Job car for unofficial business, Paul; I'd hate to lose you," laughed Diane.

The following day I called Linda into my office.

"Check with Lambeth Support HQ building for a large conference room availability on 23rd October; half day should do it."

"So, it's really happening is it?" asked Linda.

"Yes, I've briefed Diane McNulty and will now write to all BME colleagues outlining the purpose of what we are trying to achieve."

"And what exactly are we trying to achieve?" pressed Linda, who had stopped taking notes and stared expectantly at me.

"The metropolitan police are London's biggest employer of BME men and women, if we take into account all the PCSOs and civil staff. By canvassing the views of our BME staff here in Lambeth we can share any learning with the wider organisation and help improve the work environment for not only existing colleagues, but for those future recruits."

"Hmmm," nodded Linda as she scribbled furiously.

"Also, Linda, it's so important we involve someone from the Lambeth Council. I've informally spoken with Paula Williams, their Equalities officer. Can I leave that with you to make it a formal invite?"

"Will do, anyone else you need me to contact?" said Linda.

"Yes, I'll let you have a few more names tomorrow," I replied.

On Thursday 23rd October 2008, I set out for the short journey by car to Lambeth Support HQ, SE1, home to the Metropolitan Police's 24-hour emergency call centre.

On arrival, I entered the building and made my way upstairs to the main cafeteria. *I just hope and pray that my facilitators have turned up*, I thought to myself as I opened the door into the canteen.

I quickly glanced around the spacious room and in one corner I saw seated at a table two black women, one black man and one white woman. I walked over.

"Good morning ladies and gent, I'm so happy to see you here. Everyone OK?"

My greeting was met with a resounding "Yes, Sir" from all present.

"Without your help, today's very important exercise wouldn't get off the ground; so, thanks once again for giving your time and commitment," I said as I took my seat at the table.

"I looked in the briefing room a few minutes ago and checked the registration sheet. We have 36 men and women," informed Pamela.

"Happy with that, bearing in mind the whole Bristol Seminar exercise was triggered by the premature resignation of 26 black and Asian police recruits in 1989, the total recruitment of black and Asian police officers that year was 35. So, our 36 colleagues sitting in the room next door is a magical number that may just help us unlock the reasons why we as an organisation are still failing to retain and recruit black and Asian police personnel in numbers that reflect the demography of London."

"I thought this was about the Lambeth Borough?" questioned Zenobia.

"It is, but let's not forget the bigger picture. Would it be unreasonable to extrapolate today's outcome across every Borough Command Unit in London?" I questioned.

Heads shook in unison.

"Ok, great, you all have your briefing notes?" I asked reassuringly.

"Thanks, Sir, I received your briefing note including our role description for today," said Wayne.

"That's good; so, just to confirm, each of you has your theme and questions to ask?" I reiterated.

"I've got mine, just remind me what are the other themes?" said Paula.

"OK, for everyone's benefit; organisational culture is Paula, training and development is Zenobia, complaints and discipline/fairness at work is Wayne, faith issues in the workplace is Pam , and I've got 'Communicating the issues.'", I announced.

"What time do we break for lunch?" said Zenobia.

"Lunch is scheduled for 12.30pm," I informed, standing up in readiness to leave. "It's nearly 10am, let's go next door. I need to address our colleagues and give them a brief overview of what today's exercise entails."

I opened the door and my eyes quickly scanned the room; some of the faces I recognised, others I did not. They all looked in my direction and rose to their feet.

"Good morning ladies and gentlemen," I said.

"Good morning, Sir!" was the unanimous response.

"Firstly, let me express my sincere thanks to you all for taking the time out of your busy workplace to participate in this important workshop. Secondly, allow me to introduce you to your workshop facilitators for today. Paula Williams, who is an Equalities Officer with Lambeth Council, Detective Constable Wayne Blackwood, from Harrow Police, Pamela Morton, who is a Band D here in Lambeth BCU, and Zenobia Cowan Davies, also a Band D here in Lambeth BCU."

My introduction was met with a round of applause from the gathered staff.

"Thanks for that, now just a quick overview of why we are here today and what we are going to do. But can I just say, relax! Everything you say today remains anonymous; it will not be attributable to you as an individual. There will be a report compiled at the end of it but nowhere in that report will your name be mentioned. The registration sheet you completed on arrival is for logistical reasons – the canteen staff need to know how many hungry mouths to feed!" I said.

There was laughter around the room.

"I will now divide you into five groups and I want each group to go to a large table in the room, where you will be joined by one of the facilitators. The plan is for each facilitator to canvas your views on a particular theme for a period of at least 20 minutes. Please be candid in your responses. At the conclusion of 20 minutes the facilitator will move onto the next table. The exercise is complete when your table has been visited by five facilitators."

For the next 100 minutes, the thirty-six members of staff were busily engaged in facilitated debate and at the conclusion of the exercise each facilitator presented to all the assembled personnel the emerging headlines from their respective theme.

The following morning as I walked up the stairs to my office, I met Linda, who turned and followed me into my office.

"How did you think yesterday went?" she asked.

"Very happy; it went like clockwork and all delegates seemed pleased to be able to have their say."

"Yes, from what I picked up everyone was really excited, but they are now eager to see what happens next," stated Linda.

"Yes, the important bit. Once I get reports from each facilitator, I'll write up the final report and recommendations and get it disseminated to our SMT."

In the days, following the Lambeth BME Focus groups, I received notification that a Deputy Assistant Commissioner would meet with me to discuss the contents of the email exchange with the Deputy Commissioner.

DAC Alf Hitchcock's visit to Brixton police station was an anonymous affair. I watched out of my office window as the DAC's driver parked his car in Brixton's station yard and within minutes there was a knock at my door and in walked Linda.

"DAC Hitchcock to see you, Sir."

We both took seats in front of my desk and following some small talk DAC Hitchcock got down to business.

"Why is it that some communities have a propensity for knives?" he drawled in his Lancastrian accent.

I was momentarily speechless. The purpose of this meeting was to discuss the increasing disconnect between the metropolitan police and London's black communities, but the Deputy Assistant Commissioner felt it acceptable to begin our conversation with a thinly disguised stereotypical trope aimed at the black community.

"Have you contacted your opposite number in Scotland? I understand knives are the cause of nearly 50% of homicides north of the border," I said, knowing full well that white knife wielding Scots did not feed into his racialised narrative.

A smile crept across his youthful face. "Hmmm," he murmured.

Clearly, the DAC had come to discuss knife crime and there followed several questions about homicide cases in Lambeth where the victim, usually of African heritage, was slain using a knife. My attempts to steer him towards recent disorder at Notting Hill Carnival and the connected operation in Lambeth that saw black youth indiscriminately swept up in tactics designed to contain suspected gang members was deftly deflected back to his agenda.

"We've undertaken a recent health check with a sample of our BME staff here in Lambeth and the outcome suggests that all is not well and if we were to extrapolate that across the Met, future recruitment, progression and retention looks bleak," I said in a last-ditch effort to try and bring the conversation around to my agenda.

The DAC got to his feet, he smiled as he brushed imaginary pieces of fluff from his uniform. "I'd be interested to see what you've done, send me a copy."

As the DAC departed, Linda entered my office. "How was your

meeting?" she asked in a hushed voice.

"I'd like to say it was productive, but I can't lie," I laughed.

The days passed and I was finally able to put the finishing touches to the BME report that had recently consumed my life. I entitled it, *Report on Five Focus Groups conducted to establish the experiences of Black and Minority Ethnic Police Personnel working in the London Borough of Lambeth.*

I handed a copy to Linda. "Please run off ten copies and ensure each member of our SMT gets a copy."

"Can I have a read after I've done what you ask?" inquired Linda.

"You can, but I have to remind you that it's for senior eyes only at this stage; so, please do not discuss it with others."

"Of course," said Linda.

Later in the day Linda entered my office. "Sir, I've read the report. It reads very well. You haven't pulled any punches have you?"

"There's no point in dressing things up to be what they are not, that's where we fail as an organisation, particularly where matters of racism are concerned," I said.

"I've just highlighted a few quotes from the facilitators; things that might cause your senior colleagues some angst," said Linda, taking a seat opposite my desk with the report clutched in her hands.

"OK, fire away, what have you got?" I said.

Linda opened the report and began reading aloud.

'Bullying is considered to be rife - page ten."

"'*Staff commented that they found working in the MPS to be a hostile environment'* – page ten. '*A number of issues are hidden; racism nowadays is much more covert'* - page ten. '*The collective experience of BME tends not to be understood or considered important by management…this is reflected in the absence of discussion on race and diversity at senior management meetings'* – page eleven. '*Potentially contentious issues raised by BME staff are "sat on" by managers and supervisors'* - page eleven. '*PCS Union/Police Federation are not responsive to BME issues'* – page twelve. '*Little or no confidence in the annual Personal Development Review system due to: Staff left to set own objectives and targets for progression, no reviews made to ascertain whether objectives are being met, line managers fail in their duty to manage'* – page fourteen. '*Negative stereotypes of BME staff are rife and endemic in the MPS'* - page fifteen. '*The mentality of the Met is racist but there is a tendency to deny racial dimensions to a situation. Experiences of bullying, intimidation and harassment are widespread, but cases are undermined by lack of evidence. If you challenge racist jokes, you are vulnerable'* – page twenty. '*There was a view that BME staff have to be really obvious in the workplace to ensure recognition. You have to perform 110% better, it's still not enough and your performance is never rewarded'* – page eighteen."

"Ok, Linda, thanks for that," I interrupted.

"What's your honest opinion, Sir, do you think things have progressed since you started in the job?" questioned Linda as she closed the pages of the report.

"Put it like this, Linda, everything you have just read to me is an almost carbon copy of what is in the Bristol Seminar Report, written some eighteen years ago."

"I've heard about the Bristol Seminars, before my time but some black officers I know still talk fondly about them,", informed Linda.

"Yes, I can understand why. The Bristol experience certainly changed the way I viewed the job," I said.

Over the next few days, I expected to be summoned to Lambeth Borough police HQ at Frank O'Neill House, to discuss the content of my report or at least discuss the feasibility of the recommendations.

"Linda, are you sure you disseminated the reports to our SMT?"

"Yes, Sir, I've heard through my contacts at Frank O'Neill that it's been received but no feedback as yet," said Linda.

I received notification to attend the weekly SMT meeting and eagerly expected the report to be on the agenda. However, nothing was mentioned during the meeting. No acknowledgement or even a mention outside of the meeting. It was business as usual.

The days passed into weeks and with no mention or acknowledgement it became apparent that the Lambeth BME report had assumed a *persona non grata* status. I could have, of course, forced the issue, made a fuss, and approached my SMT colleagues on an informal basis. However, three weeks had now elapsed with no formal or informal recognition. That to me signaled an incredible level of apathy and/or disinterest. I decided to play along with the game and pretend the report had not been written. After all, I had done what was asked of me and clearly the result was not sufficiently important enough to merit discussion.

Nevertheless, after a time, I felt unable to let matters rest.

"Linda, would you send a copy of the Lambeth BME report to Deputy Assistant Commissioner Collins, she is the lead for 'Race and Diversity,' and also to Deputy Assistant Commissioner Hitchcock as he expressed an interest in our work?"

Two weeks elapsed and Linda walked into my office.

"A Lambeth BME Report has just been returned to us in this brown envelope, addressed to you, from DAC Collins."

"OK, that's progress. What are they saying?" I asked.

Linda pulled out the report from its brown envelope and handed it to me. On the front cover, 'Seen and noted' was scribbled on a yellow 'post-it' note.

The Lambeth BME Report had now assumed 'hot potato' status.

"Linda, see if you can get hold of Alfred John, Chair of the Black Police Association, for me."

It was not too long before I received an invitation to attend a meeting with the Metropolitan Police's Director of HR, Martin Tiplady. Martin was a member of the Commissioner's Management Board and was someone Alfred John was on friendly terms with; so, I was not surprised at the invitation.

"Excuse me, Sir, your next appointment is outside, Mrs. Roberts," announced Linda.

"Ok, Linda, just remind me what this is about."

"Her young son was photographed by police following a stop and search."

"Sure, bring her up," I said.

A few minutes later a smartly dressed black lady entered my office.

"Hello Superintendent, my name is Mrs. Roberts. Thank you for making the time to see me."

"Pleased to meet you Mrs. Roberts. How can we help?"

"It's my son, he's fourteen year's old and just recently he was stopped by your police and I was told by witnesses that the police searched him and then took his photograph. Now, being stopped and searched is bad enough but then to take my boy's photograph and not to inform me - his parent, what's going on? He's just a child."

"I understand your anguish Mrs. Roberts. Was your son carrying anything unlawful?" I asked.

"Nothing, they just searched him, took down his details, photographed him and sent him on his way."

"I'll make some inquiries to find out the circumstances of your boy's stop and search. You can leave your details with Linda, my PA, and we'll make another appointment. In the meantime, the Lambeth Community Police Consultative Group (CPCG) meets at Lambeth Town Hall this Friday. Are you familiar with the work of the CPCG?

"No," she replied.

"It's a public forum that meets once a month with Lambeth's Borough Commander. Anyone can attend; it provides Lambeth residents and those who work in Lambeth with an opportunity to raise issues with senior police officers. You may want to attend to seek their advice and support."

The day following the monthly meeting of Lambeth CPCG, Linda walked into my office.

"Did you attend last night's CPCG at Lambeth Town hall?"

"Yes, I did," I responded.

"And I'm guessing Mrs. Roberts was there?"

"Yes, she was and took the opportunity to speak, in open forum, regarding her son's recent stop, search and photograph."

"That explains why BBC news this morning carried the story," said Linda.

"That's interesting, I know the local press was in attendance last night and that the issue attracted considerable interest from the floor. I've got a senior management team meeting later; we'll see what happens," I said.

The stop search and photograph issue aired so passionately at last evening's CPCG was at the top of the Borough Commander's agenda for discussion with her four Superintendents.

"I saw and heard the strength of feeling at last night's CPCG. Do we continue with the policy of photographing young people following stop and search?"

I was the only dissenting voice in the room, "I cannot support a policy that seems to me to be wrong on so many fronts. Its continuance will foster considerable resentment from a black community that will undoubtedly be disproportionately affected by the policy."

Despite me being outvoted and without further discussion, the Borough Commander felt compelled to rescind the photograph element of stop search in Lambeth.

A few days later, I travelled on the London underground train to Hendon for an arranged meeting with Martin Tiplady, the Met's Human Resources Director, to discuss the Lambeth BME report and what I perceived as an institutional reluctance to act upon its findings and recommendations. As I walked across the expansive Hendon estate to Martin's office, I recalled a time when Trevor Phillips in his capacity as Chair of the Commission for Racial Equality (CRE), had described Martin Tiplady as "the guardian of the Met". It was a description that resonated with me for it often appeared that Martin Tiplady's raison d'être was to defend, downplay, minimise, and spin any adverse publicity associated with the Met's inability to adequately manage, promote or retain black police personnel. Something he did with startling unerring efficiency. Although Phillips' comment, I suspected, had more than likely been provoked by the increasing numbers of black police personnel approaching the CRE for representation in Employment Tribunal cases.

My one-hour meeting with the Met's Director of Human Resources had failed to disabuse me of my previously held perceptions.

Chapter 63

'Enough is Enough'

My increasingly fraught relationship with the Met's senior management seemed locked into a downward spiral, exacerbate by my frustration and inability to get the Lambeth BME report on the Met's agenda. I had taken my perceived failure to heart; I had let down junior staff members, whom I had promised to assist by bringing their views to the notice of senior management. This and other personnel matters in my place of work placed me under considerable personal stress; the like of which I had never experienced in my policing career. I sought the advice and assistance of the staff association representing Superintendents within the metropolitan police. Chief Superintendent Archie Torrance, secretary of the Superintendent's Association, was someone that listened and empathised with my plight. His support during this most difficult time of my career was unequivocal.

The signs that I was about to "dig my heels in" undoubtedly caused the Met some anxiety as the potential for yet another senior BME officer embroiled in an intractable dispute seemed increasingly likely. I picked up from my meetings with a very senior officer that the Met were willing to adopt a more conciliatory stance to try and defuse the rapidly deteriorating situation. I responded accordingly.

To: Deputy Assistant Commissioner Rod Jarman

Dear Rod,

Thank you for your letter dated 4 May 2010 where you helpfully set out your proposals for addressing the issues I raised when we recently met to discuss my grievance.

While I value your interest and personal intervention, I am disappointed that the central issue in my grievance, the Lambeth BME report, is not given a more substantive and meaningful reference in your letter. I perceive this omission as being consistent with the fear, inability and reluctance of the MPS, thus far, to grasp the report's recommendations and it is in my view symptomatic of a much wider malaise of ingrained organisational indifference where matters of 'race' are concerned. Furthermore, this apparent unwillingness to embrace and progress what are effectively organisational learning opportunities when presented at some personal risk by, for the most part, junior BME colleagues, is I feel a deplorable and somewhat shameful position for the MPS to occupy.

I am afraid that it is in this context of institutional denial that I see your well intentioned initiatives floundering and indeed withering on the vine. The recent introduction of an MPS Diversity and Equality Strategy is a further example of good intention but with little leadership commitment or thought as to how it might be implemented and sustained. Some six months after its launch we still await an effective implementation plan.

I am however grateful for the invitation to assist you in developing your proposals but for the reasons stated above, I do not feel it wise or indeed appropriate to expend more of my limited time and energy on diversity and equality issues without first an acknowledgement and discussion, with a member of the Management Board, around some of the fundamental questions raised in the Lambeth BME report.

When we met, you offered me a temporary promotion opportunity which I welcomed as an acknowledgement of my skills and ability, however, I think we both realised that such a post would be impossible for me to accept given my principled stance for improved equality of opportunity in the MPS. At our meeting you also offered to provide me with support. However, I also see next week [Employment Tribunal] as an invaluable opportunity to have a very candid and long overdue conversation about the experiences of BME staff in Lambeth, a conversation which will also provide our communities with a unique insight into how the MPS values, develops and progresses its most senior BME officers. Such issues, I feel, are in the wider public interest, certainly Lambeth's communities are very interested, and as one of the MPS's most senior black officers I feel it falls to me to present those difficult questions in a public setting as I did with some reasonable success at another public inquiry, some ten years ago.

Yours sincerely

Paul Wilson

My 'enough is enough' threshold was well and truly breached and with the support of the Superintendents' Association, I instituted employment tribunal proceedings against my employers and on the 10ᵗʰ May 2010, literally running the gauntlet of press and photographers, I found myself in the West Croydon Employment Tribunal, where in the company of Archie Torrance and watched by a packed public gallery of journalists and supporters from the Black Police Association, I rose to address the Tribunal Chair with a lengthy statement. However, just as I was about to speak, Archie leaned over and tugged on my jacket. I looked down to see Archie looking toward the back of the room. I turned to see a member of the BPA waving a cell phone. From his expression and gesticulations, it seemed that someone on the end of that phone wished to speak with me. I turned to face the Chairman of the Tribunal, who had clearly seen what was happening and ordered a short recess. I was passed the cell phone.

"Paul, it's Martin Tiplady here. We need to talk."

Following a conversation with the Director of Human Resources, I agreed to cease my proceedings against the metropolitan police service and agreed to accept a monetary award from the Met.

Chapter 64

Retirement

Following the employment tribunal, my reintroduction into life on Lambeth Borough was facilitated by Lambeth's new Borough Commander, Nick Ephgrave, a value driven Christian and a welcome breath of fresh air. Voluntarily re-located to Streatham police station, with its well-appointed Superintendent's office, complete with en-suite toilet and shower. I once again began to enjoy my new life and responsibilities when one afternoon Linda popped her head around the door.

"Phone call on line 2; it's a Detective Sergeant in Ghana."

I eagerly answered the line.

"Hello, Paul, Keith Ashong here and yes, I'm in Accra, Ghana, doing some work with the British High Commission on an advisory basis."

"Sounds like interesting work, Keith. How is Accra?"

"It's good Paul, but the police here need help and advice and that's why I'm calling. I think Accra police would benefit from your knowledge and expertise of community policing."

Keith, that's truly kind of you but my time in the Met is virtually up. I retire in a couple of months.

"That's OK, just come over for a week to see what you think; the British High Commission will foot the bill."

A few weeks later I was in Accra, a guest of the British High Commission, immersed in a truly enlightening and humbling experience that was to open my eyes to the myriad of seemingly insurmountable problems faced by officers in the Ghanaian police service.

What I had seen both depressed and at the same time encouraged me to think about the bigger picture; policing in Africa, as what I had witnessed, I suspected could well, in varying degrees, be extrapolated across the African continent. While my journey to Accra only served to confirm there to be no quick fix solution for a police service still wedded to the last vestiges of a colonial era, it, nevertheless, invoked in me a passion and determination to do something to improve matters. Each evening, I worked on my laptop computer in the hotel's communal area alongside many of the European guests, many of whom worked for multi-nationals, and began to think about how private sector money might support public services, such as the police. With only a few days remaining I started to develop the skeleton for a project, whereby private finance might be funneled through an NGO, working in partnership with the police, in support of crime reduction initiatives.

....

In September 2010, I retired from the Metropolitan Police following 32 years of service, that included my time as a member of the police civil staff. In time honoured fashion, I planned for my farewell function to mark this monumental occasion and briefly considered one of New Scotland Yard's special function rooms as is befitting for a retiring superintendent. But this was only a fleeting consideration and one that was quickly put to one side given my recent and stressful experiences.

Lambeth Borough was to be my last posting and somehow I wanted to recognise and acknowledge my fondness and close association with its community. After giving it some thought, I arranged to hold my farewell party in a Brixton nightclub venue as it just seemed to be the right thing to do. Lambeth's Borough Commander, Chief Superintendent Nick Ephgrave, very graciously agreed to host my departure attended by many friends from Black Police Associations, former colleagues, friends and family including my father, who travelled from the United States to be with me on that momentous occasion.

Following retirement, I began seeking work to keep me occupied and motivated by my recent experience in Ghana, I turned my attention to the African continent and explored several ways in which I might offer my skills and experience to African nations. I eventually contacted my old friends at South Africa's police and prisons civil rights union (POPCRU) and in 2011 I was invited to realise my dream of establishing an NGO to work in partnership with the police to reduce crime.

With my wife, Carol, we relocated to South Africa in January 2021, where I began working at the offices of the POPCRU Group of Companies 9PGC) in Pretoria and established, from scratch the Safer South Africa Foundation www.safersouthafrica.org. I was appointed its first Chief Executive Officer and developed the Foundation's 'Community and Justice

Programme,' inspired by and adapted from San Francisco Police's 'Citizen's Academy' initiative. It was introduced into many schools throughout South Africa and today, remains Safer South Africa Foundation's flagship programme.

Acknowledgements

My maiden writing voyage has, at times, proved a challenge but with copious amounts of encouragement, belief, and support, I was able to quickly extinguish the occasional flicker of self-doubt that present itself during those brick wall moments. Having reached my final destination, I can now say it has definitely been a more rewarding experience than I could ever have imagined.

To Stuart at SRL Publishing, for your belief that I had a story that deserved to be told, I thank you for your unequivocal support and encouragement throughout. And my thanks to Melody for the cover design work and to Andy Martinez for use of photographs taken in Brixton Police Station yard.

I owe an enormous debt of gratitude to those who gave me detailed and constructive comments on one or more chapters, including Susanne Schotanus, Barbra Jones and Arial King. Thank you for your patience, advice and invaluable guidance.

To Pat Gallan, Brian Paddick and Trevor Hall, thank you for your tremendously meaningful and supportive testimonials – and to Robin Oakley, for allowing me to include your deeply insightful 'institutional racism' note.

However, none of this could have ever materialised without my truly incredible wife, Carol. Her encouragement and belief inspired me to commence on this tremendous journey. It didn't stop there, either – as she relieved me of the daily domestic chores and other responsibilities, for the sole purpose of me devoting many hours a day towards research and writing. She was as important to this book getting done as I was.

To my children, Shani and Lewis, I thank you for your unwavering support, for always asking the right questions and never once doubting that I would finish it.

I thank you, David Michael, for unearthing copies of 'lost forever', memorandum. And George Rhoden, I thank you for providing a copy of the memorable 'Bristol Reunion' flyer from November 1992.

To my friends at the Metropolitan Black Police Association; Chair Janet Hills, Deborah Thomas, and Tracey Washington; thank you for your invaluable support, advice, and help with the planning and publicising of our book launch and beyond.

And last but not least, thank you to all those courageous pioneers who gathered in Pimlico, on 21st April, 1993 and helped set in motion a chain of events that would forever change the face of policing in the UK.

Annex A

INSTITUTIONAL RACISM AND POLICE SERVICE DELIVERY

1. The published report of the Police Complaints Authority states that the investigation by Kent Police into the murder of Stephen Lawrence did not produce any evidence of racist conduct by police officers who dealt with the incident and with the case subsequently. Many commentators have found this conclusion unconvincing. A key issue is what would constitute 'racist conduct' in such a situation, and how it might be identified. The aim of this note is to set out an alternative understanding of 'racist conduct' from that which seems to be implied in the PCA report, an understanding which hopefully can illuminate more clearly the challenge facing the police service in the aftermath of Stephen Lawrence's death.

2. The notion of 'racist conduct' that became established following the Scarman Inquiry was one of overt acts of discrimination or hostility by individuals who were acting out their personal prejudices. Racism was therefore a problem specifically of individual officers, of 'rotten apples' within the service who 'let the side down'. On this diagnosis, the solution to the problem would lie (a) at the selection stage, at which prejudiced individuals should be identified and weeded out, and (b) through the application of disciplinary sanctions against those who display such behaviour on the job. This conception of racism appears still to be the normal understanding in police circles, and appears also to have informed the conclusion reported by the PCA.

3. Is this analysis adequate to identify the challenge faced by the police of meeting the needs of minority communities and of providing a fair and effective service to members of all ethnic groups? Does it sufficiently explain the visible minority

communities' experience of policing over recent years? Is it reasonable to attribute the problems that have arisen to just a small number of individuals, given the fundamental shift that has taken place towards a multi-ethnic society in Britain over this period? To raise such questions is not to doubt the policy commitment of the police service to address issues of racial equality, but is to focus instead on presumptions which may underlie the policy's implementation.

4. First of all, it is quite unrealistic that minority concerns about differentials in stop and search, about the police response to racial attacks, and about police demeanour towards visible minorities generally, could be the result of actions solely of a small number of individuals. At the very least, they must be the result of tendencies among a much larger number of officers, if not the outcome of 'normal policing'.

5. Secondly, when all other major institutions are facing the need to adapt to an increasingly multi-ethnic society, it is not credible that the majority of police officers could be immune from the challenges posed. Understanding and developing respect for other cultures, recognising the pitfalls of cross-cultural communication, appreciating the impact of racism on people's lives – these together with an awareness of how one's own prejudices and ethnocentrism can affect one's behaviour are all fundamental challenges that affect every police officer in the land. They are normal challenges which are not peculiar to the police, and they affect other public service providers also.

6. For the police service, however, there is an additional dimension which arises from the nature of the policing role. Police work, unlike most other professional activities, has the capacity to bring officers into contact with a skewed cross-section of society, with the well-recognised potential for producing negative stereotypes of particular groups. Such stereotypes become the common currency of the police occupational culture. If the predominantly white staff of the police organisation have their experience of visible minorities largely restricted to interactions with such groups, then negative racial stereotypes will tend to develop accordingly.

7. The specific challenges identified above are all challenges that potentially affect all police officers. Failure to address them is liable to result in a generalised tendency, particularly where any element of discretion is involved, whereby minorities may receive different and less favourable treatment than the majority. Such differential treatment need be neither conscious nor intentional, and it may be practised routinely by officers whose professionalism is exemplary in all other respects. For these reasons, such tendencies - although extensive - may be both uncomfortable to acknowledge and difficult to detect in the individual case. By comparison, the overt acts of racism by bigoted individuals are relatively easy to identify and respond to at this level.

8. There is great danger that focussing on overt acts of personal racism by individual officers may deflect attention from the much greater institutional challenge that has been identified above. This challenge potentially manifests itself in the daily activity of each member of staff. It was potentially – though not necessarily actually – manifest in the actions of every officer involved in the events following Stephen Lawrence's murder. What were the images of Stephen as a young black person in the minds of those who attended the scene, and did they check out any possible tendencies to make assumptions of a racial nature? Did they routinely consider and also prioritise the possibility that racism could have been his attackers' motivation? Did they appreciate and respond to the concerns that a black family in particular might have when dealing with the police in these kinds of circumstances? Regardless of whether conscious or intended, any shortfalls in professional standards in such situations (such as delays, omissions, or biases) may easily be translated by others as visible manifestations of a more subtle form of 'racism' on the part of the police.

9. It would be appalling to suppose that police officers would attend the murder scene, and work on this case, and while doing so engage in overt and deliberate racist conduct. To this extent the conclusion of the Police Complaints Authority report offers little surprise. Whether there should be confidence that no racially discriminatory treatment of any kind took place, e.g. of a more subtle and unintended nature as indicated above, is an entirely different matter. In general, there are sound reasons to suppose that biased actions

could have occurred, on account of the kinds of institutional factors which have been identified.

10. The above analysis sets out a form of racism which was not conceptualised clearly in the Scarman Report, since it is usually covert rather than overt, unintended so far as motivation is concerned, acted out unconsciously by individuals, and an expression of collective rather than purely individual sentiment. Particularly on account of the latter characteristic, this may be appropriately referred to as a form of 'institutional racism'. However, by restricting the term 'institutional racism' to explicit manifestations at policy level, Scarman failed to address the more subtle and concealed form that organisational-level racism may take. This is not to say that this more covert form of institutional racism may not be expressed overtly at times, e.g. through use of racial epithets or generalisations about particular ethnic groups. Its most important and challenging feature, though, is its predominantly hidden character and its inbuilt pervasiveness within the occupational culture.

11. It could be said that institutional racism in this sense is in fact pervasive throughout the culture and institutions of the whole of British society, and is no way specific to the police service. However, because of the nature of the police role, its impact on society if not addressed in the police organisation may be particularly severe. In many other public services the challenge of institutional racism has already been acknowledged and acted upon by senior management. In the police service, despite the extensive activity designed to address racial and ethnic issues in recent years, the concept of 'institutional racism' has not received the attention it deserves. The recent report from HM Inspectorate of Constabulary *(Winning the Race: Policing Plural Communities)* moves further in this direction than before. There is a need, however, to present the challenge in the clearest and most forthright terms possible, and a need also to demonstrate how a more subtle form of 'racist conduct' may manifest itself at the level of service delivery on the street. The nature of the Stephen Lawrence Murder Inquiry provides a unique opportunity for these two needs to be met.

12. Although tackling racism in general is the responsibility of every individual officer, tackling 'institutional racism' in the above sense is

particularly the responsibility of police management and supervisors. It is the responsibility of the organisation to identify and then remove these potential barriers to professional good practice, and to ensure that front-line staff have the necessary awareness, understanding and skill to deal with racist incidents and to provide an effective service to minority ethnic communities as well as to the majority group.

13. In some respects, the solutions to these problems are already well-known, and numerous initiatives have already been taken by the police. However, by comparison with the efforts made to address equal opportunities in employment, the organisational response in addressing race issues in service delivery has tended to be piecemeal. For example, the essentials for a training strategy on racial issues were set out by an excellent Police Training Council Working Party report as long ago as 1983, yet such a strategy still remains to be fully and systematically implemented.

14. Training, however, cannot be the solution alone – any more than could reliance on selection and discipline. As in any large organisation, an overall strategic approach to tackle the problem of institutional racism must be formulated and then implemented at all levels, with the lead coming visibly from the top. However, this should not be done by the police in isolation, but by means of a fully developed 'partnership approach' in which the police service works jointly with the minority ethnic communities. Such a partnership approach is essential, both to identify and address community needs, and also to build mutual confidence and trust. Seventeen years after Scarman, the Stephen Lawrence Murder Inquiry provides a unique opportunity to get things right.

Robin Oakley

18 April 1998

References

- *Report by the Police Complaints Authority on the Investigation of a Complaint against the Metropolitan Police Service by Mr N and Mrs D Lawrence*, Cm 3822, Stationery Office, 1997
- *The Brixton Disorders 10-12 April 1981: Report of an Inquiry by Lord Scarman*, Cmnd 8427, Her Majesty's Stationery Office, 1981
- *Winning the Race: Policing Plural Communities – HMIC Thematic Inspection Report on Police Community and Race Relations 1996/97*, Home Office, 1997
- *Community and Race Relations Training for the Police: Report of the Police Training Council Working Party*, Home Office, 1983

Lightning Source UK Ltd.
Milton Keynes UK
UKHW020625110821
388445UK00002B/7/J